LAW, ORDER, AND POWER

WILLIAM CHAMBLISS, University of Delaware

ROBERT SEIDMAN, Boston University

LAW, ORDER, AND POWER
Second Edition

ADDISON-WESLEY PUBLISHING COMPANY
Reading, Massachusetts • Menlo Park, California • London • Amsterdam
Don Mills, Ontario • Sydney

Library of Congress Cataloging in Publication Data

Chambliss, William J.
　　Law, order, and power.

　　Bibliography: p.
　　Includes index.
　　　1. Law-United States. 2. Justice, Administration of—
United States. 3. Law—Philosophy. I. Seidman, Robert B.
II. Title.
KF384.A7C43　　1982　　　　347.73　　　　81-10807
ISBN 0-201-10126-2　　　　　　347.307　　　AACR2

ISBN 0-201-10126-2
ABCDEFGHIJ-AL-898765432

This book is dedicated to those who struggle for a better world, including members of our families: Neva Makgetla, Judy Parsons, and Rose, Ann, Gay, Katha, and Jonathon Seidman; Lisa and Jeana; Kent, Jeff, and Lauren Chambliss

About the authors

William J. Chambliss teaches sociology at the University of Delaware. He is the author and editor of more than a dozen books in the sociology of law and criminology. His latest works include *On the Take: From Petty Crooks to Presidents*; *Organizing Crime* (with Alan A. Block); and articles on labor racketeering, the history of opium law, and crime in capitalist and socialist societies. Since 1969 he has been a visiting professor at universities throughout the world, including the University of Ibadan, Nigeria, the London School of Economics, the University of Oslo, the University of Stockholm, and University College, Cardiff. Dr. Chambliss is a frequent lecturer and visiting scholar at universities in the United States, Europe, and Africa. He studied law and sociology at Indiana University and was a resident in Law and Sociology at the University of Wisconsin in 1966-1967.

Robert B. Seidman is Professor of Law and Political Science at Boston University. He was formerly President of the African Studies Association. Professor Seidman has been a visiting professor at the Universities of Ghana, Nigeria, Tanzania, and Zimbabwe. He is the author of many books and articles on law and the relationship between law and development. His books include *State, Law and Development* and *A Sourcebook of the Criminal Law in Africa*. Recent articles and papers cover the areas of law and population control and law and development. He is presently a visiting professor at the University of Zimbabwe, where he also serves as a consultant to the national government and is working on a revision of the country's penal law. Professor Seidman was awarded the B.A. degree by Harvard and the L.L.B. degree by Columbia University.

Preface

Awaiting the bus on a snowy December day in Madison, Wisconsin, in 1967, we began discussing the possibility of writing a "small book" on the sociology of law. We met the next day for lunch and on napkins at the student union we began the process of writing such a book. In the end we produced not a small book but a rather large one, which Addison-Wesley published in 1971. The present effort grew out of an attempt to revise that book for the 1980s.

What follows is not so much a revision as it is a new book. The field of study now known as "law and society" mushroomed in the last ten years. Theoretical and empirical developments have been so rapid that where once we suffered from a paucity of good studies we now have an embarrassment of riches. Consequently we learned a great deal and changed our minds in the face of facts and a refinement of theoretical issues not available in the 1960s.

In the first edition we relied rather more heavily than we liked on research and theory connected to the study of criminal law. Our bias was shared by those venturing into the largely unexplored area of law and society at that time. Subsequently that narrowness of vision was overcome in the field and, we hope, by us as well. While this volume still includes examples and issues from criminal law, its place is much less apparent and, concomitantly, the place of civil law is brought to the fore.

We also organize our work around quite a different set of theoretical issues. Commenting on the first volume, a British colleague, Alan Hunt, suggested we were relying for our theoretical integration on a perspective he called "radical pluralism." Today we are much more self-consciously attempting to integrate a number of theoretical perspectives which appear at present to be the most useful ideas available for making sense of law and society. Our framework synthesizes three separate themes. First is the attempt by social science to develop heuristic models of how law affects society and how society in turn influences law. Second, and in part as a result of the first, we attempt in this work to emphasize the explanatory power of dialectical theory. And finally, we take from existing ruling class and functionalist perspectives observations and perspectives which are in accord with the known facts about law and the legal order. This effort has not, however, produced an eclecticism of theoretical frameworks; rather we intend the work to provide a coherent synthesis of those perspectives currently in use by sometimes warring social scientists which withstand the test of empirical observations and logical scrutiny.

The degree to which we succeed in these efforts will, of course, have to be judged by the reader.

We intend the book to be a contribution to the scholarly study of law and society, a textbook for use in classes in this area, and a handbook for the development of social policy designed to make the law and the legal order work for the benefit of people. Hopefully, in the end, it will contribute to the emancipation of the human community from the oppression and exploitation currently experienced by so many of the world's peoples.

In preparing this book we have been aided by enough people to fill a separate volume. Some, though, we want to especially mention with heartfelt thanks: our teachers, especially Al Lindesmith, Jerome Hall, and Karl Lewellyn; many students in seminars and hallways, but particularly Kitty Calavita, Pat Donnelly, and Dan Curran; colleagues and friends who talked with us, discussed ideas, and gave of themselves in ways we can scarcely ever repay, Gerald Turkel, Alan Block, Phil Thomas, Lisa Stearns, Ann Seidman, Phil Fennell, and Maureen Cain, to mention a few. Piers Beirne and Ronald Farrell read the entire manuscript when we first submitted it to the publisher. Their detailed comments and significant insights were critically important to us in preparing the final draft. Gerald Turkel and Peter Aldridge read the entire book in its final stages and saved us from errors as well as helping us say better what we were trying to get across. Claire Blessing and Eileen Prybolsky typed the first draft with all the good humor, patience, and assistance one could possibly hope for but had no right to expect. In addition, Eileen aided immensely with a keen eye for editing, hyperbole, and logical omissions. Cheri Hoyle typed, insightfully commented on, and greatly helped in the preparation of the final manuscript. Pat Small copy edited and helped construct the index in the last hectic moments. Liz Riley of University College, Cardiff, and Carole Anderson of the University of Delaware patiently tolerated the bulk of correspondence and heavy bundles traveling between the United States, Wales, and Zimbabwe. Our editors of Addison-Wesley, especially Ron Hill and Laura Streimer, were incredibly patient and helpful from beginning to end. Finally, the copy editors, typesetters, and printers were brilliant in their ability to put together a book from the materials we provided.

No one could ask for more support and help than we enjoyed from these and other people. For their generosity and commitment we are deeply grateful. Any errors which they failed to bring to our attention or which they brought to our attention but we refused to change are entirely our responsibility.

Newark, Delaware, and Salisbury, Zimbabwe　　　　　　　　　W.J.C.
November 1981　　　　　　　　　　　　　　　　　　　　　R.B.S.

Contents

1

The study of law and society

We live on the edge of the abyss. Rarely in recent memory has society seemed to teeter so close to disaster. The economy roars out of control; international affairs threaten to overwhelm us; bureaucracy clasps us in its clammy embrace; politics becomes a theater of the absurd, and politicians, clowns.

In our era, organized political communities look not to church or clan or community for respite against social ills, but to government. We expect government to improve economic affairs, to solve international puzzles, to ride herd on bureaucracy, to improve the political climate. That era began in the Enlightenment. Then, as now, the liberal faith held that rational people, organized in political communities and exercising state power through the legal order, could instantly erase the cruelty and irrationality of social life.

It does not work that way. Just as feudal barons grew fat on the labor of serfs, so did the rural gentry grow fat on agricultural laborers, robber barons on impoverished immigrants, and multinational corporations on the people in the Third World. Those who have owned the world have run it and have kept in force legal orders to facilitate their continued rule and privilege.

They did this despite constitutions and legal orders that on their faces aimed at equality and representative democracy. The high school civics textbook blueprint tells us that the people democratically elect the legislature, which enacts laws reflecting the majority interest. The administration enforces the laws, and the courts adjudicate disputes about them. The laws, expressed in general rules, affect everyone equally. Guarantees of minority rights ensure against the majority's unrestricted tyranny.

Long ago, de Tocqueville expressed the great paradox of Western democracies. The mass, it seems, has all the power, and the rich all the money. The legal order itself supposedly ensures democratic power in the mass of the population. That we live in a sadly troubled world characterized by inequality, not equality, and authoritarianism, not democracy, expresses a failure of the legal order. In a society that looks to the legal order as the principal tool to solve our social ills, that we teeter so close to disaster expresses either our failure to use the legal order intelligently or deep-seated weaknesses in the legal order itself.

In either case, part of the explanation for our social malaise must lie in the legal order. It becomes government's principal instrument of social control. We rely upon it to maintain order in the streets, minimal harmony in the family, regularity and predictability in the marketplace, safety in the workplace, and nondiscrimination in work and places of public accommodation. We also rely upon it as an instrument of social change. If government proposes to improve economic conditions, it enacts a tax law, wage and price controls, a planning law, or laws concerning the money supply; if it strives to solve international puzzles, it operates through organs of international law like the United Nations; if it proposes to weaken bureaucracy's power, it passes new laws or enforces old ones concerning administrative accountability and decision-making power; to improve the quality of our political life, it passes laws about election finances, primary elections, and the like. The legal order becomes goverment's scalpel in operating on the body politic.

To do that adequately, government must have a great deal of knowledge about the uses and limits of the scalpel, what it can do and what it cannot do. That knowledge, by and large, however, hardly exists. No phenomenon other than law can claim to have received such intensive study generating so little knowledge. Even those most intimately involved with it—judges, law professors, attorneys, prosecutors, and law-enforcement agents—frequently become proficient in one or another of the legal order's many facets without understanding its broad expanse. In this work, we hope to introduce readers to the systematic study of the legal order. In this chapter, we first define the domain of study. We then suggest in broad outline the sort of knowledge we can expect to generate and how we propose to go about the study.

1.1 THE DOMAIN OF STUDY

We take as the domain of study the *legal order*. For some words, the culture supplies a common definition. All native English speakers know that the word "elephant" means that large moving gray mass out there. A definition of the word "elephant" need only *describe* the large gray mass in detail. Other words, like "truth" and "beauty" and "god," have only the vaguest agreed-upon meaning. For these, a *stipulative* definition serves; one says what one means by the word. "Law" is such a word, which means we must first define what we mean when we use it.

"Law" and "The Legal Order" Distinguished

The word *law* sometimes means an individual rule that has certain characteristics; at other times it means the whole complex of the legal system, involving not only the rules themselves, but the various institutions, processes, and roles that occupy themselves with those rules—legislatures, courts, administrative agencies, and lawyers, judges, police officers, legislators, administrators, jailors, bureaucrats, and so forth. To avoid that confusion, we use the word *law* in the sense of *a law*—that is, a particular rule that has the characteristics that define it as a law and not as some other sort of norm. We use the words *the legal order* to mean people doing things: Judges judging, lawmakers making law, bureaucrats administering the law, police officers making arrests and finding lost babies and sometimes beating up people illegally, and many others. The legal order, in our definition, constitutes a set of social relations governed by rules set down by the state. Its principal actors include state employees, but others participate as lawyers, litigants, and the addressees of law. Some institutions exhibit a rather tightly sealed exterior to the rest of the world, like prisons and hospitals, for example. The legal order, however, exists in large part to affect the behavior of people who often seem to be only tangentially connected with it. To study the legal order, we must of course study the actors who constitute its movers and shakers—judges and legislators and prosecutors and police officers and administrators. We must, however, also study the behavior of the law's addressees. We must cast our net wide.

Taking as our domain of study the legal order as we have described it places us in the tradition of American legal realism, a school of jurisprudence that began in 1881 when Oliver Wendell Holmes, Jr. (later a great Supreme Court justice) wrote that "the life of the law has not been logic; it has been experience."[1] The realists insisted that we must study the law-in-action as well as the law-in-the-books, the behavior that takes place in the face of the prescriptions of the law as well as those prescriptions themselves. Their case nominally won out; American legal scholars by and large accepted the proposition that to understand the legal order we must investigate the law-in-action. Lawrence Friedman expresses the realists' view as follows:

Structures [courts, police, the legal profession] and rules [laws] look one way on paper, while acting quite differently in life. Almost everyone concedes that law is to some degree a social product, and that law on the books and law in action are not inevitably the same. Rules and structures alone do not tell us how the machine really works. These provide no way to sort out dead law from living law. They do not tell us how and why rules are made and what effect they have on people's lives.[2]

The study of how laws are made, how they are implemented, and what effect they have on people's lives is called the study of law and society.

Other Definitions of "The Legal Order," "The Legal System," and "The Law"

Other writers suggest their ways of looking at law. Sometimes they have used a linguistic cover to smuggle a substantive judgment about what we ought to study. William B. Harvey adopted perhaps the most common definition of law when he suggested that the legal order (he uses the word *law,* but in the sense that we use *the legal order*) entails "a technique of social ordering deriving its essential characteristic from its ultimate reliance on the reserved monopoly of systematically threatened or applied force in politically organized society."[3] This definition implies that we misuse the words *legal order* and *law* if we apply them to systems of social control in societies that lack a centralized monopoly of force and a bureaucratic structure to determine when a violation of law occurs and to apply sanction for its breach. It limits the concept of *the legal order* to societies that have a state structure. In this view, the sorts of societies many anthropologists study do not have *a legal order* and, by definition, therefore, these societies have no law.

In an effort to find institutions common to both simple and complex societies susceptible of comparative study the American anthropologist E. A. Hoebel stipulated a broader definition of "law."[4] He saw as the "fundamental *sine qua non*" of law in any society, simple or complex, "the legitimate use of physical coercion by a socially organized agent."[5] He then defined *law* as follows: "A social norm is legal if its neglect or infraction is regularly met, in threat or in fact, by the application of physical force by an individual or group possessing the socially recognized privilege of so acting."[6]

Hoebel made a selection among the many potential attributes of what one might call *law* in a modern centralized society—the aspect of forceful sanctions—and masked his choice under a definitional guise. He did this by asserting that law *necessarily* contains force. Force becomes the *sine qua non* of law only if the concept of law exists as an essence in some unreal world of absolute, Platonic Ideas or if general agreement exists about the phenomenon to which the word *law* refers. Neither holds. In sum, by his definition Hoebel said that he had an interest in studying the use of socially approved force to sanction norms of conduct. That seems a valid area of study, but why the *sine qua non* or *essence* of law? Many other aspects of the institutions of social control can serve as the focus of study, without necessarily constituting the "essence" of the legal order: the dispute-settlement mechanism, the adjudicative mechanism, the systems of decision-making, the fact-finding mechanism, the content of the norms, the interrelationship of the norms, and a host of others.

Another tack comes from systems analysis. That discipline teaches us the difference between the system and the environment. For the systems engineer, the question of where the system and the environment separate usually appears as a factual matter. The environment consists of the unalterable conditions that affect us. The system consists of whatever appears under our control.[7] The aircraft engineer cannot change the characteristics of the ambient air; he can only do something about the design of the aircraft. The interface between the aircraft's skin and the atmosphere becomes the interface between the system and the environment.

For engineers, that seems a factual issue. For governments, it becomes a normative question. Should the Department of Agriculture accept low rainfall as part of the environment and concentrate on helping farmers in arid regions grow crops appropriate to dry lands? Or should it accept that as part of the system and concentrate on creating irrigation systems? These decisions involve normative judgments: on what *ought* government expend resources, and in what priority?

We too easily fall into the trap of asking only the factual question: what "legal" institutions seem discontinuous with society? In our society, among the various "legal" systems on first glance only courts seem discrete from society. To identify the legal system with the courts poses the problem of law and society as one of interaction between courts and society. Courts become the legal order. Many lawyers and sociologists have adopted precisely that domain of study and exclude from consideration legislatures, administrative agencies, and other aspects of state power. We think such narrowness of vision is a mistake.

Even to suggest that the words *the legal system* have no real content seems to many heretical. Language, however, poses its own tyranny.[8] Because we have a phrase, *legal system,* we assume that such a system exists. After all, we have a word, *chair,* and chairs exist, so why not legal systems too? By using that phrase, we make a value-laden decision: we mark a division between the legal system and its environment. Our own expertise misleads us into assuming that there is a discontinuity between "the legal system" and the rest of society. Some of us are lawyers. We have successfully surrounded the law with a mystique, unknowable, we assume, to those not of the guild. Others accept our claim for expertise—after all, lawyers must learn something in the three-year initiation rite we call law school. Words and expertise combine to assure us of a separate and discrete legal system. In fact, of course, government acts not only through legislatures and courts, but in a complex panoply of other institutions as well: alphabet agencies like the ICC (the Interstate Commerce Commission) and the CAB (Civil Aeronautics Board) and the NLRB (National Labor Relations Board), the police, prisons, state universities and public schools, and public corporations (AMSAT, CONRAIL, COMSAT, TVA). If we propose understanding how to use the tools that government has available to attack social difficulties, our domain must include the rules, norms, and actions of these institutions, as well as those of courts and legislatures.

By contrast, Professor Fuller (among others) excludes the rules concerning such institutions from the very definition of "law," and hence from our purview of study. It is "obfuscation," he says, to confuse "law" with "every conceivable kind of official act," so much so that "when one finds an author about to discuss, in Pound's famous phrase, 'the limits of effective legal action,' one is not sure whether the subject will be the attempted legal suppression of homosexuality or the failure of the government to convert the power of the tides into electricity at Passamaquoddy."[9]

Why Our Definition?

We prefer to stipulate our meaning of *the legal order* and *law,* and for that the test becomes utility. As we have stated, our concern has an explicitly policy-oriented thrust. We aim to develop a theory that will explain the relationship between law, the legal order, and society and that will help in solving emergent social difficulties. Organized political communities in this era invariably employ the functionaries of the state for this purpose. Typically, they do so by enacting legislation or promulgating decrees or administrative regulations—that is, normative rules for the conduct of both state functionaries and ordinary citizens. As we said earlier, therefore, we concern ourselves with the normative order in which the state and its functionaries are involved, as lawmakers, law implementors, or merely as the addressees of rules. That normative system constitutes the legal order and differs from other normative systems because it rests, ultimately, on the state's monopoly over the legitimate use of force.

This definition ranges far more broadly than some others, for it denies any sharp distinction between the legal order and the state, between legal institutions and processes and political ones. The federal government's annual budget is law (indeed, the Congress enacts it and the president signs it, just as any legislation); a proposal to make homosexuality a crime involves a proposal for a law (the norm) just as does a proposal that the Department of Energy generate electricity out of tidal power. No narrower definition will serve our purposes.

That definition of course entails a value-choice. Sawyer makes a distinction between "lawyers' law" and "the law of social administration."[10] The former denotes the rules of the private sector—contract, property, tort. The latter denotes the law concerning "collective industries, and services, collective marketing of farm products, welfare services for the masses (health, pensions, unemployment, etc.), regulation of the activities of the private sector of the economy, and the conduct of defense and foreign relations."[11] Our ideal-type of court deals with "lawyers' law" almost exclusively; the law of social administration falls before administrative agencies and sometimes never actually enters the courtroom doors. Sawyer suggests that "in a nation which gave effect to the social theories of Herbert Spencer, social administration would hardly exist."[12] Most law would be lawyers' law, occasionally amended as social change necessitated. Whatever its dominant ideology, no polity in the world subscribes to *Social Statics*. Most rules that they enact to solve emergent problems involve rules of social administration.

Our definition of *the legal order* therefore expresses our concern with the law of social administration as well as with lawyers' law. To study only the latter involves a value-choice in favor of an unreal vision of laissez-faire that today claims the adherence only of ideologies of the far right. We prefer a definition of *the legal order* that permits the study of what all governments today do, not what some laissez-faire idealists think they should be doing.

1.2 SOME MYTHS ABOUT LAW

Three myths about "the law" mislead us into thinking that the legal order serves the public interest. These myths frequently put blinders over our eyes when we try to examine the legal order. We examine these myths at length in the chapters that follow; here we only identify them.

The *consensus* myth holds that the law codifies society's value-consensus. Both the law-in-the-books and the law-in-action mirror society's "moral basis" and its "most important" values, with no gap between the law and every sound citizen's ideology.

The *normative* myth holds that what the law prescribes also describes the actual behavior of the lawyers, judges, courts, prisons, sheriffs, social workers, administrators, bureaucrats, legislators, and others who play roles in the legal order.

The *computer* myth argues that the law transmutes every social problem into a case, to which the various actors merely apply the law, acting as it were like impersonal computers: insert the facts, insert the rules of law, and they grind out "correct" decisions. In the computer myth, discretion, bias, power, and corruption do not exist or constitute at most temporary aberrations. A common aphorism catches all these: "Ours is a government of laws, not men."

A corollary to these myths, less articulated but widely prevalent, argues that despite the existence of sharp conflicts among social classes and interest groups the state (the courts, the police, the civil servants, and so forth) provides a value-neutral framework that fairly contains and resolves conflicts. Even the legislature, which is the clearest example of value-bias in the legal order with its dependence on lobbyists and institutionalized links to established interests, mouths shiboleths of value-neutrality. On rare occasions when biases are admitted the framework of elections is singled out as the ultimate neutralizing force. The legislature in this view becomes an arena within which groups reflecting society's power configurations can peacefully resolve policy disputes. That view perceives the police as enforcing the laws that the legislature enacts, and the courts as deciding on which side of a dispute truth lies, fairly and impartially applying the law to the facts, and meting out the sanction that the law itself requires.

The world contradicts these myths. We all know that the police do not treat blacks and the poor equitably; that judges have great discretion and in fact make policy in the course of "applying" the rules of law; that electoral laws in the past favored rural elements, and today still favor the rich; that most presidential candidates have great wealth; that 20 percent of U.S. senators own more than a million dollars worth of assets; that winning elections requires the expenditure of vast sums of money contributed to political campaigns by special interest groups; and that the political candidate with the most money to spend stands a far greater chance of winning than his or her poorer opponent.[13] In short:

Law discriminates. . . . First, the rules themselves . . . are by no means totally impartial even when impartially applied. They come out of the struggle for power. . . . Segregation is the law of the land in the Union of South Africa—it was the law of the land in the American South until very recently. Penal codes declare "unnatural" sex a crime. The laws punish draft dodgers, seditionists, and drug addicts. American immigration laws excluded the Chinese; public land law ruthlessly exploited the native Indians; welfare law was harsh to the poor. . . . The regulatory code, the tax laws—economic legislation in general—are geared to the needs and interests of people who own property. Rules of contract and commercial law are innocent on the surface and seem to the average person to be mere justice and common sense, but it is the justice and common sense of Western society, its economy, its dominant populations. Imperial Rome, the Cheyenne, and the China of Chairman Mao used different rules. Indeed, every area of law—land law, family law, tort law—supports the society which framed the rules and put them to work.[14]

Despite the fact that law and the legal order represent a highly selective and biased set of rules and institutionalized processes, the consensual, normative, computer, and value-neutrality myths persist. Exceptions to the exceptions of neutrality, unilinear norm enforcement, consensus, and computerized justice are dismissed as simply "aberrations" or "temporary biases" which will ultimately be resolved through the inevitable progress of law and civilization.

These myths tell lies. Far from a value-neutral framework within which conflict finds peaceful resolution, state power itself rewards the successful in the endless social conflict. The legal order in fact constitutes a self-serving system to maintain power and privilege. The black-letter texts of the law do not describe how officials behave; the law-in-action and the law-in-the-books systematically contradict each other. Far from resembling a computer, the legal order has as its main decision-making principle official discretion. We cannot study the legal order wearing blinders. To see it whole, we must shed ourselves of these myths.

1.3 WHY STUDY LAW AND SOCIETY?

Long ago Robert Lynd posed a question for academia: knowledge for what?[15] We conceive that the domain of law and society studies lies in the legal order. We do not study it for its sake alone. We study it because the organized political community necessarily implicates law in all its attempts to solve social problems.

We enact laws to solve perceived difficulties. Laws embody policies. The study of law and society ought to teach us how to generate sensible statements about how, by using the legal order, we can go about solving existential difficulties.

Consider, for example, the problem of discrimination against women and minorities in work, schooling, and the legal order. In 1954 the United States Supreme Court effectively made new law in the case of *Brown* v. *Board of Education*.[16] Basing its decision on a wealth of information from social scientists, advocates of equal educational rights, and organized groups of minority activists, and deciding a highly controversial issue in the face of massive demonstrations throughout the nation, the Supreme Court concluded that "separate but equal" educational facilities were inherently discriminatory and unconstitutional. The issue had been brought before the Court before and the decision had gone the other way. In 1954, however, the Court reversed previous decisions and made illegal an entire body of state law that established separate educational institutions for minorities—especially for blacks.

Twenty-five years later there is an abundance of evidence that the antidiscrimination laws, including the *Brown* v. *Board of Education* Supreme Court decision, have had only a slight effect on discrimination in education. Separate schooling for blacks is still ubiquitous throughout the South and is prevalent in many parts of the North as well.[17]

The study of law and society requires that we look keenly at this process of lawmaking—why in 1954 did the Supreme Court reverse itself on earlier decisions? Why did antidiscrimination laws emerge in most states following the 1954 decision? And why, given the lofty goals expressed in the decision and in the halls of legislatures when antidiscrimination laws were passed, has there been so little change in educational discrimination?

Or consider another example—the problem of discrimination against women in faculty positions in higher education (colleges and universities). Title VII of the Civil Rights Act of 1967 provided an elaborate machinery for solving the problems of discrimination against the employment of blacks, other minorities, and women. The statute expressly exempted universities. By 1972, however, Congress had received massive evidence that in their academic employment decisions universities and colleges discriminated against women. Under the sway of the normative myth, Congress believed that Title VII worked as prescribed. In 1972, it swept universities under Title VII's coverage. By 1979, at least forty academic women had instituted lawsuits claiming that they had not received tenure on grounds of gender. Despite the massive evidence of continuing sex-based discrimination in universities, until 1980 *not one* of these forty women had won tenure through a court decree. It defies common sense that not one of them was the victim of sexist discrimination.

How to solve problems of this sort? The study of law and society should give us a disciplined agenda to follow, whose probable outcome will advise us how to solve these difficulties through the legal order. We cannot manufacture solutions to problems out of gossamer and dreams. We must use past experience to solve new difficulties. How to use the experience with the legal order's response to discrimination in education, industry, and universities to fashion a solution to discrimination?

Every human situation has unique qualities; two people never view the moon from precisely the same angle. Factories differ from universities. How do we learn from always unique experience something helpful about a new situation which is itself necessarily unique? With respect to the legal order, that plainly calls for knowledge of two sorts: knowledge about the uses and limits of law, a methodology for acquiring usable knowledge, and knowledge about the methodology of making workable policy judgment. What sort of knowledge can at once derive from unique, nonreplicable human experience, and at the same time teach us something useful about a new, unique problem? We try to characterize the sorts of knowledge required in the following section.

1.4 KNOWLEDGE ABOUT THE LEGAL ORDER

Sensible problem-solving through the legal order requires extensive knowledge about how the legal order works. Just as a cabinetmaker cannot expect to produce well-designed, long-lasting furniture without extensive knowledge about the capacity of his tools and woods, so we cannot solve our problems through the legal order without knowledge about its limits and potentials. We conceive that the study of how the legal order actually works becomes a necessary, but not sufficient component of an adequate theory of justice. Justice theory must concern itself with the question, What ought the law to be? The ought supposes the can, or the question becomes idiotic. For example, in 1954 it appeared that the institutionalized patterns of discrimination in education would be permanently destroyed with the decision in *Brown* v. *Board of Education*. Almost thirty years later, buttressed by streams of federal and state legislation and numerous court decisions designed to achieve racial equality in education the problem has scarcely been touched. In 1972, it appeared that to ensure equal employment opportunities for academic women required only that universities in their roles as employers change their behavior to act in a nondiscriminatory way. Machinery to accomplish that already stood in place, created for industry by the Civil Rights Act of 1967. Under sway of the normative myth, how easy it was to assume that the Civil Rights Act secured the rights it purported to do, and sweep under its scope university women. A sophisticated decision-maker might have asked what we could learn about the problem from the industrial experience in the five years since the enactment of Title VII, and more generally from law and society studies. How to use the experience of trying to solve employment discrimination in industry to resolve employment discrimination in the academy? How to learn from experience?

That general problem has a long provenance. It is evident that underpinning attempts to control the world must lie knowledge of the world. Long ago, Sir Francis Bacon put the objective of learning to be the discovery of the "secret motion" of things, to the end that people could control their environment.[18] An airplane designer ignores the law of gravity at peril. Lawmakers equally at risk ignore the "secret motion" of people-in-society. Solutions aimed at symptoms rarely succeed. We must first understand causes—the "great motion" of things.

The difficulty is that *people* and *things* have different characteristics. The eighteenth-century conception of society copied that of the physical sciences, taking as its model the clock. A rubric expressed its central principle: "same causes, same effects." Lawrence Friedman and Stuart Macauley have the same model in mind when they argue that "the ideal for the social sciences is the situation in the physical sciences; what is true of falling bodies in New York is true of them in Brisbane tomorrow and Nairobi yesterday. It is a view which assumes that there are systematic, universal ties between law and society and that these ties can be uncovered through the methods of the physical sciences."[19]

Laws of course embody *purposes, plans, policies, desires, ends, goals, anticipations*—that is, they embody conscious choice. If society really does constitute a giant clockwork, then choice disappears, for even our sense of choosing becomes only an illusion. Material causes, it seems, make our choices inevitable. Law embodies choice. Unless we have some degree of freedom in choosing, the creative use of law to solve existential problems disappears.

Karl Popper and a host of others have pointed to the miscomprehension of the natures of people and society implicit in the clockwork model.[20] Human beings have consciousness. Every human situation is therefore in a sense unique. It is precisely that consciousness and that uniqueness that distinguish people from inanimate objects; it is these qualities that distinguish *social* science from *physical* science.

History demonstrated the naivete embodied in the clockwork view. No sooner did social scientists develop "laws" about human behavior than eternal human cussedness proved them less than invariant. Society came to resemble a cloud of midges, whose only governing principle requires one to turn back if too far from the swarm. The first view made it seem as though the amorphous cloud of society in fact operated as a clock. The second view (supported by developments in physics) made it seem that all clocks only masked a cloud. The new principle appeared to be "same causes, who knows what effects?"

If all clocks only mask clouds, however, then prediction becomes impossible. If prediction becomes impossible, then purpose disappears in the world. On that view of the world, one might as well plant a stone as a seed; what emerges depends on random chance. Like the all-clouds-are-clocks model the all-clocks-are-clouds model too made law impossible. The one denied choice, the other denied purpose.

Two positions emerged in the face of the insufficiency of both clocks and clouds. Mainstream social science asserted a sharp difference between the Is and the Ought. The world that Is became a clock; the world of the Ought became a cloud. Purpose lived, for prediction about what Is remained possible. Choice, too, lived, for the cloud remained the model for the Ought. The conventional language of ends and means captures this position. In the world of the Is, clockwork reigned, prediction became possible, and values disappeared. Propositions about the world of the Is caught unvarying relationships. true everywhere and always. In the world of the Ought, however, clouds reigned, prediction became impossible, and values determined everything. All propositions embodying a decision about what we ought to do ultimately rest upon values and sentiments. The philosopher David Hume preached the discontinuity of the Is and the Ought, and that reason should always serve as slave to passion.[21] In that view, a proposition urging that government should enact a law of a particular sort to solve a particular problem expressed policy. Since that involved ends, it must rest upon the personal predilection of the decision-maker. Experience could only tell us the likely consequences of alternative courses of action, not whether any of these ought to come about. The personal tastes or desires of lawmakers hardly serve to justify public policy.

In this view all law—including the 1954 Supreme Court decision and the 1972 decision to include universities under Title VII—constitutes no more than the personal value-choices of those making the decisions: judges and Congressmen and women. The decisions involved the ends of ensuring equal educational opportunity for minorities and equal employment opportunities for women in universities. Furthermore, experience must be irrelevant to the decisions—they rest entirely upon the subjective values of the people. Research might explain what formed their consciousness—past socialization, interest group pressure, personal interest, and so forth. The experience of educational and employment discrimination against minorities and women could not bear upon the issue of choice and ends, however, because experience is not supposed to advise us about ends. Only values can do that.

Such a point of view, still quite common among those social scientists who identify with an extreme form of sociological positivism, is severely myopic and misleading. Attempting to divorce social science from social policy by circumventing the problems of making choices inherent in human social relations is no solution. The problem does not disappear by fiat. Social science by its very nature discovers relationships that have political and policy implications. The output of law and society studies necessarily consists of intellectual tools appropriate to the solution of real-life troubles. However, every historical situation is unique. How to learn from one unique situation something useful for solving another problem, in another place, involving different people is at the very heart of the study of law and society. A concomitant problem is how to use the empirical investigations of social science that ineluctably deal with past events in order to understand and guide problem-solving in the future.

To accomplish these ends requires a different vocabulary than ends and means. It requires a vocabulary that does not implicitly distinguish between Is and Ought, between fact and value. John Dewey called a proposition expressing what we ought to do to solve a particular problem an *end-in-view*.[22] People are starving; we seek to do something about it; we develop a plan to transfer food from one place to another. These constitute an end-in-view.

In the 1960s organized demonstrations, political mobilization, and lobbying by women's groups created a problem for the government of Great Britain, as it did for governments throughout the world. In Britain the government responded by passing the Equal Pay Act of 1970. This act, which came into force in 1975, made it illegal for employers to pay women lower wages than were paid to men for the same work. Ten years later, despite the Equal Pay Act and a number of other laws designed to accomplish the same goal, "women's average earnings remain at 64 percent of those for men."[23] The point of view that sees social science studies of law as solely concerned with the "Is" and as unable to suggest how to make law more effective denies that we can learn from this experience.

We do not agree that social science must deny the political and social implications of our work. Instead of the language of ends and means, we suggest the language of problem-solving as appropriate to the study of law and society. Difficulties, explanations, proposals for solution (or ends-in-view) are all part of the outcome of social scientific inquiry. Every proposition about the world has a value-content; every proposition also has a factual component. The task of social inquiry is to stipulate how these different facets of social inquiry mesh together.

The methodology implied by the point of view that sees problem-solving and social science inquiry as inextricably intertwined results in a variety of propositions about the world. These propositions base themselves to some extent upon knowledge about past experience. Their utility, however, lies in solving new and different difficulties. How to use past experience to generate knowledge useful in future situations?

We believe that the answer to that question lies in the concept of the *heuristic*. Propositions based on experience in one time and place cannot state reliable predictions about how people will behave in a different time and place. Human behavior too closely resembles a cloud to make those predictions very reliable. On the other hand, social behavior has some clock-like characteristics. That particular factors explain behavior in one time and place at least suggests that by examining similar variables in some other time and place we can economize our research.

We mean by a heuristic a general proposition causally relating two or more categories of experience. In policy-oriented research, heuristics focus our attention. In searching for the causes of a troubled situation, the researcher learns from heuristics that if one looks in particular areas, one will likely discover those causes. For example, research has long suggested that review agencies have great difficulty in holding accountable officials or agencies who exercise broad discretionary power. Employers always claim that the decision of which particular person deserves an appointment calls for difficult, highly subjective judgment that only management can make—that is, they claim that management must have great discretion in deciding who shall be employed. From this one might derive a tentative explanation for the failure of the 1972 amendment to help academic women to resist discrimination: courts cannot easily hold accountable university tenure decisions because they involve the exercise of broad discretion.

That proposition does not state how the world goes in every case. It does not state that universities win every Title VII lawsuit involving women only because universities successfully conceal discrimination behind the vague contours of discretionary choice. It does state that if one seeks an explanation for the general failure of courts to solve women's Title VII difficulties with universities, it might prove useful to look at the issue of scope of discretion and accountability. Only if one has made an investigation, however, can one discover actual causes of the behavior at issue. "No historical situation can be understood by 'applying' such laws, as one applies laws to particular occurrences in natural science. Indeed, it is only insofar as one has an *independent* historical grasp of situations like this that one is able to understand what the law amounts to at all."[24]

There is an important paradox in the study of law, then, that must be recognized. Law, as Pashukanis argues, is "historically specific," but at the same time it "parallels a real history which unfolds itself not as a system of thought, but as a special system of social relationships." The study of law, thus, must not only recognize the uniqueness of law and the legal order in a particular historical period, it must also take into account the historical development of these social phenomenon in order to comprehend the potential for as well as the limits of change. This in turn requires empirical investigation. Chairman Mao Tse Tsung put it pithily, "No empirical investigation, no right to speak."[25]

Given a new rule of law a proposition about its likely impact not only serves to put the law in its proper historical context but also serves as a prediction of behavior. The proposition that review agencies have great difficulty holding accountable agencies that exercise wide discretion now becomes a prediction that if universities continue to have great discretion in awarding tenure, courts will likely continue to fail to hold them accountable.

Knowledge of this sort ordinarily falls under the rubric, "the limits of law." "To optimize legal impact, we must honor the limits of law."[26] Our knowledge about these limits takes the form of propositions, general in form, stating the probable causal relationships between law and social variables—sometimes called "theories of the middle range." These "seek to map, and proclaim the propriety of mapping, the social world in a limited way—province by province, sector by sector."[27]

However dogmatically phrased, a proposition purporting to express knowledge about human affairs can never hold through all times and places. Knowledge about human affairs necessarily derives from past experience. A proposition purporting to express knowledge only tells us that in the particular times and places from which it derived, it held. It contains no warranty that it will hold in some new time or place. Nevertheless, it sums up the lessons of experience. It can serve to guide problem-solving in a new arena, but it comes with a built-in warning not to trust it implicitly. We live in a world both of clocks and of clouds.

We learn through experience. We can generate theory only by experience; we can understand experience only through theory. What we learn through doing finds its expression in heuristic propositions of the middle range.

Taken together, these heuristic propositions of the middle range constitute a statement of existing knowledge about the ways that law influences society, and its limits. Generating knowledge of this heuristic sort we take as a core task for law and society studies about the legal order. The limits that society imposes upon the law's capacity to change behavior explain how society determines what rules get enacted, and why, and what rules get enforced, and why. The study of law as an instrument to mold society becomes paradoxically but inevitably also a study of society as mold of law. The enterprise of generating knowledge of that sort cannot succeed if we wear the blinders of myth; we can learn through experience only to the extent that we look squarely at the data. As Gunnar Myrdal said, "Facts kick."

1.5 THE ELEMENTS OF THEORY ABOUT LAW AND SOCIETY

As we conceive it, the outcomes of the study of law and society ought to consist of propositions about how to solve existential social problems, that is, ends-in-view. To do that requires heuristic propositions embodying existing knowledge about how the legal order works. It also requires heuristic propositions advising how to go about solving social problems through the legal order. We call this body of knowledge *theory*.

The subject matter of the study lies in the world of "fact," of "data," of flesh and blood. Yet propositions do not arise out of data by mere inspection. The aimless collection of "facts" will no more lead to reliable knowledge (save by serendipity) than will the ditty bag of an idiot contain only gold and precious stones.[28] Blindly to examine forty unsuccessful Title VII cases may only end with a catalog of plaintiffs' names, or details about the length of the opinions.

The exploration of the vast mazes of reality demands a guide. Before a geographer can construct a map, he must have in mind a process that will, if followed, yield a reliable map. Before a navigator can use the map safely, she must have knowledge about a process by which she can relate the map and the existential world. Neither geographer nor navigator observes stars or mountains or rivers at random. Each follows a procedure believed to result in the acquisition of reliable knowledge. We subsume those procedures under three headings: methodology, perspectives, and vocabulary (or concepts). Here we discuss methodology; in Chapter 2, perspectives, and Chapter 3, vocabulary.

1.6 METHODOLOGY

How to generate reliable heuristics about the legal order? Facts do not come packaged as sentences. Propositions do not lie immanent in fact. Knowledge, not facts, has a logical form. Methodology has as its central task moving from an apprehension of experience to reliable heuristics expressing causal relationships in the real world.

Law and society research usually begins with a discontent. Management uses its position to injure shareholders; the police do not investigate rape complaints with sufficient vigor; or (in the cases we earlier mentioned), antidiscrimination laws do not seem to afford women and minorities relief against discrimination. That in turn comes down to *whose* discontents one will investigate—an issue we return to later.

Second, having defined a particular trouble, one must propose alternative explanations for it. That calls for the invocation of heuristics drawn from past experience. For example, one might begin with four possible explanations for the failure of courts to give much relief for university employment sex discrimination. (1) In a period of raised consciousness, members of an allegedly subordinate group will bring many frivolous claims alleging discrimination; or (2) women as a class have less competence than men do to serve as professors; or (3) where judges share the same class and gender prejudices as defendants, they will rarely find against those defendants; or (4) review agencies have great difficulty in holding accountable officials or agencies who exercise broad discretion in decision-making.

How to choose between these alternative explanations? People can dream up a broad range of heuristics; only a few of them seem to help in solving problems. Those that do help to solve problems have two principal characteristics, falsifiability and empirical warrant. An explanation that one could not in principle falsify through experience does not rest upon experience. It rests upon intuition, definition, or mysticism. It defies the central proposition—that we can only learn through experience. An explanation that the real world does not deny may prove unreliable; one that experience falsifies cannot serve at all. We learn through experience by generating heuristics that seem to fit the available data, and then using those heuristics as preliminary guides to examine the problem under review.

Third, having eliminated most of the candidate explanations and thus identified the "causes" of the difficulty at hand, one can propose alternative solutions addressed to those causes. For example, if it develops that courts in fact have found it impossible to review tenure decisions because they are based on unstated discretionary standards, perhaps the law ought to require universities to state precisely their standards for tenure or perhaps it ought to create a body of independent experts to review tenure decisions, applying the discretionary standards of academia but charged to ensure that no discrimination intruded in the decision.

Finally, the research requires implementation, monitoring, and evaluation of the selected solution. Any failure of the action taken to resolve the original difficulty (and no solution ever works completely) falsifies to that extent all the previous steps. The failure in any particular of the bridge falsifies not only the engineering design, but perhaps also the theoretical mechanics upon which the design based itself. The failure of antidiscrimination laws falsifies the proposition that the passage of these laws is sufficient to ensure compliance. Thus do we learn by doing (Dewey). Marx and Sartre called it *praxis*.

In this agenda, the law-in-the-books constitutes always a proposal for solution. The law-in-action constitutes its implementation. A systematic variance exists between the law-in-the-books and the activity it induces. That gap constitutes a new trouble, requiring in turn explanation and solution. Thus the gap between the promises of antidiscrimination laws and their failure to counteract discrimination constitutes a new trouble.

In the course of proposing explanations, we must articulate major premises in the form of general propositions. If it works in one case, a proposition has some status as knowledge, i.e., as a heuristic. The principal task in the generation of knowledge consists in generating and trying to falsify heuristics. The general stock of knowledge consists in the main of these "middle level" propositions (hypotheses, theories), all of them heuristics, and therefore none of them ever more than problematical. "Policy," "instrumental" or "problem-solving" research, and academic or "theoretical" research in this view constitute parts of the same enterprise.

1.7 VOCABULARY (CONCEPTS) AND METHODOLOGY

An adequate theory of law and society requires a set of categories to guide empirical investigations. If we have no category within which to classify an item of data, it becomes meaningless. English has only a few words for different sorts of snow: slush, powder snow, corn snow. The Eskimos, it is said, have thirty-two words, each for a different sort of snow. We lose the differences that Eskimos perceive between one kind of snow and another, because we lack categories into which to classify the information.

We cannot, however, simply increase the number of categories *ad infinitum*. Of course every nugget of experience differs from every other. Unless we reduce the infinity of experience into a relatively small number of categories, we lose all ability to deal with it. A map of the world on a one-to-one scale would cover the world. It would not lose detail, but its very detail would deny its utility. Only by the inevitable loss of detail involved in creating categories of thought can we understand.

Any choice of categories (or vocabulary) entails an evaluation.[29] To create a category expresses a judgment that the category helps to explain the phenomenon at issue. The British rulers of the Gold Coast Colony in Africa solemnly recorded of every prisoner his tribal origin and his religion. They did not record his social class, his family situation, his mental or his educational level, his criminal record, his living conditions, or whether he lived in an urban or rural setting. The categories selected contained a criminological theory relating crime to tribe and religion, and rejecting other possible causative variables.

1.8 PERSPECTIVES AND METHODOLOGY

In addition to a methodology and categories, any social theory requires a *perspective*. Like every methodology for generating knowledge, the one we put forward here requires discretionary choice. Consider, for example, the four possible explanations for university discrimination against women faculty. All express various sorts of sentiments, or "values": about the psychology of oppressed groups and their response, about the competence of women, about male biases, about the nature of discretion and review. We must make choices at every step in the research agenda: in deciding to research what questions, what candidate explanations, what modes of testing explanations, what proposals for solutions, and so forth. How do we make these choices? Problem-solving without explicit control over value-choice too easily becomes muddling through—i.e., adopting the smallest possible change to help to alleviate the difficulty. In that case, problem-solving ends up a device for tension-management and a handmaiden to the status quo.

In research, discretionary choices appear to arise out of the personal consciousness of the researcher. They may arise out of mere self-interest, or out of the dark, irrational drives or "residues" or "values" of which social scientists warn us. They guide research, but unconsciously. Unless the researcher "delivers his domain assumptions from the dim realm of subsidiary awareness into the clearer realm of cool awareness, where they can be held firmly in view, they can never be brought before the bar of reason or submitted to the test of evidence."[30] One must begin by articulating one's domain assumptions and thus confronting them. The researcher who takes as his explanation for testing that women and minorities do not have sufficient capacity for the education and work they seek ought at least to declare the perspective from which he views the problem. Mere declaration of bias, however, will hardly do for law and society studies. Matters of public policy require public justification. If intellect and science can ever enlarge their control over lawmaking, public justification must rely upon appeals to reason, not to unreason.

Stating one's values as domain assumptions, however, inevitably leads to attempts at rationalizing and harmonizing them. Together, they become the researcher's ideal-typical "model of society" or paradigm.[31] The neoclassical model of capitalist society, legal liberalism, the political scientist's model of political pluralism, and Marxism constitute examples. Such ideal-typical models serve the same function in problem-solving inquiry as do "values": they guide discretionary choice.

Ideal-typical models frequently embody proposals for solution, for they put forward programs (or "ends") that their authors think desirable. Like all proposals for solution, they either state or imply explanations, whose stated causes they address. Adam Smith did not write a tract exalting free enterprise or capitalism; he wrote an explanation for the wealth of nations.[32] So also Karl Marx: *Das Kapital* did not propagandize for a socialist society (the word "socialism" does not appear in its four long volumes).[33] He wrote a description of and an explanation for mid-century English capitalism.

In principle, every end constitutes a proposal for solution. It therefore implies an explanation. The great trick in law and society research lies in converting proposals for law reform (i.e., proposals for solution, themselves not testable) into explanations for solution, in principle subject to the tests of falsifiability and falsification. Every overarching end implies an equally overarching explanation—some call those explanations "grand theory" or "perspectives." Using grand theory to guide discretionary choices in research should lead to the same results as using the "values" or ideal-typical model with which the grand theory resonates.

For example, that antidiscrimination laws fail because male judges share the prejudices and empathize with the white male-dominated ruling class rests upon a domain assumption that ruling class males tend to have prejudices against minorities and women. That domain assumption translates into an ideal-typical model that holds that discrimination against minorities and women will persist until minorities and women make decisions about themselves. That ideal-typical model rests upon an explanation for the world that holds that people generally (and judges in particular) make decisions because they respond to their subjective values. Because social science rarely can do experiments, we cannot likely discover now if women judges in the future will *actually* make different decisions than do men. We can make an empirical test only of the explanatory proposition.

How to test such overarching theories? The articulation of "grand theory," like the articulation of any explanation, requires discretionary choices. How to guide *those* discretionary choices? How to test grand theory itself? Ultimately, its test lies in praxis, in learning through doing. The process of problem-solving inquiry requires implementation and monitoring. Implementation generates data to test all the preceding process. Just as building a bridge tests not only its particular design, but the general theoretical propositions that underlie it, the successes or failures of particular social interventions may test the grand theories upon which they were based. Ultimately, however, even that answer becomes unsatisfactory. By what standards do we measure the success or failure of the intervention? That asks not merely by *what* standards, but by *whose?* Just as the choice of *whose* trouble determines the domain of study, so the research must decide from whose perspective to judge success or failure. Researchers can no more avoid choosing sides in the great social struggles of our time than can anyone else.[34]

1.9 CONCLUSION

In our era, government's principal technique of social control consists of law and the legal order. That legal order is supposed to contain within it a panoply of liberal, democratic values that ensure democratic control over the state, equality before the law, and the protection of essential minority interests. That the times seem so out of joint, therefore, implies a failure of the legal order to carry out the functions it is alleged to have. Since we take as our domain of study the legal order we must explain its seeming failure.

That study, we believe, takes its significance from the legal order's significance. Without invoking the legal order, no government, whatever its intent or ideology, can mold society to its policy prescriptions. Without it, ruling classes or elites cannot sustain their domination. Without it, whatever their content, democratic liberties lie at risk. As a community, we must rely on the legal order to solve the problems that face us. Without knowledge about how the legal order works, we cannot use it effectively.

To understand the legal order, we must first generate a theory with which to approach its study. That calls for a methodology, perspectives, and vocabulary. We advanced a methodology that purports to aid in generating heuristics, that is, propositions that will guide investigations of particular existential problems. We suggested the function of perspectives to aid in taming the biases that value-sets ineluctably give to research and policy prescription. We argued the function of vocabulary (or categories) in research. In the following two chapters we discuss the various perspectives and vocabularies employed in the study of law and society. First (Chapter 2) we contrast formal social control systems in stateless and state societies, taking the occasion to discuss a few of the broad theoretical perspectives that scholars have urged for law and society studies. In Chapter 3 the discussion of vocabularies and theories continues with an emphasis on theories of law and categories for studying law and legal order in state societies.

NOTES

1. Oliver Wendell Holmes, Jr., *The Common Law* (Boston: 1881).

2. L. Friedman, *The Legal System: A Social Science Perspective* (New York: Russell Sage Foundation, 1975), pp. 1-2.

3. William B. Harvey, *Law and Social Change in Ghana* (Princeton: Princeton University Press, 1966), p. 343.

4. E. A. Hoebel, *The Law of Primitive Man: A Study in Comparative Legal Dynamics* (Cambridge: Harvard University Press, 1964), p. 26.

5. *Ibid.*, p. 28.

6. *Ibid.*

7. W. Ross Ashby, *An Introduction to Cybernetics* (New York: John Wiley & Sons, 1956), pp. 106, 227, 228. Walter Buckley, ed., *Modern Systems Research for the Behavioral Scientist* (Chicago: Aldine Publishing Co., 1968), pp. xx, 204, 490-491.

8. Robert B. Seidman, *The State, Law and Development* (London: Croom Helm, 1978), pp. 16-17, 72-78, 23-24, 345-346.

9. Lon F. Fuller, *The Morality of Law* (New Haven: Yale University Press, 1964), pp. 169-170.

10. Geoffrey Sawyer, *Law in Society* (Oxford: Oxford University Press, 1965).

11. *Ibid.*

12. *Ibid.*

13. Congressional elections and campaign funding.

14. Friedman, *Legal System*, pp. 180-181.

15. Robert Lynd, *Knowledge for What* (Princeton: Princeton University Press, 1939).

16. *Brown v. Board of Education*, 347 U.S. 483 (1954).

17. A. D. Freeman, "Legitimizing Racial Discrimination through Anti-Discrimination Law: A Critical Review of Supreme Court Doctrine," *Minnesota Law Review* 62 (1978): 1049.

18. John M. Robertson, *The Philosophical Works of Francis Bacon* (London: George Rutledge & Sons, 1905), pp. 39-176.

19. L. Friedman and Stewart Macauley, *Law and the Behavioral Sciences* (Indianapolis: Bobbs-Merrill, 1969), pp. 915-916. Also see D. J. Black, "The Boundaries of Legal Sociology," *Yale Law Journal* 81 (1972): 1086-96.

20. Karl Popper, *The Logic of Scientific Discovery* (New York: Harper & Row, 1968), and Norwood R. Hanson, *Patterns of Discovery* (Cambridge: at the University Press, 1958).

21. David Hume, *A Treatise of Human Nature* (London: Everyman's Library, 1972), p. 127.

22. John Dewey, *Logic: The Theory of Inquiry* (New York: Henry Holt & Co., 1938), pp. 496-497. Also see John Dewey, *The Theory of Valuation* (Chicago: University of Chicago Press, 1939).

23. Jeanne Gregory, "Sex Discrimination, Work and the Law," in Bob Fine, *et al., Capitalism and the Rule of Law* (London: Hutchinson, 1979), p. 145.

24. Seidman, *State, Law and Development*.

25. Piers Beirne and R. Sharlet, eds., *Pashukanis: Selected Writings on Marxism and Law* (London: Academic Press, 1980). Also see Mao Tse Tsung, *Selected Readings from the Works of Mao Tse Tsung* (Peking: Foreign Languages Press, 1971).

26. J. A. Robertson and P. Teitlebaum, "Optimizing Legal Impact: A Case Study in Search of a Theory," *Wisconsin Law Review* (1973): 663.

27. Alvin Gouldner, *The Coming Crisis of Western Sociology* (New York: Avon Books, 1970).

28. N. R. Hanson, *Patterns of Discovery* (Cambridge: at the University Press, 1958).

29. Gouldner, *Coming Crisis*.

30. *Ibid.*, p. 35.

31. A. Inkeles, *What Is Sociology?* (Englewood Cliffs, NJ: Prentice-Hall, 1964), pp. 28-29.

32. Adam Smith, *The Wealth of Nations* (London: J. M. Dent & Sons, 1957).

33. Karl Marx, *Capital,* translated by S. Moore and E. Aveling. Edited by Frederick Engels. (New York: International Publishers, 1967).

34. *Ibid.*

2

Theoretical perspectives: stateless and state societies

Our domain of study—that normative system which comprises law and the legal order—focuses on societies in which a state structure exists. Societies exist that have no state, that is, in which nobody fills formal roles whose only function relates to one of the many manifestations of governance. We can learn much from comparing these stateless societies with those in which power is exercised through a state structure.

Our interest in the legal order centers on its social control functions. Every society has a system that serves that function. Consider one aspect of it, dispute-settlement: moots and conclaves in tribal society, cadis in Moslem systems, the Curia Regis in medieval England, "juries" of six hundred citizens in classical Athens, and military tribunals in junta-controlled Chile all serve functions roughly analogous to our courts.

In this diversity, however, some patterns emerge. In all their differences, the normative systems of pre-industrial states have some striking similarities; so do the legal orders of industrial states. How to explain the diversity of normative systems, even between states superficially similar? How to explain the underlying similarities of legal orders within the broad categories mentioned? From the study of similarities and differences, in this chapter we try to tease out some factors that differentiate the legal orders of state societies from their functional surrogates in stateless societies. We begin with the diversity of normative systems.

2.1 THE DIVERSITY OF NORMATIVE SYSTEMS

The many societies that the world has known contain a wide variety of normative systems. Countries side by side, in seemingly the same general circumstance, develop widely different systems—the United States and Mexico, for example, or Greece and Yugoslavia, or China and India. Even states of the United States whose culture seems identical have quite divergent rules on many specific matters, for example, capital punishment, marijuana smoking, and rape.

That diversity seems, if anything, even more striking when we consider "simple" societies based on low technologies. These stand sharply contrasted with more complex societies, a distinction that has excited social scientists for two centuries. An anthropologist, Max Gluckman, wrote:

When we contrast tribal society with modern society we are . . . working with a distinction the implications of which have been elaborated by many sociologists and anthropologists: the difference between Durkheim's mechanical and organic solidarity, Tonnies' *gemeinschaft* and *gesellschaft,* von Weise's sacred and secular societies, Weber's traditional and bureaucratic societies, Stalin's patriarchal and industrial societies, Redfield's folk society and urban civilization.[1]

Today, practically all social scientists agree that technology has great force in explaining societal differences and similarity. How does one explain diversity among societies whose low levels of technology seem markedly alike?

Out of a naive Darwinism, an earlier generation of social scientists generalized that societies like species developed linearly from simple to complex. Technology does change; it constantly grows more complex. That does not necessarily constitute progress. To paraphrase Milton Mayer, a society in which one cuts off friends' heads with a two-toned convertible and enemies' with a flame thrower has not much progressed over a society in which one does these tasks with a machete. As a concept, "progress" must entail a culture-bound set of values. It will not serve as an explanatory construct.

Confronting variations in law-like systems, some anthropologists tried to explain their difference by placing them on a continuum from the most simple to the most complex. They postulated that their continuum represented a historical progression through which every "legal" order must pass. The historical materials seem too scanty to warrant such a thesis; what evidence exists is ambiguous.[2]

The study of law-like institutions in nonindustrial as compared with industrial societies can, however, yield dividends. By contrasting and comparing the legal orders of industrialized, bureaucratized societies with their analogues in traditional, nonindustrialized societies, one might discover useful propositions relating social structure and legal order. Here we first consider the range of law-like norms in technologically underdeveloped societies.

Technology and Simple Societies

Nonindustrial societies have simple technologies. The tools lack complexity, and the various tasks required to produce the necessities of life do not fall readily into easily learned, repetitive bits. In a technologically complex society, on the other hand, unbelievably sophisticated tools require the division of the tasks involved into small, easily learned and repetitive actions. A modern automobile manufacturing plant creates fantastically complicated automobiles by people each of whom does a comparatively simple job.

These differences in technology create a range of consequences that become important for our study. First, the simpler the technology, the smaller the number of differentiated jobs in the economy. That does not say that everyone in simple societies does the same thing. Even in a Bushman band, living on as simple a technological level as exists in the world, women do different sorts of jobs than men. But the variety of jobs has a much narrower range, and the jobs seem much less differentiated from each other than they do in complex societies.

Second, the simpler the technology, the less likely that its use *requires* much cooperation between the owner of the means of production and those who do the actual work. A women who owns a short-handled hoe does not need to hire another person to help her to use it. The owner of an automobile factory, however, cannot build cars alone. She must hire other people to work in her factory.

Third, primitive technologies entail privation. In many instances, they hardly produce the minimum required to satisfy hunger, let alone a surplus. Thus the phrase "subsistence economy," frequently used to describe the economies of simple societies, has a dual meaning. On the one hand, it implies quite literally that the standard of living does not rise much above the subsistence level. On the other hand, since roles lack much differentiation, people do not exchange many goods and services. Everyone provides for herself and her family, rather than exchanging what she uniquely produces for what others uniquely produce.

Social Control in Technologically Simple Societies

Nevertheless, even in societies gripped by harsh environments and low technological levels, and whose populations' common lot entails fear and privation, social forms and law-like structures richly proliferate. Villages located side by side, with seemingly identical technological levels, sometimes have different cultures, organizations, and religions. One Ibo village on Nigeria's Niger River may have as its dominant mode of production agriculture; the next village downstream, fishing. The one village may worship an earth god, the next, a river god. In the one village taboos may prohibit fishing, with the fish believed to embody the ancestral spirits, while downstream, analogous beliefs inhibit farming. One task posed by these cultural variations is to explain such different sets of norms in what appear to be such similar circumstances.

Whatever their differences, every society, simple or complex, has some system of social control. In a classical passage, Hobbes wrote, "It is manifest, that during the time men live without a Power to keep them all in awe, they are in that condition which is called Warre, and such a warre, as is of every man against every man."[3] Hobbes erred. All the available evidence falsifies his famous pronouncement. No matter how simple the society, no matter how innocent of state structure and legal order, its normal condition does not consist of war and turmoil. Though there may be conflict and change, not "warre" but stability constitutes the norm. The anthropologist E. E. Evans-Pritchard described the social control system among the Nuer of the Sudan in Africa.

The Nuer live in a flat savannah country on both banks of the White Nile as it flows northerly from northern Uganda across the southern Sudan toward Khartoum and Egypt. Clayey, parched, and bare during drought, the land floods and glows verdantly during the rainy season from June through December when the rivers overflow their banks. When it rains, flooded swampy areas separate the villages, which lie on sandy ridges rising out of the water. On these ridges, along which the villages stretch for a mile or two, people and cattle live, isolated. In the dry season, all becomes dry and sere; great cracks open up in the hard clay soil and, lest the cattle die, the villagers must set forth to find water. Then the villagers burn the grass to provide for new pasture. They live in small camps near water holes. When the rains set in, they return to the safety of their ridge-top villages, to begin again the unchanging cycle of their lives.

The harsh environment and the very simple technological level that the Nuer have achieved demand that the members of the community work cooperatively against the ever-present threat of famine. Evans-Pritchard, whose work on the Nuer forms the basis for most of our knowledge about them, says that the Nuer

are generally on the verge of want and that every few years they face more or less severe famine. Under these conditions, it is understandable that there is much sharing of food in the same village, especially among members of adjacent homesteads and hamlets. . . . [Moreover, the] paucity of raw materials, together with a meagre food supply, contracts social ties, drawing the people of village or camp closer, in a moral sense, for they are in consequence highly interdependent and their pastoral hunting, fishing and, to a lesser degree, their agricultural activities are necessarily joint undertakings.

He concludes:

Thus, while in a narrow sense the economic unit is the household, the larger local communities are, directly or indirectly, cooperative groups combining to maintain existence, and corporations owning natural resources and sharing in their exploitations. In the smaller local groups the co-operative functions are more direct and evident than in the larger ones, but the collective function of obtaining for themselves the necessities of life from the same resources is in some degree common to all local communities from the household to the tribe.[4]

Arising out of the two different conditions of life, Nuer society faces two different problems in the maintenance of public order. During the rainy season, the principal problem becomes maintaining order within the isolated village—a close-knit community in which practically everybody relates to everybody else, and both as an economic unit and for mutual welfare everyone depends on the village's corporate cohesiveness. During the dry season, the same requirements obtain, but in addition the herdsmen must move safely through the countryside without fear of attack by other Nuer from other villages moving through the same country.[5]

The Nuer meet these two different kinds of problems in maintaining public order through their systems of organization. The Nuer organize themselves into tribes, and further divide and subdivide each tribe on a territorial basis into primary, secondary, and tertiary tribal sections. They divide each tertiary section into villages, and villages into domestic groups.[6] Though a tribal segment has a territorial orientation, each relates to others through common lineage in a complex way, so that each segment of the tribe, though including persons not of the same lineage, nevertheless often regards itself as connected to a particular agnatic group ("agnatic" meaning related through the male line).

As a result of this system of division and subdivision, every Nuer becomes a member of a host of corporate groups. He holds membership in his own village; and vis-à-vis another village, even one within his own tertiary section, he owes allegiance to his own village. Within his own tertiary section, however, he is allied with every village in it vis-à-vis other tertiary sections; and so goes the association with respect to all the tribal divisions up to the tribe itself.

The Nuer maintain public order, by the norms of conduct determining who must join, and on whose side, in any situation involving force. In the event of violence between two persons, others ought to support whichever of the two persons holds membership in their smallest corporate group. Thus if a member of Village A kills a member of Village B, all the other members of Village B ought to support the aggrieved parties (the family of the deceased) against the killer; and Village A's members ought to support the killer. On the other hand, if Z tertiary section includes both Village A and Village B in a similar case between any member of Z tertiary section and X tertiary section, then all the village members of both A and B will unite behind the member of their tertiary section.

What outsiders might regard as a mad anarchy centered on the "barbaric" and "primitive" concept of blood feud thus becomes the significant regulating force of the society. A man hesitates to violate the norms of peaceful conduct for fear of visiting upon his head the wrath not only of his victim, but of all those within the relevant corporate group of the victim as well. Although no doubt the expectation that in such an event one's own in-group will support him somewhat offsets this fear, the expectation of support depends on whether one knows that one has or has not complied with socially approved norms. Whether as victim or as aggressor, the amount of opposition one stirs up and the amount of effective support one can expect become functions of whether the conduct involved does or does not match the role-expectation of others in the community.

Such a system of maintaining public order provides no way of resolving bona fide disputes concerning whether a person in fact violated the norm, or the content of the appropriate applicable norm. It seems reasonably appropriate for maintaining order, however, among relative strangers, for the fear of setting off serious group conflict, with all its dangers to oneself and to one's close relatives and associates, tends to deter breach of the acceptable rules of conflict.

These rules become less satisfactory within the village community and between closely neighboring villages. Following a killing, mystical sanctions operate that forbid persons between whom a blood feud exists to eat and drink from the same vessels. Were they to do so, they believe, they would die.

Yet within the same village and between adjacent villages common economic and familial bonds tie people together. Women from one lineage or village may marry men from another lineage or village. A feud may place a man and his sister's children— particularly close relations—on opposite sides. The cooperation on which Nuer existence depends may lie at risk.

The Nuer do have an official of sorts, a man whom they call, rather loosely, a leopard-skin chief because he has the right to wear a leopard skin. His title notwithstanding, the leopard-skin chief has no authority over anybody else. Within the village, if a man's action excites resistance—for example, if a farmer claims that another man owes him a bullock and he proceeds to take it by self-help, with resistance on the part of the owner—others will try to persuade the disputants to ask the leopard-skin chief to mediate the dispute in an effort to avoid the difficulties of unresolved feud.

The leopard-skin chief has more than a merely passive role. When a man has killed another man, he may neither eat nor drink until a leopard-skin chief has cut his arm until the blood flows. Moreover, the hut of the chief constitutes a sanctuary. A killer usually stays in that hut to avoid vengeance. Meanwhile, the leopard-skin chief actively tries to persuade the kin of the deceased to accept cattle in compensation for the killing. He has no authority, however, to impose any decision.

The chief is not asked to deliver a judgment: it would not occur to Nuer that one was required. He appears to force the kin of the dead man to accept compensation by his insistence, even to the point of threatening to curse them, but it is an established convention that he shall do so, in order that the bereaved relatives may retain their prestige. What seems really to have counted were the acknowledgement of community tie between the parties concerned, and hence of the moral obligation to settle the affair by the acceptance of a traditional payment, and the wish, on both sides, to avoid, for the time being at any rate, further hostilities.[7]

Thus "the leopard-skin chief does not rule and judge, but acts as mediator through whom communities desirous of ending open hostility can conclude an active state of feud."[8]

The Nuer have a fixed scale of compensation—said to have been forty to fifty head of cattle until recently—regardless of the actual status or position of the deceased, or of the number of persons dependent on him. A ritual cleansing and atonement, performed by the leopard-skin chief, accompanies payment.

In lesser disputes than homicide, usually over ownership of cattle, the leopard-skin chief and the elders act as mediators. The chief does not, however, act as judge in this instance either; he has no power to summon the parties or to compel compliance with his decision. He can only visit the defendant with the plaintiff and some elders and inquire whether the former and his kinsmen will settle the matter. If the defendant agrees, the parties can submit the matter to arbitration by the chief in consultation with the elders. Even this decision, however, calls for general agreement and "in a large measure, therefore, arises from an acknowledgement by the defendant's or plaintiff's party that the other party has justice on its side."[9]

The seeming anarchy of Nuer life is an illusion. The Nuer society maintains order because its social structure consists of a set of positions defined by norms that describe a system for the peaceful resolution of disputes.

Nuer society seems extremely simple, homogeneous, and unstratified. Most people know the simple norms and internalize them. The intangible and largely unconscious sanctions and rewards of ordinary social intercourse suffice to enforce these norms. At the same time, harsh environment and simple technology combine to teach that compromise, with the concomitant restoration of social cohesion, constitutes a more pressing social imperative by far than the winner-takes-all norm enforcement solution. As a result, the dispute-settlement mechanism becomes a device, not for imposing punishment for the breach of norms, but for the restoration of social cohesion. No special agencies exist for norm enforcement; the feud, which involves the whole society, becomes the sanctioning institution.

Norm Creation in Technologically Simple Societies

Though every society has some sort of a social control system—that makes it a society, and not anarchy—these vary widely between societies. How to account for these differences? To answer that question, we must consider how norms get created. In a complex society such as the United States, formal rules of law emerge from particular institutions charged with creating law: legislatures, administrative agencies, appellate courts. In simpler societies, however, those institutions do not exist. How do those norms that seem analogous to our rules of law come about? Here we examine four of the many theories that scholars have advanced, those by Seagle, Von Savigny, Malinowski, and Hoebel. Then we will put forward an explanation that focuses on *choice* and *conflict* as an explanation for diversity.

Seagle. In his book *The Quest For Law* (1941), lawyer William Seagle entitled a whole section "Custom Is King." As he put it:

The great reality of primitive law is not "civil" law, or "criminal" law, but custom. . . . While there is no automatic submission to custom, there is an automatic sway of custom. Somehow, marvellous to relate, the savage recognizes the binding character of his customs although they are not backed by specific judicial sanctions of a repressive character, as in civilized society. It is obeyed merely because it is the custom.[10]

Seagle noticed a frequently reported fact: that in simpler societies, breaches of the norms occur relatively less frequently than they do in more complex societies. To blame that on personality structure or the genes, however, runs in circles. The relative infrequence of deviance calls for explanation. Seagle explains this by "custom." To "prove" the existence of the custom, however, he can only point to the relative infrequence of deviance. That chases its own tail.

Von Savigny. Explanations that postulate "instinct" as the original source of the norms of a given society tend to explain the differences in the normative structures of societies in terms of the specifically different instincts belonging to different populations. In the early nineteenth century the German jurisprudent Friedrich Carl von Savigny popularized that view. He sought the ultimate source of law in the *Volksgeist* or "common consciousness" of a people. He argues:

In the earliest times to which authentic history extends, the law will be found to have already attained a fixed character, peculiar to the people like their language, manner and constitution. Nay, these phenomena have no separate existence; they are but the particular faculties and tendencies of an individual people, inseparably united in nature and only wearing the semblance of distinct attributes to our view. That which binds them into one whole is the common convention of the people.

The kindred consciousness of an inward necessity excluding all notions of an accidental and arbitrary origin . . . law grows with the growth, and strengthens with the strength of the people and finally dies away as a nation loses its nationality. . . . The sum therefore of this theory is that all law is originally formed in the manner in which ordinary . . . language is said to have been formed, i.e., that it is first developed by custom and popular faith, next by jurisprudence, everywhere therefore by internal silently operating powers, not by the arbitrary will of a law-giver.[11]

Von Savigny's explanation suffers from the same weaknesses as the notion that "custom is king." It runs endlessly in circles, for the *Volksgeist* explains precisely the behavior that evidences it. Von Savigny acknowledged this. He said that one who does not hold membership in the community cannot recognize the *Volksgeist,* and one who does, knows it without evidence. To try to account for the differences in normative structures in terms of "custom" or "instinct" or *"Volksgeist"* merely pins a different label upon observed phenomenon. It does not explain it.

Malinowski. Perhaps more than any other modern anthropologist, Bronislaw Malinowski introduced the scientific spirit into his discipline. Partly by accident, but also because he was no longer content with the random jottings of intrepid travelers, he went to live with the inhabitants of the Trobriand Islands for three years, recording what he heard and saw with a care and diligence that has since become the standard for anthropological field work.

Malinowski found that the central force cementing Trobriand society was a complex of interrelated economic ties, arising out of reciprocal economic obligations. Fishermen exchange bundles of fish with inlanders who await them on the shore. The inland villagers repay the fisherman with vegetables:

"Civil law," the positive law governing all phases of tribal life, consists then of a body of binding obligations, regarded as a right by one party and acknowledged as a duty by the other, kept in force by a specific mechanism of reciprocity and publicity inherent in the structure of their society.... Law is the specific result of the configuration of obligations, which makes it impossible for the native to shirk his responsibility without suffering for it in the future.[12]

There is in every act a sociological dualism: two parties who exchange services and functions, each watching over the measure of fulfillment and the fairness of conduct of the other... in all the manifold activities of economic order, the social behavior of the natives is based on a well-assessed give-and-take, always mentally ticked off and in the long run balanced.[13]

A variety of anthropologists questioned Malinowski's formulation. Plainly, as Gluckman said, a web of interrelationships exist in every society. To call all of these "law" troubles even those who want to use the word "law" for many aspects of the normative systems of nonstate societies. If we substitute the expression "social rules and social control" for the word "law" in Malinowski's statement, many of the difficulties in Malinowski's statement disappear.[14] Robert Redfield, however, complained that that approach to the problem of "law" in traditional society suffers from overbreadth. Were one to follow Malinowski down this road, "one has not too little to talk about but too much."[15]

In any event, as explanatory variable, the interchange of goods and services does not seem to cut very deep. The economic activities that give rise to exchangeable goods and services themselves follow norms of conduct. Why and how do *these* norms become the social facts of these societies? Why do fishermen fish in canoes rather than with nets from the shore or with fishtraps? Malinowski's explanation assumes a static society, in which fishermen have always fished and inland dwellers have always produced vegetables. Like Seagle and Von Savigny, he assumes concensus. His explanation does not reflect the central fact that norms imply a choice, for there always exists some choice about what people ought to do. Unless possibility for alternative behavior existed—that is, for *choice*—why the norm?

Hoebel. The American anthropologist E. A. Hoebel saw in the fact of choice the principal challenge in describing a system of norms. Every society exists in a milieu that permits choice—not an infinite choice, but choice within a range imposed by the external constraints of time and place. He quotes Ruth Benedict:

The cultural pattern of any civilization makes use of a certain segment of the great arc of potential human purposes and motivations—the great arc along which all human behaviours are distributed is far too immense and too full of contradictions for any one culture to utilize even any considerable portion of it. Selection is the first requirement.[16]

What constraints determine what choices any particular society makes? At any moment in its history a given society has a culture. In large part, that culture takes its shape from choices the society earlier made, for rationalizations and justifications for what exists make up much of the culture. William Graham Sumner said long ago, "The folkways are the 'right' ways."[17] Religious ideologies, economic theory, mythological explanations, philosophy, moral and secular literature all tend to provide rationalizations and indeed imperative reasons for the selections made.

People must choose within the constraints of time and place. In the nature of things, they must also choose in light of the existing conceptual patterns. Hoebel, following Pound, called these conceptual patterns "jural postulates." Hoebel quoted Julius Stone: "The jural postulates . . . are generalized statements of the tendencies actually operating, of the presuppositions on which a particular civilization is based. . . . They are ideals presupposed by the whole social complex, which can thus be used to bring the law into harmony with it, so that the law 'promotes rather than hampers and oppresses it.' They are, as it were, directives issuing from the particular civilized society to those who are wielding social control through law within it."[18] Hoebel would argue that not only "civilized" societies, but every normative system, "primitive" or "civilized," legal or law-like, has its jural postulates.[19]

Hoebel's choice model teaches us that people constantly face new problems. New technologies, natural disaster or new natural opportunities, war, human ambition, and perversity constantly create new difficulties that press for solution. People solve those difficulties in the light of existing constraints and resources—existing technologies, knowledge, institutions, material wealth, and so forth. To solve those problems, of course, they must think about them, and to do that they can only draw on the stock of jural postulates and other domain assumptions that they presently have on hand. Thus do people create new norms. In state societies, call them law.

Like Hoebel's, the model we put forward in Chapter 1 rests upon the notion of choice. To say that choice exists of course argues against an iron determinism that perceives human activity as channeled by implacable forces, whether of mind or the material world. As Hoebel puts it, however, only ideology constrains choice. Plainly, material factors too constrain choice: geography, technology, social institutions, class and other economic relations, and so forth.

We live in a world both of clocks and of clouds. Perceiving human beings either as programmed by acculturated values and attitudes ("custom" or *Volksgeist* or "jural postulates") or as channeled down a narrow track by material conditions (technology or the mode of production) envisions the world as a clock. The world-as-clock can explain diversity between seemingly similar cultures only by invoking a faith that *something* must differ between them, or else why would they differ? That faith makes the central proposition nonfalsifiable. Without choice, diversity becomes inexplicable.

Choice alone, however, does not explain diversity in similarity. To explain that requires that we combine choice with a conflict model.

Consensus and Conflict

Any theory of choice must ask, Who makes the choices for the society? If everyone in the society really has the same set of jural postulates (''values''), then the choices anyone in the society makes will not differ from those that anyone else in the society makes who faces the same difficulties with the same range of constraints and resources. If not consensus but conflict best models society, however, then *society* has no jural postulates. ''Society'' makes choices only metaphorically. Particular persons— appellate judges, legislators, administrators, presidents, and so forth—make law. Whose demands get embodied into law, and why, becomes a fundamental sociological question.

The rules of law invariably respond to demands made by some part of the population, mediated by circumstances. Demands invariably call for new rules that require some other part of the population to behave differently. In the United States, black people's demands for the right to vote require white voting clerks to change their discriminatory behaviors. Newspaper demands for a harsher law against student protestors require students to moderate their protests. Business demands for tax advantages require tax collectors to permit them to retain more of their earnings, and to require other segments of the population to increase their tax contributions. Women's demands for equal rights impinge on men's legal right to suppress women.

That demands for new law entail demands for new behaviors results from law's *normative* character. Every rule of law carries a freight of the Ought. It describes how people ought to act—voting clerks, students, tax collectors, and so forth. Rules of law *ineluctably* prescribe; they do not purport to *describe*.

Our form of language misleads us about the law's normative trust. The sentence, ''This book is brown'' has the same form as ''This book is mine.'' Because the former plainly describes, we too easily come to think that the latter, too, describes. It does not. It prescribes. Unpacked, it says, ''Anybody but me ought not meddle with this book! And if you do, you become liable to arrest, trial, fine, or imprisonment.''

Every law, therefore, expresses a valuation. It embodies an idea about how people ought to behave. Even the law that commands us to drive on the right-hand side of the street expresses value-choices: of order over chaos, of the property interests of car owners over the interests of car manufacturers and car dealers. (How much would your present car, with its steering wheel on the left-hand side, fetch in the secondhand market the day after we changed to a left-hand driving system? When Sweden changed from left-hand traffic to right-hand traffic, the government set aside a substantial fund to recompense car owners disadvantaged by the change.) As Philip Heck puts it: ''The fundamental truth is that each command of the law determines a conflict of interests; it originates in a struggle between opposing forces. . . . It operates in a world full of competing interests, and, therefore, always works at the expense of some interests. This holds true without exception.''[20]

A society comprises individuals occupying roles engaged in repetitive behavior patterns. Every change in the rules to the extent that it in fact leads to changed behavior, therefore, to that extent changes society. Because every rule entails a valuation, consciously inducing social change through law entails a valuation. By the same token, a decision to retain a given rule in the face of demand for change also entails a valuation. How do societies make these valuations?

On the highest level of generalization, jurisprudents and social scientists offered two sorts of answers. One perceived the state and the legal order as comprising a value-neutral framework within which struggle takes place. The other perceived the state itself as an integral part of the unending social struggle between society's antagonistic interests and classes. The one assumed that the state's lawmaking, law-applying, and adjudicating machinery reflects a fundamental value-consensus. The other proposed that control of the state and its awesome machinery of compulsion itself becomes the prize for which antagonistic interests struggle.

This question becomes crucial to a study of law and society. If people share a basic set of domain assumptions—that is, propositions that explain generally what makes the world go, and what considerations ought to guide our choices—then the state might, and plainly should, represent that consensus. As its central problem the legal order must assure only that individuals do not substitute their own, deviant motivations and behaviors for those the polity prescribes. If, on the other hand, consensus does not exist, then the issue becomes: whose interests does and ought the state represent?

In a more innocent era, perhaps one could understand a naive belief that upon every important issue every polity has a value-consensus. The law's ineluctably normative nature, however, falsified that naive view. If so wide-reaching a consensus existed, demands of new law would not always take the form that somebody else change their behavior. Why do demands for new law always create conflict?

A variety of social theorists offered a modified form of the value-consensus position to answer this question: even if conflict does rack society generally, the state itself embodies value-neutrality. In this view, the state represents all-of-us, but only to a limited degree. Every specific law of state activity has a value-content, but the machinery by which the state comes to decide whether to create and enforce a particular law itself retains value-neutrality, permitting conflict to work itself out peaceably. This pluralist position held that while particular laws contain a burden of values, the legal order as a whole remains value-neutral.

Conflict theorists denied that any modern polity has even a limited value-consensus. In the unceasing wrestling match that society's more or less peaceable facade conceals, state power has a determinative role. Whoever controls the state uses its power in their own interest. Moreover, the structures that make up the state—the very structures that consensus theorists assert embody value-neutrality—come into existence as the result of law and therefore of conflict. Particular laws create and define courts, legislatures, police forces, administrative agencies, the civil service, jails, armies, and public universities. Since all laws have a value-component, it defies credibility that the institutions that those laws define could miraculously become value-free. The institutions and processes by which the state reaches decisions and which determine who will succeed in winning state power ineluctably favor one group or the other. A law that permits parties to hire their own lawyers favors those with the money and resources to hire the best attorneys as against those who cannot hire a lawyer at all. Election laws that permit unlimited corporate contributions to election campaigns to that extent favor large corporations as against the poor.

Most writers without extended discussion assume either a consensus or a conflict position. Roscoe Pound, for example, an American jurisprudent who invented the phrase "social engineering through law," urged that in a democratic society, the law ought to respond to the values of those to whom it applies. He therefore urged the cataloging of the claims and demands made upon the legal order, synthesizing the values subsuming them, and using those values to determine the serial order for pay-out. His system rests on the assumption that every society has a basic consensus of values that the totality of social demands reflects.

Talcott Parsons and the structural-functionalist sociological school made exactly that claim. As Ralf Dahrendorf points out, Parsons based his model on four principal assertions:[21]

1 Every society has a relatively persisting configuration of elements.

2 Every society has a well-integrated configuration of elements.

3 Every element in a society contributes to its functioning.

4 Every society rests upon a consensus of its members.

Given a consensus like that, as Pound held, a legislator need only determine the values that society in fact holds.

Against that model Dahrendorf and others urged a conflict perspective that opposed the structural-functionalist model at every point:

1 Every society constantly changes; social change never ceases.

2 Every society experiences at every moment social conflict; conflict never ceases.

3 Every element in a society contributes to its change.

4 Every society rests on the constraint of some of its members by others.[22]

More generally, we can discern a whole series of disagreements between the functional and conflict models:

1 Functionalists view society as a social system with various built-in needs that it must meet. Conflict theorists view society as the setting within which various struggles take place. In that view, "society" has no needs. Only particular people and collectivities have needs (water, food, shelter), desires, wants, and interests.

2 Functionalists view the governing body of modern society—the state—as a value-neutral agency within which various struggles take place. Conflict theorists see

the state as a most important agent participating in the struggle on the part of one side or another. Functionalists argue that coercion plays only a minor role in society and that inequality arises as a necessary consequence of society's general consensus on its most important values. Conflict theorists emphasize the state's monopoly of legitimate coercion (usually in the form of law or war-making institutions) as the chief factor creating and maintaining social institutions such as private property, slavery, and others that give rise to unequal rights and privileges.

3   Functionalists have stressed hard work, innate talent, and selection by others, etc., as the route by which some and not others obtain economic advantages. In the conflict view, social and economic inequality arise because of the operation of coercive institutions. Advocates of this view lay great emphasis on force, fraud, and inheritance as the chief avenues for obtaining rights and privileges.

4   Functionalists generally minimize the existence of social conflict and see conflict as stemming from man's nature, not from the structured inequality of society. Conflict theorists see social and economic inequality as a chief source of social conflict.

5   Functionalists see the state and law as organs of the total society, acting basically to promote the common good. Conflict theorists regard them mainly as instruments of oppression employed by the ruling classes for their own benefit.

6   Functionalists regard the concept of social class as a heuristic device calling attention to aggregations of people with certain common characteristics. Conflict theorists view classes as social groups with distinctive interests that inevitably bring them into conflict with other groups with opposed interests.

7   Both functional and conflict theorists seek to understand the consequences that particular social events have for the society. The functionalist analysis generally stops when the consequences have been described. The conflict analysis goes on to ask who benefits from the established social relations that produce those events. Cicero's famous question "cui bono?" becomes central to social inquiry. Whether they are studying war, social class, or deviant behavior, functionalists ask what functions it serves; conflict theorists add, for whom is it functional?

We can best examine these various disagreements in the study of particular social phenomena. The concepts used, the questions asked, and the empirical data gathered depend upon the model from which we begin our inquiry. Nowhere does this more clearly appear than in the study of the legal order.

Dahrendorf denied that one can use empirical data to choose between these two sets of assumptions. "Stability and change, integration and conflict, function and 'dysfunction,' consensus and constraint are, it would seem, two equally valid aspects of every imaginable society."[23] Like the two theories of light (wave and quanta), each model may serve to explain specific aspects of social processes.

In this book we intend to demonstrate that Dahrendorf erred. The legal order itself falsifies his assertion that one cannot choose between conflict and consensus models. Briefly put, the value-consensus model cannot account for the shape of the legal order: it does not even raise sociologically relevant questions about it. By contrast, the conflict model, with all its shortcomings, does have considerable heuristic value for analyzing the legal order. Furthermore, the very existence of a legal order, enforcing prescriptive rules by employing society's hit men—police and gaolers and sheriffs and the National Guard and the Army, all official armed enforcers—falsifies the consensus model. If consensus existed, we would not need the hit men.

Many social scientists who perceive conflict as the dominant mode of complex societies nevertheless assert that consensus dominates simple societies. In such societies, specialized institutions for creating norms do not exist. The community rarely makes choices explicitly and consciously. Individuals make their choices, and the norms that emerge become those of most members only because they all live in the same society, face the same difficulties with much the same constraints and resources for their solution. Living by the same norms they acquire in time the same value-sets. Consensus reigns.

We disagree. Even simple societies do not match the ideal type suggested by consensus theory. If such a consensus existed, one would expect consensus—i.e., near unanimity—about the content of customary rules with respect to such central matters as land tenure, descent and distribution, or rights and duties among family members. In a number of cases that came before the British colonial courts in West Africa, however, that supposed consensus did not exist.

Britain imposed a strange mixture of English and customary law on its West African colonies. The general law followed English common law, equity, and "statutes of general application"; Africans, however, retained rights under customary law (with some exceptions). A dual system of courts existed, for Africans and for non-Africans. Both ended in the same appellate courts, British-created and British-manned. Unlike customary courts, the judges there did not know "native" law. The litigants had to inform them about it. When a case came on appeal in a matter, say, of land tenure between Africans, both parties frequently claimed rights under customary law—but their versions of customary law frequently differed. Consensus plainly did not exist. Even in the simplest societies, conflict, not consensus, tends to reign.

Which of these two perspectives—consensus and conflict—best explains the manifold diversities of normative systems? Consensus perspectives can only explain diversity between societies with seemingly identical matrices by postulating something innate to each society that differentiates it from others—"custom" or "instinct" or the *Volksgeist*. As we have seen, like Seagle's notion of custom, that runs in circles. Only a choice model coupled with a conflict perspective can explain diversity:

1   Rules of law and law-like norms always require some role-occupants to behave in ways they otherwise would not; they ineluctably hit differently situated persons differently.

2   In every society, different sets of people have different interests, and therefore they demand different sorts of laws and law-like norms.

3 In every society, different sets of people at different times have differing capacities to get the rules they desire enacted as law, or accepted as law-like norms.

And, therefore, the legal orders and normative systems of different polities, no matter how similar, must differ. Thus do choice and conflict join to explain diversity.

2.2 THE SIMILARITY OF NORMATIVE SYSTEMS

Yet, normative systems in all their diversity have some similarities. Along at least three dimensions, the normative orders of non-state societies differ in similar ways from the legal orders of state societies. (1) The dispute-settlement systems of simple societies tend toward compromise, or "give-a-little, get-a-little"; the official dispute-settlement systems of most complex societies tend toward "winner-takes-all." (2) The norms concerning property in simple societies tend to subsume themselves under the general concept of Status, while those of complex societies tend to fall under the general rubric of Contract, or Command. (3) The norms of a simple society usually aim only at one set of addressees. These norms consist only of what H.L.A. Hart calls "primary norms." The rules of law in a complex society always have a double face. They include both primary norms, addressed to the principal actors, and secondary norms addressed to officials. In each of these three ways, the normative orders of non-state societies and the legal order of state societies to a remarkable degree resemble the others in the same category. How can a choice model explain this similarity in diversity?

Choice and Similarity

The question, "Why does a person choose this or that?" usually elicits an answer depending upon subjective valuations by the actor. In individual matters, that becomes a matter of taste (about which we all concede the bootlessness of argument), or, in social affairs, of social psychology—that is, these explanations relate the interior workings of the personality to the social situation. Alistair MacIntyre agrues cogently that that narrow question embodies a common mistake in the social sciences. Choice raises not one, but two questions. The usual question that social science answers only asks, "Why did this individual or group choose as they did, taking the range of constraints and resources they face as given?"[24] A more fruitful additional question requires that we ask, "Why *that* range of constraints and resources?" If one learns that farmers in a western state suddenly begin to raise coyotes in pens, one might suppose that they did that because they valued coyotes. Nothing of the sort. They did that because a law required county agricultural agents to pay a bounty for every pair of coyote ears presented to them, and farmers discovered that they could make a profit raising them. Any explanation that ignored the law and how that changed the farmers' arenas of choice would not really explain very much.

This theory of choice explains why societies similarly situated frequently emerge with roughly similar sorts of normative systems and legal orders. If two societies have very arid climates, one might expect that water, not land, would become the scarce resource about which the normative system would build many protections. In other countries, with abundant water but scarce land, land law becomes paramount. In each of these sets of countries, lawmakers face ranges of constraints and resources similar along at least the dimension of aridity; their options become similarly limited; and their choices must therefore crowd within the narrow range imposed by the constraints of their arenas of choice.

The similarity of the normative and legal orders of different sorts of societies seems consistent with the choice model as MacIntyre explains it. These different sets of societies must have similar characteristics, which present the actors in these very different societies with some similarities. That in turn leads to some similarity in their range of options, in their arenas of choice. We turn now to try to explicate these similarities in the arenas of choice, and their consequences for law-like behavior and institutions.

The Style of Dispute-Settlement

Following the lead of the anthropologist Laura Nader, we can categorize all dispute-settlement systems into a give-a-little, get-a-little and winner-takes-all, the former predominately in relatively unstratified, simple societies, the latter in complex, stratified ones like our own. Here, we first suggest an hypothesis to explain this difference; then we examine some of the consequences of these different sorts of dispute-settlement.

Compromise versus norm enforcement. Disputes arise because one party does not act as the other wants or expects her to do. Norms express role-expectations. Disputes necessarily take the form of a claimed breach of a norm. When the matter comes for decision before a third party, each party must appeal to commonly held norms to justify her position. Whether compromise or rule enforcement dominates the mode of dispute-settlement, in each case the argument centers on the claim of rule violation.

As common human experience teaches, the consequences on the future relationship of the parties in conflict depend, to a degree, on their sense of equitable treatment in the conflict. Where parties want or must have continuing interactions of a nonantagonistic nature after the dispute, both must leave the dispute-settlement procedures without too great a sense of grievance. If, however, the parties need not live together thereafter, then it becomes irrelevant whether either of the parties continues to be antagonistic to the other after the proceedings.

As a result, whether dispute-settling has as its principal objective continued relationships or not influences whether the tribunal will base itself on "give-a-little, get-a-little" or "winner-takes-all." As we have seen in the Nuer case, in simple societies the dispute-settling process entails a bargaining relationship. The bargain aims not to determine that one side or the other breached the norm at issue so much as to discover a compromise solution that will leave neither party so strongly aggrieved as to prevent future amicable relationships. If, on the other hand, the tribunal does not care whether the parties will live together after the dispute-settlement, then it tends to determine unequivocally whether the defendant in fact violated the norm, and to award a decision based on the principle of "winner-taking-all."

In our society, "give-a-little, get-a-little" becomes the appropriate principle of decision-making in cases where the dispute on its resolution anticipated a continued relationship. Stewart Macauley demonstrated that businessmen do not bring lawsuits against customers whose trade they want to keep after settling the particular dispute.[25] Married couples who want to preserve their marriage do not take their disputes to courts; they take them to marriage counselors, who usually try to help find compromise solutions. Because they must continue their relationship after a dispute, trade unions and employers favor arbitration.

"Winner-takes-all," on the other hand, typically controls dispute-settlement when no one wants to continue the relationship. When a person gets injured in an automobile accident, usually he had no prior relationship with the other party and anticipates no future relationship. In such cases, the parties typically expect in the end that if necessary they will settle their dispute in court on a "winner-takes-all" basis. So also in criminal matters: either the accused is guilty or not guilty.

In every "winner-takes-all" situation, of course, bargaining may take place, and often compromise controls the actual disposition. But the objective of such a compromise differs markedly from the objective of compromise in a true "give-a-little, get-a-little" situation. Bargaining over a negligence claim only aims at saving the parties the time and expense of an actual trial. They bargain, not in an effort to make possible a future relationship, but in light of their estimates of the probabilities of a favorable outcome of the potential "winner-takes-all" litigation. Guilty plea bargaining in criminal cases likewise arises from the convenience of avoiding a "winner-takes-all" result of the potential trial. (This case is complicated by the fact that, although the criminal and the prosecutor do not anticipate a continuing relationship, defense counsel and prosecutor do, and hence they may bargain in an attempt to preserve that relationship.)

A one-sided decision has the consequence of sanctioning the breach of a norm. A compromise solution does not necessarily have that consequence. The man who has committed a first-degree murder, but is permitted by the prosecution to plead guilty to manslaughter (with a considerably lighter penalty), has not been sanctioned to the degree consistent with the norm relating to murder. The man who breaches a contract, but ultimately compromises the claim at much less than the applicable norm, has not received full sanctions for his breach.

We can therefore regard the difference between "give-a-little, get-a-little" and "winner-takes-all" as the difference between the objectives of dispute-settlement and of norm enforcement. One can hypothesize that the difference between the objective of dispute-settlement processes in simple and in complex societies results from the different imperatives imposed by the differences in constraints, resources, and social structures.

Viewing the various types of societies globally, we see that two marked characteristics exercise significant constraints on every social institution: the relative differentiation of roles and the relative degree of stratification. In explaining the difference between traditional and modern societies, Durkheim fastened particularly on the relative differentiation of roles. In a society marked by what Durkheim called "mechanical solidarity," each individual does many different sorts of tasks. With its low lever of technology, the society merits the name "subsistence" society. Little interchange of goods ensues. In a stratified subsistence economy, even the chief or leader may live no more elegantly than does a lesser member, and his actual day-to-day activities may not differ very much from those of the ordinary member. More advanced technologies created role-differentiation—that is, specialization. That led in turn to the exchange of their specialized products. That sort of society Durkheim characterized as one of "organic solidarity."*

Societies with marked role-differentiation have many more norms than do societies with smaller amounts of it, for norms create roles, and the greater the number of roles, the greater the number of norms. In such societies, roles become more complicated and sophisticated, and hence the norms become more complicated and sophisticated. Simpler societies have not only fewer norms, but less complicated ones as well.

As a consequence, complex societies require different sorts of dispute-settlement institutions to maintain social solidarity—that is, to ensure that the several role-occupants perform their duties. In a society with low technology—a *subsistence* society—every person depends upon the others for support in a harsh environment. An individual Bushman cannot survive for long; together, the family or small Bushman group might make it. Social solidarity becomes all-important. The extended family buttresses all social relationships. Difficult communications force people to remain close to their birthplace all their lives. The close ties between neighbors and relatives do not readily dissolve. People learn relatively simple norms of behavior through elementary socialization. Community-enforced sanctions—scorn, disapproval, anger, even group excommunication, or rewards and approbation—serve instead of the bureaucratically enforced punishment that dominates law in complex societies. These societies do not need formal institutions to sanction breach of the norms; they require institutions to maintain social solidarity. Dispute-settlement institutions become devices not to sanction a breach of the norm, but to enforce social solidarity.

In a complex society the opposite holds. While economic existence depends on a fantastically complex interchange of goods and services, the goods and services, not

---

* Of course, these categories constitute ideal-types. A pure society of mechanical or of organic solidarity exists only in the sociologist's heaven. On the contrary, in this real world societies fall on a continuum from simple to complex, from mechanical to organic solidarity. The ideal-type, however, helps us to understand and thus escape the real world's pervasive disorder.

the identities of the individuals performing those services, become important. The relatively high level of technology reduces the threat of starvation and death, and hence lowers the requirement for future mutual support between any particular individuals. Easy communication at once raises the level of interdependence upon the system as a whole, but reduces the interdependence of specific individuals on each other. In a fashionable term, alienation increases. The institutionalization and enforcement of complex norms and roles in conditions of alienation require more formal processes. In such conditions, whether or not litigants ''live together'' after the dispute does not loom importantly.

The dispute-settlement processes of the two kinds of societies therefore become markedly different. We may formulate, therefore, the following proposition: the lower the level of complexity of a society, the more emphasis in its dispute-settling process upon reconciliation; the more complex the society, the more emphasis on rule enforcement.

Durkheim inferred precisely the opposite conclusion. He separated juridical rules into ''two great classes, according as they have organized repressive sanction or only restitutive sanctions.''[26] He reached his conclusion by first asserting that ''the only common characteristic of all crimes is they consist . . . in acts universally disapproved of by members of each society.''[27] He found the source of this disapproval in the ''collective'' or ''common conscience'' of the society, which he defined as ''the totality of beliefs and sentiments common to average citizens of the same society,'' and which formed a ''determinate system which has its own life.''[28] The same collective conscience is the source of repressive punishments. ''Because they are found in all consciences, the infraction committed arouses in those who have evidence of it or who learn of its existence the same indignation. Everybody is attacked; consequently, everybody opposes the attack.''[29] Hence the relative strength of this reaction becomes a function of the solidarity of the collective conscience.

Durkheim then reasoned that the small differentiation of roles, obtained in some societies—i.e., societies in which all the members of the group resemble one another—reinforces the common conscience.[30] Hence he concluded:

There exists a social solidarity which comes from a certain number of states of conscience which are common to all the members of the same society. This is what repressive law materially represents. . . . The part that it plays in the general integration of society evidently depends upon the greater or lesser extent of the social life that the common conscience embraces and regulates. The greater the diversity of relations wherein the latter makes its action felt, the more also it creates links which attach the individual to the group; the more consequently, social cohesion derives completely from this source and bears its mark.[31]

Restitutive law—i.e., law in which the sanction is ''not expiatory, but consists of a simple return in state''—indicates, Durkheim said, a society with relatively highly differentiated roles.[32] The infraction of rules that apply only to a specialized segment of the community does not strike at the common conscience, and hence does not elicit the retributive passions occasioned when a delict violates the beliefs that animate the entire body politic.[33] Hence the more differentiated the roles of a society, the more restitutive its law.

Durkheim, however, failed sufficiently to take into account the very real community of interests of the members of simple societies, largely arising out of the difficult and indeed dangerous environment of practically all societies of mechanical solidarity. Whether the law of these societies becomes repressive and punitive or whether it becomes conciliatory raises an empirical question.

A great deal of attention has been given to Durkheim's theory by students of law and society. There is, of course, considerable difficulty in trying to test such abstract notions as "mechanical" and "organic" solidarity or even types of law such as "repressive" and "restitutive." As Gerald Turkel recently suggested, it may mislead to judge a broad theoretical position by the accuracy of particular claims.[34] Although Turkel's argument is cogent, it defeats itself. If we cannot judge broad theoretical schemes according to the degree to which the facts they assume or postulate turn out to exist in the real world, then there is no way to assess theories at all save "as critical and insightful programmatic interpretations of societal development and constitution that can be elaborated through empirical research."[35] If we cannot use data—that is, experience—to test theory, we can never use experience to guide choice. If we cannot use experience to guide choice, we can never learn through experience. Is there any other way to learn?

We do not agree with such an approach. Whatever the merits a theory may have as a guide to interpretations we side with that branch of the philosophy of science which sees as the task of scholarship the accumulation of knowledge and the development of sound social policy. That task has no meaning apart from an assessment of theory by empirical facts.

In this light, Schwartz and Miller attempted to test Durkheim's proposition that restitutive law would characterize societies of mechanical solidarity. Cross-cultural data from a large number of societies studied by anthropologists revealed no such correlation. They found that, contrary to Durkheim, restitution characterized "mechanically solidary" societies.[36] Baxi criticized Schwartz and Miller's methods. He pointed out the limitations of data gathered from cross-cultural summaries of anthropological studies.[37] The criticism suggests the use of caution in interpreting the Schwartz-Miller findings. Similar results by Spitzer[38] and Wimberly,[39] however, support the findings of Schwartz and Miller. Spitzer concludes that repressive law (the use of punishment) appears less frequently in simple than in complex societies.

Although these findings do not "disprove" Durkheim's theory, they raise important questions about it. We argue that Durkheim's theory fails because of its "domain assumptions." First, an explanation for types of law cannot rest solely upon the organization of morality in a society. Morality constitutes an important variable, but only one variable. Legal institutions result from choices made in a material environment by people with particular interests and ideologies (moralities). Repressive or restitutive legal forms arise from those choices. In modern society we see both restitutive and repressive legal sanctions playing important roles depending on the choices people have made and are making in dealing with problems arising in their historical location. Durkheim reifies ''society'' and makes it a living thing rather than a complex of people occupying roles and struggling for things they believe in, want, and think are worth having. Second, Durkheim's underlying methodology is deterministic: it assumes that we can locate universal laws about the evolution of societies. History proves that viewpoint false. No sooner do social thinkers propose universal laws than people ''turn the laws on their heads.'' Knowledge—generalizations about why or how people behave—become part of the process determining how and why people will behave. In so doing people's actions disprove the generalizations. Knowlege consists not of deterministic laws, but of heuristics.

People in society create institutions in order to deal with disputes. These institutions vary depending on their purposes. Where an institution purports to reconcile the parties so that after resolving the breach they can live together amicably and cooperatively, one would expect to find the institution to emphasize mediation and compromise. If the institution mainly aims at rule enforcement, then a bureaucracy probably develops to determine the precise content of the norms, whether someone has breached one, and to assess and enforce the sanction.

A second variable is social class. It too comes from technological change. Until the technology permits an economic system that produces a surplus, social classes have little point economically; not enough exists to make domination worthwhile. Moreover, so long as every woman can own her own hoe, in order for her to produce, the technology does not require her to employ anybody else. As societies grow technologically more complex, rival groups may scramble to control surpluses and the means of production. For a wide variety of reasons—greater aggressiveness or competence of individuals, territorial conquest, superior weaponry, accidental control of significant resources, and so forth—people differentiate themselves in terms of wealth and their respective roles in the productive process. Some become owners and commanders, others become workers and receive the commands. One could rank order societies in terms of stratification. That does not necessarily represent historical evolution; it is no more than a classificatory device, it is not a description of a historical progression.

Economic stratification always entails control of the surplus by the upper class, and struggle for a more equitable share by the lower class. The upper classes inevitably look for coercive means to maintain their superior position. They must have the norms of property and contract enforced, not compromised. One does not bargain with a thief in order to find a compromise position that will enable all of us to live together amicably from here on. The central theme of dispute-settlement becomes not reconciliation, but rule enforcement.

Thus we can formulate a second proposition: the less stratified a society, the greater emphasis its dispute-settlement processes are likely to place on reconciliation; the more stratified, the more emphasis is put on rule enforcement.

We combine these two propositions into a simple four-cell table. This table tells us that in less stratified, less complex societies, we would expect a maximum emphasis on reconciliation of disputants; in a more highly complex, stratified society, on rule enforcement. In less complex, stratified societies we would expect emphasis to be placed ambiguously on both; the same would be true in complex, less stratified societies (if any exist).

	Less complex societies	More complex societies
Less stratified societies	reconciliation reconciliation	rule enforcement reconciliation
More stratified societies	reconciliation rule enforcement	rule enforcement rule enforcement

An example of reconciliatory procedures in an African society. An anthropologist, P. H. Gulliver, in 1963 described a dispute and its settlement occurring among the Arusha, a group of agriculturalists living in Tanzania.[40] Arusha society—at least, its dominant male component—organizes itself around age-sets. Age-sets tend to support their own members; each age-set has a particular affinity with the age-set once removed from it. Different sorts of dispute-settlement procedures exist, depending upon the relationship between the parties. In the case that Gulliver described (Kadume against Soine), the matter came for disposition before a moot, an institution used to settle disputes between relatives.

About ten years earlier, Kadume's mother separated from his father, Makara, and took Kadume to live some miles away with her own family. Makara lived alone on the farm, relying more and more in his old age on his neighbor and half-brother, Soine. When Makara died, Soine occupied Makara's land. Kadume, now married, obtained from his dead father two cattle and three goats; these he left to graze in Soine's paddock.

About a year after his father's death, Kadume claimed all his father's land, which Soine cultivated as he had for the past four or five seasons. Soine refused to surrender the land, and, after quarreling with Kadume, refused to allow Kadume to graze his beasts in the paddock.

After some inconclusive earlier negotiations in an inner-family conclave, Kadume persuaded his lineage counselor, an elder, to convene a moot. All the members of the inner lineage, the counselor, and nine members of the maximal lineage living nearby attended. At the moot, Kadume's spokesman claimed that brothers did not inherit land, but that sons did (a norm apparently well accepted by everyone). Soine responded by pointing to his own shortage of land, to his claimed rights in Makara's land, which had come to Makara through the estate of their common father, and to Kadume's land that he had received through his mother. Other members spoke, appealing to Soine not to break lineage unity. In the moot, as in all Arusha dispute-settlements, each age-group tended to support its member. After extensive discussion, Soine proposed a compromise: to divide the land. After some bargaining, the members of the moot came to a consensus that the division made sense, and Kadume accepted it. In the result, despite the norm that sons inherit, not brothers, Soine got half the land. The moot ended with all its members going to Soine's household to drink beer together. Its members congratulated both Soine and Kadume on the success of the agreement.

We make two observations about the proceedings. First, the norms of descent and distribution played a subordinate function to the norms of dispute-settlement. The overriding dispute-settlement rule called for reconciliation and amicable conclusion of the dispute. Gulliver reports that the Arusha articulate these dispute-settlement norms; ''We discuss and discuss the matter (in dispute) and then we agree. When we agree, that is the end. What else is there to do?''

The process of establishing a settlement consists of discussion and negotiation, argument and counter-argument, offer and counter-offer, between the disputants' parties in an endeavour to find an area of mutual agreement. Being mutually accepted, the question of enforcement does not arise, or at least only marginally. This is perhaps an ideal statement, but essentially it represents the aim of the Arusha. For them, the emphasis lies in the joint participation of the conflicting parties so that the settlement of their dispute emerges from within—that is, from them together. It is not an imposed decision, a judgment, on the disputants from outside, however rational and equitable that decision might be.[41]

Second, the settlement did not arise in a vacuum. Each party had the support of his age-set. The agreement also had the support of the different age-sets, which participated actively in the discussion. A party may not greatly like the settlement reached; perhaps he would prefer to continue litigating. He must, however, listen to his age-mates. He lives with them; indeed, he cannot live without them. Only a very self-willed litigant, or one who felt supremely confident of his own competence to succeed without his age-mates' support, could ignore their recommendations for settlement. The compromise that Arusha disputants agree to comes not out of their estimate of success in litigation—that does not exist in our sense of the term—but out of the various community pressures. Arusha dispute-settlements reflect society itself.

From Status to Contract—And Beyond

In one of the seminal generalizations of jurisprudence, in 1861, Sir Henry Maine said:

The movement of the progressive societies has been uniform in one respect. Through all its course it has been distinguished by the gradual dissolution of family dependency, and the growth of individual obligation in its place. The individual is steadily substituted for the Family, as the unit of which civil laws take account. . . . Nor is it difficult to see what is the ties between man and man which replaces by degrees those forms of reciprocity in rights and duties which have their origin in the Family. It is Contract. Starting, as from one terminus of history, from a condition of society in which all the relations of Persons are summed up in the relations of

Family, we seem to have steadily moved towards a phase of social order in which all these relations arise from the free agreement of individuals.

All the forms of Status taken notice of in the Law of Persons were derived from, and to some extent still are coloured by, the powers and privileges anciently residing in the Family. If we then employ Status . . . to signify these personal conditions only, and avoid applying the term to such conditions as are the immediate or remove result of agreement, we may say that the movement of the progressive societies has hitherto been a movement *from Status to Contract*.[42]

"Status" and "contract" became metaphors into which various writers poured their own contents. Maine himself focused on conditions of personal liberty, and not on property ownership. A proper Victorian gentleman, he believed that Britain exemplified par excellence "progressive" societies, and that individual freedom developed there as a consequence of the great transition to contract. Other writers have demonstrated, however, that Sir Henry may have spoken more accurately than he knew, for status does control property relationships in every society of low-level technology—that is, every subsistence economy.

Max Gluckman gives a striking example of property relationships among the Lozi (of Barotse), who live in Zambia on the flood plain of the Zambesi River. There, the river floods annually. People must build their villages on small mounds that rise above the flood waters; at the heights of the floods, they must move from these to temporary villages along the banks. The mound village has arable land around it that the flood waters renew every year, and the village becomes the center of fishing.

All land and its products "belong" to the king, by whose bounty all live on the land. He can therefore demand allegiance from anyone who settles in Barotseland; he can distribute unsettled land; he can ask people to surrender land that they use. He can claim land that has no heirs; he can determine where people build homes. He cannot, however, drive people off the land that they rightfully use, even though their right to use it in theory derives from an ancient grant from the king or his predecessors. The king has many duties, too. He must give every subject land for living and cultivating; he must permit a subject to fish in public water, to hunt and gather, and to use clay and reeds and iron ore and grasses; he must protect them from marauders.

Ownership intertwines closely with personal relationships. The king allocates land in the first instance not to individuals but to village headmen, who receive what Gluckman calls an "estate of administration." That gives the headman (and his descendants) the right to allocate land in the village, not to work all of it. The headman has the obligation of giving land to all heads of household in the village, and each head of household in turn must distribute the land among his dependents and himself. Thus, rights to land in the village come from membership in the village (usually by birth), and the power to distribute from descent from a headman. Gluckman observes:

This system of land-holding was an essential part of the organization of social relationship from the king downwards through the political units of villages, into the hierarchy of kinship relationships. The king may be called "owner of the land" only as trustee or steward for the nation. He granted a primary estate of rights of administration to all titles of heads of villages, including himself in his capactiy as head of many villages. Each head of a village then broke his estate into secondary heads of households in the village, including himself. These holders of secondary estates might allocate tertiary estates of this kind to dependent heads of households, but usually secondary estates were broken up and allocated in parcels of land to be worked as arable or as fishing sites by the holders. . . . Thus at the bottom of the series there is an "estate of production." Land-holding in these tribes is thus an inherent attribute not only of citizenship, but also of each social position in the total political and kinship hierarchy.[43]

Rights in cattle, like rights in land, intertwine with social relationships. Gluckman states:

In cattle-owning tribes it is almost impossible to work out who is the "real" owner of cattle in a herd. . . . When a Lozi girl marries as an ostensible virgin her bridegroom presents two beasts to her kin. He pays the first beast to make the girl his wife, the second is for her untouched fertility. Should he divorce her and she has not conceived, he is entitled to recover the second beast handed over with its progeny. This is therefore called "the beast of herding": i.e., the bride's kin merely herd it for the husband until he has impregnated their daughter. They have the right to hold it and to sue for it, against the world including the groom, but it is not theirs; it is still the husband's though he cannot claim it without divorcing his wife.[44]

In modern, technologically complex societies, relationships of property readily distinguish themselves from personal relationships. When one purchases a bundle of groceries from the unfriendly neighborhood supermarket, the transaction could not become more impersonal. You take the goods from the anonymous shelves, an impersonal computer reads off the prices, an all-but-faceless clerk takes the money and gives the change. The supermarket probably belongs to a conglomerate that engages in only one real endeavor—making money—but turns to a variety of tasks to do so: movies and mining and real estate and supermarkets, for example. In traditional society, however, property and personal relationship so commingle that one defines personal relationships in terms of property relationships, and vice versa. Gluckman writes:

Material objects thus gain high symbolic value, for they stand for the range of social relationships which form the very fabric of society. . . .
    Once we look at the situation of property from this point of view, we understand why a man pays cattle or other goods for a bride. He is not purchasing a woman to be a concubine or a slave; a wife's rights are very different from those of such a person. He is validating the transfer of certain rights over the bride from her kin to herself, and establishing "friendship"—in-law relationship—with those kin. The marriage-gifts also signify that he accepts the obligations of his status as husband, and that his own kin, who contributed to the payment, accept obligations to their new daughter or sister-in-law and the rest of her family.[45]

All this exemplifies Maine's generalization about status.

It stresses that in the early law of Europe, as in the law of tribal society, most of the transactions in which men and women are involved, are not specific, single transactions involving the exchange of goods and services between relative strangers. Instead, men and women hold land and other property, and exchange goods and services, as members of a hierarchy of political groups and as kinsfold or affines. People are linked in transactions with one another because of pre-existing relationships of status between them. . . . We can only describe the Law of Property in these types of society by describing also the law of Persons, or status; and we can only discuss the law of status by talking about ways of owning property.[46]

How to explain the regularity with which status systems occur in subsistence economies? Low technology approaches subsistence in the sense that each person does many different sorts of work, and produces many different sorts of goods, but mainly for family consumption. High technology entails a high degree of specialization and exchange. Beginning with these premises, we explain the observed nexus between low technology and status systems as follows.

1   Traditional societies have low levels of technology.
2   With low levels of technology, the ownership of productive assets (especially land) and the labor on those assets are closely integrated.
3   Having low levels of technology, such societies are geographically static.
4   Such societies have social orders that depend primarily upon kinship ties for social solidarity, rather than social solidarity that arises from the interchange of goods and services.
5   Such societies remain relatively impoverished, and population tends to be low in relation to available land.
6   Given these propositions, no market exists for the interchange of factors of production, or for the interchange of customer products.
7   Without such a market, norms define right to land in terms of the existing organizing principle of social solidarity, i.e., status deriving from kinship relationships.

Societies with low levels of technology must have legal orders sounding in status. It does not hold, however, that societies with high technology need have legal orders sounding in contract. Many do. Historically, all the western European countries developed high specialization and exchange through market systems—and that required contract. As we examine below, contract delegates to the parties the power to determine the rules for their transaction. Where contract unlimited defines the economic system, private persons, not officials, determine the shape of the economy.

Other ways to organize a high technology economy exist. In the welfare state, the law delegates only partial authority to private parties to determine the rules of economic exchange. In classical laissez-faire and contract, employers can hire small children or pay any wage for which they can get workers. All welfare states prohibit child labor and require a minimum wage—that is, to that extent, they withdraw authority from the contracting parties to decide these rules. Or, in lieu of contract or welfare state, a polity may institute a command economy, in which all the rules of economic exchange find their source in an authoritative, centrally adopted and enforced plan.

In 1861 Maine correctly said that all previously existing progressive societies had always moved from status to contract. Those do not constitute the only categories for law. Low technologies require a status system, but high technologies still leave room for choice.

From Primary Rules to Primary Plus Secondary Rules

The legal orders of complex societies differ from those of simple societies along a third dimension besides compromise/norm enforcement and status/contract or command: between normative systems having only what H.L.A. Hart called "primary rules," and those that he characterized as having both primary and "secondary" rules.[47] As we shall see, this states for the normative system the consequences of a bureaucratized legal order.

Hart begins by imagining a society "without legislature, courts or officials of any kind."[48] The norms defining such a social structure he calls "primary rules of obligation."[49] Such a normative system suffers from three serious drawbacks. First, no procedure exists for settling the authoritative form of a rule; the system lives in *uncertainty*. Second, a system like that has no capacity for intentional change; save for slow accretion and atrophy over time, it must remain *static*. Finally, a system of that sort has no means of adjudication of disputes except personal vendetta; it suffers *inefficiency*. The cure becomes rules aimed at officials who will specifically address each of these deficiencies—the secondary rules. *Rules of recognition* tell officials how to identify authentic laws from mere customs, rules of etiquette, and so forth. *Rules of change* instruct lawmakers how to create new law. *Rules of adjudication* provide for dispute resolution.

Behind Hart's analysis lurk two assumptions. First, he assumes that, unless a rule has sufficient precision so that adjudicators can recognize its scope, it does not qualify as "law." Without rules of recognition, it becomes impossible authoritatively to determine the content of a rule. That is to say, without rules of recognition a normative order does not qualify as "law" or a legal order. Hart, like us, would deny the name "law" to the normative system of the Arusha, or any other society that puts rule enforcement at a lower priority than dispute-settlement. To enforce a rule requires its precise statement. Compromise, on the other hand, resonates happily with a vagueness that permits contending parties to find a version of the rule with which both can live. That is, Hart makes a stipulative definition of the word "law" but masks it behind his discussion of the secondary rules. Put another way, however, Hart makes an important statement: normative systems with relatively greater precision in their substantive norms likely have specialized officials to interpret the norms and rules of recognition to prescribe their behavior. Seen as explanation, what seems no more than a convoluted way of asserting a stipulative definition becomes a useful hypothesis about why normative systems of a particular sort get that way.

Second, Hart explicitly assumes a society with a legislature, courts, and officials—in terms of the usual American high school civics text, legislative, judicial, and executive branches. Hart's secondary rules become the rules that define and direct the state—for of what does the state consist beyond these? Hart's definition of law matches our definition of the legal order: the normative system in which the state has a finger. Hart gives us more precise categories to consider, which explain how the state performs its functions of rule creation, rule definition, and judication. Every normative system that operates through a state structure will have secondary rules; without it, they will not.

The existence of the state and secondary rules bears a relationship to the system of dispute-settling. As the Arusha case suggests, a dispute-settlement system based on compromise needs no separate adjudicatory or enforcement system. One based on norm enforcement does. The same societal variables that determine the characteristics of dispute-settlement also determine whether the policy will have a regime of secondary rules or not—that is, the complexity of the normative system and the degree of stratification.

2.3 SUMMARY AND CONCLUSION

Considering the global range of systems of social order and social change, explaining their remarkable diversity and underlying unities becomes central to the study of law and society. A consensus model offers no adequate explanation. A conflict, choice model is suggestive but that also fails when it addresses only the selection of an alternative among the limited range available. An adequate model must also ask, "Why that range of options?" A conflict model and choice can explain diversity; they can also explain why simple societies tend to have give-a-little, get-a-little dispute-settlement institutions, status property systems, and only primary rules, while complex societies have their opposites. High technology makes complexity inevitable and stratification not only likely, but, so long as the polity does not take conscious steps to eschew it, inevitable.

These systematic results come about because in all the diversity of the world's different social, political, and economic relations the people who create these different systems do so within sets of "external" or "material" constraints and resources; they do not fashion their world out of the gossamer of their own ideas, nor are they impotent to effect their reality. People always devise legal orders out of materials at hand; they choose within the constraints and resources of the world confronting them. Within those constraints and resources, choice exists. We have freedom to create our social existence, but only within the constraints of necessity. Freedom—choice—exists, but only within the constraints of necessity circumscribed by the actor's arena of material and ideological factors that make up his or her world.

NOTES

1. Max Gluckman, *Politics, Law and Ritual in Tribal Society* (Chicago: Aldine Publishing Co., 1965), p. 213.

2. Richard D. Schwartz and James C. Miller, "Legal Evolution and Societal Complexity," *American Journal of Sociology* 70(1964): 159-160.

3. Thomas Hobbs, *Leviathan* (Oxford: B. Blackwell, 1946), Chapter 13.

4. M. Fortes and E. E. Evans-Pritchard, eds., *African Political Systems* (London: Oxford University Press, 1940), pp. 273-274. Published for International African Institute.

5. Lucy Mair, *Primitive Government* (Baltimore: Penguin Books, 1962), p. 23.

6. Fortes and Evans-Pritchard, *African Political Systems*, pp. 278-283.

7. *Ibid*, pp. 291-292.

8. *Ibid*, p. 293.

9. *Ibid*.

10. William Seagle, *The Quest for Law* (New York: Alfred A. Knopf, 1941), p. 33.

11. Wolfgang Friedman, *Legal Theory* (London: Stevens & Sons, 1953), p. 136.

12. Bronislaw Malinowski, *Crime and Custom in Savage Society* (London: K. Paul, Trench, Trubner and Co., 1926), pp. 58-59.

13. *Ibid.*, p. 26.

14. Gluckman, *Politics, Law and Ritual*, pp. 205-206.

15. R. Redfield, "Primitive Law," *University of Cincinnati Law Review* 33(1964): 1, reprinted Paul Bohannan, ed., *Law and Warfare Studies in the Anthropology of Conflict* (Garden City, NY: Natural History Press, 1967), p. 4.

16. Ruth Benedict, *Patterns of Culture* (New York: Houghton Mifflin Co., 1934), p. 237.

17. William G. Sumner, *Folkways* (Boston: Ginn & Co., 1911), p. 28.

18. Julius Stone, *The Province and Function of Law* (Cambridge: Harvard University Press, 1961), p. 337.

19. E. A. Hoebel, *The Law of Primitive Man: A Study in Comparative Legal Dynamics* (Cambridge: Harvard University Press, 1964), p. 16.

20. P. Heck, *Interessinjurisprundenz in Recht and Statt in Gefenwart*, 1930, trans. M. M. Schock, quoted in M. M. Schock, ed., *The Jurisprudence of Interests: The Selected Writings of Max Rumdm et al.* (Cambridge: Harvard University Press, 1948), pp. 29, 34.

21. Ralf Dahrendorf, "Toward a Theory of Social Conflict," *Journal of Conflict Resolution* 2(1958): 170-183.

22. *Ibid.*, p. 174.

23. *Ibid.*, pp. 174-175.

24. Peter Laslett and W. G. Runciman, eds., *Philosophy, Politics and Society* (Oxford: Basil Blackwell, 1969), p. 48.

25. Stewart Macauley, "Non-Contractual Relations in Business: Preliminary Study," *American Sociological Review* 28(1963): 61.

26. Emile Durkheim, *Division of Labor in Society* (New York: The Macmillan Co., 1933), p. 69.

27. *Ibid.*, p. 73.

28. *Ibid.*, p. 79.

29. *Ibid.*, p. 102.

30. *Ibid.*, p. 105.

31. *Ibid.*, p. 109.

32. *Ibid.*, p. 110.

33. Talcott Parsons, *The Structure of Social Action* (New York: Free Press, 1937), p. 318.

34. G. Turkel, "Testing Durkheim: Some Theoretical Considerations," *Law and Society Review* 13(1979): 721-738. See also R. K. Merton, "Durkheim's Division of Labor in Society," *American Journal of Sociology* 40(1934): 319-328.

35. Turkel, "Testing Durkheim," p. 736.

36. R. Schwartz and J. Miller, "Legal Evolution and Societal Complexity," *American Journal of Sociology* 70(1964): 159.

37. U. Baxi, "Durkheim and Legal Evolution: Some Problems of Disproof," *Law and Society Review* 8(1974): 645. See Schwartz's rejoinder, R. Schwartz, "Reply," *American Journal of Sociology* 70(1965): 627.

38. S. Spitzer, "Punishment and Social Organization: A Study of Durkheim's Theory of Social Evolution," *Law and Society Review* 9(1975): 613.

39. H. Wimberly, "Legal Evolution: One Further Step," *American Journal of Sociology* 79(1973): 78.

40. P. H. Gulliver, *Social Control in an African Society* (Boston: Boston University Press, 1963), pp. 255-258.

41. *Ibid.*

42. Henry Sumner Maine, *Ancient Law*, ed. by Fredrick Pollock (London: John Murrary, 1930), pp. 180-182.

43. Gluckman, *Politics, Law and Ritual*, p. 40.

44. *Ibid.*, p. 44.

45. *Ibid.*, p. 47.

46. Maine, *Ancient Law*, p. 3.

47. H.L.A. Hart, *The Concept of Law* (Oxford: Clarendon Press, 1961), pp. 77-96. For an excellent discussion on the ambiguity of Hart's concepts see Peter Hacker and J. Raz, *Law, Morality and Society: Essays in Honor of H.L.A. Hart* (London: Oxford University Press, 1977).

48. *Ibid.*, p. 89.

49. *Ibid.*, p. 89.

3

Perspectives and vocabularies: social structure and the legal order

Methodology, perspectives, vocabulary: these elements make up every social theory. In this chapter we discuss the various vocabularies (categories, concepts) and theoretical perspectives employed by social scientists, including lawyers, in an effort to understand and use law and the legal order. In this chapter we will also develop more fully the theoretical perspective which we believe to be the most useful and the most consistent with known facts about law and society.

The vocabulary we choose to study a phenomenon ineluctably places blinders on us. It must do this or else we see so much we cannot understand it. Like methodologies and perspectives, vocabularies guide us to relevant data. In the conventional language of theory, vocabularies in general terms identify independent variables, dependent variables, and relevant conditions correlated with the social facts we wish to describe and explain. In the language of the problem-solving methodology we earlier advanced, propositions concerning categories constitute heuristics useful in directing attention to explaining (theory).

There is a fundamental paradox in this process of developing categories and perspectives. No matter how we try, we can never make our minds blank slates. To examine requires that we use a vocabulary. To be useful a vocabulary (or categories) must help in explaining the phenomena under examination. We dare not use our existing vocabulary unexamined, or else our explanations will merely reflect our present biases. Before doing the research designed to explain the legal order, paradoxically, we must generate an explanation for it out of which to generate categories to guide the research. Accomplishing that becomes the principal task of the "ideal-type."

The ideal-type expresses what, based on present knowledge, the theorist supposes constitute the key variables, put together in a pattern whose form derives not from detailed data (for gathering the data constitutes the purpose of the research), but from logical inferences based upon preliminary excursions into the domain of study. Investigators deep in their subject create the great ideal-types, such as Hans Kelsen's model of the legal order, Max Weber's of bureaucracy, or Karl Marx's of capitalism. Such an ideal-type may, facially, prescribe a Utopia, but it may base itself explicitly or implicitly upon an explanation. That explanation, necessarily in general terms, identifies outcomes, causative factors, and conditions and specifies how these logically interact with each other. In law and society studies, ideal-types concern themselves more directly than does "grand theory" with the working of the legal order.

Consider, for example, the vocabulary suggested by H.L.A. Hart.[1] Hart divides the law into "primary" and "secondary" rules. Plainly, that constitutes an ideal-type. Hart does not describe any particular state society when he discusses the character and function of primary and secondary rules. In his book, we find scant reference to any *particular* legal system. Hart argues, however, that to understand any particular legal order we must distinguish between "primary" and "secondary" rules. By primary rules Hart means those rules of law which are simultaneously addressed to the citizen and government officials (for example, the judge). A rule prohibiting the sale of heroin is addressed to the citizen and warns him or her that they may be punished if they engage in this act; this rule also tells the judge that if someone is found engaging in the sale of heroin the judge is to punish them. But, Hart argues, equally important for an understanding of the legal order are the secondary rules: these are rules addressed solely to the administrators of the law, a rule requiring that a judge conduct a trial in a certain fashion, for example.

We discuss Hart's theory of law in more detail in Chapter 8. For now we simply want to point out that by providing this language, these categories for inquiry into law, and creating this particular ideal-type Hart is structuring our vision. He provides a set of categories and implicitly a theory about how law works which excludes from our vision a multitude of other facts and focuses our attention on those facts which he believes to be crucial for an understanding of the legal order. Whether or not he is correct in choosing the vocabulary he does, creating the ideal-type he creates, and implying the theory implied, will in the end be determined by the theory's ability to explain what actually happens and by the theory's utility in providing usable propositions for changing existing conditions.

With this orientation in mind, then, let us examine a few of the most influential vocabularies and perspectives employed by social scientists in an effort to understand the legal order. It must be borne in mind, in the discussion that follows, that ideas, like all other social facts, exist within the constraints of a particular historical period. There are, of course, resources available for transcending existing knowledge. This is necessary for ideas to change. Nonetheless, the ability to manufacture new perspectives and vocabularies is itself linked to the inherited *Weltanschauung* (world view) of a particular generation. Thus, to understand today's vocabularies and perspectives it is necessary to delve into the history of these ideas and see first of all what political, economic, and social relations existed at the time of their creation. We object as much as anyone to thumbnail sketches of the lifetime works of profound and sometimes prolific scholars. We urge students to read the works of the authors discussed in the original. We recognize, however, that not everyone has time for that; so we include these condensations as a handy index to these writers and no more than that.

3.1 THE RULE OF LAW

One of the most lasting conceptions of law and the legal order is summarized under the concept the "Rule of Law." Scholars, lawyers, politicians, and laypersons alike have employed this perspective on the legal order for centuries. The "ideal-type" assumed by this model sees the law as a set of rules, norms, and institutionalized processes which function to create predictable, comprehendible rules that limit the discretion of state officials. This perspective on the law emerged in England during those centuries when England's political economy was undergoing a transition from feudalism to capitalism.

Late eighteenth- and early nineteenth-century England saw a dramatic conflict between the older landed gentry and the newer entrepreneurial classes. The former struggling to maintain its hold on state power, the latter trying to dislodge it. At stake lay command over the English economy and the use of state power to bolster directly and indirectly the one class or the other.

The English common law courts developed out of the continuing struggle between the Crown and the great feudatories. Under feudal constitutional law, a feudatory had in effect his own government and his own courts; the power to govern came with the land. The Crown early tried to eat away that jurisdiction by sending the king's judges into the countryside to try cases on a winner-takes-all basis. The substantive law they applied purported to arise from custom, not from the Crown's will. For example, while primogeniture (inheritance of property by the eldest son) prevailed for distributing a dead person's estate, in those parts of England that followed the custom called *gavelkind,* courts distributed property equally to the deceased's children. The judges purported to apply not laws that they invented, but only customary norms. As a body of decisions accumulated, judges came to follow not the statements of witnesses about the content of the custom, but what the earlier, precedent cases declared it to be. Even legislation at first took its force from the claim that it only embodied custom, as the rules concerning the overseas reach of British law demonstrates.

English law declared that Englishmen colonizing overseas—for Britain, the world's greatest empire, an important occupation—carried their law with them as a birthright. That law, however, did not include *all* the law of England, but only part of it: the common law, "and all statutes *in affirmance of the common law* passed in England, antecedent to the settlement of a colony. . . ."[2]

As we discuss in greater detail below, courts that decide cases by "applying" rules must in some cases create law. Some fact situations fall clearly either within or without a rule. Some, however, fall within the rule's gray areas, in which reasonable lawyers disagree about whether the rule properly subsumes the facts. In deciding whether the rule does or does not control the case, the court in effect must rewrite the rule, expanding it a bit to include the troublesome facts within its embrace, or contracting it to exclude them. To that extent, courts inevitably make new law.

In undertaking this task, the common-law judges wavered between two alternative theories. On the one hand, the common-law judges (at least until the middle of the nineteenth century) perceived themselves in the aristocratic tradition. The common law, they said, resided in their breasts; they announced it from time to time and usually made few bones about their creative role. On the other, they sometimes denied that they created law. Purporting to enforce custom, they readily attributed any change in the law to the slow transformation of social values and standards. To warrant the title of custom, a norm must embody the custom of "all-of-us." In common-law theory, custom and law become the resultant of *community* determination. It assumed that a society had a common set of values, manifested in its common choice of norms. It perceived law not as the molder of society or creator of institutions, but as a newly institutionalized form of norms earlier developed in society's bosom.

The notion that courts did not create norms, but merely enforced "the custom of the realm" conformed nicely to the emerging theme of contract as the principal form of economic cooperation. In feudal England, economic cooperation rested upon customary institutions, upheld by state power. The serf had certain obligations to the owner of the manor; the vassal, to his lord. These obligations ensured that the economy would function and extract the surplus for the benefit of the feudatories. They ensured that the serfs would perform the labor upon which the whole edifice rested. Other norms give the serf rights required to ensure that the labor force would reproduce itself. For example, the serf had certain customary rights to land and the right to physical protection against marauders.

In the sixteenth century, feudalism was in rapid decline. The mercantilist theory was rapidly coming to dominate political and economic thought and practice:

The Mercantilists aimed at amassing in their own country the greatest possible amount of treasure. To this end Navigation Acts attempted to confine trade to English ships so that the navy could be kept strong. Bounties were paid to exporters of corn since corn exports were held to encourage agriculture and to bring in treasure and home industries were protected with tariffs. This was the theory held by the Government and the bourgeoisie in England right up to the Industrial Revolution.[3]

By the eighteenth century, English feudalism had long since died. Britain lay gripped by a mercantilist economy and an aristocratic constitution. State power supported and created an economy in which privilege received a monopoly position. The legal order served the interests of the landed gentry, who governed the countryside as justices of the peace and controlled the tight London circles of Parliament and government.

Meanwhile, in the very heart of mercantilism, new forms of enterprise arose. British and Scotch mechanics began the spate of invention that created the Industrial Revolution. New people, both canny and daring, saw vast opportunities for profits in manufacturing and selling goods. In an unplanned economy, commodity exchange rests upon each economic actress trying to seize her chance as she perceives it. Contracts replaced feudal custom as the economy's glue. Employers hired employees; importers sold to wholesalers, wholesalers to retailers, retailers to consumers, suppliers to manufacturers. Entrepreneurs entered upon large undertakings with one another, based upon their agreement to cooperate in specified ways.

Contract became the legal form of a free-market economy. Mercantilism denied the free market. The form of law associated with mercantilism made contract law—the law of the free market—difficult. The privilege-ridden mercantilist legal ardor made it difficult to estimate how courts and the state would deal with investment, contracts, and property—and above all else, businesswomen must calculate what might happen to their enterprise.

New philosophies arose to express the world views of the new free-market economy entrepreneurs. In economics, Adam Smith explained the relative wealth of nations (why some nations were rich and others poor) by the free market: those nations with free-market economies encouraged invention and productivity, those with other economic forms discouraged these developments.[4] It followed therefore that England was by rights wealthy and Asia poor, for example. In philosophy, jurisprudence, and law, Jeremy Bentham created a theoretical perspective that resonated easily with Adam Smith's daring new notions of the value of laissez-faire capitalism. Bentham argued that people were motivated by an overwhelming concern to maximize pleasure and minimize pain. In law these ideas translated into a utilitarian philosophy in which the state's responsibility was to see that undesirable behavior was swiftly, certainly, and severely punished while desirable behavior was rewarded by the acquisition of material wealth.[5] These new social theories implied a legal order that located economic decisions in the heads of entrepreneurs. Contract law embodied its typical modality. Contracts embody the operative norms of capitalist economic life. From the law businessmen demanded the exclusive power to determine those norms and the law's subsequent aid in enforcing them. (See Chapter 4 for an elaboration on contract law in capitalist society.) That called for a legal order whose courts served mainly to decide conflicts over the performance of bargains, in which entrepreneurs (or their lawyers for them) could predict the decision with reasonable certainty. To do that, a court had to treat those who appeared before it as formally equal, for it would not serve the cause of predictability if the well-born could expect the court's favor for no better reason than the blueness of their blood. A court had to decide pursuant to rules well known in advance, without the intrusion of the judge's personal values; it would not do to make every case depend upon what the particular judge ate for breakfast. A court had to require government officials, too, to act only pursuant to rules that made their behavior predictable. The capitalist dreamed of a static legal world, whose courts decided cases like computers, and legislation had no role. In one of the several ideologies of the common law, the bourgeois jurisprudents found a congenial set of norms prescribing how courts ought to behave. In laissez-faire ideologies of the law, the common-law courts became the very core of the legal order.

Nowadays we call such a legal order the "rule of law." The rule of law arose out of the demands of the new entrepreneurial classes for a form of state power commensurate with laissez-faire that would so far as possible endow them with power and that would discipline bureaucrats not to interfere with that power. All the usual attributes of the rule of law resonate with that conception, e.g., judicial independence, narrow discretion, equality before the law, due process, and judicial review of administrative action.

So stated, the ideology of the rule of law constitutes a normative model, a statement, not of how things are, but of how they ought to be. Such ideologies easily fall prey to the normative fallacy, the belief that they describe how things actually are. So with the rule of law: many people fondly believe that we have a society in which the rule of law operates, with at best minor aberrations. Whether the rule of law actually describes the legal order, or whether it in fact mystifies it and why, becomes a central issue for an adequate study of law and society.

The rule of law, moreover, readily fits a consensus model. That model argues that every society has a particular set of values, upon which practically all its members agree. If people do share basic values, then a democratic state must represent that consensus. The only legal problem becomes one of ensuring that individuals do not substitute their own deviant motivations for the values of the polity. A common variant of the consensus perspective holds that, although the polity of course contains conflict, the state itself does not take sides. No matter how antagonistic the contending classes or straits, on this much they must agree, that the peaceful settlement of conflict serves all-of-us better than violence. In this view, the state represents all-of-us, but only for the limited purpose of containing conflict. Every specific law or activity of the state carries its burden of values, but the machinery by which the state comes to the decision to create and enforce any particular law operates impartially.

The rule of law theory par excellence embodies this variant of the consensus model. Its strictures aim at ensuring the value-neutrality of the state machinery. Under the value-neutral state's benign aegis, people (read entrepreneurs) can work out their own destiny, permitting the invisible hand of the market to determine the best allocation of goods and services, made possible by the perfect predictability ensured by the value-neutral state and the rule of law.

In jurisprudence, the dominant school in this tradition became that of analytical positivism; in sociology, that of Max Weber. Here we discuss Weber's theory of law.

Universalistic Rules, Autonomous Legal System, and Legalistic Reasoning

Max Weber wanted to explain why industrial capitalism arose in the West, but not elsewhere. He sought to relate his concept of the unique characteristics of western

European law to the rise of nineteenth-century capitalism.[6] A system where profit maximization makes each the other's enemy seems opposed to technological demands for cooperation. Exchange through markets resolves this tension. Every bargain accommodates these two disparate forces. From the actor's point of view the exchange brings control over resources. If a party withdraws from a bargain it loses its purpose. Custom loses power and cannot ensure the calculability demanded by modern entrepreneurs. A legal order becomes necessary to enforce agreed-upon bargains. That legal order rests upon three pillars: an autonomous legal system, universalistic rules, and legalistic reasoning. The very notion of a market economy, open to every person, requires sanctions pursuant to universalistic rules that apply to all similar transactions. Market bargains define the norms of economic interchange, within the framework of the general rules of property, tort, and criminal law. Courts sanction violations of these rules. Calculability requires a system where each actor can discover what law will apply in a particular situation. He can discover such rules only under publicly known procedures for determining the law, adhered to by judges who exercise little discretion. That condition presupposes that judges (and lawyers) can find the rules by logical processes—that is, that the law exists as a "seamless web" and that if gaps seem to exist, sources within the legal order can fill them. This system of law-finding we call "legalistic." Its great expression in the English jurisprudence became analytical positivism.

Weber thus defined the ideal-type of capitalistic law. In Weber's view, "legalism supported the development of capitalism by providing a stable and predictable atmosphere; capitalism encouraged legalism because the bourgeoisie were aware of their own need for this type of governmental structure."[7] How well do its categories serve to study law and society in our century?

As we have already argued with respect to the category of an autonomous legal system (Chapter 1), the concept of universalistic rules requires that we ignore most of the law of social administration in favor of lawyers' law. That entails a value-judgment in favor of those solutions which lawyers' law serves—i.e., solutions consistent with an extreme version of laissez-faire. No government in the real world accepts so narrow a limitation upon its powers. If we want to study what governments in fact do, we must adopt categories adapted to studying not only lawyers' law, but also the law of social administration. As a category, universalistic rules read too narrowly.

Legalistic reasoning as a category of study too cannot serve, but for another reason: it does not exist any place except in some jurisprudents' heaven. Judges cannot decide "trouble" cases solely with materials drawn from the universe of norms. The law is not a gapless web.[8]

How would Weber's categories explain the failure of antidiscrimination laws? How would it explain the failure of academic women to receive much comfort from Title VII? His model suggests that laws' failure must result from a legal system insufficiently autonomous, or legal reasoning insufficiently legalistic. He argued that legal rationality worked best when both monopoly power and social interests were weak. Rational legality was undermined by particularistic demands characteristic of democratic governments or governments in societies where one class possessed a virtual monopoly of power. A rule permitting its addressee great discretion in deciding how to obey does not fit the model of universalistic rules, because it in fact consists not of one prescription for action applicable to everybody equally, but a delegation of power to the authority holder to act with little regard for any particular rule. Title VII permits universities unlimited discretion in deciding the criteria for employment, promotion, and tenure. Its only injunction states a negative: the university may not give adverse weight to the gender of the applicant. By leaving the rest of the criteria for employment decisions in the university's discretion, however, Title VII creates wide opportunities for discrimination to lurk behind the impenetrable fog of subjective and discretionary criteria.

Weber's theory does not lack interest, but it does not go very far. The solution that it suggests—more narrowly drawn rules, which limit the criteria officials such as university administrators may use in deciding cases—may defy accomplishment. In any event, plainly a multitude of factors, not merely the rules, affect behavior. The explanation for the legal orders' behavior cannot lie in the rules themselves, but must lie in the interweaving of rules and these other factors. Because Weber's categories point us away from behavior to the texts of the positive laws, they cannot serve to solve existential problems of law and society. That domain requires us to consider constantly the tension between the law-in-the-books and the law-in-action. With their emphasis on legalism, Weber's categories point us away from the law-in-action.

Like the rule of law model generally, the Weberian categories impose a strong ideological bias upon law and society investigations. Those categories impose a pre-cut pattern upon the range of potential explanations and hence of potential solutions. They require us to ask only the narrow question: what will serve to develop or strengthen a legal order appropriate to a market-oriented, privately controlled, laissez-faire economy? It will not do to study today's world of monopoly capitalism, multinational corporations, state corporations, and social administration.

3.2 THE FAILURE OF THE RULE OF LAW THEORY

Eighteenth-century thinkers "worked on a series of assumptions: that a society such as the American and its form of government by the state were bound together inseparably; that both could be made more perfect—and hence that the progress of society and progress of the state were one and the same. Eighteenth century optimism was based on legislative reform, conscious political judgement and action. Revolution was the servant of the legislature and the legislature was the servant of the people."[9]

The nineteenth and twentieth centuries overwhelmed that sanguine temper. The world created by the rise of capitalism and the Industrial Revolution defied control. The government promised to be structured in the interests of the people but developed instead large-scale organization, bureaucracy, and bases of decision-making that contradicted and undermined the lofty ideals and theories that justified their existence. The early nineteenth century found people revolting against the prevailing order, demanding political rights, and struggling to expand liberal democracy. The "Rule of Law" theory was shaken by the onslaught of people's actions expressing and illuminating the contradictions that existed between the ideal of law and society and the reality of most people's experiences.

A variety of theories of law and society arose to explain the failure. Most of them accepted the rule of law model and sought to explain its failure by people's innate characteristics—their values and attitudes, their interests, or their endemic resort to bargaining instead of rational planning processes. Almost alone, Marxism questioned the central premise of the rule of law model. We discuss each in turn.

The *Volksgeist*; Custom and Law; The Legal Culture

A variety of theories hold that society itself determines law. These mainly rest upon notions of value-consensus. Here we discuss the historical school, the notion that law merely institutionalizes custom, and the concept of the legal culture.

Carl von Savigny developed a jurisprudence that applied mystical Hegelian notions to the problem of law. He held that ''in the general consciousness of the people lives positive law.... It is by no means to be thought that it was the particular members of the people by whose arbitrary will law was brought forth.... Rather it is the spirit of a people living and working in common in all the individuals, which gave birth to positive law, which therefore is to the consciousness of each individual not accidentally but necessarily one and the same.''[10]

Some sociologists took over a central notion of historical jurisprudence. William Graham Sumner put it in an extreme form: stateways cannot change folkways.[11] Law reflects custom, or it remains immured in the books. Paul Bohannan stated the claim in a sophisticated form:

Customs are norms or rules ... about the ways in which people must behave if social institutions are to perform their tasks and society is to endure.... Some customs in some societies are reinstitutionalized at another level; they are restated for the more precise purposes of legal institutions....

A legal right (and, with it, a law) is the restatement for the purpose of maintaining peaceful and just operation of the institutions of society, of some, but never all, of the recognized claims of the persons within those institutions....

Law is never a mere reflection of custom, however. Rather law is always out of phase with society, specifically because of the duality of the statement and restatement and of rights.[12]

Lawrence Friedman proposed that the legal system comprises three elements: structural, substantive, and cultural.[13] Structure includes ''the number and types of courts, presence or absence of a constitution, presence or absence of federalism or pluralism, division of powers between Judges, legislators, Governors, Kings, juries, administrative officers; modes of procedure in various institutions and the like.''[14]

The substantive component embodies the output side of the legal system: ''the 'laws' themselves—the rules, doctrines, statutes and decrees, *to the extent that they are actually used by the rulers and the ruled,* and in addition, all other rules which govern, whatever their formal status'' (emphasis added). ''The legal culture''—the cultural element—consists of ''the values and attitudes which bind the system together, and which determine the place of the legal system in the culture as a whole . . . . [It is] the term we apply to those values and attitudes which *determine* what structures are used and why; which rules work and which do not and why'' (emphasis added).[15]

In sum, Friedman translated the term ''legal system'' into the concept of society itself, consisting of the state, the society's normative structure, and its values and attitudes. But he built into his definition an *explanation* of how the legal system affects behavior: ''values and attitudes'' determine behavior.

Despite minor variations, these three theories explain behavior with respect to the legal order by dark, irrational, subjective attitudes of mind—the *Volksgeist*, custom, or the ''legal culture.'' All would explain the failure of law to have the effect anticipated in similar ways. Laws that fail ''run against the grain.'' However denoted, white and male dominance so pervades our culture that white male educators and white male judges who try antidiscrimination cases behave in discriminatory ways as part of their values and attitudes. Employers and educators continue to defy antidiscrimination commands and judges find ways to avoid enforcing the laws.

All these theories assume their central proposition, that behavior reflects values and attitudes. They hold that we can therefore discover values and attitudes by examining behavior and inferring from it the values and attitudes of the actor. Because in the past courts did not upset university decisions concerning academic women, we infer from that behavior values and attitudes generally favorable to males and to established authority and then invoke those values and attitudes to explain continued similar behavior. That becomes only a convoluted extrapolation: it is not an explanation.[16]

Interest Jurisprudence

The historical and sociological schools that explained behavior with reference to the values, attitudes, customs, or *Volksgeist* formed by ''society'' spawned another philosophy of law based on the assumption that all human beings share in common certain inalienable interests. Beginning with Van Jhering (1781-1843), exponents of this philosophy generated lists of six, seven, eight, or twelve ''interests'' common to all people. The protection of these ''interests,'' it was argued, must be the cornerstone of all civilized legal systems. Examples of the interests that the law must protect included health, safety, wealth, shared power, respect, enlightenment, skill, and so forth.[17] The lists differ depending on the author.

These lists of interests tell us nothing about what the law and legal order consist of nor do they tell us how the law came to be as it is. The lists tell us only what one person believes the law should look like. Why the legal order favors the rich, discriminates against blacks and women, undermines rather than enhances equality of opportunity; these and a myriad of other questions are simply brushed under the rug by a perspective seeking to discover that set of interests presumably necessary for human society. Interest jurisprudence invokes a normative, not an analytical theory. Ironically, even as a normative prescription for what ''ought'' to be interest jurisprudence is a failure. The prescribed interests necessarily become highly generalized and abstract. Even if ascertainable, therefore, they have little practical use.[18]

Roscoe Pound proposed a theory of jural postulates that consisted of a sophisticated sort of interest jurisprudence.[19] He purported to discover people's vital interests from the subject of the law. He thus turned interest jurisprudence on its head. Instead of a form of natural law, based on the inherent nature of humans, it became a device to satisfy actual claims and demands:

I am content to think of law as a social institution to satisfy social wants—the claims and demands and expectations involved in the existence of civilized society—by giving effect to as much as we may with the least sacrifice, so far as human wants can be satisfied or such claims given effect by an ordering of human conduct through politically organised society.[20]

Underlying those claims and demands, he thought, lay the jural postulates, statements of value-sets so encompassing that they subsumed practically all the claims and demands that the people in any given society made. In 1942, Pound put forward five jural postulates that he believed underlay society in the United States as it then stood:

1   In civilized society men must be able to assume that others will commit no international aggressions upon them.

2   In civilized society men must be able to assume that they may control for beneficial purposes what they have discovered and appropriated to their own use, what they have created by their own labour and what they have acquired under the existing social and economic order.

3   In civilized society men must be able to assume that those with whom they deal in the general intercourse of society will act in good faith and hence
    a) Will make good reasonable expectations which their promises or other conduct reasonably create
    b) Will carry out their undertakings according to the expectations which the moral sentiment of the community attaches thereto
    c) Will restore specifically or by equivalent what comes to them by mistake or unanticipated or not fully intended situation whereby they receive at another's expense what they could not have reasonably expected to receive under the circumstances.

4   In civilized society men must be able to assume that those who are engaged in some course of conduct will act with due care not to cast an unreasonable risk of injury upon others.

5   In civilized society men must be able to assume that those who maintain things likely to get out of hand or to escape and do damage will restrain them or keep them within their proper bounds.[21]

Consider the claims and demands which would not find a home among these five. By 1942, for the eighty years after the Civil War, blacks had hammered on the doors of American society claiming equal treatment. Nothing in Pound's postulates expresses those claims. For generations the poor demanded a more equitable share of the goods they helped to produce; nothing in Pound's statement addresses that. Universities had discriminated against women for three centuries; Pound's postulates do not touch on women's claims. Harold Laski caustically observed: "After his long journey through the immense literature of legal theory he arrives at a framework of principles which are the obvious outcome of his affection for the country town of Lincoln, Nebraska

[Pound's birthplace] . . . they are framed, that is to say, for a community of small owners such as the Middle West knew in the epoch first following the Civil War.''[22]

It need hardly be stated that the postulates that Laski could so characterize do not offer much help in explaining specific problems, e.g., gender discrimination. The legal order of the mid-nineteenth century, far from resisting, supported gender discrimination. If it provided the source for Pound's jural postulates, it seems unlikely that his postulates could help scholars to understand why Title VII gave women such cold comfort.

Interest jurisprudence finally asserts that people have particular interests, which flow from "human nature," and that the law does and should reflect those interests. That becomes only a sophisticated form of natural law, a philosophy that holds that the law does and ought to reflect "natural" tendencies, whether coming from God or from human beings' inherent nature. Nobody has ever stated in a way that becomes subject to falsification either what deity commands or what constitutes people's "inherent natures." Natural law (as Pareto remarked) reflects people's claims and demands, dresses up in a quasi-philosophical form. It becomes worthy of study in order to learn what people demand; it does not serve as an explanation for what happens in the real world.

The Bargaining Model

The mechanisms of the rule of law model implies what Professor Lon Fuller called the enterprise of governance by rules.[23] That suggests the Englightenment model: rational people intelligently analyzing problems, deciding upon appropriate solutions, and instituting them through rules of law. The failure of an Enlightenment model that excited the historical, sociological, and interest schools also excited the bargaining model.

Bargaining pervades not only the marketplace but every human relationship. Scholars have invoked it to explain such diverse phenomena as "primitive" law,[24] relationships in a maximum security penitentiary,[25] and why businessmen avoid courts.[26] That model denies that coercion serves as the operative control mechanism. Bureaucrats obey rules only if they do not too strongly oppose them. Superiors therefore ordinarily issue only those orders that will elicit voluntary obedience. The nominal superiors have only a "fiction of superior authority. Even though physical force is involved and even under the extreme condition of battle, when the regime is nearly absolute, authority nevertheless rests upon the acceptance or consent of individuals."[27] Nobody runs the machine; the nominal heads only tend it. Rational planning backed by the coercive power of bureaucratic superiors dissolves into accommodation arising from bargaining and agreement.

The pervasiveness of bargaining generalizes into the pluralist notion of government. The entire structure of government itself becomes a vast arena within which coalitions form and split and in effect bargain with each other to achieve a working compromise. The "bargaining model" of law and society deals "mainly with the fact that individuals and groups with differing values exist, with the power they possess and with the processes of adjustment among these groups in the working of government."[28] The rules of law emerge from these various bargains and so do the methods to implement them. Logrolling, long thought to be a specific technique of legislating, becomes an iron law; social change, a chain of group bargains.

The bargaining postulated by the model, of course, does not take place overtly and explicitly. Only rarely do the leaders of the various interest groups sit down at a table to negotiate. Instead, the bargaining model instructs us to examine their behavior as if they had done so. Bargaining reflects power vectors. To say that law results from bargaining asserts that law reflects the configuration of power.

How would the bargaining model explain changes in racist laws over the past hundred years? Slaves in pre-Civil War America never bargained with the slave owners—both slavery and its demise were thrust onto the African-American population without bargaining. Prisoners did not bargain for changes in the law of an accused's right to counsel (although one particular prisoner brought the case to court through the aid of an organization composed mainly of white middle-class men who had never themselves been in prison but who sought legal reform). Academic women as a group never bargained with university administrators as a group about claims of discrimination.

Some theories view power as arising from successfully mobilizing resources and allies *within* the existing working rules; others see it as having been created by the working rules themselves. The bargaining model purports to explain particular decisions as they occur within the existing working rules. The model does not, therefore, concern itself with "non-decisions."[29] The working rules themselves always admit for consideration only a limited range of issues, explanations, data, proposals for solution. Those that never enter the system never fall for decision—that is, they become "non-decisions." Because they decide whose claims, explanations, data, and solutions to accept and whose to ignore, the working rules therefore create power. By unquestioning acceptance of the rules behind a seeming consensus the bargaining model masks the brutishness of power. Bargains, after all, occur upon assent to the same set of clauses in an agreement. The bargaining model directs attention toward comfortable middle-class notions of harmony and compromise and away from coercion, toward the civility of the negotiating table and away from the barbaric horror of maximum security prisons.

The bargaining model of law therefore reflects the status quo. "Ascendent groups of course tend readily to proclaim a just balance of power and a true harmony of interest, for they prefer their domination to be uninterrupted and peaceful."[30] Precisely because the bargaining model examines how people make decisions within the existing framework, it can direct attention only to incremental changes within that framework. It does not and cannot suggest radical change in the very structure. "The balance of power theory . . . is a narrow focus view of American politics. With it one can explain temporary alliances within one party or the other. It is also narrow focus in the choice of time span: the shorter the period of time in which you are interested, the more usable the balance of power theory appears."[31]

The bargaining model gains its greatest acceptance among the yea-sayers of American academia. Most public discourse in American postwar politics focused on questions of incremental change, with decisions occurring through accommodations among power centers within the existing institutional framework. That was generalized into a prescriptive model of the Good Society and dominated the postwar public philosophy. It failed; the war on poverty did not produce solutions to poverty, but only the inclusion of poor people on boards dealing with poverty.[32]

3.3 SOCIOLOGY, JURISPRUDENCE, AND LEGAL REALISM

Eugene Ehrlich (1862-1922) lived in the Duchy of Bukovina, which was then part of the Austro-Hungarian Empire. Bukovina was the home of at least nine distinct ethnic and religious groups. Each had its own informal rules: for marriage and divorce, descent and distribution, landlord and tenant. They followed these norms, not the formal Civil Code. Ehrlich called these informal norms the "living law" in contrast to the formal legal order. He argued that the living law should rank the priorities of payment of the various claims and demands different people and groups made upon the law:

When the jurist is asked to draw the line between the conflicting interests independently, he is asked by implication, to do it according to justice.... The catch phrase about balancing of interests that is so successful at the present time is not an answer to this question, for the very question is: What is it that gives weight to the interests that are to be balanced? Manifestly it is not the balancing jurist, writer or teacher, Judge or legislator, but society itself.... Justice therefore does not proceed from the individual, but arises in society.[33]

In short the legislator or jurist should adjust the formal law to match the living law.

The sociological school, in the wing represented by Ehrlich, ultimately asserted not merely that formal law reinstitutionalized custom, but that it ought to do so. It contributed to studying law as social engineering by distinguishing the living law from the formal law—a lead that the legal realists, coming from a different, positivist tradition, would follow.

While the sociological school began to explore the tensions between formal law and living law, the realists in the United States moved rapidly in the same direction. As noted earlier, Oliver Wendell Holmes fired the opening gun in the long engagement between the realists and the analytical positivists in a lecture at Harvard in 1881. "The life of the law," he said, "is not logic, the life of the law is experience."[34] He accepted the positivist view of law as a human affair, decided by human beings. He added the pragmatic notion that one ought to base the decision on what the law ought to be upon considerations of community expediency.

The realists began, as did the positivists, by considering primarily what happened in courts. They learned that one could not explain the decision of courts in "difficult" cases, that is, those of first impression, by the elegant rationalizations that the judges, following analytical positivism, gave in their opinions. They explained what judges did and ought to do: to formulate new rules in light of how they thought the rule would operate in society. That is to say, they invoked the categories they called the law-in-the-books and the law-in-action.

These categories, formal and living law, law-in-the-books and law-in-action, plainly become the basic building blocks for any science of law as social engineering. Law as social engineering supposes the use of law to influence behavior directly. The lawmaker can only change the formal rules. Lawmakers cannot, however, punch and pinch people and society like balls of clay. Unless they are quite mad, they will try to shape a legal order that effectively induces desired behavior. The way formal law in fact affects social behavior embodies the influence of the formal law on a society. The way social behavior constrains the choice of lawmakers expresses the influence of the living law on the formal law. The study of formal law and living law, of law-in-the-books and law-in-action, embodies the study of the interaction—the dialectic, if you please—between law and society.

The gap between the formal and the living law only opens up the problem. The study and explanation of that gap can lead to reliable knowledge about why some laws work and others do not. Without that knowledge, society can never purposively solve its troubles.

The realist perspective poses problems; it does not help much with solutions. In the case of university women and Title VII, it tells us that we must study the difference between the promise of Title VII in-the-books and how it affects the behavior of the various actors involved—here mainly the universities involved and the federal judges charged with Title VII's enforcement. That marks the beginning of wisdom about the problem, for it asks the right questions. It tells us nothing about how to go about answering the questions posed.

The study of the gap between the law-in-the-books and the law-in-action too easily leads to research that serves merely as a handmaiden to power. If research explains only why people disobey, its findings will more likely teach how to induce obedience and not question policy itself. The study of the gap between the law-in-the-books and the law-in-action sometimes seduces the researcher into studying threats to power, not poverty and oppression. Students of law and society ought not become hired guns, ready to travel on demand.

The perception of the gap between the law-in-the-books and the law-in-action, however, initiates the generation of reliable knowledge about the limits of law. But, it is only a first step. That study requires a methodology which lends itself to studying ends as well as means, the morality as well as the practicality of the legal order.

3.4 MARXISM AND DIALECTICAL MATERIALISM

All the jurisprudence theories we have thus far examined, except the "sociological jurisprudence" of Eugene Ehrlich, assume (usually without explicitly so stating) a consensus society. Marxism, like many other theories, arose to explain why the Englightenment's dream failed. Unlike those other theories, however, it postulated a conflict society. In that society, the haves generally had both privilege and power. They exercised their power to maintain their position and to exploit the masses. In that view, the rule of law model did not work the way some dreamed it might, to alleviate mass misery.

Until recently Marxist theories of law were virtually ignored in capitalist countries, despite the fact that the writings of Marx and Engels contain some fertile observations on law.[35] Furthermore Marxist theory generated a large number of researches, policies, and treatises on law,[36] and it influenced the legal orders of nations from the Soviet Union and Eastern Europe to Cuba and China.

As a result of the bias against seriously considering Marxism in studies of law and society, most references to Marxist theory grossly distort it. Dennis Lloyd, for example, although recognizing Marxist theory as worthy of inclusion in the sociology of law, nonetheless distorts its perspective and claims. He asserts that for Marx the law was merely an epiphenomenon reflecting the economic relations of capitalism.[37] More recent works give a more sensitive and sophisticated rendering of Marxist contributions to law.[38] It rests upon two pillars. Piers Beirne clearly articulated the first: "In the analysis of any phenomenon Marx always looked for the basic internal contradiction which determined the movement of the whole; ideological forms such as State, law, religion and so on are explained by reference to the contradictions of the capitalist mode of production."[39]

The basic contradiction in capitalist societies rests upon the production of commodities as a public event. Production requires everyone's labor. And we might add, socialist law (as in the Soviet Union, China, and Cuba) reflects contradictions of the socialist mode of production (see Brady and Bahro). Only the capitalist, however, owns the product. Only he decides how to dispose of the product. The legal order develops in response to the conflicts and inconsistencies of that system of production: calling slaves inhuman but relying on their human qualities; stigmatizing women as inferior but depending on them for survival and the maintenance of essential social relations; defining the talents of workers as less valuable than the talents of administrators but being unable to produce a nail without the workers' labor. To legitimize the inconsistencies and irrationalities born of the contradictions of the economy the legal order constitutes myths, creates institutions of repression, and tries to harmonize exploitation with freedom, expropriation with choice, inherently unequal contractual agreements with an ideology of free will. Socialist economic systems must harmonize the inefficiency of decentralized productive systems with a commitment to rapidly improving the standard of living of "everyone" and industrializing in competition with already industrialized capitalist countries.

The second pillar of Marxist sociology of law consists of the dialectical relationship between scientific explanation and social praxis, the essence of Marxist methodology. Ideas do not change by the force of their logic. New discoveries in social relationships and understanding society do not emerge merely from people's heads. Reliable knowledge arises and can only arise in the course of people's efforts to change their world. Scientific socialism and reliable scientific knowledge about the processes and forces of history, then, come from our efforts to change the world in accordance with the implications of our understanding (our theories) about that world.

Thus Marxism diverged from consensus models both theoretically and methodologically. It diverged in its perception of both the appropriate vocabulary and the appropriate methodology of social inquiry. The vocabulary employs *contradictions* as the central analytical concept. The methodology rests upon the dialectical unity of theory and practice, thought and action, ends and means. To generate theory, engage in social practice; to produce good social practice, generate good theory.

Marxism stresses that society constantly changes in a dialectical process. It holds that the "ruling class" is neither unified nor omnipotent. Laws change as a consequence of the unending struggle between social classes and within social classes. The legal gains of the women's movement in the last hundred years, however slow, Marxism explains as process. The history of the struggle for equal rights for women disproves both the consensus model and the Weberian theory that the law changes according to its own logic and ideological commitments. As Sachs and Wilson put it:

A study of sexism in the legal systems . . . explodes the notion that legal systems evolve according to inherent principles of logic and procedure. The great changes in gender status have come about not through the harmonious unfolding from within of legal concepts, but through vigorous attacks against the legal system from outside . . . forced to a more egalitarian position by the challenge . . . the record shows each step forward has had to be strenuously campaigned for.[40]

So also of improvements in workers' wages, work conditions, and child labor, of legally institutionalized racism, poverty, discrimination, and colonialism: they changed as the result not of the internal logic of the law, but of class conflict.

Marxist theory posits the salient role of struggle, contradiction, and conflict in the historical process as determinants of social and legal change. Other theories ignore or give little credence to the importance of this characteristic of human societies. Marx and Engels explained why legal forms took the shape they did. Marx wrote that "my investigation led to the result that legal relations as well as forms of state are to be grasped neither from the so-called general development of the human mind, but rather have their roots in the material conditions of life, the sum total of which Hegel . . . combines under the name of 'civil society.' "[41]

This reflected Marx's explanation for what later sociologists called "culture." The economic system constitutes the base; the culture—law, political forms, ideologies, art—the superstructure. Engels wrote that "according to the materialist conception of history, the *ultimately* determining element in history is the production and reproduction of real life."[42]

At first blush, Marxism seems only a special form of the sociological school. Law reinstitutionalizes the forms of society itself with economic affairs as the key variable. Some Marxists so construed their doctrine.[43] In that view, the interests of the ruling class required discrimination against women in academia and blacks in school; the court decisions denying women Title VII relief and the institutionalization of racial discrimination in spite of antidiscrimination laws result from the court's subservience to ruling class power.[44] Since the academic women involved hardly consisted of proletarians, only in indirect ways could ruling class interest require defeating their claims. The ruling class has a strong interest in a divided working class and therefore fosters an ideology of female inferiority. Judges subservient to that ideology, therefore, unwittingly served the ruling class by defeating academic women's Title VII claims.

Engels himself denied so mechanical an interpretation of the base-superstructure metaphor. He wrote:

If somebody twists [the notion of the primacy of the base] into saying that the economic element is the *only* determining one, he transforms that proposition into a meaningless, senseless phrase. The economic system is the basis, but the various elements of the superstructure—political forms of the class struggle and its results, to wit: constitutions established by the victorious class after a successful battle, etc., juridical forms, and even reflexes of all these actual struggles in the brains of the participants, political, juristic philosophical theories, religious views and their further development into systems of dogmas—also exercise their influence upon the course of the historical struggles and in many cases predominate in determining their form.[45]

The principle of the dialectic saved Marxist legal theory from economic determinism. Opposites interpenetrate each other. So do the base and the superstructure and even the different elements of the superstructure itself. Law interacts not only with economic base, but with religion, philosophy, custom, tradition, and ideology. Law simultaneously affects and is affected by each of these.

Law can affect both the base and the superstructure because each of these inevitably contains contradictions and multifarious purposes and tendencies—in short, a potential for change. The law and the state can as it were nudge society along one or another of these alternative courses, although they cannot alone determine society's shape.

These contradictory tendencies ultimately stem from the relationships of production.[46] Classes arise in every society based upon private ownership of the means of production. The owners of property require workers to produce goods and profits. Capitalists ineluctably exploit their workers; their profits arise out of that exploitation. Capitalist society therefore inevitably produced classes with antagonistic interests.

Since the base and its class struggle in a sense "cause" the superstructure, the culture reflects the class struggle itself. Law, as part of the superstructure, cannot avoid taking sides in the class struggle. It cannot become a neutral consensus of all-of-us, for a society of antagonistic classes knows no consensus. The state becomes a weapon of a particular class. Law emanates from the state. Law in a society of classes must therefore represent and advance the interests of one class or the other.

"The nature of law is determined by economic relationships *via* the political demands of the dominant class."[47] Our legal order embodies not the rule of law, but the rule of class struggle. In this respect, Marxism opposed most other schools of jurisprudence. Marxism perceived societies everywhere in struggle and conflict. The state and law serve as weapons in that struggle. Most other schools and writers assumed a consensus—the common consciousness, the legal culture, custom, and so forth. Marx was right. As we argued in Chapter 2, all contemporary polities embody conflict. Law and the state inevitably represent one or another class in that conflict. The opposite proposition is simply false. Since many in the nonsocialist world regard these as highly controversial statements, however, any theory of law and society must take them as problematic, not primitive propositions.

The perception of the dialectical relationship between base and superstructure, between economy and law, pointed toward the notion of law as a means of social engineering. "The legal superstructure ensures organization in social life, facilitates the conscious solution of the problems which confront it and enables members of the public to assimilate the principles and ideals of the future socialist community."[48] The existence of modern forces of production creates the possibility of a socialist and ultimately a communist order of society. "But the transformation of possibility into reality is not automatic. A decisive role is played by . . . the state."[49]

The Marxist notion of the state and law therefore falls between the positivist and the sociological schools. For Hans Kelsen, a notable positivist, the state serves as "an immanent intelligence, directing social change, rather than as a social agency."[50] The sociological school—or at least one branch of it—understands the state and law merely as reflecting the customs and demands of "society." Marxism understands it as both simultaneously. Law reflects social organization, but at the same time and to a degree affirmatively directs its change. The dialectic embodies this perspective.

3.5 A PERSPECTIVE, VOCABULARY, AND METHODOLOGY FOR THE STUDY OF LAW AND SOCIETY

We have considered a wide variety of variables that scholars have urged determine the ways that the legal order and society interact. Some of these turn out to serve normative rather than analytical purposes, e.g., universalistic rules, autonomous legal system, and legislative reasoning. Some seem quite nonfalsifiable, such as the *Volksgeist*, custom as determining law, and the legal culture. Others—the Marxist categories, calling attention to the importance of power, contradiction and the dialectic, and the law-in-books/law-in-action dichotomy urged by the legal realists—have greater utility in analysis. Alone, none of these theories seems completely adequate for the domain of study we have staked out.

There is, however, a corpus of categories, methodologies, and perspectives which can be culled from the theories that we take as a starting point for any adequate study.

All theories recognize that members of a group, collectivity, society, or nation inherit patterns of social relations from their past. Furthermore it is generally acknowledged that those features of the past which are of paramount importance in shaping the present include the economic structure (e.g., capitalism, feudalism, socialism), political organization (e.g., democratic, authoritarian, popular justice), and culture (e.g., norms, values, roles). In other words, all social theory recognizes that historically rooted institutions are fundamentally important influences over present-day events. It is also generally recognized as analytically useful to study both the *material* (economic) and the *ideological* (cultural) conditions inherited from the past, an important quality of which are the extant contributions within and between material and ideological structures.

Other concepts employed by practically everyone who has studied the relationships between law and society incorporate a sociological vocabulary: role, position, norm, institutions, power, conflict, interaction. We will discuss those various concepts in turn.

Sociological inquiry often begins by describing people in terms of the *positions* they hold in society: Father, Mother, Sister, Judge, Professor, Derelict, Thief, Lathe-operator, Carpenter, Churchmember, Atheist, Political Activist, etc. The observed regularities of the position, i.e., its content, arise because the persons who occupy it fulfill a complex of obligations and exercise a complex of rights associated with the position. These "rights" and "obligations" may differ from the rights and obligations that lawyers customarily associate with the terms "right" and "duty," for most of them do not derive from the state's edict. One may have an "obligation" to surrender his seat in a train to an elderly person, but in most places the state will not punish you if you do not. Hence, this "obligation" does not comprise a *legal* duty. The complex of obligations that define a social position we denote collectively as its *role* and the equivalent complex of rights, its *status*.

These obligations and rights find their definition in prescriptive rules called *norms*. These have varying degrees of articulation. Relatively little precision defines the position of Father, although children may let their Father know unmistakably when he acts in a way that to them seems to violate his role. (Act your age, Daddy!) Other norms, such as some embodied in law, have highly explicit contents.

Human societies exhibit a high degree of regularity of behaviors. We denote any regular behavior by people in various positions as an *institution*. A university in this view constitutes an institution because it consists of many people—administrators, students, teaching staff, clerks, secretaries, and many others—all behaving in particular, repetitive patterns.

Animal and insect societies, too, exhibit a high degree of regularity of behavior. The human condition, however, differs from that of the lower orders. People have consciousness, with which they can create and shape their institutions, their material conditions, and their ideology. The intricate interactions of an ant colony or a beehive, like those of a prairie dog village, rest mainly on the instinctive reactions of natural and social stimuli. To understand the structure of human societies, however, to explain human behavior, we must deal with the symbolic conscious forces that accompany human action. "Consciousness" and "ideology," then, are concepts (categories) essential for our analysis.

One can ask a wide range of questions about norms and social structure: what constitutes the content of the norms and how relevant do they seem to the tasks which people perform? To what extent are the norms institutionalized, that is, to what extent do the persons in the system accept the norms, treat them seriously, and expect the norms to guide the behavior of others? How are norms sanctioned? To what extent are they articulated? How closely does one's actions match the expectations of those concerned? To what extent do the consequences of compliance with the norm match the anticipations of the persons affected?

As one consequence of the normative system, action manifests consciousness and consciousness manifests action. Norms reflect the subjective, internal conceptions that human beings hold, about how people occupying certain positions ought to act. They state the *role-expectation* for the position. *Role-performance* refers to how people in fact act, either in pursuit of the norms defining the position or, deviantly, in defiance of the norms.

The rules of law constitute a particular order of norms. Like all norms, they define how people or collectivities ought to act. Some, like the laws against murder, address everyone. Some, like traffic laws, address only a particular category of persons (automobile drivers). Others apply to very specific positions (such as the laws that define the role of the president of the United States). Still others address collectivities (corporation law). The commands of Title VII, requiring universities not to discriminate on the basis of sex in employment decisions, address university faculties, administrators, and trustees. All constitute norms.

They also constitute laws. All the rules that laymen call "law"—statutes, case law, administrative regulations—constitute norms. To understand how these function, we must understand three central "law-jobs": law creation, sanctions, and dispute-settlement. In a centralized state, the state or its agencies create these norms. Every society has as one of its law-jobs the creation of rules of law, the principal task of legislatures, appellate courts, and administrative agencies.

Second, besides understanding the creation of the norms and the determination of their content, we must also understand the enforcement of the norms—their accompanying sanctions. In a centralized state, state authority enforces most (but not necessarily all) rules of law. If one violates a criminal law, the initiative of a state official (the policeman or the prosecutor) sets the sanctioning system into motion and other state officials (the jailer) actually inflict the punishment. If one violates other sorts of law—e.g., one forbidding negligent automobile driving—one may become liable for damages at the behest of the injured party, who can enlist state power to enforce the judgment. Under Title VII, a woman against whom a university discriminates has the right to ask a federal district court for an order requiring the university to "make her whole" by giving her the job she would have had but for the unlawful discrimination and to pay her back pay to recompense her for any losses occasioned by the discrimination. That order has behind it the federal court's contempt powers, and behind that a gaggle of armed people—sheriffs, jailers, the National Guard, the Army.

Thirdly, disputes arise concerning a variety of issues in connection with the normative system: the content of a norm or whether the person in question actually violated it. To resolve these conflicts, a dispute-settling machine emerges. All these various "law-jobs" constitute a set of processes: the processes of creating law, defining the content of the norms, administering the rules, settling disputes, sanctioning breach. For us, these processes constitute the legal order. Thus viewed, the legal order in a centralized state becomes more than a mere body of rules. Rather, it becomes a dynamic process involving every aspect of state action, for state action will involve at some point creation of a norm, adjudication about its content, administration, adjudication of violation, or sanctioning breach.

The Legal Order and its Components

Like every social subsystem, the legal order performs a myriad of functions; it resolves disputes, creates official norms, educates the people in certain value-sets, provides employment for a professional class, etc. In studying so complex a system comprising so many functions, to what sorts of data ought one direct attention? What categories should we use? Here we put forward a bare-bones outline of a model that we find useful.

We start from the observable fact that people make certain demands upon the bureaucratic organization that constitutes the state. They demand that the state settle disputes, perform certain services, redistribute resources, and make certain kinds of decisions. These demands lead either to the creation of new norms or to a change in the application of existing rules. Every norm, whether legal or nonlegal, aims at the activity of a role-occupant. With most norms, the sanction takes place through direct interaction between the person aggrieved by the breach of the norm in question and the role-occupant. If my children disobey me, my parental role authorizes me directly to punish them; if my employee displeases me, I can rebuke him or her or (in the absence of a union) discharge the said employee.

A relatively small group of norms, rather formal in character, have separate sanctioning institutions. Law constitutes the outstanding example. Other, law-like norms exist sanctioned by separate, although non-state bodies. As Hans Kelsen pointed out, practically every norm of law that addresses a role-occupant simultaneously commands that if the prosecutor proves to a judge that someone has committed murder, the judge shall apply a sanction. Thus the same demand by people that a rule-creating institution formulate a new norm of conduct for a citizen simultaneously demands a new norm for the rule-sanctioning agencies, instructing them to impose a sanction if someone breaches the primary norm. Thus the safety at work laws which command employers to maintain safety standards simultaneously command judges in a proper case to order the employer to remedy unsafe conditions, subject to sanctions for contempt of court if the employer disobeys.

We can, therefore, very tentatively and very abstractly diagram the flow of demands into the legal system, their conversion by rule-making and rule-sanctioning institutions into norms, addressed both to role-occupants and to the rule-sanctioning agencies, and into sanctioning activity (see Fig. 3.1).

Every normative system induces or coerces activity. The normative system we have defined as the "legal order" uses state power to this end. Our model, therefore, suggests that demands come from various segments of the population and that the state through the legal order exercises its power to induce or coerce certain desired behavior by some set of role-occupants. In the nature of things, demands of this sort respond to the interest of those making the demands. They call for the exercise of state power to induce or coerce the desired activity because the law's addressees do not necessarily want so to act. The legal order, thus defined, becomes a system by which one part of the population uses state power to coerce another segment. It becomes a system for the exercise of state power.

The diagram in Fig. 3.1 does not purport to provide a guide for investigations into the real world. It only traces the flow of demands: demands put to the state by segments of the population, demands that rule-making institutions make upon role-occupants and upon role-sanctioning institutions. The sanctioning activity it refers to concerns the sanctioning activity the appropriate institution ought to apply. It tells us nothing about how in fact any of these various actors behave. It says nothing, for example, about who has the *power* to influence the state.

Law cannot succeed in its ostensible purposes of affecting the behavior of its addressees unless lawmakers can predict accurately the actual behavior of a law's addressees in the face of the rule. The law-in-action concerns behavior, what in fact takes place, not what ought to take place. How can we in general understand why people do or do not obey a rule of law? To answer that question, what general categories of data ought we to examine?

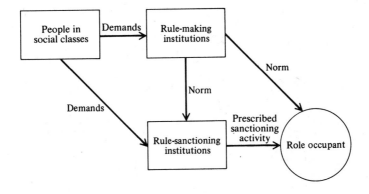

Figure 3.1

We take as our most general model of society people and collectivities making choices among all the myriad forces of their social environment, in the light of what goes on inside their heads—i.e., in the face of the ideological and material forces that make up their milieu. Every role-occupant makes an analogous choice when he obeys or disobeys a norm. Where the legal order defines the role, however, special forces exist that the law's addressee must take into account. First, the role-occupant must take into account the general respect or disrespect that other citizens may accord obedience or disobedience to the law. Universities, for example, cannot today openly discriminate against women on their faculties (as many of them did only a few short years ago) because they may lose respect and esteem (not to speak of financial support) from people who believe that a moral imperative requires obedience to law. More importantly, perhaps, where the law addresses a role, officials exist to adjudicate and enforce it. The role-occupant's arena of choice now includes among the forces that compose it the activity of officials. Since 1972, whenever universities decided whether or not to discriminate against women, they had to take into account the possibility of administrative or judicial action if they did discriminate.

We might diagram the relationships thus presented as shown in Fig. 3.2. The critical factors that a role-occupant must take into account in deciding how to behave consist of the norm addressed to him, the expected activities of law-implementing agencies and officials, and all the material and ideological factors that constitute his

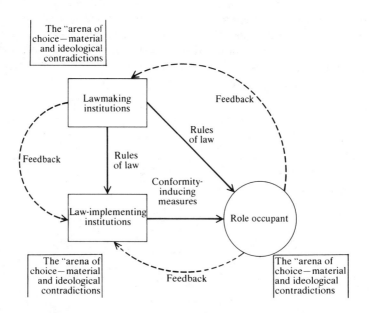

Figure 3.2

PERSPECTIVES AND VOCABULARIES

arena of choice. But, the lawmaking and the law-sanctioning agencies do not operate in a vacuum. They, too, consist of people—role-occupants—making choices within a milieu of material and ideological forces, including rules of law defining their positions and the activities of others.

People do not remain passive in the face of undesirable material and ideological or legal conditions. They protest, they resist, they complain, they threaten, they rebel, they revolt. Throughout history, revolution, rebellion, and opposition to the extant legal order occur everywhere. United States history is a catalog of constant rebellion, riot, revolution, and civil disorder.[52] Even our most heavily oppressed class, slaves in the antebellum South, revolted; more than four hundred black slave revolts took place before the Civil War.[53] As a result, the law changed, sometimes slowly, as people won small gains from those in power, sometimes radically, as they succeeded in changing not only the people who operate the levers of state power, but the very structure of the state itself. The legal basis for a contract, for crime, for land ownership changes radically in every country over the years. In our time, following revolutions, they changed radically in Algeria, Cuba, China, and the Soviet Union. Laws have no immortal existence. People make them, people change them. The operative mode by which the people bring this about we subsume under the word "feedback." This category, in turn, contains the idea of the dialectic.

In what sense can we denote Fig. 3.2 a "model"? We earlier argued that no single, autonomous legal system exists discontinuous with society. A vast number of specific systems, involving particular laws, bureaucracies, and feedbacks, do exist. How do the model and its existential referents relate?

Models organize thought. No matter how detailed, a physical model of an airplane only *represents* the airplane. It is not the airplane itself. A diagrammatic representation of the legal system affecting agriculture only represents that system. The model put forward here only represents the form of a variety of legal systems. It directs attention to particular categories of data for investigation, that is, it constitutes a heuristic, a perspective to guide discretionary choice in social inquiry. It is an agenda for research. In principle, one can test it, however, by seeing if there are instances in which significant variables not subsumed by the model do affect behavior in response to a rule of law. Testing will be facilitated, however, after closing the vague boxes labeled "arenas of choice."

This model implies a definition of law that addresses law's function in channeling behavior. *Law is a process by which government structures choice.* Law as a device to structure choice expresses at once law's usual marginality in influencing behavior and its importance as the principal instrument that government has to influence behavior. Since a people's history itself determines the arena of choice in most respects, that history determines the limits on law. We can understand law only by understanding it as part of a people's history and present conditions.

The model assumes that society does not have a consensus. The arenas of choice of lawmakers, of law enforcers, and of the addressees of law do not necessarily have the same content. Lawmakers and some law enforcers come from or have close alliances with the upper ranks of society. Some laws address their equals; most address members of society with very different backgrounds. Mainly white male Congressmen wrote Title VII and in 1972 stretched it to cover women academics. Mainly white male judges enforce the law against mainly white male university administrators, at the behest of mainly white female claimants. The women claimants and the other actors plainly do not all have the same arenas of choice—i.e., the same material, social and ideological environments within which they choose and therefore act.

3.6 CONCLUSION

Analytical positivism asserted the independence of law from society. In response, sociological jurisprudence and some crude versions of Marxist jurisprudence claimed that law was merely an epiphenomenon. Neither proposition matched reality. The legal order structures society simultaneously with society's structuring of the legal order. The model we have advanced purports to explicate this complex relationship, by examining how the various actions in the system behave and analyzing that behavior in terms of constrained choice. The constraints that limit choice represent the influence of society on the legal order; the fact of choice represents the legal order's potential for influencing society.

The model depicts a deeply authoritarian legal order, where lawmakers promulgate law, enforcers implement it, and the rest of us respond to it. It assumes that the governors remain distinct from the masses of the people. That authoritarian structure, with its sharp dichotomization between we and they, between the mass and the governors, lies at the heart of the felt deficiencies of the legal order.

The model is admittedly ambiguous. The arrows that represent the arenas of choice of the several actors are no more than signposts. So open a set of residual categories must render a model nonfalsifiable. All we hope to accomplish with the model is to provide a rudimentary vocabulary and the beginnings of a theory for studying and understanding law and society.

The remainder of this book is an attempt to elaborate and complete the suggestions contained in this model. In the next chapter we look at the laws of contract and property. We intend to demonstrate with this example how our historical-sociological model helps us to understand law and the legal order. In particular we intend to open up that part of our perspective which stresses the important role of power in social and legal relationships.

NOTES

1. H.L.A. Hart, *The Concept of Law* (Oxford: Clarendon Press, 1961); Chapter 2 above.

2. Robert B. Seidman, "A Note on the Gold Coast Reception Statute," *Journal of African Law* 13(1969): 45.

3. A. L. Morton, *A People's History of England* (London: Lawrence & Wishart, 1938), p. 163.

4. A. Smith, *The Wealth of Nations* (Oxford: Clarendon Press, 1880).

5. J. H. Burns, ed., *The Collected Works of Jeremy Bentham* (London: Athlone Press, 1970).

6. M. Weber, *Law in Economy and Society,* ed. by Max Rheinstein (Cambridge: Harvard University Press, 1954). Also see M. Weber, *The Protestant Ethic and the Spirit of Capitalism* (London: G. Allen & Unwin, 1930). For discussions, see D. Trubek, "Max Weber on Law and the Rise of Capitalism," *Wisconsin Law Review* (1972): 270; M. Abrow, "Legal Positivism and Bourgeois Materialism: Max Weber's View of the Sociology of Law," *British Journal of Law and Society* 2(1975): 14-31.

7. Trubek, "Max Weber on Law," p. 270.

8. O. W. Holmes, *The Common Law* (Boston: Little, Brown & Co., 1938).

9. L. Krader, *Formation of the State* (Englewood Cliffs, NJ: Prentice-Hall, 1968), p. 2.

10. Friedrich Carl von Savigny, *Ueber den Beruf unserer Zeit zur Gesetzgebung und zur Rechtswissenschaft,* 1814, trans. A. Howard (London, 1832), pp. 24, 27, 30; quoted in Wolfgang Friedman, *Legal Theory* (New York: Columbia University Press, 1967), pp. 159-160.

11. William G. Sumner, *Folkways* (Boston: Ginn & Co., 1911).

12. P. Bohannan, *Law and Warfare* (Garden City, NY: Natural History Press, 1967), pp. 47-49.

13. L. Friedman, "Legal Culture and Social Development," *Law and Society Review* 4(1969): 29-44.

14. *Ibid.,* p. 34.

15. *Ibid.,* p. 34.

16. For the inadmissibility of tautologies as scientific explanation, see, K. Popper, *The Logic of Scientific Discovery* (New York: Harper & Row, 1968).

17. See, for example, C. A. Auerback, L. K. Garrison, *et al.,* eds., *The Legal Process* (San Francisco: Chandler Publishing Co., 1961).

18. George W. Paton and David P. Derham, *A Textbook of Jurisprudence,* 4th ed. (London: Clarendon Press, 1972).

19. R. Pound, *An Introduction to the Philosphy of Law* (New Haven: Yale University Press, 1954).

20. *Ibid.*

21. R. Pound, *Social Control through Law* (New Haven: Yale University Press, 1942), pp. 112-116.

22. H. J. Laski, *The American Democracy* (New York: Viking Press, 1948), p. 443.

23. L. Fuller, *The Morality of Law* (New Haven: Yale University Press, 1964).

24. B. Malinowski, *Crime and Custom in Savage Society* (London: K. Paul, Trench, Trubner & Co., 1926).

25. Gresham Sykes, *Society of Captives* (Princeton: Princeton University Press, 1958).

26. S. Macauley, "Non-Contractual Relations in Business: Preliminary Study," *American Sociological Review* 28(1972): 55-66.

27. C. S. Barnard, *The Functions of the Executive* (Cambridge: Harvard University Press, 1954), pp. 170-183.

28. C. Wright Mills, *The Power Elite* (New York: Oxford Univeristy Press, 1959). See also L. Friedman and J. Ladinsky, "Social Change and the Law of Industrial Accidents," *Columbia Law Review* 67(1967): 50-82.

29. Peter Bachrach and Mortons Baratz, *Power and Poverty: Theory and Practice* (Oxford: Oxford University Press, 1970).

30. Weber, *Law in Economy and Society.*

31. Mills, *Power Elite,* p. 4.

32. T. S. Lowi, *The End of Liberalism* (New York: Norton, 1969).

33. E. Ehrlich, *Fundamental Principles of the Sociology of Law* (New York: Russell & Russell, 1962), p. 200.

34. Holmes, *Common Law,* p. 1.

35. See, for example, Maureen Cain and Alan Hunt, *Marx and Engels on Law* (London: Academic Press, 1979).

36. For example, D. Fraser, *The Evolution of the British Welfare System: A History of Social Policy since the Industrial Revolution* (New York: Barnes & Noble, 1973). Also see, Q. Haore and G. N. Smith, eds., *Selections from the Prison Notebook of Antonio Gramsci* (London: Lawrence & Wishart, 1971); P. Beirne and R. Sharlet, eds., *Pashukanis: Selected Writings on Marxism and Law* (New York: Academic Press, 1980); K. Renner, *The Institutions of Private Law and Their Social Functions* (London: Routledge & Kegan Paul, 1949); G. Rusche and O. Kirchheimer, *Punishment and Social Structure* (New York: Columbia University Press, 1939); R. Stammler, *The Theory of Justice* (New York: The Macmillan Co., 1925).

37. M. Cain, "The Main Themes of Marx and Engel's Sociology of Law," *British Journal of Law and Society* 1(1974): 136.

38. Max Weber, "R. Stammlers' 'Surmounting' of the Materialist Conception of History," trans. M. Albrow, *British Journal of Law and Society* 3(1976): 17-43. Z. Bankowski and G. Mungham, *Images of Law* (London: Routledge & Kegan Paul, 1976). P. Hirst, *On Law and Ideology* (Atlantic Highlands, NJ: Humanities Press, 1979). A Hunt, *Marxism and Democracy* (London: Lawrence & Wishart, 1980). C. Sumner, *Reading Ideologies* (London: Academic Press, 1979). The Critique of Law Editorial Collective, *Critique of Law: A Marxist Analysis* (New South Wales, Australia: University of New South Wales, 1978). J. P. Brady, "Political Contradictions and Justice Policy in People's China," *Contemporary Crises* 2(1977): 127-159. More generally consult the following journals: *Contemporary Crises: Crime and Social Justice; British Journal of Law and Society; International Journal of Law and Society.*

R. Bahro, *The Altenative in Eastern Europe* (New York: Schocken Books, 1978).

39. P. Beirne, "Marxism and the Sociology of Law: Theory or Practice," *British Journal of Law and Society* 2(1975): 78-81.

40. A. Sachs and J. Wilson, *Sexism and the Law* (New York: Free Press, 1979), pp. 225-226.

41. Karl Marx and Friedrich Engels, *Selected Works* (Moscow: Progress Press, 1969).

42. *Ibid.*

43. R. Miliband, *The State in Capitalist Society* (London: Wiedenfeld & Nicholson, 1969).

44. A. D. Freeman, "Legitimizing Racial Discrimination through Anti-Discrimination Law: A Critical Review of Supreme Court Doctrine," *Minnesota Law Review* 62 (1978): 1049-1119.

45. Marx and Engels, *Selected Works.*

46. For Pashukanis the link was between the commodity form and the legal system. See Beirne and Sharlet, *Pashukanis.* See also I. Balbus, "Commodity Form and Legal Form: An Essay on the 'Relative Autonomy' of Law," *Law and Society Review* 2 (1977): 571-585.

47. Marx and Engels, *Selected Works.*

48. *Ibid.*

49. *Ibid.*

50. H. Kelsen, *General Theory of Law and State* Cambridge: Harvard University Press, 1946), p. 50.

51. *Ibid.*

52. R. Rubenstein, *Rebels in Eden: Mass Political Violence in the United States* (Boston: Little, Brown & Co., 1970).

53. E. Genovese, *Roll Jordan Roll: The World the Slaves Made* (New York: Pantheon Books, 1974).

4

Facilitative law: contracts, property, and corporate law

In the last three chapters we explored extant theories, paradigms, methodologies, definitions, and categories for studying the relationship between law and society. We concluded the last chapter with a general model which seems to us an appropriate starting point for our inquiry. In this chapter we propose to add flesh to the bare bones of our model by analyzing one of the cornerstones of modern capitalist societies: the laws of contract and property. We refer to these laws as "facilitative law." They constitute mechanisms by which the state through law copes with some of the principal contradictions inherent in capitalist societies—contradictions born of the public nature of production and the private ownership of what is produced (see discussion in Chapter 3).

Our model assumes the centrality of authority. Lawmakers promulgate commands; law implementors enforce commands by applying measures to subjects. Criminal and tort law fit this model nicely. Mostly, however, the model does not seem to fit our common perceptions of the legal order. Every time you pay for groceries or work for a wage, you enter into a "legal" relationship. Rarely does one perceive these relationships as coercive. Contract law does not *require* anyone to enter into a contract; property law does not *require* owners to do anything with their property; corporation law does not *require* that a person form a corporation. These laws only facilitate such social and economic relationships. Facilitative law therefore seems to free us from the coercion of state power. To the extent that facilitative law does in fact defy authoritarianism, the model earlier put forward cannot account for it. But does facilitative law break the legal order's coercive bonds—or does it only create an illusion of doing so? We denote two alternative answers to this question, the classical and anticlassical views. The former equates facilitative law and freedom; the latter identifies it and all law with coercion. Before describing these views in detail, we set out a case study: corporate power and how facilitative law contributes to it.

4.1 A CASE STUDY: FACILITATIVE LAW AND CORPORATE POWER

The Problem Stated

The largest U.S. corporations hold the greatest concentration of wealth that the world has ever known. In 1971, 1.5 percent of all U.S. corporations received 85 percent of all corporate receipts and 71 percent of all business receipts. The hundred largest manufacturing corporations held almost half (48.9 percent) of all manufacturing assets and the two hundred largest held 61 percent. The largest fifty companies produced almost one-fourth (24 percent) of all the value added by manufacture in 1970 and the largest two hundred produced 43 percent.[1] The fifty largest corporations each has larger total incomes and employs more workers than the total revenues and employment of most of the fifty states.

The gross volume of business of the fifteen largest corporations in the U.S. exceeds the gross national product of all but a dozen or so countries in the world. General Motors' sales receipts are greater than the total revenues of New York, New Jersey, Pennsylvania, Ohio, Delaware, Massachusetts, Connecticut, Rhode Island, Maine, Vermont, and New Hampshire *added together*. In comparison to other corporations, the top one hundred dominate the economy in ways that are truly amazing: out of a total of 300 thousand firms, the largest one hundred corporations account for over one-third of the total volume of business produced by all 300 thousand. These one hundred firms also employ 25 percent of the total work force in manufacturing and own about 50 percent of all assets in manufacturing. Furthermore, this concentration of assets, employment, and wealth in a few firms is a trend that has been apparent in American and European industrial growth since the 1900s and it shows no signs of easing. Since World War II the largest one hundred firms have expanded their control of the total market from 23 to 33 percent; the two hundred largest manufacturing corporations control over 60 percent of all manufacturing assets, an increase of 10 percent from less than twenty years ago (since 1950 the total assets of the two hundred largest corporations have increased from 50 to 60 percent).

Beneath the world of the one thousand or so largest corporations, the United States has an economic subsystem in which live some 400 thousand smaller corporations and many unincorporated businesses. We do not here concern ourselves with that "market" or "informal" sector. Its corporations do not have the sort of market power the great corporations do. Their legal problems have little in common with those of the great corporations, save their common title of corporation. General Motors, with millions of shareholders and 35 billion dollars in assets, has practically nothing in common with a "mom-and-pop" grocery store.

The power that these great businesses have over all of us hardly needs example. When one purchases a new automobile, the seller presents a form contract. Although one may bargain a little about the price, if the buyer wants the automobile, he or she must accept the contract's terms. Great corporations sytematically pollute our water and our air: for example, the notorious Love Canal in New York, where a chemical company so poisoned a small waterway that the state had to evacuate permanently the people who lived nearby; Duluth, where the Superior Mining Corporation endangered the drinking water for a great city; and the Three Mile Island disaster, in which malfunction of a nuclear power plant almost caused a meltdown of the reactor core similar to the situation depicted in the film *China Syndrome*. Large corporations create serious hazards for their employees—in asbestos (whose workers contract asbestosis, a fearful lung disease), coal mining (brown lung), nuclear energy (radiation disease), lumbering (amputated hands, legs, and fingers). They create all sorts of dangerous consumer products, such as automobiles that require recall for design changes, tires that blow out, airplanes whose mechanisms for attaching the engines to the wings fail in takeoff, and hair dryers that blow lethal asbestos fibers at the user. They slaughter beef too young for good flavor, but profitably; they give us bland and tasteless apples because they have greater shelf life and milk whose butterfat content they systematically reduce to the minimum required by law. They rent us apartments and lend us money based on terms they have written.

Yet we all willy-nilly suffer these insults to our physical, personal, and financial integrity. We must purchase automobiles, so we accept their contracts and the defects that plague the gas-guzzlers; we must live in industrial societies, so we accept the pollution industries cause; we must earn wages working in their plants and taking our chances with asbestosis, brown lung (pneumoconiosis), and radiation; we must fly in their airplanes, so we accept whatever seats we can get in whatever planes they make available; we must eat, so we purchase tasteless beef, tomatoes, and apples; we must have shelter, so we rent on their terms; we must borrow money, so we accept their loan agreements.

Conventional economic theory "explains" corporate power by giving it another name: market power. That theory holds that the absence of competition explains market power. Adam Smith taught long ago that when the market consists of so many buyers and so many sellers no one can know everybody, purchasers will shop around to find the most favorable bargain. Economists put forward a slew of graphs and formulae that purported to show how in those conditions supply and demand create a market that acts as an Invisible Hand, protecting each of us from the other's market power. The United States has a whole series of antitrust statutes such as the Sherman Antitrust Law designed to ensure a free market. They do not succeed in preventing market power; antitrust at best prevents worse concentration. In few sectors of the economy of the United States does the market in practice match Adam Smith's ideal, or come even close to it; where a free market does prevail the great corporations do not operate.

Some lawyers explain corporate power by the failure of the antitrust laws. A negative "explanation," however, does not explain. It merely makes a disguised assertion that a proposed solution will work and therefore, but for that solution's absence, the difficulty would not exist. So, if antitrust succeeded in ensuring competitive markets, by definition market power would not exist. That does not tell us anything about *why* corporate market power exists. Faithfully to our model and domain of study, we must explain corporate power in terms of the legal order and how it so shapes corporate arenas of choice that the great corporations can adopt courses of behavior that result in market power. First, however, we need to explain what we mean by "power."

Law and Power

Writers on law and politics use the word "power" as a central concept. We define it in terms of our choice model. One's course of action depends on the choices one makes and the choices made depend in main part on the range of constraints and resources that one faces—the arena of choice. Whoever can alter the arena of choice has to that extent power over the person. Since usually one can simultaneously affect the other's arena of choice, a diagram of the relationship rarely has its arrows pointing in only one direction. But parties to a relationship rarely have symmetrical power over one another. An unskilled laborer affects the range of choice of General Motors when he or she turns up at their factory gate for a job. That does not fit symmetrically with how General Motors can change his or her arena of choice by denying or giving him or her the job. Our thesis concerning facilitative law holds that the rules of property, contract, corporation, and other sorts of facilitative law, together with special perquisites the legal order gives them, clothe the great corporations with power to affect most Americans' arenas of choice in ways decisive for their existence.

Property Law

"Property" has a dual usage. Sometimes it refers to a thing, sometimes to a set of relationships between people. We speak of my pipe as my property, but that concept unpacks into a set of role-relationships between myself and others with respect to my pipe. Without my consent, they cannot legally take or use it. The material thing that "property" seemingly denotes becomes property in the sense of a role-relationship, however, only to the extent that it becomes subject to conflicting claims. Is the air we breathe property? Is water in a stream that passes my land property, if I enjoy the view but do not otherwise make use of the water? Does it become property if I use the water to irrigate my land? Is the long-existing light that comes through my windows property, so that when my neighbor builds on his land in a way that blocks out my windows, he takes my property?

These questions only arise when what I want to do with something rubs against what somebody else wants to do with it, or does not want me to do with it. I dig a basement on my land. Must I shore up your land to prevent it from caving in? Suppose that your land would cave in only because you have a huge pile of metal slag on it. Does the way you use your land impose an additional burden of support on me that I would not have had if you had left the land in its natural state? I own a factory. May I shut it down for whimsical reasons, regardless of what it does to the lives of my employees? Do I have the right to throw away the milk produced by my cows when people in other parts of the world are starving?

The rules concerning property always grant different amounts of power and privilege to people who have different relationships to the thing. The persons we conventionally label owners in our culture have more power over property than, say, workers. Not always, however: the shareholders of a corporation nominally "own" the corporation, but in reality have little control over it. The managers of the corporation work for the corporation. The managers of the corporation, nominally its employees, however, generally have more power over the corporation and its assets than the shareholders do. Until relatively recently (and even today in some places), a husband had more power over property nominally owned by his wife than did his wife, a landlord more power over an apartment or house than did the tenant.

We usually think about property as embodying power over things. Because property entails norms that affect the relationships between people, however, the power that owners and others acquire from property always entails power over other *people*. I own my car; I can drive it, sell it, rent it, or not. These propositions embody statements about my power over others. I drive on the road and deny that portion of the road to others; I decide not to sell and thus determine whether another gets the car; I decide to rent and thus determine whether my lessee has this car to use for the weekend. Power entails the ability to structure choice for another. The norms give me the capacity to structure another's choice. They grant power. They also grant some immunity from another's power. If I own my own home, for example, landlords cannot control my choice of dwelling as much as they could if I had to rent from them.

The rules that define what I can do to specific others with respect to my things determine that quantum of power with which property law endows me. Property law embodies these rules. They vary from place to place and from time to time. In the United States, owning a factory gives one the power to employ in it as many workers as one chooses. In Yugoslavia, a factory owner cannot employ more than seven workers; in Poland, one hundred; in the Soviet Union a factory owner may not employ any. Not so long ago, the fact that I owned a factory gave me the power to employ workers at whatever rate of pay I could get them to work for; now, for factories involved in interstate commerce, federal minimum wage laws put bottom limits on rates of pay.

The rules of property law of course reflect the relative political power of different strata. That for centuries laws gave husbands power over the property of their wives reflected the relative political strength of man over woman. Property rules do more than reflect power; they also create it. For example, eighteenth-century property law conferred upon a landowner power to prevent a use of a neighbor's land that interfered with his quiet enjoyment of his land. Two potentially contradictory theories emerged from this principle. One "limited property owners to what courts regarded as the natural uses of the land and often 'natural' was equated with 'agrarian.' "[2] The other "amounted to rule that priority of development conferred a right to arrest a future conflicting use."[3] So long as "natural" meant "agricultural," both rules plainly favored agricultural over newer industrial uses. During the nineteenth century, these doctrines capsized. A new doctrine, that of reasonable use, became dominant, which sought "to define the extent to which newer forms of property might injure the old with impunity."[4] The new theory permitted judges to decide which of two competing uses best advanced societal interests. The judges tended to favor the newer forms of use as against older ones. In the nineteenth-century context, that meant industrial rather than agrarian uses. The extent of property interests, their very content, changed with time.

Property law today is an important factor in the rise of corporate power. The state protects property against violent depredation or theft, even if the thieves steal out of desperate hunger.[5] The factory owner has the inherent right to determine the production technology used.[6] Absent an antidiscrimination statute, the right to property implies the absolute right to employ whomever the owner wishes, whether or not on discriminatory grounds.[7] The owner of property can insist that her or his employees wear the clothing that he or she requires them to wear, come and go at the hours he or she stipulates, and organize the work in the way that he or she wants. The owner can determine the product mix as he or she likes. The owner can close down the plant or change its location, without let or hindrance from any of the people these drastic actions affect.[8]

No place does property power have greater reach than in the employment relationship. Except that we have become so deeply acculturated to accept them, the rules of property defy common sense notions of how best to organize the workplace. It is evident that either trained managers or, since they have the richest experience, the workers themselves must know best how to organize the work. Instead, the owner has that power, no matter how limited his or her sense or capacity. (We justify that on the ground that he or she has the greatest interest in the property and therefore the greatest incentive, on the theory that owners become so money-mad that to earn more they drop all interest in wine, sex, sport, art, hobbies, or intellectual pursuit and as though great incentive automatically endows owners with great acumen.) Our folklore has as a standard stereotype the self-made man of great drive and competence whose children can do nothing better than run through a gaggle of husbands or wives, follow the sun for pleasure, or drive expensive cars at ruinous speeds; yet, after they inherit, they, neither the workers nor trained executives, have the power to run the factory.

Part of our mythology instructs us that people should receive the fruit of their labor. Property law works otherwise. The person who actually produces the goods receives a contracted wage. The shareholder, who lifts not a little finger to produce, may receive far more than the worker who does. Indeed, an employee who produces the goods has so little claim to them that the law denotes it theft if he or she takes for personal use one of the articles that he or she produces. For a hatmaker in a factory to take a hat he or she makes for his or her own use subjects that worker to the laws' penalties.* In capitalist societies, property brings with it power—a vast, unclassified, and probably unclassifiable set of specific powers that affect every human relationship.

Three statements about the rules of property law are relevant to corporate power. First, their enforcement, like the enforcement of all law, rests upon state power. During the scoundrel time of McCarthyism, a colleague, close friend, and former graduate student of a university professor whom McCarthy attacked refused to testify that his close friend and academic patron, to his knowledge, did not hold membership in the Communist party. The professor could call on neighbors and passersby to deplore this violation of elementary norms of friendship and loyalty; the legal order and the state did nothing. But let someone take the professor's hat and he can invoke a whole panoply of state employees, many of them armed to the teeth, to defend his interests.

Second, except for some bargains' explicit requirements, in our era the powers and privileges of property do not require the property owner to return anything to those over whom her property gives her power. In the feudal era, the knight had vast powers over his land and those dependent on the land. In exchange for the serf's labor, however, the knight had to protect him against marauders. A master not only had to pay his apprentice a small cash wage, but provide him a home, sustenance, and education, i.e., a place in the family. A farmer had to do the same for his agricultural laborers. In our era, in law *noblesse oblige* is dead. All these obligations have become subsumed in the cash nexus, where labor is bought and sold.

Third, the authority implicated in property flows from the relationship to the thing. I may sell or bequeath my factory to any ninny that I will, and he succeeds to all the power that I had. In most other role-relationships, that cannot happen. During my lifetime, I cannot very easily transfer to someone else my paternal authority.

Property entails power. Property law helps to explain corporate power because *property law delegates authority to property owners*. Out of the role of owner and the relationships that role implies, one becomes the *commander*. And the great corporations become the greatest commanders of them all.

Most of the power that property gives its owner lies, like the coiled power of a spring, inchoate and unrealized. The factory owner has power to exclude people from her factory; that helps to protect against thieves, but does precious little good when she needs hands to work the machinery. The manufacturer has power to determine the sorts of goods she will make; that protects her almost absolute management prerogatives, but gives her small comfort when, to turn a profit, she must conform her choices to consumer tastes. Property power gets exercised mainly in the form of contracts—of employment and sale and lease and mortgage and loan and a thousand others. In these contracts, the property owner bargains away part of the power that property gives her,

---

* In rare instances, the person who produces does have a property claim, as in the case of mechanics' liens.

usually in order to get what she wants from the other party. An owner has a property right to employ those she wants to employ and to fire those she does not want to keep. If a union bargains for it, however, the employer by contract may agree to a grievance procedure, the result of which is that she may have to retain an unwanted employee. A manufacturer need not give any warranty at all on the sale of most goods. If she does not, however, and expressly denies them, she may not be able to sell the goods. By agreement at the time of sale, she may agree to a warranty.

The power that workers and consumers have over property owners only sets limits upon the outer extremes of property power. Workers must work, or starve; consumers must buy what appears in the stores, or go without heat, shelter, or food. The great corporations try to legitimize their power by denying it. They assert that consumer power, not corporate power, controls the economy. They badly overstate the case. Property gives its owner capacity to alter other people's arenas of choice. That power usually exerts its force through contract law. The rules of contract serve with property law as pillars to corporate power.

Contract Law

Contract law, like property law, has undergone a metamorphosis over the centuries. Here we discuss it in three phases: its eighteenth-century, precapitalist phase; its nineteenth-century, laissez-faire heyday; and its present-day conformation.[9]

Eighteenth-century contract law. Eighteenth-century notions assimilated contract to the law of property and permitted a court to refuse to enforce a contract if it thought its terms unjust. The contracts served mainly to transfer title to the specific thing contracted for. That all but eliminated an action for the recovery of damages for failure to deliver the goods. Instead, the appropriate action would be specific performance, i.e., for an injunction commanding the seller to deliver the goods, or the buyer the price. That suited well eighteenth-century conditions, for it assumed that no real market for goods existed. Bargains arose because one party wanted the goods for her own use, not ordinarily for resale and profit. Specific performance was therefore an appropriate remedy.

Because contracting parties did not ordinarily use contracts as a device for profit making, but merely to transfer title to goods, courts felt small pressure to sustain inequitable contracts on the ground that profit taking lay at their heart. Instead, the dominant rule permitted the courts to set a contract aside if it seemed inequitable. As late as 1817, South Carolina's chancellor wrote:

It would be a great mischief to the community, and a reproach to the justice of the country, if contracts of very great inequality, obtained by fraud, or surprise, or the skillful management of intelligent men, from weakness, or inexperience, or necessity, could not be examined into, and set aside.[10]

Contract law at this time, therefore, set its face against the commercial classes. ''The law did not assure a businessman the express value of his bargain, but at most its specific performance. Courts and juries did not honour business agreements on their face, but scrutinized them for the substantive equality of the exchange."[11]

The will theory and expectation damages. By the middle of the nineteenth century all this changed. When markets arise, businessmen purchase goods expecting to resell them as the market rises. The title theory of contract made that impossible. So did the rule that a court would inquire into the fairness of the price, for that notion challenged the legality of purchasing with knowledge of facts that might lead to an increase in price.

The question arose first in the sale of securities, perhaps because a market for them appeared very early. *Davis* v. *Richardson* (1790), a South Carolina case, first established the rule permitting the recovery of speculative profits.[12] That involved a "short sale." The defendant borrowed some stock, contracting to return it with interest in the future. Of course, he sold the stock, expecting that the price would drop and that when the time came to return the shares to the owner he could purchase substitute stock on the market at a lower price.

Instead, the market rose, so that the defendant could not replace the stock except at a loss. Defendant offered to pay the price of the stock at the time that he borrowed it. The court announced the new rule: "Whenever a contract is entered into for the delivery of a specific article, the value of that article, at the time fixed for delivery, is the sum a plaintiff ought to recover."[13] The South Carolina courts sustained the rule in 1793, in *Atkinson* v. *Scott*, against counsel's claim that the rule brazenly permitted usury—a claim with considerable susbstance, for in *Atkinson* the disputed securities appreciated 850 percent in one year.[14]

Permitting expectation damages changed the basis for contract law from a theory that contracts concerned primarily the transfer of title to specific property and that permitted a court to assess a contract's inherent equity to a theory that perceived contract as part of a market economy, whose usual purpose was to purchase fungible goods for resale and whose test lay not in inherent fairness, but whether the parties appeared to make a bargain, i.e., whether a "meeting of the minds" took place. Supporting that shift lay a changed notion of value and of justice. As Horwitz states:

In a society in which value came to be regarded as entirely subjective and in which the only basis for assigning value was the concurrence of arbitrary individual desire, principles of substantive justice were inevitably seen as entailing an "arbitrary and uncertain" standard of value. Substantive justice, in the earlier view, existed in order to prevent men from using the legal system in order to exploit each other. But where things have no "intrinsic value," there can be no substantive measure of exploitation and the parties are, by definition, equal. Modern contract law was thus born staunchly proclaiming that all men are equal because all measures of inequality are illusory.[15]

The will theory and expectation damages became the law appropriate to laissez-faire capitalism and the free market. In place of the "subjective" valuations of individual judges and juries, the Invisible Hand substituted its impersonal valuations.

In place of uncertainty over what individual judges might do to a businessman's expectations, predictable rules now controlled. Instead of discretion, easily warped by aristocratic privilege, judicial decision came to depend upon rules.

The markets of the early and middle nineteenth century that forged the new law of contracts in the main concerned what in today's terms we would call small businessmen. In 1800 four out of every five Americans employed themselves; by 1979 only one out of every five Americans did so. Where contracting parties have actual as well as fictitious equality in bargaining power, the laws of contract may approach the classical perspective. But those same laws applied to plainly unequal parties reached self-evidently inequitable results.

Laissez-faire contract law and concentration. In an ideal-type world, where parties have equal bargaining power, where the Invisible Hand prevents either from having great market power over the other, the rules of contract law seem sensible enough. Applied to parties so vastly unequal as an ordinary consumer or an ordinary laborer and a corporation controlling vast enterprises, the legal rules easily permit what lawyers sometimes call "overreaching," i.e., injustice arising out of market power. We discuss here three of these rules: offer and acceptance, the parol evidence rule, and the law of damages.

Offer and acceptance. Every contract consists of a number of terms: in a sales contract, for example, the description of the goods, their price, the terms of payment, the delivery date, the warranties that accompany them; or, in a lease, the description of the property to be rented, the rent and how the tenant will pay it, the responsibilities of landlord and tenant to each other, and so forth. In the language of sociology, the terms of the contract constitute norms prescribing the behavior of the role-occupants. The price term of the contract constitutes a rule for the behavior of the buyer: he ought to pay a particular amount of money on stated terms (cash or in installments) to the seller. The description of the goods also constitutes a norm prescribing the seller's be-havior: he ought to deliver goods that match the description. In effect, a contract becomes private legislation for the conduct of the parties.

The rules of offer and acceptance purport to govern the formation of contracts, that is, they specify the procedures that, if followed, have as their end product a contract that courts will enforce. By analogy, a legislature too must follow particular rules of procedure: if it does not, what emerges may not count as legislation. For example, a legislature pasing a statute without a quorum present may not have enacted anything.

Today's rules do not vary much from those of the nineteenth century; every law student learns them early in her first year. Starting from the laissez-faire proposition that contracts enforce bargains (not gifts), and bargains arise out of agreement, contract in law early developed two principal categories to define the occasions when an agreement arises out of haggling. The *offer* embodies on an expression by one party from which the offeror intended to be bound on stated terms to the other. In the terms of the law, that clothes the offeree with the power to accept the offer and thus create a binding contract between the parties. The acceptance involves an expression by the offeree from which the other as a reasonable man could infer a willingness to be bound by the same terms. If the offeree, instead of accepting the offer, proposes new terms, that proposal acts as a refusal of the offer and as a counteroffer, to which the original offeror now has the power to accept or not. In the language of our choice model the offer changes the arena of choice for the offeree; by accepting or not, the offeree changes the arena of choice for the offeror.

Nineteenth-century law developed an additional category, that of the invitation to make an offer. When a merchant exhibits, say, a pair of shoes in her shop window with a price tag on it, does she offer the goods for sale, so that anyone who comes in and says, "I accept," by so doing creates enforceable obligations to buy and to sell? Courts early held that that did not happen. They characterized the merchant's action not as an offer, but as an invitation to the public to make offers for the goods at the stated price. Thus, when the purchaser entered the store and said, "I will buy the shoes at the advertised price," no binding contract arose. The buyer's statement constituted the offer; the merchant could still decide not to sell at the advertised price, for good reason or for no reason. In general, courts came to characterize advertising not as an offer, but merely as an invitation to make an offer. The difference lay in this: an offer empowers the offeree to accept and, by accepting, to create binding legal obligations between the parties. An invitation to make an offer does not create any power in anyone.

These categories plainly provide useful concepts for analyzing bargaining. Where greatly disparate power positions make bargaining impossible, these categories do not much help analysis. The invitation to bargain becomes the critical category rather than a mere auxiliary to the process, for that invitation sets the terms of the ultimate contractual arrangement. Moreover, it does not even matter that the offerree know the details of the invitation to make an offer. When a store advertises a refrigerator for sale, the customer enters the store, sees the price, and purchases the refrigerator. A few days later the refrigerator arrives. When the customer opens it, inside he finds a number of documents, including something entitled "Limited Warranty." That warranty in fact ordinarily extends to the buyer fewer warranties for the goods than the law would otherwise apply. Nevertheless, the warranties become part of the contract. The original invitation to make an offer included everything that lay inside the refrigerator, including its warranties. Or, if an insurance company claims it sells fire insurance policies, when I call my insurance agent and he gives me a binder on my property, the company's liability on the binder finds its basis in the policy that it has not yet issued and that I have not yet seen.

Offer and acceptance resonated easily with a society in which bargaining ordinarily preceded the agreement. In our society, that rarely occurs and almost never between consumers and one of the thousand great corporations. Those corporations hold themselves out as willing to entertain offers on the terms they decide. The rest of us have a relatively simple choice: to take the offer on the corporation's terms or to forego the goods or services that the corporation sells. In a society based on specialization and exchange, one cannot readily refuse to deal with the vendors of what one needs. One can retire to New Hampshire's hills and "drop out," but not easily.

The parol evidence rule. Where genuine bargaining exists, typically the parties make many invitations for offers, rejections, and counteroffers before coming to agreement. Where that agreement finds final form in a written document, in an action on the contract it makes obvious sense to insist that the parties draw all their rights from the written document and to bar them from even introducing into evidence testimony that would tend to vary the written terms. The written contract purported both to put down the terms of the final bargain and to exclude everything that the parties had discussed but had not agreed upon. The rule therefore evolved that where a written document exists the parties cannot, except in exceptional cases, introduce parol evidence (i.e., oral or written evidence outside of the "four corners" of the document) that would tend to change the written document.

Applied to cases where no equality in fact exists, where one party imposes his written contract on the other, in circumstances in which the weaker party either does not or cannot read and understand it, that rule opens the door to mass fraud. It becomes easy for the stronger party to induce the weaker to enter the contract by all sorts of oral representations, then give him a written document that does not bear out the terms of the oral representations. When sued, the stronger party has a powerful ally in the parol evidence rule.[16] That rule permits what Slawson called "lawful fraud" in many areas of life: insurance of all sorts (the contract of insurance comes long after the actual bargaining takes place and the purchaser ordinarily has no opportunity to bargain over the details)[17]; warranties on consumer goods (written bits of paper tucked into the package that the consumer takes with her from the store and never sees until she gets home); leases (the residential tenant signs a binder and puts down the first month's rent and another month's rent as security on the real estate agent's say-so; later on, after credit checks and frequently only after moving in, she gets a copy of the lease itself); mortgages (the mortgage commitment from the bank embodies the terms upon what the parties actually agreed, if any written document does; the mortgage itself contains acres of small print, most of which the commitment never mentioned); contracts for the purchase of durable goods (what the car salesman says about the car rarely finds complete expression on the printed form contract that he has no authority to vary); and many others.

In all these cases the parol evidence rule gets transformed into a somewhat different operative rule. Slawson calls it "the doctrine of the conclusive contractual status of the standard form—a standard form, no matter how tenuous its relationship to what the parties actually agreed, is conclusively the parties' contract."[18] Slawson observes that "this doctrine will not be found in any case or treatise. Judges, lawyers and law professors assume it. . . . And all of us—Judges, lawyers and professors alike—are mesmerized by printed forms. If it is printed and at *some* time given to the buyer we assume it is a contract."[19]

A transformation similar to the one that changed the parol evidence rule also affected the rule concerning anticipation damages.

Anticipation damages. One of the striking changes that nineteenth-century contract law wrought in eighteenth-century doctrines concerned, as we have seen, anticipation damages. Now a party could recover not only specific performance or the price, but damages for profits on anticipated resale as well. What anticipated profits did that notion subsume? The British Court of the Exchequer in 1854 decided *Hadley* v. *Baxendale*, a leading case that first-year law students still peruse.[20] There a mill's crankshaft broke; the carriers failed to deliver the new one as promised; the mill had to shut down for a few days, with resulting losses of anticipated profits. The court, however, refused to permit recovery of those anticipated profits, but limited recovery to damages that it labeled the "natural consequences" of the breach. That came to mean, in most cases, the difference at the time of breach between the price stipulated in the contract and the market price for similar goods or services.[21] The rule makes sense for businessmen in a market of fungible commodities, all easily available on the market. If a seller refuses to deliver an order of nails at a few cents less than a pound than the market price, it makes sense to limit the buyer's damages to those few cents per pound. In effect, that agreement requires the buyer to dash out into the market and buy up equivalent nails at the then market price. That measure of damages diminishes the frequency with which an aggrieved party will sue on the contract. Since in most cases the contract and market prices equal each other, what profit is there in a lawsuit?

Ordinarily, businessmen themselves can remedy a breach without harm to themselves and without invoking the courts. In the usual case, the rule of *Hadley* v. *Baxendale* holds that no legally compensable damages occur. Applied to payments of money, that rule holds that consequential damages can hardly ever occur for the failure to pay money on time (aside from legal interest payments). Subsequent courts expanded *Hadley*'s rule to include some losses for anticipated profits in exceptional cases, but in the main the rule holds.

That rule makes sense in transactions between businessmen, where the buyer or seller has ready access to a market for similar goods. A seller on the Grain Exchange whose buyer breaches a contract for the purchase of a thousand bushels of wheat can immediately sell it on the market and sue the defaulting buyer for the difference between the contract price and the market price. The rule, however, wreaks injustice when applied to a transaction between a consumer and a large corporate seller. If the ordinary consumer signs a contract with an automobile dealer for an automobile and the seller does not deliver the car in time, the consumer has little choice but to wait until in its own good time the manufacturer delivers the car to the dealer. Only a rare consumer has the resources necessary to run out and buy a substitute vehicle as soon as the seller breaches.

Within a barter economy, where bargaining existed in fact, and where each party had genuine alternatives to buy and sell, these rules of contract law make some sense. They make no sense when one party has excessive market power over the other. Contract law in these cases, like property law, becomes a device by which the economically superior party can alter the other's arena of choice, that is, she has power over the other. Then, if a party breaches the contract or violates the property interest, the aggrieved party can summon the law's coercive apparatus to her aid.

The utility of the perspective and vocabulary developed in Chapters 1 through 3 should be becoming clearer. Between the eighteenth and twentieth centuries the state slowly forged a set of *institutionalized* processes of lawmaking and law implementation the content of which—the rules articulated, the norms developed, and the procedures for adjudicating disputes—reflected the political, economic, and social relations of each historical period and how people responded to their inherited constraints and resources. With respect to property and contract law, the inherited distribution of power was reflected in the law. Those with access to state power through the legal order were able to shape the law in their own interests. Under the guise of creating equitable roles the law *in fact* came increasingly to represent the interests of the capitalist class. At each juncture in the development of our present legal order people were making decisions that were not determined by what was "natural," "necessary," "logical," or "right," but that were the result of the interplay of ideological, material, and social relations existing at the time. The law could have consistently developed in ways that would have given the worker, the consumer, the tenant, and "the people" protection against owners, manufacturers, landlords, and bureaucrats. Instead, in both property and contract laws forged over the past two hundred years the overwhelming thrust has been to buttress the power of property owners at the expense of the masses. Thus did contract law provide owners—and today this means large corporations that own more than anyone else—the modality to affect lives, making kenetic the potential power with which property law clothed them.

Sometimes slowly, sometimes overnight the law changed, giving the owners of the means of production and private property complete control over how their property and profits were to be used. These changes did not go unnoticed by the people over whom the owners were gaining increasing control. People forced by cloth manufacturers to transfer their work from their homes to mass-production factories rebelled by smashing the machines that were transforming their labor into meaningless monotonous tasks.[22] Villagers used to hunting, fishing, and gathering wood on open land fought against emerging laws of private property that cut them off from traditional sources of sustenance.[23] In these instances the people most affected by the legal changes lost their struggle. As we shall see, this is not always the case. These cases serve as a reminder that, although "the ruling class" may often have its way in the development and implementation of law, it is not omnipotent and does not run roughshod over the masses without creating resistance. That resistance in turn has its effects on the law. The case of landlord-tenant relations is illustrative.

True to the logic applied to the owner's rights to do whatever she chooses with the property she owns, landlords in the United States have been protected against responsibility for accidents or health hazards experienced by tenants.

The acknowledged rule since the country's beginnings had been just the opposite of strict landlord's liability: absent special agreement to the contrary a landlord was considered to owe her tenant no duties regarding the physical conditions of the leased premises except to disclose non obvious defects known to the landlord.[24]

It is not mere chance but predictable from our model that these laws would change when and only when tenants became sufficiently mobilized to demand protection against exploitative landlords. This came about in the 1960s and 1970s. Twenty years of civil rights movements (beginning in the 1950s), antigovernment demonstrations on university campuses and in cities, riots and rebellions in urban ghettos and at national political gatherings forced a veritable sea change of law including a fundamental alteration of the laws governing landlord-tenant relations. During the 1960s and 1970s "help was increasingly appearing in the form of municipal housing code ordinances. These ordinances set forth minimum health and safety standards for dwellings often characterizing them as minimum standards of decency for human habitation and typically branding as a criminal offense . . . a landlord's act of marketing housing accommodations not meeting code standards."[25]

These cases serve as a reminder of the dialectical nature of legal relationships. We shall develop this point more fully below. Before doing that, however, we need to understand in greater depth how the laws of property and contract came to give corporations the power they presently have over everyone's life. To understand this we must consider yet a third area of law, the area generally known as corporation law.

Corporation Law

A standard legal dictionary defined a corporation as follows:

An artificial person or legal entity created by or under the authority of the laws of a state or nation . . . ordinarily consisting of an association of numerous individuals, who subsist as a body politic under a special denomination, which is regarded in law as having a personality distinct from that of its several members and which is, by the same authority, vested with the capacity of continuous succession, irrespective of changes in its membership, either in perpetuity or for a limited term of years and acting as a unit or single individual in matters relating to the common purposes of the association, within the scope of the powers and authorities conferred upon such bodies by law.[26]

(In Chapter 5 we consider why lawyers write non-English.)

How did it come about that an "artificial person or legal entity" has the power to affect our lives? How did property and contract law somehow attach power to a fiction, a mere concept, a piece of paper? Fictions do not exercise power. People do, flesh and blood people, with desires and interests, sentiments and passions. People in fact exercise the power with which property and contract law endow corporations. How does the law explain that? The answer lies mostly in the body of rules that law students learn as corporation law.

Like contract and property law, corporation law passed through a metamorphosis from the agrarian societies of the eighteenth century down to our own era. From early days, the legal order had to deal with collectivities of people, e.g., cathedrals and monasteries, guilds of artisans, cities and towns, and shipping ventures with many participants. Their membership changed over time, but the collectivity continued. Lawyers solved the problem (as they so frequently do) by inventing a convenient fiction, by which they applied to new subjects a set of laws earlier developed for other categories. Courts treated these collectivities as if they were unitary individuals and thus gave birth to the fiction of corporate personality. The law attached contract and property rights to these mythical persons, just as it did to real persons.

The law of corporations developed in a series of stages. First, in the early part of the nineteenth century, the law of private, business corporations separated from that of municipal and other public corporations. Second, during the later nineteenth century, the law forged devices to protect corporations from legislative interference, to provide some protection for investors from insiders, and to protect centralized management in business decisions against investor interference. Finally, during our era, the law concerning the great corporations with their thousands of investors who do not know each others' identities in many respects branched off from the law of smaller, closely held corporations.

In the beginning, courts treated collectivities as unitary persons, i.e., as corporations, only exceptionally, when the sovereign had granted a charter to them for that purpose. Today, that theory notionally persists, but a general incorporation law grants the charter as a matter of course to anyone who carries out the simple procedures it stipulates—mainly, registration with the secretary of state. In the eighteenth and most of the nineteenth century, however, a corporation had to receive a special charter from the legislature.

Most of these characters incorporated collectivities that had a plainly public purpose: municipalities, churches, charities. Private business won a few charters; before 1800, only a handful were for business and, of these, almost all were transportation companies (turnpikes, canals, bridges).[27] In most of these instances, the state granted the privilege of acting like a corporation. In exchange, private capital fulfilled functions that government wanted to have accomplished, the building of a canal or turnpike, for example. The corporate charter not only granted the privilege of acting like a corporation, but it usually granted an exclusive, monopoly power to a small group of investors. Incorporation and an exclusive franchise seemed inextricably intertwined. They intertwined because, to bring about necessary or desirable economic development in that early era, governments had to use whatever resources of men and capital lay at hand. To achieve that, governments granted exclusive franchises and, along with them, the privilege of corporation.

In England, the first great corporation, the East India Company, which came to dominate not only world trade but several nations as well (India especially), was formed in the sixteenth century and foretold what was to become the dominant economic form of the future:

From the start [the East India Company] was a company of a new kind, better adapted for large scale trade and making a more flexible use of capital. Such a body as the Merchant Adventurers was not a company at all in the modern sense. It was rather an association of merchants doing a similar trade in a particular area and combining for mutual aid and protection. Inside the association each merchant traded with his own capital, making his own profit and bearing his losses. It was, in fact, somewhat the commercial counterpart of the simple association of labor that marked the manufacturing stage of industry. The East India Company was the first important Joint Stock Company, its members investing so much capital to be pooled and used jointly and receiving a proportionate share of the common profit.[28]

Down to and including the nineteenth century corporations came increasingly to differ only marginally from governments.

As more advanced technology developed, businessmen saw opportunities for larger enterprises that required more capital than any individual entrepreneur wanted to or could hazard. A class arose that had accumulated sufficient surplus to invest in enterprises in which the investor did not spend most of his time as manager or supervisor. That required a form to make possible centralized management, so that every investor need not participate in every managerial decision. Investors will not readily invest in an enterprise if by so doing they expose not only their investment but all their assets to the unlimited claims of creditors; that called for limited liability. Most of all, the corporate form of investment and enterprise had to enjoy the same predictability with respect to state action as private property and contracts enjoyed.

These different desiderata came about by different channels. Centralized management and limited liability arose mainly as clever lawyers drafted corporate charters that included them and then successfully lobbied (or bribed) their way through state legislatures. In *Dartmouth College* v. *Woodward* the Supreme Court decided the most important issue: the applicability to corporations of the rules protecting private property against state interference.[29] In that case, private persons had developed Dartmouth College as a charitable corporation. New Hampshire enacted an amendment to Dartmouth's charter, providing for a new set of trustees selected by the state. The old trustees resisted. At stake lay the immunity of corporate property from state action not by universalistic rules, but by particularistic action; and underlying that stake lay the entrepreneurial requirements of foreseeability, predictability, and "certainty" in law. If the corporation in fact did no more than serve the state in the same sense as any branch of government, it seems at least arguable that the state could amend the statute creating the corporation just as it could amend any other statute creating a branch of government. We see here a clear case where the decision made in law will have far-reaching consequences for the relative power of private interests in conflict with the state and public interests. The court decided on the side of private interests. It held that a state cannot arbitrarily change a corporate charter and thus impair the corporation's relationship to its property. It did this by denoting the corporate charter a "contract" and subsuming it under the clause of the United States Constitution that forbids a state from impairing the obligation of contract. By reserving a right to amend a corporate charter, the states quickly found a way around the narrow holding of *Dartmouth College*; its larger message lived.

Thus by the early years of the nineteenth century, private corporation law had separated from the law of public corporations. The movers and shakers in the great economic expansion of the nineteenth century seized the corporate form as a useful device for exploiting opportunity. The thrust of the law concerned two different conflicts. First, populist criticisms tried to curb the new behemoths, while corporate managers sought (and generally found) legal shields from interference. Second, shareholders and creditors tried to prevent the worst excesses of managerial grab-and-get; the managers lost that battle de jure (in theory) although de facto (in practice) they still managed to do what they wanted.

The nineteenth century became the century of corporate expansion. By 1927 giant corporations dominated the American economy and American politics.[30] Two-thirds of the corporations reporting incomes in that year earned less than $5000 each. The average corporations (excluding banking corporations) had an *average* income of $22,000 and gross assets of only $570,000. By comparison the giant corporations had already far outstripped the small ones. American Telephone and Telegraph in 1927 was equivalent to over 8000 average-size corporations. As early as 1920 the largest 200 corporations in the United States accounted for over 33 percent of the total net income by all nonfinancial corporations. The next 800 largest corporations accounted for only 19 percent of the total income. Thus shortly after the turn of the century the relative economic power of the largest corporations far outweighed the economic power of the smaller ones. By 1930 the discrepancy had increased to the point where the 200 largest corporations controlled over 40 percent of the total income of all corporations (see Table 4.1).

Writing in the 1930s Adolf Berle and Gardiner Means pinpointed the tendency:

The corporate system has done more than evolve a norm by which business is carried on. Within it there exists a centripetal attraction which draws wealth together into aggregations of constantly increasing size, at the same time throwing control into the hands of fewer and fewer men. The trend is apparent; and no limit is as yet in sight.[31]

Widespread populist criticism attacked the "soulless" corporations that, in the critics' views, threatened American democracy:

This typical, American fear was the source out of which the system of checks and balance had grown. It was a fear of unbridled power, as possessed by large landholders and dynastic wealth, as well as by government. An influential segment of the public was willing to try many techniques to prevent concentration of authority and to offset the corrosive effect of money and power. The triumph of the corporation as a form of business association was therefore neither painless nor noiseless. The corporation was an object of great controversy in the first half of the nineteenth century.... Corporations were creatures of state, endowed with breath for the sole purpose of holding franchise or privilege, that is, some power or right that no one else could lay claim to. Most corporations were transportation monopolies, banks, insurance companies— aggregations of "capital," representing the "few" against the "many."[32]

To this fear the latter half of the nineteenth century added others: the fears of bigness, trusts, and monopolization. Standard Oil became a name for hissing. An entire capitalist class was labeled "Robber Barons"; corporation managers and large investors found themselves in conflict with populist forces that wanted to control them. The populist forces made violent, vociferous demands and carried with them considerable social power. Theirs was a reaction to the contradictions inherent in an exploitative capitalism tacked onto an egalitarian ideology. State legislatures and the federal Congress moved in many ways to regulate and limit corporate power. For example, the Congress created the Interstate Commerce Commission, the first major

TABLE 4.1   Growth of large corporations as indicated by relation of their statutory net income to that of all corporations *

	Net income of all non-financial corporations (million dollars)	Estimated net income of 200 largest non-financial corporations (million dollars)	Per cent by largest 200 corporations (million dollars)	Estimated net income of 800 next largest non-financial corporations (million dollars)	Per cent by next largest 800 corporations
1920	$6,899	$2,307	33.4	$1,305	19.0
1921	3,597	1,354	37.6	708	19.6
1922	6,076	1,958	32.2	1,151	19.0
1923	7,453	2,445	32.8	1,386	18.6
1924	6,591	2,378	36.0	1,247	19.0
1925	8,060	2,993	37.1	1,522	18.9
1926	8,337	3,335	40.0	1,564	18.7
1927	7,459	2,865	38.4	1,360	18.2
1928	8,646	3,493	40.4	1,618	18.7
1929	9,456	4,081	43.2	1,808	19.1
Average 1920-1923	$6,006	$2,015	33.5	$1,137	18.9
Average 1926-1929	$8,474	$3,444	40.7	$1,587	18.7

* Derived from Statistics of Income for the respective years. Net income of all non-financial corporations equals statutory net income of all corporations reporting net income less that of financial corporations reporting net income. Income for the largest 200 was estimated by taking the net income of all non-financial corporations reporting income over $5,000,000 including nearly 200 companies and adding to this an estimate of the income of additional companies to make the total of 200. In each case the few additional companies were assumed to have a net income of $5,000,000. (If the average income of the added companies had been $4,500,000 it would have lowered the estimate in 1927 only from 38.4 to 38.2 per cent. In other years the change would have been very much less. As in each year there were approximately 800 companies having incomes between $1,000,000 and $5,000,000, it is unlikely that the average income of the few companies necessary to make up the 200 largest would have been below $4,500,000 and was probably closer to $5,000,000. The assumption of the latter figures would not, therefore, lead to appreciable error.

Income for the next largest 800 was estimated by taking the income of all non-financial corporations reporting statutory net income of over $1,00,000 (approximately 900 corporations each year) and adding an estimate of the income of additional companies to make a total of 1,000, the extra companies being assumed to have an income of $1,000,000. From the resulting figure the estimated income of the largest 200 was substracted. (Error due to the probability that the additional companies had an average income of somewhat less than $1,000,000 would be negligible. If the average in 1927 had been $900,000 it would have reduced the percentage only from 18.2 to 18.1. As there were nearly 1,000 corporations having incomes between $500,000 and $1,000,000, the average income of the added companies must have been more nearly $1,000,000 than $900,000. In other years the error would have been even less.)

From Adolf A. Berle and Gardiner C. Means, *The Modern Corporation and Private Property*, rev. ed. (New York: Harcourt, Brace & World, 1968), p. 39.

regulatory agency, and in 1890 passed the Sherman Antitrust Act. Populist elements supported these laws as tools with which to control corporate power, but the corporations themselves supported many of these laws as a way to defuse populist agitation: to legitimize, as it were, the capitalist economic system.

Against these efforts to control them, corporations turned for protection to the courts. In the case of *Dartmouth College*, the judges insulated corporations from particularistic legislative interference disguised as an amendment to the corporate charter. Other restrictions on corporate power also fell. Earlier cases emphasized the ultra vires doctrine, which in effect prohibited corporations from doing acts outside the powers defined in the charter. That doctrine aimed at ensuring that management use corporate assets in the enterprise in which the shareholders had invested. Its effects, however, victimized third persons dealing with the corporation, whose contracts became invalid because of ultra vires. In form, the doctrine survived; in practice, it died, as courts became adept in finding anything a corporation did within the implications of the charter powers. "The courts were aware that corporations were becoming indispensable. The [ultra vires] doctrine was a nuisance and an obstacle to corporate credit."[33]

The judges found a powerful defense of corporations lurking in the Fourteenth Amendment of the U.S. Constitution. That amendment provided that no state might deprive any "person" of life, liberty, or property without due process of law. It aimed at protecting newly freed slaves. It ended by protecting corporations. Courts had long talked loosely about corporate "personality" as a shorthand way of dealing with the collectivity in a unitary way. Using the same words and then defining due process in a way that protected property, courts insulated corporations against many legislative interferences.

In our time, too, courts have furthered corporate interests by the same device. The Constitution prohibits states or their creatures from discriminating on grounds of race; it does not prohibit discrimination by private persons. Courts held that corporations had the same privilege to discriminate as a private person. (Since the directors and management made the decisions, this left the decision to discriminate to their prejudices, disguised as business judgment. Contradictorily, however, it is rare that an individual in a corporation is held criminally libel for criminal acts committed by the corporation.)

Again, courts argued that the First Amendment guarantees freedom of expression. Its privileges run to corporations. Therefore, these courts argued, a state cannot prevent a corporation from spending its funds to oppose legislation.[34] Even advertising came under the protection of the First Amendment.[35]

Against the forces of nineteenth-century populism, corporations emerged the clear winners. Nineteenth-century courts and legislatures actually produced more law with respect to another set of conflicting interests, that between shareholders and managers, and on that issue the score did not emerge so one-sided. By the middle of the nineteenth century, a few shrewd, unscrupulous spectators, the Jim Goulds and Jay Fisks, learned how to manipulate the corporate form to milk their fellow investors and corporate creditors. The principal thrusts of the law attempted to curb corporate promoters and managers from defrauding shareholders and creditors—a classic example of the legal order's function to discipline discordant elements of the ruling class itself. We mention two examples of these rules. First, to protect creditors, the so-called trust fund doctrine treated the capital originally invested in the corporation as a fund for the payment of corporate debts, so that the managers could not distribute it to shareholders and then declare the bankruptcy of the empty corporate shell. Second, to protect shareholders, corporate promoters had imposed upon themselves a duty of trust to their investors (courts labeled it a "fiduciary" duty, making a rough analogy to the duties of trustees in ordinary trust relationships). That required them to deal openly and candidly with shareholders. For example, a popular device of corporate promoters was (and is) stock watering. A promoter owned a down-at-the-heels factory with a fair market value of, say, $10,000. She would sell shares in a corporation to manufacture the same sort of goods and, by dent of hard selling, would raise (let us say) $100,000 in small stock subscriptions. She then would offer the factory to the corporation for an additional $100,000 worth of stock. Because at that early stage in the corporation's life the promoter de facto would usually control it, she would cause the corporation to accept the offer. In return for her $10,000 factory, the promoter would end up with a half interest in a corporation with capital actually worth $110,000 ($100,000 raised from shareholders and a factory actually worth $10,000), but with a book value of $200,000. The promoter would have watered the stock to the value of $90,000. Various nineteenth-century rules tried to reduce a promoter's power to water stock, more or less unsuccessfully. It was not until the Securities and Exchange Act of 1933 that an adequate legal remedy for this practice emerged. Difficulties of enforcement, however, continue to make the practice of watering stocks not uncommon.

In the tug-of-war that pitched investors against managers and directors, the managers and directors found a useful aid in the diversity of the states. Some states, dominated by populist sentiment, enacted laws to curb corporations. Other states, either dominated by great corporate power (for example, Delaware, where the Dupont Corporation virtually owns the state) or simply in a mad scramble to pick up a little tax revenue (New Jersey, for example), enacted corporation laws that would attract business to incorporate in their state. Under the U.S. Constitution's Commerce Clause, a corporation can do business in any state no matter where it is incorporated. Not surprisingly, this clause makes states competitors for corporations to register in order to gain taxes and perhaps to locate more plants inside a state's borders thus increasing jobs and generally enhancing the economy. Some states, therefore, passed laws which were very favorable to corporations. Among other advantages offered by some states, such as Delaware and New Jersey, was considerable protection for the managers of the corporation from supervision by shareholders or state officials by allowing corporations legally to withhold information. To this day Delaware remains the state of record for thousands of corporations, including many with connections with organized crime, which do practically no business in the state.

Corporate theory assumed that the corporation actually comprised a group of investors, concerned with the enterprise, who selected directors and, through the directors, the managers to run the enterprise for them. By the mid-twentieth century, that model no longer fit very many of the great corporations. A few still had a great family as its major shareholder. Most had thousands of investors. In these, professional managers had long since taken over from directors and shareholders the corporation's de facto governance. Because share ownership became enormously fragmented, management frequently became a self-perpetuating clique. So long as they produced adequate profits and a satisfactory increase in share price, their power suffered the threat not of shareholder revolt so much as takeover via a proxy fight by a competing team of management wolves. Shareholders bought shares not because they proposed to involve themselves in the business of the firm, but in the same general sense as a bettor punts on a horserace. I buy shares in, say, I.B.M. or General Motors not because I propose to participate in the business or even to exercise my vote for directors—that never occurs to me as a possibility—but because I think them good risks. If I become dissatisfied, I do not agitate to change directors or management, but sell my shares and invest in some other corporation.

Slowly the legal order came to recognize that change. For example, if investment has as its purpose the actual participation in the particular business, then if the business should expand the shareholders must have a concern to maintain their proportional interest. A nineteenth-century rule (first judge-made, later legislative) gave a shareholder a so-called preemptive right to a proportional amount of any new issue.[36] After about 1890, corporate charters began specifically to exclude that right and courts did not object. By the 1930s, statutes permitted corporations to eliminate preemptive rights, and most large corporations did so.[37] The shareholders had become market players, not participants in a business enterprise.

In a small corporation, the directors supposedly "represent" shareholder interest. Subject to the corporate charter and bylaws, they have the entire responsibility for running the enterprise. They appoint managers, who operate the firm on a day-to-day basis. New Jersey and Delaware gave directors broad power to amend the corporation's charter and bylaws. Where the directors can amend charter and bylaws without reference to the shareholders, they no longer "represent" the shareholders. Directors can even change the basic line of business of the enterprise, or its basic institutional relationships, without canvassing the shareholders. Directors still have responsibilities to them, of course; the corporation, after all, operates on the shareholders' investments, just as banks operate on depositors' funds. Both owe special duties of care.

The only nexus that holds shareholders to directors and management in a large corporation therefore becomes their common interest not in the business of the firm, but in its profits. Emerging twentieth-century corporation law emphasized the cash nexus and built a body of law protecting shareholder interest in profits. In *Dodge* v. *Ford*, the majority shareholder had for some years refused to pay dividends (except some very small ones) out of the incredible profits earned by the Ford Motor Company in its early years.[38] When sued for an order compelling a dividend payment, Ford defended on the ground that he wanted to reduce the price of the Ford car as a charity to the American people. The court forced him to pay dividends, holding that directors cannot treat the company as an eleemosynary institution. In other cases, courts had struck down outright and overreaching fraud. The Securities and Exchange Act created a vast administrative machinery to protect shareholders against fraud and overreaching in share promotion, advertising, and insider trading and profits.

Beyond that, however, the directors and managers could do very nearly what they liked. Nobody expects a punter to tell the jockey how to run the race; nobody expects an ordinary shareholder to tell management how to run the business. The business judgment rule protected management against any challenge to its decisions. The rules with respect to proxies and corporate elections made it impossible for any but the most well-heeled even to try to challenge their tenure.

In 1932, Berle and Means described the new breed of corporate managers and directors holding the power property usually held by owners.[39] Property, they said, entailed the power to deal with assets and, therefore, with people. Corporate management had that power with respect to corporate assets. With respect to those assets they exercised all the power that contract and property law extend to the property owner.

Against these new "owners" of corporate property, populist movements beat unceasingly but with only moderate success. In 1937, a radical shift in the Supreme Court majority weakened the court as the last line of defense for corporate and managerial power. The corporations had earlier learned, however, that their piles of pennies and patience topped those of reformers. The agencies that supposedly curbed business (and in our era, therefore, corporate power)—the Interstate Commerce Commission, the Civil Aeronautics Board, the Federal Communications Commission, the Federal Trade Commission—in time fell themselves under the sway of their corporate subjects. Congress and state legislatures, too, became increasingly amenable to corporate blandishment. Where in the preceding century, business had run to the courts for protection against populist attempts to curb them, now the corporate managers ran to Congress to reverse court or agency rulings that threatened their interests. For example, in *United States* v. *Philadelphia National Bank Company* (1967),[40] the Supreme Court unexpectedly held that the Sherman Antitrust Act applies to banks. The banking community speedily persuaded the Congress to reverse that decision. Under the Bank Holding Company Act of 1964 Congress placed control over bank mergers in the federal agencies that had always dealt with banks sympathetically rather than in the courts.[41]

Special Legal Perquisites

In terms of the legal order, property, contract, and corporation law provide the broad framework that explains corporate power. In addition, however, practically every large corporation or its industry receives special favors from the legal order. We mention only a few here.

To the extent that a particular taxpayer or class of taxpayer does not pay tax according to the same rules that apply to others, in effect the state gives that taxpayer a subsidy equal in amount to the tax she saves. The tax laws contain innumerable special favors for particular categories of taxpayers. If I own a machine that will stop working after ten years, in each year I rightly ought to include in the cost of the goods one-tenth of the machine's value. Increasing the cost of the goods reduces my profit, my taxable income, and therefore my tax. The tax laws generally permit everyone a deduction of this sort, called depreciation. Certain selected industries, however, receive a percentage depletion deduction. For many years, for example, the oil industry could arbitrarily deduct 27½ percent of its income as a "depletion" allowance, regardless of the actual depletion or its original cost. As a result, oil companies paid very small taxes and the rest of us paid correspondingly more.

The customs laws of the United States, too, respond to particularist forces. Every year they include special breaks for special industries. For example, for years they imposed a prohibitive duty on the import of barber chairs. The United States has only one barber chair manufacturer. The duty in effect gave it a monopoly of the U.S. trade in barber chairs.

Usually these rules have a universalistic phraseology that conceals their particularistic impact. For many years federal tax law permitted recipients of interest municipalities to borrow money, giving in return their bonds. The law permitted recipients of interest on those bonds to exclude it from their taxable income. The municipalities paid less interest and the federal government received less tax than it otherwise might have done. Massachusetts (and other states) then enacted a statute permitting municipalities to borrow money, secured not by their general promise to pay, but by the income from a specific property. The municipality would then borrow money at a low interest rate, secured by a mortgage on a particular factory. It would then lend the money at the same interest rate, on a mortgage, to a business firm. In effect, the business firm got a low interest rate for its mortgage and the lenders received less interest but paid no tax on it (and therefore did not lose anything), but the U.S. government did forego tax it would have received from the lenders if the transaction had not received tax shelter. The bottom line meant that the businesses which received the favors (almost all corporations) received a very low interest rate mortgage. To subsidize them, the rest of the taxpayers paid a higher federal tax. In Massachusetts over many years, General Electric Company, one of the nation's largest, received the lion's share of this largess. The mass of federal taxpayers came to that extent to subsidize General Electric.

Sometimes, however, the fig leaf of universality and equality disappears. Regularly, the federal government comes to the rescue of large firms. It bailed Lockheed Aircraft out of bankruptcy by guaranteeing loans of $250,000,000. It did the same for the Chrysler Corporation, guaranteeing $1.5 *billion* in loans. Since 1968 the federal government has guaranteed over five billion dollars in loans to private corporations.[42] In some industries, defense for example, government constitutes the sole market; without it, the entire industry would die. In the case of highways, the federal government maintains a trust fund created by the proceeds of the gasoline tax. Despite a widespread belief that, rather than more super highways, the country needs more public transit, the law has not changed, except incrementally.[43] The highway trust fund remains dedicated to building more highways, i.e., providing highway contracts for contracting firms.

The list is almost endless. All of these perquisites to corporations have their defenders; many of them no doubt have a basis in sound public policy. The hypothesis here urged, however, has nothing to do with that. It only argues that part of the explanation for corporate power lies in the legal order's grants to specific firms of special perquisites.

4.2 FACILITATIVE LAW: ALTERNATIVE EXPLANATIONS

The laws of property, contract, and corporations stand at the cornerstone of capitalist economic systems. Not surprisingly there is considerable controversy over why these laws have taken and currently possess the particular characteristics they do. In general the argument flows from two broad theoretical perspectives: the classical and the anticlassical models.

Classical Perspectives

Property law protects individuals in their ownership of things. The classical school of thought argues that without that protection individuals will not likely enter the market economy. Nor can the market economy easily exist without contracts. These promote social cooperation. The division of labor requires manufacturers to buy from suppliers, employ labor, and sell to customers; landlords to rent to tenants; wholesalers, retailers, and consumers to buy and to sell goods. Without planned organization of these exchanges, every man must seize his own opportunity. Through contract, the parties create their private norms, thus exercising personal freedom to conduct their own affairs. To the extent that the legal order enforces these norms, it ensures freedom. So goes the classical perception.

Contract law only embodies "freedom" if the market matches its laissez-faire ideal-type. If perfect competition and knowledge prevail, then by definition no seller can charge, nor will a buyer pay, more than the market price. Other potential bargaining partners, offering their services or goods on competitive terms, protect a person from another's arbitrary power. The market becomes an Invisible Hand to protect every person.

What ideal-type of legal order will achieve this ideal economic order?[44] A customer will not buy goods unless his ownership will be exclusive. Property and tort law purportedly guarantee rights of peaceful possession. The law of contract purports to ensure that promises, once made, will be kept.[45] These laws do not ensure competition, but without them a market cannot exist.

The classical view of property and contract law neither describes nor explains reality. Instead, it holds that "freedom" from arbitrary economic power requires two necessary (although not efficient) conditions: the market, an Invisible Hand to protect everyman, and the state, a value-neutral framework to create and maintain the conditions for the market. These imply dual discontinuities: the legal order, sharply discontinuous from the private sphere, and state action, clearly distinct from state non-action. If a genuinely free, competitive market and a genuinely neutral state existed, then by setting the framework for these facilitative law would ensure voluntariness and freedom, not manipulation and coercion.

The Anticlassical Perspective

The anticlassical perspective argues that the classical model cannot achieve these conditions. Both perceptions agree that facilitative law permits the parties to negotiate a transaction to determine for themselves the norms defining their interchange and provides coercive state machinery to enforce them. "From this point of view, the law of contract may be viewed as a subsidiary branch of public law, as a body of rules according to which the sovereign power of the state will be exercised in accordance to the rules agreed upon between the parties to a more or less voluntary transaction.''[46] In terms of our earlier general model the contracting parties participate in lawmaking, that is, they create rules that the organs of the state enforce. Facilitative law delegates to the parties a portion of state power.

When a person bargains, she makes choices within her arena of choice. In every case, presumably she chooses the best available alternative. Some arenas of choice permit only limited alternatives. The robber who allows his victim only to choose between surrendering his money or his life permits a choice, albeit starkly limited. So limited a choice we denote coercion. When the choices open to a bargaining party have a narrow range (e.g., if she lives in a company town in which she must work for the company or leave her home, or if sellers offer only a very narrow range of goods of a certain sort), she has a choice of sorts, but that choice still bears the label coerced. To the extent that contract law enforces bargains arising out of limited arenas of choice, it embodies not freedom but coercion. Is it significantly different to say to a person, "I will pay you a wage if you will work for me," rather than "You will get no wages unless you work for me." Two hundred years ago Lord Chancellor Northington expressed it succinctly: "Necessitous men are not, truly speaking, free men."

In a bargaining situation, to give unequals legal rights against each other ensures that the stronger will dominate. No equality exists between a casual laborer and the Ford Motor Company or U.S. Steel. A worker for whom a much lower paying job or even welfare loom as the only alternatives to a job in a radioactive nuclear plant cannot easily decline the employment. Facilitative law in a society of unequals effectively transfers equal power to create legally enforceable norms, i.e., rules of law, to the economically strong. In this view, between unequals facilitative law entails not freedom but coercion.

Their explanations for corporate power. How would these two schools, the classical and the anticlassical, explain the way that law relates to corporate power? In a sense, both can claim that they accurately describe the relationships between corporations and the rest of us. The law does not compel a laborer to work for pennies for a great mining corporation in Africa, or a consumer to buy shoddy or dangerous goods, or a tenant to rent on a lease every clause of which adds yet another weapon to the corporate armory. In an abstract sense, of course, each of these has "freedom" to say yea or nay. Unlike the case of ideal-type of status society, each has some control over her destiny. If the mining corporation in Africa gives too little for the labor of its employees, they will remain on the farm; if the goods at too great a price carry too heavy a burden of danger (and the consumer knows about it), many consumers will decline to buy the product; if the lease at too high a rent has too many onerous clauses, no doubt tenants will find other accommodations, even if it means moving in with the in-laws. Contract law endows each of us with the power to enter into the contract or not, as we choose.

In that restricted sense, the classical view argues, contract law does create the legal conditions for freedom. Since contract law ensures freedom, it cannot contribute to corporate power; on the contrary, it limits it, because in order to attract laborers and customers and tenants, corporations must make their offers acceptable to them. So goes the classical view.

The classical perception resembles the elementary choice model that examines only the choice that the role-occupant makes and ignores the context, the arena of choice, within which she chooses. The anticlassical perspective, on the other hand, focuses on the range of constraints and resources within which the actor chooses as well as the reasons why she chooses as she does. The laborer must work, the consumer buy, the tenant rent. Their choices respond to these imperatives.

One cannot understand the range of constraint and resources within which the actor chooses without considering other social institutions. Property and corporation law, as well as contract, structure my arena of choice so that corporations and their managers have great power over me. Without alternatives, they can withhold jobs or offer them on onerous terms; they can decide what sorts of goods I can buy and at what prices and what premises I can lease and on what terms. They can decide this with precious few constraints from government or from shareholders. In that view, contract law indeed ensures my liberty to say yea or nay to particular bargains that corporations invite me to propose to them, but in the sector of the economy dominated by the great corporations that range of options usually constitutes "freedom" in a sense so limited as to become ludicrous.

So understood, the aura of freedom that hovers about the institution of contract law contributes to the pervasive belief that law, far from constituting a coercive order, in fact liberates from coercion. If one accepts the institutions of society as given, then truly contract law does "liberate," for notionally one can say yes or no to any proposal. To the extent that I depend on the great corporations for subsistence, however—and in our society almost all of us do—that so-called freedom diminishes. To the extent that, contrary to fact, we believe that contract liberates us, contract law substantially contributes to the hegemony that the legal order creates. It helps to persuade us that the very legal order that creates and maintains coercive power in fact liberates us from it.

The economist J. K. Galbraith reached an analogous conclusion. We all have illusions (and orthodoxy systematically cultivates them) that consumers have choice and that the economic system in final analysis responds entirely to aggregated consumer choice. "And if choice by the public is the source of power the organisations that comprise the economic system cannot have power, they are merely instruments in the ultimate service of that choice."[47] That ideology serves to maintain power. "If the goods that [the firm] produces or the services that it renders are frivolous or lethal or do damage to air, water, landscape or the tranquility of life, the firm is not to blame. This reflects public choice. If people are abused, it is because they choose self-abuse. If economic behaviour seems on occasion insane, it is because people are insane."[48] Power holders maintain their power today not by naked coercion, but mainly by persuasion. If power holders can persuade all of us that we, not they, hold power, we will explain our difficulties by our own tastes, values, and attitudes, not the interests of those who truly hold power. Facilitative law masks coercion under a facade of choice and consumer sovereignty. In the legal order, the classical perspective in contract law becomes the analogue of the economic ideology of consumer choice and corporate powerlessness.

These propositions about facilitative law entail four corollaries concerning the potential for a free market and for a value-neutral state, the distinction between state action and state *non*-action, and conflict versus consensus models.

Law and the Free Market

If the anticlassical perception holds, then all economic choices must take into account the legal order and the institution it bolsters. These constitute, however, not the unfettered choices of consumers in a "free" market, but constraints imposed on the market by the state. Contract, property, and corporation law and the perquisites specially granted to corporations, like all law, constitute some of these constraints. The market can serve as an Invisible Hand only when unfettered consumer interests constitute the entire arena of choice of sellers and when the price incorporates every cost. To the extent that a seller's arena of choice includes "externalities," that does not exist. An externality exists when a seller can exclude a cost from the price; for example, if a seller can throw soot into the air, imposing unrecoverable costs of repainting upon home owners, the price of the goods will not include their total actual cost. The cost of repainting constitutes an externality. Most costs or benefits imposed by law constitute externalities. If a particular manufacturer has a tax advantage, or if his road is paved before others, or even if contract law gives him special advantages, the price will not reflect all the costs and he will make his choices in terms of the law as well as the aggregate desires of consumers. To the extent that law (or custom, which serves the same function) exists, externalities must exist and the market as the Invisible Hand disappears. But, markets can only exist in society. A "society" with neither law nor custom becomes not society, but anarchy. At the very point at which a genuinely free market might appear, society disappears. A genuinely free market *cannot* exist. It becomes a concept analogous to the concepts in physics of absolute zero or absolute vacuum. It can never exist, although as a hypothetical concept it may serve to elucidate real-life difficulties.

In short, the anticlassical view holds that outside of economic theory, a free market can never exist. Behind the Invisible Hand, the state cannot avoid putting a thumb on the scales. Gunnar Myrdal makes the same point: "Prices are manipulated. They are not the outcome only of the forces in the market; they are in a sense 'political prices,' depending also on the regulating activity of the state, of quasi-public and private organizations and of private businesses. The state interferences in the price system are, in a sense, the ultimate ones...."[49]

Law and the Value-Neutral State

The anticlassical perspective also denies the possibility that the state, which inevitably must put its thumb on the scales, can never be value-neutral. The law defines what property owners can and cannot do with their property. It protects them in their ownership and thus largely defines their relative power in the contractual relationship. The law, too, defines lawmaking and law-implementing processes, that is, law defines the state. Since, as we have seen, rules of law can never become value-neutral, the state they define cannot become value-neutral. The rules of contract, property, and corporation law that emerge from the state's lawmaking institutions cannot achieve neutrality either.

State Action and Non-Action

Solutions imply explanations. If the legal order (i.e., state action) did not "explain" behavior then one could not devise a "legal" way to change behavior. In that case no meaningful science of directed social change through law could ever exist. Throughout the world, however, governments of course make massive efforts to change their societies. In the Third World, development efforts consist of the state trying to bring about change through the legal order. In our country, we make efforts to use the legal order to prevent inflation, solve problems of race discrimination, and strengthen our energy position. The classical perception of contract law, by emphasizing the discontinuities between the private sector and the legal order and between state action and non-action, instructs the policy maker not only to look for nonlegal explanations for behavior, but to find solutions that do not depend upon the state for their success and to turn to laissez-faire, contract, and private action rather than to their opposites. If we accept the anticlassical perception, then we must perceive in what seems state non-action a decision by the state to intervene through facilitative law rather than through other, more direct devices. That may constitute the desirable course; but nobody should deceive himself that it does not constitute state intervention. When the state stands by and permits a landlord to discriminate against blacks, or an employer against women, that constitutes state intervention to achieve that result just as much as if the state explicitly forbade the employers to discriminate in those ways. The question never becomes one of intervention or no intervention, but only of what sort of intervention. A state cannot avoid decision.

Conflict or Consensus

Finally, we earlier adverted to two alternative perspectives of society, conflict and consensus. The former assumes that the state can act neutrally; the latter that in a society of unequals "neutrality" cannot exist. The anticlassical perspective specifically denies the *possibility* of state neutrality. If the anticlassical perspective holds, then the notion that the state can exist as a neutral adjudicator also falls.[50]

4.3 DISCUSSION AND CONCLUSION

In this chapter we have looked in some detail at the development of those sorts of rules we label facilitative law—property, contract, and corporation law. Harkening back to the discussion in Chapters 1 through 3 of methodology, perspectives, and vocabularies appropriate to the study of law and society, it should now be clear why we chose the model we did. The history of property, contract, and corporation law marks the absurdity of the consensus model. These laws quite apparently reflect the power of merchant, capitalist, and corporate elites in various epochs. They reflect this power, however, in the face of opposition from other social classes and groups struggling against them.

More generally, the process by which laws are created and implemented is a response by people to problems (conflicts, struggles) generated out of contradictions in the political, economic, and social relations of the period. Eighteenth-century legislators created law to deal with an agricultural economy, without major markets for fungible goods. Initially, property law favored earlier, agricultural uses; contract law adapted to transfers of property mainly for personal use; corporation law endowed business collectivities with power to carry out quasi-governmental functions.

The nineteenth century saw the development of industry, the creation of markets for more or less fungible goods, and the need for the large agglomerations of capital that more advanced technology demands. When these changes created contradictions and conflicts between agrarian economic demands and a capitalist economy, lawmakers created (1) property law which favored industrial over agricultural uses; (2) contract law, by developing notions of noninterference by courts in the terms of the bargain and permitting expectation damages; and (3) corporation law, by separating the law of private from that of public corporations, protecting centralized management, and endowing corporations with the power to hold property and enter upon contracts as free from state intervention as private entrepreneurs.

The late nineteenth and twentieth centuries experienced a new phenomenon: an economy dominated by enormous, concentrated market power. The same rules of property and contract law that emerged from a small-holder, market economy and worked tolerably in the less oligopolized sectors of the economy became oppressive when manipulated by the great corporations. Corporation laws ensured management's control of the corporation, but protected investors from insider cheating. New efforts tried to curb corporate contract and property power, mainly through the use of administrative agencies. However, old rules of contract, property, and corporation law, generated to solve problems for an earlier, less centralized economy, were inadequate to the task: they did not satisfy the needs of the emergent giant corporations. Furthermore, the emergence of the giant corporations generated massive resistance from those whose lives were most affected by the change. This resistance, which often took the form of riots and rebellions, forced changes in the law, as we have seen.

In the next chapter we continue the discussion of lawmaking, adding more flesh to the skeleton of the theory, methodology, and vocabulary we are constructing in order to help us to understand law and the legal order.

NOTES

1. U.S. Statistical Abstracts, 1971. See also Richard J. Barber, *The American Corporation: Its Power, Its Money, Its Politics* (London: Macgibbon and Kee, 1970).

2. M. J. Horwitz, *The Transformation of American Law: 1780-1860* (Cambridge: Harvard University Press, 1977).

3. *Ibid.*, p. 32.

4. *Ibid.*, p. 34.

5. *State* v. *Moe*, 17 Wash, 203, 24 p. 2d 638 (U.S. Supreme Court, Washington, 1933).

6. Austin Painter's District Council 22, 64 n.w. 2d 550 (Michigan, 1954).

7. In re Parrott, 1 Fed. Rep. 481 (Circuit Court, California, 1880).

8. *Paul* v. *Neechem* (N.Y. Supplement, 1938).

9. Horwitz, *Transformation of American Law.*

10. *Ibid.*, p. 165.

11. *Ibid.*, p. 167.

12. *Ibid.*, p. 174.

13. *Davis* v. *Richardson,* in *ibid.*

14. Horwitz, *Transformation of American Law,* p. 175.

15. *Ibid.*, p. 161.

16. For an interesting exception to this rule see *Stevens* v. *Fidelity and Casuality Co.* 58 Cal. 2d 862, 377 p. 2d 284, 27 Cal. Rptr. 172, 1962.

17. W. D. Slawson, "Mass Contracts: Lawful Fraud in California," *California Law Review* 1(1974): 48.

18. *Ibid.*

19. *Ibid.*, p. 4.

20. *Hadley* v. *Baxendale*, 397 U.S. 50 (U.S. Supreme Court, Washington, 1970).

21. H. C. Black, *Black's Law Dictionary* (St. Paul: West Publishing Co., 1979), p. 307.

22. Geoffrey Pearson, "Goths and Vandals: Crime in History," *Contemporary Crises* 2(1978): 119-139.

23. E. P. Thompson, *Whigs and Hunters: The Origin of the Black Act* (New York: Pantheon Books, 1976).

24. Frank J. Michelman, "Norms and Normativity in the Economic Theory of Law," *Minnesota Law Review* 62(1978):1016.

25. *Ibid.*, p. 1017.

26. Black, *Black's Law Dictionary*, p. 307.

27. L. Friedman, *The Legal System: A Social Science Perspective* (New York: Russell Sage Foundation, 1975), pp. 166-167.

28. A. L. Morton, *A People's History of England* (London: Lawrence and Wishart, 1938), pp. 206-207.

29. *Dartmouth College* v. *Woodward*, 4 Wheat, 518, 4L ed. 629 (U.S. Supreme Court, 1819).

30. Adolf A. Berle and Gardiner C. Means, *The Modern Corporation and Private Property*, rev. ed. (New York: Harcourt, Brace and World, 1968), pp. 18-46.

31. *Ibid.*, p. 18.

32. Berle and Means, *Modern Corporation*, p. 171.

33. *Ibid.*, p. 454.

34. *Bigelow* v. *Virginia* 421 U.S. 809 (1975).

35. Advertising was determined to be protected by the First Amendment in the case of *Va. Pharmacy Board* v. *Va. Consumer Council*, 425 U.S. 748, 48L ed. 2d 346, 96 S Ct. 1817 (1976).

36. Willard Hurst, *The Legitimacy of the Business Corporation in the Law of the United States: 1780-1970* (Charlottesville: University of Virginia Press, 1970).

37. *Ibid.*, p. 127.

38. *Dodge* v. *Ford*, 204 Mich. 439, 170 N.W. 668 (1919).

39. Berle and Means, *The Modern Corporation*.

40. *U.S.* v. *Philadelphia National Bank Company*, 296 U.S. 601 (1934).

41. Bank Holding Company Act 1966, 12 U.S.C. sec. 1841 *et seq.*

42. Gerald Turkel, "Rational Law and Boundary Maintenance: Legitimizing the 1971 Lockheed Loan Guarantee," *Law and Society Review* 15(1980-81): 41-77; G. Turkel, "Situated Corporatist Legitimacy: The 1979 Chrysler Loan Guarantee," in S. Spitzer (ed.), *Research Law and Sociology*, vol. 4 (Greenwich, Conn.: JAI Press, 1982).

43. Alan A. Whitt, "Toward a Class-Dialectical Model of Political Power: An Empirical Assessment of Three Competing Models," *American Sociological Review* 43(1979): 81-99.

44. D. Trubeck, "Max Weber on Law and the Rise of Capitalism," *Wisconsin Law Review* 270(1972).

45. *Dartmouth College* v. *Woodward*.

46. M. R. Cohen, *Law and the Social Order* (New Haven: Yale University Press, 1964), p. 69.

47. J. K. Galbraith, *Economics and the Public Purpose* (Boston: Houghton Mifflin Co., 1973), p. 5.

48. *Ibid.*, p. 6.

49. G. Myrdal, *Economic Theory and Under-Developed Regions* (New York: Melliner, 1967), p. 49. The alternative and the value-neutral are not, as is sometimes argued, a conceptualization of the state as an evil cabal of a few powerful men. There is no evidence, for example, that the colonial office legal advisers who wrote the initial reception statute which imposed English law on Africa had anything in mind except to do what was "fair" to devise a set of laws that would guide the courts in Africa in dispute-settlement and which were within bureaucratic means. See Chapter 2 above.

50. K. Renner, *Institutions of Private Law and Their Social Functions*, ed. O. Kahn-Freund (London: Routledge and Kegan Paul, 1949).

5

The language of law

It is in the nature of things that we cannot say everything at once. We have thus far outlined and to some extent elaborated the methodology, vocabulary, and perspective which we feel most adequately describe and explain the relationship between law and society. We will return to these issues in the chapters that follow. In this chapter we want to apply our model and add another dimension to our knowledge of law and society by examining the "language of law" and why it came to be as it is.

For the legal order to induce social change through consciously conforming behavior, its addressees must learn what the law requires. The law, however, has its own language. It has its own vocabulary, requiring special dictionaries to translate it into ordinary speech. Words and phrases like *respondent* and *habeas corpus* and *fee simple* and *demurrer* abound, each with meanings peculiar to the law. Lawyers also use a special, arcane writing style, for example, the use of multiple redundancies (*null and void*; *give, bequeath, and devise*; *in full force and effect*).[1] Between specialized vocabulary and arcane style, the very language of the law defies lay understanding.

From the Republic's earliest days, officials and laymen protested the law's incomprehensibility. Thomas Jefferson wrote that Congress decided

to reform the style of the later British statutes and of our acts of Assembly, which from their verbosity, their endless tautologies, their involutions of case within case and parenthesis within parenthesis, and their multiplied efforts at certainty, by *saids* and *aforesaids,* by *ors* and *ands,* to make them more plain, do really render them more perplexed and incomprehensible, not only to common readers but to the lawyers themselves.[2]

More than a century and a half later, President Jimmy Carter ordered that the federal agencies write regulations ''in plain English,'' ''understandable to those that must comply'' with them.[3] A law school dean wrote in 1978:

We lawyers cannot write plain English. We use eight words to say what could be said in two. We use old, arcane phrases to express commonplace ideas. Seeking to be precise, we become redundant. Seeking to be cautious, we become verbose. Our sentences twist on, phrase within clause within clause, glazing the eyes and numbing the minds of our readers. The result is a writing style that has according to one critic, four outstanding characteristics. It is: ''(1) wordy, (2) unclear, (3) pompous, and (4) dull.''[4]

The written rules through which the legal order purports to influence our conduct have three principal categories: the rules of the common law, found mainly in appellate court opinions; the contracts, wills, deeds, insurance policies, warranties, and similar documents that control much of our economic lives; and statutes and administrative regulations. Here we discuss the language that lawyers use in writing legal documents and formal rules; we defer discussion of appellate opinions to later chapters.

5.1 THE LANGUAGE OF DOCUMENTS OF "PRIVATE LEGISLATION"

Most laypersons never read an appellate opinion or even a statute. Everyone reads (or tries to read) contracts, insurance policies, leases, deeds, wills. These embody norms prescribing behavior. A will, for example, prescribes rules that a dead person's executor should follow in distributing the estate. A fire insurance policy prescribes what the insurance company should do if fire damages the property. A lease lays down the rights and duties of landlord and tenant.

If a person violates a norm prescribed by one of these documents, an injured person can bring a lawsuit for relief. To sanction the offending party, the plaintiff summons the panoply of state power: courts, sheriffs, bailiffs, gaolers, police, and ultimately the army. That sort of case does not differ in principle from a case in which plaintiff claims that defendant violated a statute. In both cases, the plaintiff invokes the legal order to sanction a breach of a norm. In one case state officials laid down the norm, and in the other some private party. The machinery to deal with them does not differ very much. Wills, contracts, leases, deeds, and so forth in this sense constitute ''private legislation.''

Of the documents that embody private legislation, practically all have lawyers as authors. They employ a strange language. If at table I said, ''What lovely raspberries! Please pass the said raspberries,'' my friends would view me with concern. We expect that sort of gobbledygook in formal documents. Deeds begin with ''Know all men by these *presents*''—and precisely what does *presents* mean? (It is an anglicized, abbreviated version of the medieval Latin *presents scriptum*, or "present writing.")[5] It proceeds to an equally mystifying, "For One Dollar and Other Valuable Considerations"—except that the one dollar is never paid, and what are the other "valuable considerations"? (Consideration in the seventeenth and eighteenth centuries became the "magical essence of contractness."[6] The magic words guarantee that the contract would work.) It ends with signatures and the initials *L.S.*—and what does *L.S.* mean? (It stands for "locus sigilli," or "the place of the seal";[7] since the law of seals practically expired some years ago, *L.S.* has today literally no significance, legal or otherwise.) *Such* and *hereinabove* and *subject to* and *provided, however,* and similar barbarities abound like thickets in brush country. One expression, *ss.,* appearing in affidavits and other notarized instruments has no known meaning, although guesses abound.[8]

The common myth has it that lawyers use these strange words because they bring precision to private legislation. Sir Ernest Gower, a lawyer, paid flowery compliments to the language in his books *Plain Words* and *Plain Words: Their ABC:*

The "inevitable peculiarities" of the language of the law "come from a desire to convey a precise meaning. . . ." [It is] a language "obscure in order that it may be unambiguous." An afterthought makes this "almost unnecessarily obscure . . ." and a later edition acknowledges "room for improvement. . . ."[9]

Laymen have repeated Gower's observations: "The wording of documents may be tedious, polysyllabic, repetitious, cacophonic, and humorless, but to anyone not panic-stricken at the sound of 'whereas', it usually makes the meaning clearer than it otherwise would be."[10]

These writers repeat myths. Legal language falls far short of exactness. All words have a core meaning and a penumbra. The core meaning of words subsumes all the situations that native speakers would agree fall under it. The penumbra includes those situations where reasonable native speakers would have doubts about subsumption. Linguistic precision in one sense means using words that reduce the size of the penumbra. A contract that calls for delivery on *March 13, 1979,* in this sense has greater precision than one that calls for delivery *within a reasonable time.*

A great deal of legalese does not help precision. Phrases like *know all men by these presents* or *in the premises* or *the day and year first above mentioned* or *in witness thereof* all have no real content that adds anything to legal documents; they add nothing to precision. For example, note the following comment on legal writing from the fifteenth century: "Sir, the law is as I say it is, and so it has been laid down ever since the law began; and we have several set forms which are held as law, and so held and used for good reason, though we cannot at present remember that reason."[11] Nor do tautologies aid clarity: *to have and to hold; all that certain lot, tract, or parcel of lands; last will and testament; fit and proper; null and void; force and effect; give, devise and bequeath; rest, residue and remainder;* the list seems endless. Long sentences continue to exist, meandering on, losing readers at every new line. Lawyers pat themselves on the back for their linguistic precision; nobody else finds it precise and, frequently, neither do courts. H. Alan Cairns, himself a law professor, repeats the myths about the linguistic precision of the law, but admits that "there seems to be a constant failure of communication within the realm of legal discourse."[12]

Why then do lawyers continue to use these tautologies, verbosities, words without meaning, conventional phrases, and other barbarisms? Precision remains the answer, but in a different sense: precision as exactly-the-same-way. That has a double edge, one instrumental and the other not. Sometimes, lawyers use language to trigger particular desired results. When Ali Baba said, "Open, sesame," that the enchantment concerned sesame and not mustard seed did not matter. The ritual brought a desired result. A great deal of law consists of the ritual use of language to bring about particular results.

Consider the phrase, always used in deeds transferring title to land, conveying the land "to Doe and his heirs." At first blush, it does not seem illogical to think that the land granted by the clause went to (a) Doe and (b) the heirs of Doe. Until Doe died, nobody could ascertain his heirs. Therefore, the grant seems to give the land to Doe for life, and after his death to his heirs. Doe could not, therefore, sell the land during his lifetime. He did not "own" it. An early case, however, rendered that the grant "to Doe and his heirs" constituted a grant to Doe of the full ownership of the land.[13] Ever since then, lawyers have always used the full phrase "to Doe and his heirs" to grant full ownership to Doe. They never adopted a simpler form, for example, "to Doe as full owner." Indeed, authority exists for the seemingly ridiculous proposition that the phrase "to Doe," when used alone, grants not full ownership but a life estate. The mystical words "and his heirs" came to mean exactly the opposite of a grant to the heirs (since Doe could sell the land before anyone inherited it). Lawyers keep using the phrase as incantation; it triggers a known result, just as "open, sesame!" triggered a known result.

If all phrases in the law constituted incantation, their archaisms might amuse, but they might enhance precision. "To Doe and his heirs" does create some certainty; no court today would declare that it meant anything except full ownership. Most of the language that clogs our documents of private legislation, however, does not even have ritualistic value. It merely confuses, confounds, and fails to elucidate (as lawyers are used and wont to say, write, or otherwise commnicate). A variety of influences made the law long-winded. The popular eighteenth-century style suffered the same fault; for a variety of reasons, the courts came to insist upon technicalities in language, so that drafters multiplied them lest they fault by omission. Scriveners received their pay by the length of the document, and they increased their returns both by reducing the number of words per page and by increasing the total number of words. Most documents embodying private legislation, however, found drafters not among lawyers but among clerks, many without legal competence. Rather than drafting their own documents, they followed form-books. The principal modality that perpetuated the prolixity and inexactness of legalese exists in the form-books that these clerks (and many lawyers) followed.

The same history repeated itself in the United States. From England, the colonists took the language of Coke and Littleton. Form-books soon followed, soon devised specifically for the American condition. These found their origins, however, in English forms. Their authors did not attack the received forms with a rigorous blue pencil. They roamed through the case reports to find examples that they might copy, frequently without regard to the precision or legal consequences of the form they used. A contract to produce a play, "Peg o' My Heart," drawn in 1912, came to litigation in 1918-20. The producer won in District Court. The Second Circuit affirmed, 2-1. The United States Supreme Court reversed, 7-2. The "Peg o' My Heart" contract was an eligible contender for an award for imprecision. It found a place, however, "its stains of battle unwashed and unnoted," in a 1955 form-book.[14] The forms used in form-books have no virtue except this, that they stand ready for use. Lawyers keep using them and keep replicating their mistakes, vagueness, ambiguities, and, above all else, their inscrutability.

Why do lawyers do so? Most of the absurd non-English that lawyers use confuses rather than illuminates. Why then do they use it? Part of the answer must lie in the institutionalization of patterned transactions. Legal stationers sell printed forms for many, perhaps most instances that require private legislation: deeds, leases, contracts for the sale of real property, simple wills, building contracts, mortgages, chattel mortgages, conditional sales. Lawyers and non-lawyers alike use these forms for reason of speed and efficiency. They repeat the language obtuseness that has been carried on for centuries. More important reasons for the strangeness of legalese, however, are found in the dialectics of the legal order as a class-based institution.

5.2 THE LANGUAGE OF STATUTES AND REGULATIONS

To laymen, most statutes defy comprehension. Consider section 9-108 of the Uniform Commercial Code:

Where a secured party makes an advance, incurs an obligation, releases a perfected security interest, or otherwise gives new value which is to be secured in whole or in part by after-acquired property his security interest in the after-acquired collateral shall be deemed to be taken for new value and not as security for an antecedent debt if the debtor acquires his rights in such collateral either in the ordinary course of business or under a contract of purchase made pursuant to the security agreement within a reasonable time after new value is given.[15]

It hardly scans. Most laypersons simply throw up their hands at it. So unreadable became legislation that committees in the United States Congress wrote translations so that Congressmen could understand what they voted for. Consider the difference between the Administrative Procedures Act of 1946 and its paraphrase:[16]

The Act	*The Paraphrase*
There shall preside at the taking of evidence (1) the agency, (2) one or more	The hearing must be held either by the agency, a member or members of the board

members of the body which comprises the agency, or (3) one or more examiners appointed as provided in this Act; but nothing in this Act shall be deemed to supersede the conduct of specified classes of proceedings in whole or in part by or before boards or other officers specially provided for by or designated pursuant to statute. The functions of all presiding officers and of officers participating in decisions in conformity with section 8 shall be conducted in an impartial manner.

which comprises it, one or more examiners, or other officers specially provided for in or designated pursuant to other statutes.

All presiding and deciding officers are to operate impartially.

As we have seen (in Chapter 4) nineteenth-century entrepreneurial demands for predictability, certainty, and cognoscibility in law had enormous impact in creating the law's dominant "grand theory." Following those demands, statutory drafting went through a metamorphosis. We first examine that history.

Legislative Drafting: History

Drafting before Sir Henry Thring. Many imagine that present-day statutory drafting has a history stretching into antiquity. It does not; rather, it formed part of a distinct nineteenth-century movement. A parliamentary report recently summarized its early history:

In the earliest times statutes were drafted in Latin or Norman French, by a committee or judges, counsellors and officials, in response to a petition or bill which asked for a remedy but left the terms of the remedial act to the King in Council. In the fifteenth century, the practice began of drafting bills in the form of the act desired. By the end of that century this became the established method and the earlier practice had been discontinued. After 1487, Parliament appears to have handed over the drafting of bills (in English) [the first Commons Bill in English was 1414] to conveyancers and from the laconic and often obscure terseness of our earliest statutes, especially when in Latin, we swung in the sixteenth, seventeenth and early eighteenth centuries to a verbosity which succeeded only in concealing the real matter of the law under a welter of superfluous synonyms.[17]

By the middle of the nineteenth century, the verbosity, prolixity, and helter-skelter organization of British statute law made it a marvelously confused stew. Consider, for example, a *single* sentence of the notorious Black Act (1723):

Be it enacted . . . that if any person or persons, from and after the first day of June in the year of our Lord one thousand seven hundred and twenty-three, being armed with swords, firearms or other offensive weapons and having his or their faced blacked, or being otherwise disguised, shall appear in any forest, chase, park, paddock, or grounds enclosed with any wall, pale or other fence, wherein any deer have been or shall be usually kept, or in any high road, open heath, common or down, or shall unlawfully and willfully hunt, wound, kill, destroy, or steal any red or fallow deer, or unlawfully rob any warren or place where conies or hares are usually kept, or shall unlawfully steal or take away any fish out of any river or pond; or if any person or persons from and after the said first day of *June* shall unlawfully and willfully hunt, wound, kill, destroy or steal any red or fallow deer, fed or kept in any of his Majesty's forests or chases, which are or shall be inclosed with pales, rails, or other fences, or in any park, paddock, or grounds inclosed, where deer have been or shall be usually kept; or shall unlawfully and maliciously break down the head or mound of any fish-pond, whereby the fish shall be lost or destroyed; or shall unlawfully and maliciously kill, maim or wound any cattle or cut down or otherwise destroy any trees planted in any avenue, or growing in any garden, orchard or plantation, for ornament, shelter, or profit; or shall set fire to any house, barn or out-house, or to any hovel, cock, mow, or stack of corn, straw, hay or wood; or shall willfully and maliciously shoot at any person in any dwelling-house, or other place; or shall knowingly send any letter, without any name, subscribed thereto, or signed with a fictitious name, demanding money, venison, or other valuable thing; or shall forcibly rescue any person being lawfully in custody of any officer or other person, for any of the offenses before mentioned; or if any person or persons shall, by gift or promise of money or other reward, procure any of his Majesty's subjects to join him or them in any such unlawful act; every person so offending, being thereof lawfully convicted, shall be adjudged guilty of felony, and shall suffer death as in case of felony, without benefit of clergy.[18]

Those 367 words in one sentence contain 14 different sets of felonies, each containing many separate offenses, often overlapping with different sorts of required mental states usually without apparent reason. Similar miseries pervaded almost all legislation.

Statutes so poorly drafted gave judges great arenas within which their discretion might roam, plainly defeating the ideals of predictability and certainty. The common law itself reached a similar result. Presented by a case controlled by common law, a judge must first by deduction from the precedent cases derive a general proposition that might serve as a major premise to a syllogism whose minor premise consisted of the facts of the case and whose conclusion constituted the judgment. That gave the judge considerable discretion to decide what the law ought to be—whatever the state of the precedents. Clear, precise statutes and codifications of the common law seemed one way to cut down judicial lawmaking and achieve predictability in law.

As we have seen (in Chapter 4) the demand for predictability arose out of the conditions of eighteenth-century English life. Uncertain statutes and imprecise case law demand construction; they therefore endow judges and administrators with discretion. Everywhere, decision-makers tend to use discretion to increase rewards and reduce strains for themselves and the organizations they serve. In eighteenth-century Enland the landed gentry and aristocracy held enormous power and could readily extend rewards or impose strains upon judges and officials. Formal judicial independence, nominally born in 1688, had not yet reached a vigorous maturity. The judges sucked at the thumb of power. In eighteenth-century poaching cases in Cannock Chase, for example, the justices of the peace frequently asked Lord Paget, the local great landowner, how he wanted them to deal with an accused poacher. With respect to the game laws, the judge's discretion in part flowed from the confusion of the statutory stew. That pattern replicated itself at many places in the law.

By the middle of the nineteenth century, therefore, the form of statutes became perhaps the most arcane of the many arenas where the interests of old landed classes and new bourgeoisie clashed. The old way of writing statutes increased discretion; that favored the aristocratic interest. The new way enhanced certainty and predictability; that favored entrepreneurial interest. The rules that determined how bills got drafted determined what sorts of bills emerged. Rather than value-free, technical instructions embodying a consensus on how to write statutes, the rules of statutory drafting involved policy choices. They became another focus of social conflict.

Parliamentary counsel and precision, harmonization, codification, confined discretion. Lawyers and laymen repeatedly criticized the confusion of English statutory law. During the Commonwealth, two committees examined the question of consolidating the statutes "for the more ease and clearer understanding of the people," but nothing came of it. The subject slumbered until the end of the eighteenth century.

Beginning in 1796, a series of parliamentary committees reported on various aspects of the form of British statutes. A report of that year led to an improvement in the classification of statutes; another in 1806 began the long course, still unfinished, of consolidating all the statutes; in 1826 Sir Robert Peel began the consolidation and amendment of much of the then existing criminal law; the Statute Law Commission of 1826 undertook to make a consolidated penal code and to report on the possibility of consolidating other branches of English law; a commissioner in 1845 and again in 1852 undertook to complete the work of the 1826 commission; in 1854 a temporary Statute Law Board became the Statute Law Commission that revised and codified some areas of law and, finally, recommended that "perhaps nothing satisfactory towards the improvement of future legislation can be effected until either a board or some other persons are appointed, whose duty it shall be either to prepare or revise and report upon all bills before they are brought into Parliament, and to watch them during their progress through the two Houses. . . ."[19] In the following two decades, various sorts of statute law revision commissions followed each other with bewildering rapidity.

These various commissions and reports finally came to fruition in the last third of the century. They produced the Office of Parliamentary Counsel, a new procedure for creating legislation and legalese. The Office of Parliamentary Counsel became the principal institution for bill drafting.[20] In the beginning of Queen Victoria's reign the home secretary ordinarily took responsibility for initiating government's most important legislative measures. In 1837 he appointed the first of a series of counsel to help with that task; Thring occupied the post from 1861. The work load swamped him, and the ministries began again to employ independent counsel to draft bills. The costs were great; no uniform style prevailed; even uniformity of principle in government bills vanished, so that different departments got inconsistent bills enacted; no check on the financial consequences of legislation existed.[21]

To resolve these difficulties, in 1869 the chancellor of the exchequer instituted the Office of Parliamentary Counsel. The procedures counsel then used did not differ very much from those of today.[22] At bottom, they created a sharp split between policy and bill drafting. The ministries and their departmental solicitors represented the policy makers; parliamentary counsel, holding an independent brief as scrivener, represented the legal order. Policy emerged from the political process. Administrative (i.e., senior) civil servants then worked out the "means" and devised a legislative program expressed in the instructions the department drafted for parliamentary counsel. The departmental solicitor reduced the department's policy to a request for changes in the law, which he incorporated in his Instructions to Parliamentary Counsel, sometimes accompanied by a laymen's draft of the proposed bill. Parliamentary counsel's expertise lay not in devising substantive solutions to perceived problems, but only in chaining words together. A minister usually refused to put down a bill or an amendment unless drafted by counsel. In debate, parliamentary counsel attended the minister to pass on any proposed amendments as they arose.

The developed British system differed from analogous institutions elsewhere. In most of the western world today no discontinuity exists between substantive and formal decision-making. In France,

the drafting of a law is done in the ministry originating it by an officer in the section responsible for the topic with which the law deals. He may or may not be a lawyer, but he is never a "draftsman." . . . The French principle is that the drafting of a law, decree, etc., is best placed in the hands of those who have expert knowledge of the subject involved. . . . There is no such thing in France, at any rate in the legislative field as a specialist draftsman, a lawyer (or layman) who acquires and applies a particular technique for chaining words together to form a law.[23]

In Sweden, too, "the processes of consultation deliberation and drafting are *all one*."[24] In the Federal Republic of Germany, "there are no specialized draftsmen of legislation, nor is any training given in drafting. Those who write the laws are the ministry officials handling the subjects, as a rule, lawyers."[25] In Britain, exactly the opposite occurred. The substantive ministries prepared a legislative program. This became a set of instructions for parliamentary counsel, a specialized, central agency that drafted all government bills; and in a parliamentary system, only government bills ordinarily get enacted. The same small set of drafters handled bills dealing with taxes, crimes, electrical energy, shipping, land law—everything.

Greater precision in drafting also demanded new rules for the use of language. Institutional and linguistic changes both found their hero in Henry (later Baron) Thring. He drafted his first bill in 1850; appointed counsel to the Home Office in 1861, he became Britain's parliamentary counsel in 1869.[26] The office that he established became the principal source of all legislative drafting for Britain. The statutory style he orginated became the model for the common-law world.

The English tradition had four principal elements: linguistic devices that aided precision but not readability; internal consistency; codification, and explicit limits upon discretion.

Since Thring's day, draftspeople have played only minor variations on his two principal themes of clarity and precision. Every text parliamentary draftsmen wrote echoed them.[27] Thring's text, for example, included five pages about the "mode in which a draftsman should prepare himself to draw Acts" and 107 pages on the arrangement of the subject matter of an act, the composition of sentences, and such matters as the preamble, the short title, and the commencement of an act. In all this, "clearness is the main object to be aimed at in drawing Acts of Parliament."[28] Clearness, he held, "depends first, on the proper selection of words; secondly, on the arrangement and construction of sentences."[29] Thring quoted Mr. Justice Stephen: in statutory drafting, "it is not enough to attain a degree of precision which a person reading in good faith can understand; but it is necessary to attain, if possible, to a degree of precision which a person reading in bad faith cannot misunderstand."[30]

An Irish drafter, F.A.R. Bennion, a century later said of the Constitution of Ghana (which he drafted):

1   It is a mechanism, and all its operative provisions are intended to have the precise effect indicated by the words used—no more and no less.

2   It is drafted on the assumption that the words used have a fixed and definite meaning, and not a shifting and uncertain meaning; that they mean what they say and not what people would like them to mean; and that if they prove unsuitable, they will be altered formally by Parliament and not twisted into new meaning by "interpretation."[31]

He summed up the draftsman's ideal as handed down from Thring's time.

The rules of drafting seek to ensure that unattainable ideal. Use words with rigid consistency. Use "and" conjunctively and "or" disjunctively. Avoid squinting modifiers ("He gave the pen to the little girl filled with green ink"). Use "shall" to impose a duty, "may" a right or privilege, "will" to indicate the future tense. Write briefly and concisely, but unpack complex concepts. Every subhead in a tabulation must read with the introductory and conclusory phrases. The rules make a fair-sized packet.

Next to precision, fitting the new statute smoothly into the law's corpus held high place. "When instructions for an Act are given to a draftsman, his first step should be to acquaint himself with the *whole* of the existing law relating to the subject-matter of the Act which he is directed to prepare."[32] If not, dreadful things might happen: the draftsman, "by the alteration of a definition or the introduction of a superfluous provision, may unintentionally subvert a settled principle of common law or disturb a series of legislative enactments."[33] That would destroy predictability.

Thirdly, the new statutory style looked to the codification of the commercial law.[34] These codes did not purport to state new substantive rules, but only by changing their form to enhance their predictability. Their authors believed the codes enhanced predictability because of a particular perception of the judicial process. Presented with a case involving uncodified law, a judge must first by deduction derive from the cases a general proposition that might serve as a major premise for a syllogism whose minor premise consisted of the facts in the case, and whose conclusion constituted the judgment. If the case involved a code, however, the propositions of law are stated in the authoritative words of the legislature. When a particular case arises, the sole question is whether it falls or does not fall within some given statement in the code. The process of reasoning is purely deductive, and the code supplies the major premise in the syllogism.[35]

Finally, drafters made heroic efforts to limit discretion. Dicey contrasted the Rule of Law "with every system of government based on the exercise of persons in authority of wide, arbitrary or discretionary powers of constraint."[36]

The new drafting rules did not, however, aim to make legislation understandable to the laity. It did not make radical changes in the vocabulary that lawyers used nor in many of their accustomed redundancies and circumlocutions. Lawyers still spoke to lawyers and judges with *whereas* and *provided, however, that* and *null and void* and *fee simple* and *cestui que trust*, some defining concepts that lawyers need to use, some of no known instrumental utility. Statutory drafting continued to defy ordinary native speakers of English. Consider the British order of 1946 providing that a launderer no longer need notify the Board of Trade if he intends to close down his business: "The Laundry (Control) Order, 1942, as amended by the Laundry (Control) (No. 2) Order, 1942, shall have effect as if subparagraph (3) of paragraph (2) were omitted, and the Laundry (Control) (No. 2) Order, 1942, is hereby revoked."[37]

Drafting in the United States. These changes in British drafting had a lineal descendant in the Office of the Legislative Counsel of the Congress of the United States, established in 1918 after six years of legislative efforts. From the beginning, the proponents of the office had in mind the British model. At the 1912 House hearings, Lord Bryce, the British ambassador, gave a detailed description of the drafting function of the parliamentary counsel in Great Britain. In 1913, Senator Elihu Root argued that "the fundamental idea of the bill is . . . to perform the function that is now performed to great advantage by the officers who are called counsel in the British House of Commons. . . ."[38] The specific objectives of the office did not differ from those put forward by Thring almost half a century before. In Root's words:

The idea is to have a more or less permanent officer who is familiar with existing legislation and with the decisions of the courts, who can take a measure that has been drafted with the slender opportunities for examination and research which we have here and see how it fits into the existing laws of the country, and what its effect will be under the existing decisions of the courts and suggest better, clearer, more unambiguous and more effective forms of expression.

A very large part of the litigation and miscarriages of intention on the part of law-makers of the country and the failure of our people to get by legislation the relief which they wish to have which their representative in Congress wish to give them comes from the fact that laws are carelessly drawn; that laws are drawn without a sufficient study or a sufficient understanding of what is going to be existing laws under existing decisions.[39]

As in Britain, so in the United States: the central theme of the proponents of the new way of drafting bills was the need for predictability and clarity in court. The legislative drafter had to "arrest, as far as possible, the tendency more or less due to the pressure of circumstances, to prolixity, disorder and uncertainty in statutory enactments.'"[40]

The several state legislatures have different drafting institutions. In some (for example, Minnesota), a full-dress, well-organized office of legislative counsel exists. In others, such as Massachusetts, drafting seems relatively disorganized, with most legislators getting their own drafting done on a catch-as-catch-can basis.

Thring's crusade for clarity, predictability, and certainty in statutes succeeded in the creation of a new specialty within the profession, that of legislative draftsman. Statutes, like contracts and case law, however, remained inaccessible, written in a language that defied ordinary lay understanding. What explanations suggest themselves? What consequences ensued?

5.3 EXPLANATIONS AND CONSEQUENCES

Why did legalese continue in documents of private legislation and statutes? Lawyers explain it by the demands for precision. As we have seen, that states a myth. Except for its specialized vocabulary and "open, sesame!" incantations (and that leaves most of it) legalese does not perform an instrumental function. *Ss.* today has neither meaning nor function, and nobody remembers what it once meant or did, yet, like the buttons on the sleeves of men's jackets that no longer button anything, it hangs on. That lawyers use form-books helps to explain legalese's survival, but it hardly goes far enough. Why does it continue in the form-books? We discuss three alternative explanations: social lag; theories that ascribe to law various kinds of legitimating, mystifying, symbolic, or hegemonic functions; and what we denote an institutionalist explanation.

Social Lag

In 1922, F. Ogburn said that "when one part of culture changes first through some discovery or invention, and occasions changes in some part of the culture dependent upon it, there frequently is a delay.... The extent of this lag will vary ... but may exist for ... years, during which time there may be said to be a maladjustment.'"[41] He later specified his hypothesis more precisely:

The theory of cultural lag . . . calls for the following steps: (1) the identification of at least two variables; (2) the demonstration that these two variables were in adjustment; (3) the determination by dates that one variable has changed while the other has not changed in greater degree than the other; and (4) that when one variable has changed earlier or in greater degree than the other, there is a less satisfactory adjustment than existed before.[42]

Yehezkel Dror made the concept central to his theory of law and social change.[43]

The theory of social lag as thus set out does not suggest any causal explanation. It does no more than to state the problem that calls for explanation. Why does the institution "lag"? Obviously, that does not happen in a fit of social absentmindedness. "When, in the face of changed technology and new problems, a social arrangement stubbornly persists, there are social reasons why this is so; there are explanations why no change or slow change occurs.''[44] What explanations can we suggest to explain the ''lag''?

The Noninstrumental Functions of Law

Max Weber and Marxist theorists argued that law serves a noninstrumental function. Weber suggested that governments cannot rule easily through force or threat of force; instead, they seek to win the consent of the governed.[45] The developed, capitalist, western countries accomplish this in part through ''legal-rational legitimacy''—that is, a legal order that operates through universalistic rules, based upon legalistic law-finding by judges, where the legal order appears discontinuous with the social system, and where the law contains discretion. Weber examined how the rulers maintain their control with the cooperation of the dominated in societies in which the rulers used their control for their own benefit. He asked, ''What claims to authority do the rulers make? How do these serve the interests of the rulers?''[46] Marxists capsized that question, asking instead, ''What illusions do the dominated have that blind them to their own potential for changing affairs?''[47] Both sought to explain how the powerful retained their rule in an unjust society. Weber's concept of legitimacy pointed to solutions for the problems the rulers have in maintaining power; Marx's concept of false conscious-ness, to the difficulties the masses have in liberating themselves.

The Italian Marxist Gramsci held that the masses' false consciousness mirrors ruling class hegemony.[48] Ideas affect the way that people perceive the possibilities and the means of changing their circumstances. A class achieves hegemony to the degree that ideas that serve its own interests permeate society. ''People who are objectively members of the working class acquire a bourgeois subjectivity. As a result each member of the ruled class becomes an instrument of his own oppression. Herein lies the essence of hegemony.''[49] A legal system has normative rules enforced by coercion (its coercive aspect) and a set of values (its hegemonic aspect). ''In a bourgeois legal system these latter will include such ideas as equality before the law, separation of powers, due process, the rule of law, fairness, and so on. The direct interests of a dominant class will not always determine the outcomes of particular cases. Instances will arise when the hegemonic aspect is determinative.''[50]

In this view, legalese serves a mystifying and hegemonic function. When a court bailiff requires a witness to tell ''the truth, the whole truth and nothing but the truth,'' or a lawyer tells a layperson to put her signature to a contract that ends ''in witness thereof, we have hereunto put our hands and seals the day and year first above written,'' the non-lawyer must feel the awe and majesty of the law. He succumbs to its hegemony.

The hegemonic and legitimization explanations make some sense but they do not go far enough. Nobody today questions that people act pursuant to their domain assumptions, their concepts about and explanations for the world. Certainly, legalese mystifies the law and makes laypersons incapable of dealing with it. The hegemonic and legitimization explanations, however, sometimes imply that legalese exists *in order to create* hegemony, that, inevitably, "the law" created legalese. The law, however, does not *do* anything. People do things. Legalese gets used because particular groups find it necessary or convenient to use it. It may serve a hegemonic or legitimizing function, but the consequence (function) of a social fact does not explain its existence, except teleologically. Furthermore it is not inevitable that legalese will serve hegemonic or legitimizing functions. Theories of hegemony too easily make it seem as though the rules of law adopted its hegemonic characteristics (such as legalese) by processes both ineluctable and mystical. In this logic "law" like "society" are reified and lead to errors of factual reason.

An Institutionalist Explanation

The choice model earlier advanced holds that people act as they do by making choices within the constraints and resources of their environment as they perceive it. Linguistic behavior arises in the same way. Legalese arose for all the reasons that professional vocabularies flourish in other professions. Its continued use in statutes and private legislation, however, betrays a particular ideological bent.

Every professional field develops its own vocabularies out of necessity. Professionals communicate with other professionals about matters of shared concern. They develop a special vocabulary to express the concepts they need in their professional work. Physicists need words like *molecule* and *mass* and *velocity* to communicate to other physicists about matters of mutual interest and concern. So lawyers need words like *beneficiary* and *testator* and *certiorari*. Doctors and musicians and accountants and engineers each have their specialized vocabularies. All these get socialized into their professions through specialized education and training, a large part of which consists of learning to communicate in the appropriate specialized vocabulary.

That does not explain the noninstrumental words and dysfunctional style of legalese. Why the mystic *ss.*? Why *L.S.* and *to have and to hold* and *all that certain lot*, *tract or parcel of land* (with *lot, tract,* and *parcel* meaning the same thing)? All ingroups have their own style, reinforced by education. (Have you ever tried reading a scientific article on, say, microbiology?) In the same way, legal education and training perpetuate legalese. No doubt some lawyers imagine that, because they learned it in school, it must have value. Other lawyers talk to them in legalese, and they respond in it. We all believe that social institutions exist for a reason although often enough the reason arose *after* the institution, in order to explain it. Legalese becomes the "right" and "only" language in which to write statutes and private legislation. One of the authors conducts a legislative drafting service, in which students draft for Massachusetts legislators. The students learn to draft in relatively simple, common English. Not infrequently a lawyer-legislator insists that the student redraft the bill, adding more "legal" terms to make it sound "more legal."[51]

People write for an expected audience. That lawyers use legalese in writing documents of private legislation and statutes argues that they expect that lawyers and judges constitute their principal readership. Behind that proposition, however, lurks the ideology of law that we earlier characterized as legal liberalism. That ideology constituted the legal expression of laissez-faire. Law does not directly affect the behavior of private parties; the market does that. Before the dictate of marginal utility, all else must fail. Courts exist to decide disputes between parties. Case law, private legislation, and statutes in this view become the rules of the litigation game, not norms to guide behavior outside the judicial forum. Case law, private legislation, and statutes use legalese because their authors believed that only judges and lawyers need read them.

That does not explain why legalese continues in use. In a society of unequals, every norm (except perhaps very trivial ones) affects different people differently. To understand the consequences of a rule, we must examine how the rule advantages and disadvantages people in the society. Only with that information can we begin to understand the continued existence of particular rules. The consequences of a social fact, institution, social relationship, or common practice cannot explain the fact's existence but it will often give us a clue why those with the power to change it do not do so.

It is evident that the use of legalese has the direct consequence that only legally trained people learn how to read statutes. That does not say that only legally trained people know their content. People who use a law or a contract daily of course learn its content. Bureaucrats in government and in business know the laws that ought to control their behavior. They become experts not only in the subject matter involved, but in its legal environment. That becomes a principal source for the power of lawyers, and of all the people who use a law repeatedly, over laypersons without the expertise that arises either from knowledge of legalese or from experience with a particular area of law. Insurance companies defend their use of legalese in insurance policies; banks and appliance sellers in consumer credit sales; real estate brokers and agents in real estate contracts and leases.

Knowledge is power, and no place more than with respect to the law. The legal order constitutes the system of social control supported by the immense organization, resources, and ultimately the armed might of the state. Whoever can manipulate the legal order to his or her benefit has an enormous advantage against those who cannot. Lawyers play a central role in the legal order. Because they come in relatively small numbers compared to the total populace, they do not come inexpensively.

That becomes a principal consequence of the obscurity and inaccessibility of law brought about by the case system and legalese: lawyers become indispensable, and that inevitably enhances the power and control of those who have the money to pay for lawyers. The obscurity of the law ensures that result.

That result came about as a consequence of the ideology of liberal legalism. That ideology perceives the legal order as distinct from the social order, with the law coming into play only to resolve emergent disputes. It sees courts as the principal institutions of the legal order. Courts serve par excellence as the arena for lawyers and judges. Only they need to know and understand the law. The result is that liberal legalism leads to elitism in the legal order and to creating opportunities that can more readily be seized by those who already have power and privilege than by the ordinary person. The very form of the law, expressed in practically innumerable cases and statutes, written in a language that laypersons cannot comprehend, endowed lawyers with disproportionate power, and enhanced the power and privilege of the already powerful and privileged.

That an institution enhances the power and privilege of a social group does not demonstrate that that constituted the motive for creating the institution. The early lawyers who first used the mystic *ss.* on affidavits did not do so to enhance the power and privilege of lawyers in the twentieth century. That an institution has as a consequence the enhancing of the power and privilege of a particular group or stratum, however, does help to explain why that group does not try to change it. Why should lawyers or those who control legislation seek to change a language system that helps them to maintain power and privilege? Why should those who can afford lawyers try to change a system that gives them an advantage?

This explanation can conveniently be restated as a theory to explain the continued existence of the noninstrumental aspects of legalese:

1   The process of a problem-solving institution and its ruling ideas permits it to address some difficulties and not others, and permits only some outcomes and not others.

   a) Legislative and other legal drafting by lawyers, and the ideas that supported them, tended to produce statutes and documents of private legislation that spoke mainly to lawyers and judges in the language used by lawyers and judges.

2   An institution and its associated ideas tend to create interest groups that support them, always including their own functionaries.

   a) Lawyers formed an interest group that supported the use of legalese.
   b) Those with sufficient power and privilege to retain lawyers in the ordinary course of affairs formed an interest group that supported the use of legalese.

3   Those interest groups come in time to prize the institution and its associated ideas for their own sake, without regard to their instrumental uses or, sometimes, even their own self-interest, and devise explanations to justify that prizing.

   a) Lawyers came to prize legalese and devised the myth that precision in drafting required legalese as a justification for its use.

It seems possible to test part of this explanation empirically. In recent years, various legislatures have enacted statutes requiring simple language in insurance contracts (Massachusetts), contracts generally (New York), and consumer credit contracts (federal). Drafters can write these instruments in simple language without losing precision. Jeffrey Davis rewrote a typical consumer credit contract that contained 1100 words and tested at a 16th to 17th grade reading level (that is, beyond the ordinary college graduate level) into a 480-word contract that tested at the 11th to 12th grade level. Overall, that led to a 26 percent increase in the understanding of the contract of a sample of consumers.[52] The objection to the simplication of statutes cannot rest upon claimed impossibility of drafting them in simple language.

If our explanation serves, however, one would expect that opposition to the simple language statutes came from lawyers and from the large corporations that use documents of the sorts at issue. That, of course, constitutes precisely the hard core of the opposition to the bills. Opposition in fact came from exactly those sources.

New York's Sullivan Law provides that all consumer contracts and leases "must be written in non-technical language and in a clear and coherent manner using words with common and every day meanings."[53] The bill kicked up formidable opposition. The opponents included the New York State Bankers Association; the Association of the Bar of the City of New York's Committee on State Legislation; the New York State Council of Retail Merchants, Inc.; the New York State Bar Association's Business Law Committee; and the New York County Lawyers' Association's Special Committee on Consumer Agreements.[54] Massachusetts enacted a lay language insurance law.[55] The opposition there came from the same general groups: lawyers and the large firms that in fact have drafted most of the contracts at issue (in the Massachusetts case, the great insurance companies).

5.4 CONCLUSION

The language of the law arose because the structure of the legal order and the ideology that dominated most of its professional actors created lawyers as a specialized profession that created a specialized dialect, and then used that dialect to draft both private legislation and statutes. It had the direct consequence of bolstering the power of lawyers and other professional actors in the legal order, and of those with the sophistication and money to pay for lawyers. Thus did the language of the law reflect both the social milieu and the existing forces in it, and in turn change and re-create the social milieu in its own image.

The language of law reflects social relations, political and economic forms. The most important sources of law in the Anglo-American legal order are the legislatures and the appellate courts. We turn then to a consideration of these lawmaking institutions in the next chapters.

NOTES

1. L. Friedman, "Law and Its Language," *George Washington Law Review* 33(1964): 563-579.

2. T. Jefferson, *The Writings of Thomas Jefferson* ed. Lipscomb, issued under auspices of Thomas Jefferson Memorial Association of the U.S. (1903).

3. Executive Order #123044, 43 Federal Regulation 12, 661, 1979.

4. R. C. Wydick, "Plain English for Lawyers," *California Law Review* 66(1978): 727. Quoting Ralph Nader, "Gobbledygook," *Ladies Home Journal*, September 1977, p. 68.

5. D. Mellinkoff, *The Language of the Law* (Boston: Little, Brown & Co., 1963), p. 92.

6. *Ibid.*, p. 180.

7. H. C. Black, *Black's Law Dictionary* (St. Paul: West Publishing Co., 1979), p. 1090.

8. M. Jordan, "The Cryptic 'ss,' " *University of Boston Law Review* 8(1928): 117.

9. Sir E. Gower, quoted in Mellinkoff, *Language of the Law*, p. 291. See also J. B. White, *The Legal Imagination* (Boston: Little, Brown & Co., 1973).

10. B. Evans, *The Spool of Spooks and Other Nonsense* (New York: Alfred A. Knopf, 1954), p. 265.

11. Mellinkoff, *Language of the Law*, frontispiece.

12. H. Cairns, "The Language of Jurisprudence," quoted in R. N. Anshen, ed., *Language: An Inquiry into Its Meaning and Function* (New York: Harpers, 1957), pp. 232, 259.

13. *Wolfe* v. *Shelley*, 76 Eng. Rep. 1-9, 76 Eng. Rep. 206 (K.B. 1779-81).

14. D. Mellinkoff, see *American Journal of Law Forms* 12(1955): 619.

15. Uniform Commercial Code, sec. 9-108.

16. Administrative Procedure Act, 5 U.S.C.A. (1001 et seq.), 7 (c).

17. *The Preparation of Legislation: Report of a Committee appointed by the Lord President of the Council* (London, 1975), Cmnd. 6053, p. 27 (hereinafter, the *Renton Report*).

18. E. P. Thompson, *Whigs and Hunters: The Origin of the Black Act* (New York: Pantheon Books, 1976).

19. D. Hay, "Poaching and the Game Laws on Cannock Chase," in D. Hay *et al.*, eds., *Albion's Fatal Tree* (New York: Pantheon Books, 1975), pp. 189, 242.

20. C. Ilbert, *Legislative Methods and Forms* (Oxford: Oxford University Press, 1901), p. 46.

21. *Ibid.*, p. 58.

22. *Renton Report*.

23. A. Keon, "Drafting a Bill in Britain," *Harvard Journal of Legislation* 5(1968): 253.

24. *Ibid.*

25. R. Dale, *Legislative Drafting: A New Approach* (London: 1977), p. 115.

26. H. Thring, *Practical Legislation: The Composition and Language of Acts of Parliament and Bureau Documents*, 2nd ed. (Boston: Little, Brown & Co., 1902), pp. 4-5.

27. A useful bibliography appears in R. Dickerson, *Legislative Drafting* (Boston: Little, Brown & Co., 1954), p. 125.

28. Thring, *Practical Legislation*, p. 60.

29. *Ibid.*

30. *Ibid.*, p. 9.

31. F.A.R. Bennion, *Constitutional Law of Ghana* (London: Butterworth's, 1962), p. 111.

32. Thring, *Practical Legislation*, pp. 5-6.

33. *Ibid.*, p. 22.

34. See R. B. Ferguson, "Legal Ideology and Commercial Law Codes," *British Journal of Law and Society* 4(1977): 18.

35. *Ibid.*

36. A. V. Dicey, Introduction to *The Study of Law and the Constitution* (London: MacMillan, 1939), p. 188; see also F. S. von Hayek, *The Road to Serfdom* (Chicago: University of Chicago Press, 1944), p. 72.

37. S.R.O., 1946, No. 890. Quoted in C. K. Allen, *Law in the Making*, 6th ed. (London: Oxford University Press, 1958), p. 539.

38. 50 Congressional Record 2376 (1913). Quoted in F. P. Lee, "The Office of Legislative Counsel," *Columbia Law Review* 20(1967): 381, 384.

39. *Ibid.*, pp. 381-384.

40. J. B. Mooke, "Forward to the Office of the Legislative Counsel," *Columbia Law Review* 29(1929): 379.

41. William F. Ogburn, *Social Change With Respect to Culture and Original Nature* (New York: Viking Press, 1922), p. 201.

42. William F. Ogburn, *On Culture and Social Change* (Chicago: University of Chicago Press, 1964), p. 89.

43. Y. Dror, "Government Decision Making: Muddling Through," *Public Administration Review* 24(1964): 154.

44. Ogburn, *Social Change,* p. 201.

45. C. Wright Mills and H. H. Gerth, *From Max Weber: Essays in Sociological Theory* (New York: Oxford University Press, 1946).

46. *Ibid.* See also Gerald Turkel, "Rational Law and Boundary Maintenance," *Law and Society Review* 15(1980-81): 41-77.

47. Maureen Cain, "Gramsci, the State and the Place of Law" in David Sugarman, ed., *Legality, Ideology and the State* (London: Academic Press, 1982).

48. Antonio Gramsci, *Letters from Prison* (New York: Harper and Row, 1973), p. 129.

49. Antonio Gramsci, *Selections from the Prison Notebooks* (London: Lawrence and Wisehurt, 1971), p. 245.

50. A.W. Gouldner, *The Coming Crisis of Western Sociology* (New York: Avon Books, 1970).

51. Friedman, "Law and Its Language, p. 563.

52. J. Davis, "Protecting Consumers from Over Disclosure and Gobbledygook: An Empirical Look at the Simplification of Consumer Contracts," *Virginia Law Review* 63(1977): 841.

53. N.Y. Gen. Oblig. Law Sec. 5-701 (b) (1), McKinney supp. 1977.

54. 23 N.Y.L.S.L. Rev. 824: Note "The Plain English Law: Let the Buyer Beware."

55. 1977 Mass. Acts Ch. 801 Sec. 1 M.G.L.A. Ch. 175 Sec. 2B.

6

Lawmaking: the dialectics of problem-solving

If we are to understand law and the legal order, our model must account not only for the development of laws affecting the propertied and corporations (see Chapter 4) but also for laws directed toward the poor and the workers. We must not only account for why the legal profession obscures and mystifies law through legalese (see Chapter 5) we must also understand the way law responds to the problematics of a particular historical era.

There are literally thousands of laws enacted each year. In the United States with fifty state legislatures and the federal government passing laws, and with the enactment of thousands of municipal and county ordinances, the sheer magnitude of law is overwhelming. In addition, there are court decisions at the state and federal level which often constitute the creation of new laws as well. Other nations, such as most European countries and Scandinavia, where the lawmaking function is more centralized, do not produce quite the magnitude of new law each year that the United States does, but it is nonetheless a very prolific enterprise, this business of making law.

It is not surprising, then, that attempts to generalize about the processes that lead to the creation of law should be wanting. Some laws are clearly passed for the specific interest of an individual; others emerge out of lobbying by groups representing substantial portions of the population; yet others, perhaps the majority, are no more than an expression of the views and interests of legislative committees.

Despite this, however, there remains the need for generalization to aid understanding. Fortunately, we are not hopelessly mired in an endless number of laws, for as it happens not all laws are equally significant. In fact, most of the bills and statutes passed by legislatures are concerned with tinkering and diddling with existing law. What we should thus be concerned with is not the mountain of minutia produced as law but the critical events: the points at which laws are produced that provide a new approach to a problem, a basic revision of the existing relationships between state, polity, government, and fundamental institutions; new innovations in the conception of legal contracts, or the rights of children vis-à-vis parents or of women at work. These laws are the ones that constitute the important turning points in the historical process and are therefore the ones about which we should be concerned to develop adequate sociological theory.

Most cases, to be sure, are merely cumulative in their effect, moving in well-beaten paths, with some inevitable deviation but by and large within the lines laid down. Occasionally, however, comes a case of tremendous importance.[1]

These are the cases which "strike out in a new direction."

6.1 EXPLAINING THE CREATION OF LAW

The consensual and conflict theories earlier outlined each gave birth in the 1960s to an offspring: the pluralist theory (from the consensus perspective) and the ruling class theory (from the conflict perspective). Each of these theories has in turn given way to more sophisticated explanations; it will nonetheless help to keep developments in the study of law and society in perspective if we review briefly the pluralist and instrumental Marxist theories.

Lawrence Friedman expresses an eclectic pluralist view of the relationship between ideology and economic structures, but his emphasis in the end is on the importance of consensually held values rather than economic relations as the determinant of law. He articulates the pluralist position that law reflects a struggle of competing interest groups, some of whom are more powerful than others: "What makes law, then, is not 'public opinion' in the abstract, but public opinion in the sense of exerted social force."[2] Friedman goes on to recognize that some groups (and social classes) will be more successful in exerting social force to create law than will other groups. A more naive pluralist view simply argues that the world is composed of competing interest groups which are equal before the law. Friedman at least recognizes differentials in power.

The greatest problem with the pluralist position is how little it tells us about the creation of law; if all we can say is that those who will succeed are those who succeed, we know nothing. How does one know whether or not one interest group is more powerful than another? The only measure Friedman suggests is whether or not they succeed in getting their chosen law enacted. Friedman recognizes this tautological aspect of his theory but is unable to suggest a way out of the dilemma. In the end even a sophisticated rendering of consensus theory ends in tautology.

The instrumental Marxist (or ruling class) theory borne of the conflict paradigm does not fare much better. The instrumental Marxist theory is a stepchild of the classic statement from Marx that "in every era the ruling ideas are the ideas of the ruling class."[3]

There is an abundance of research on law creation which bears on this issue. Gabriel Kolko, in a classic study of the meat-packing industry, demonstrated an important fact: law which appears to conflict with ruling class interests may in fact be a clever device for maintaining those interests.[4] Kolko studied the legislative history of the law requiring federal inspection of the slaughter of animals and the preparation of meat for sale. The industry had been attacked in the press and books for its unsanitary practices and for the appalling state of working conditions for its employees. The large meat-packing firms were suffering financially in competition with smaller firms which were able to undersell them. The entire industry engaged in incredibly unsanitary processing practices that resulted in widespread illness. The larger firms were also being hurt by the fact that the often unhealthy meat sold abroad was reducing the demand in Europe for American meat products. A solution to both problems for the large corporations was legislation creating government inspection of meat processing. This would, of course, raise the cost of producing the meat but for the large firms the increased cost would be minimal as it could spread over a large output. For the small firms, however, the increased cost would destroy their competitive advantage. Simultaneously, meat-inspection laws would improve the health qualities and thereby enable American manufacturers to compete favorably for European markets. Realizing this, the large meat-packers lobbied for federal regulations to control the industry. The government responded to these pressures by passing laws making it a crime to produce meat under unsanitary conditions. The legislation thus aided the large meat-packers in their competition with smaller firms. Upton Sinclair, who inadvertently popularized the unsanitary conditions in the meat-packing industry (he was mainly concerned with working conditions when he wrote in 1904 but it was sanitation that became the issue), accurately described both the reason for passing and the effects of the meat-packing regulations:

The Federal inspection of meat was, historically, established at the packer's request; . . . it is maintained and paid for by the people of the United States for the benefit of the packers; . . . men wearing the blue uniforms and brass buttons of the United States service are employed for the purpose of certifying to the nations of the civilized world that all the diseased and tainted meat which happens to come into existence in the United States of America is carefully sifted out and consumed by the American people.[5]

During the legislative debates establishing federal inspection of meat, the large meat-packers were consulted and helped in drawing up the bills. Samuel H. Cowan, the lawyer for the National Livestock Association, was asked to write a bill acceptable to the packers, which he did. When President Roosevelt criticized the bill, Senator Wadsworth responded: "I told you on Wednesday night when I submitted the bill to you, that the packers insisted before our committee on having a rigid inspecting law passed. Their life depends on it. They placed no obstacle in our way."[6]

When the bill was finally passed and the head of the Department of Agriculture announced to a gathering of the meat-packers his department's intention to enforce the new laws strictly and rigidly, he was greeted with a round of applause from the industry. For the new laws would, as George Perkins wrote to J. P. Morgan, "be of very great advantage . . . as it will practically give [the meat-packers] a government certificate for their goods."[7] At the time, the legislation was heralded as a triumph for "the people" when in fact it was a triumph for monopoly capital.

The pluralist and ruling class theories are equally untenable as an explanation for these events. Pluralist theory suggests only that the large meat-packers were the "organizer interest" who succeeded. But the theory cannot tell us except tautologically why they succeeded or why the interests of the small meat-packers failed.* Ruling class theory suggests the large meat-packers should succeed but the fact that the small meat-packers who lost are also part of the ruling class (as owners of the means of production) suggests an important dimension to the struggle of lawmaking that is obscured by ruling class theory: namely, that the ruling class is often divided in its interests. A valuable theory must inform us of how the process works when ruling class consensus is lacking as well as when it prevails.

The history of legislation is replete with examples of members of a divided ruling class quite openly fighting one another for favorable legislation. Calavita's research on the history of immigration laws in the United States is a good illustration.[8]

In the 1800s the burgeoning Industrial Revolution in the United States produced a demand for labor much greater than was available in the population of the nation. Cheap labor is most prevalent when there is an abundance of labor; when there are more jobs than there are people looking for work, the work force's power vis-à-vis employer's increases, demands for higher wages and improved work conditions have a greater likelihood of success, and the amount of the surplus produce produced by labor that the owners can expropriate declines. One solution to a labor shortage problem, from the point of view of owners, is to allow immigration from countries where there is a labor surplus. During the 1800s U.S. immigration laws clearly reflected the state's adaptation of this solution. There is, however, a contradiction here: if the influx of

---

* There is an important logical parallel here with Darwin's evolutionary theory. Darwin's central postulate that "the species that survives is the most fit" becomes a useless tautology if "fitness" is defined in terms of survival. What saves Darwinian theory from this scientifically indefensible error is that "fitness" is defined independently of "survival," thus providing a testable, scientifically useful theory. By the same token, if pluralist theory defined organized interest groups' likelihood of success independent of the passage of their sought-after legislation, then the theory would not be tautological; it would be empirically false, as we shall see in the following pages.

labor grows beyond the numbers that can be easily integrated into the labor force there is a potential for labor unrest as workers band together to demand more jobs. In the case of U.S. history there was also the fact that workers from Europe brought with them a conscious realization that the interests of workers and owners were inherently in opposition to one another; they brought with them a history of involvement in socialist and communist politics. Thus, as the labor market was gradually filled and the initial phase of industrialization subsided a large unemployed urban labor force was left behind. Militant labor movements and open rebellion were one of the consequences. Some legislators and some businessmen saw a solution to the unrest and rebellion in laws restricting immigration. Some industries, however, continued to depend on a large surplus labor force for maximum profits. Thus while the bankers and clothing manufacturers sought restrictions on immigration, the steel industry sought to keep immigration policies open. Eventually the steel industry lost and in 1921 the nation's first general law restricting immigration was passed.

Karl Klare's research on labor law provides another example. He notes that the National Labor Relations (Wagner) Act of 1934 "was perhaps the most radical piece of legislation ever enacted by the United States Congress."[9] He goes on to point out that this law was

enacted in the wake of the great strikes of 1934, at an unusually tense and fluid historical moment, it represented, in the words of one historian, "an almost unbelievable capitulation by the government. . . ." A small number of the most sophisticated representatives of business favored passage of the Act on the theory that some such measure was essential to preserve the social order and to forestall developments toward even more radical change. Nonetheless most employers, large and small, bitterly opposed passage of the Act.[10]

But of course the mere passage of the act by the legislature did not therefore change the legal order nor mean that the law would necessarily be effective.

The Wagner Act did not fully become "the law" when Congress passed it in 1935, or even when the Supreme Court ruled it constitutional in 1937. . . . The Act "became law" only when employers were forced to obey its command by the imaginative, courageous, and concerted efforts of countless unheralded workers.[11]

Can these laws be explained by ruling class theory? They can, of course, if one argues that the "real interests" of the ruling class were served. If the only evidence for this claim is that the laws were passed, then the explanation is a tautology: the event is explained by the existence of the event. Some ruling class theorists argue, however, that the "real" interests of the ruling class are served by these laws because they "maintain the system."[12] In capitalist societies laws that appear to conflict with ruling class interests in fact legitimize the existing class relations, reduce class conflict, and thereby contribute in the long run to the maintenance of the political economy.

Like the pluralist theory, there is in this argument the danger of tautology. So long as the political and economic system survives, by this logic, the law must be serving ruling class interests. Not only is such a theory nonfalsifiable it begs the very question it should seek to answer, namely, how does law change? Feudal law ''supported'' the feudal political economy until it changed. Feudal law led to bourgeois law that supported capitalists in their struggle against feudalism.[13] English and American laws supporting the right of capitalists to demand sixteen-hour work days at low wages supported early capitalist economies, but eventually changed. Why did they change? It tells us very little to say simply that these laws changed because it was ''in the interests of the ruling class.''

On the other hand, to argue that the ruling class theory is totally inapplicable to the legal process is to throw out the baby with the bath water. Examples of ruling class intervention in and control of the legal order abound: the asbestos industry attorneys recently drafted a piece of legislation which would make it illegal for employees to sue their employers or trade unions for damages resulting from illnesses caused by working in asbestos—and this industry, infamous for health hazards to workers, is expected to claim at least 400 thousand lives in the next twenty years; lawyers employed by the pharmaceutical industry play a major role in drafting drug legislation; representatives of the largest meat-packing firms in the nation controlled the legislation establishing meat inspection standards for the industry; the banking industry writes legislation ostensibly controlling banks, the aerospace industry participates in legislation settting safety standards for airplanes, etc.[14] That there is ruling class interest and influence in vast areas of law cannot be denied. That it is the only force responsible for law creation or law implementation, however, is erroneous. What is called for is not a theory that argues either for total control by the ruling class or for no control at all, but one that recognizes both the strength and the limitations of ruling class influence on the legal order.

The Dialectics of Lawmaking

An alternative model that avoids the tautological tendencies of pluralist and ruling class theory employs the logic of the dialectic: the theory that every society, nation, economic system, and historical period contain within them certain contradictory elements which are the moving force behind social changes—including the creation of law. The dialectic stresses what we have emphasized throughout: that people, not ''systems,'' ''societies,'' or ''the legal order,'' but people make laws, people acting in the face of extant resources and constraints.

The traditional distinction in Marxist theory between the ''base'' and ''superstructure'' is a useful metaphor for it provides a guide for where to begin analysis: one should begin with the most basic problem faced by human beings, that of organizing work to the end of accumulating sufficient food and shelter for survival and, if there is a surplus produced, how it will be distributed.[15] The dialectic, however, insists that not only does the base ineluctably constrain the social relations contained in the superstructure, but the social relations contained in the superstructure affect the choices poeple make with respect to the base:

A land reform law that restricts the size of a holding to ten acres forms part of the superstructure, yet it sharply constrains behavior with respect to the mode of production. So do laws prohibiting any individual from having more than seven employees [as in Yugoslavia], giving benefits of various sorts to cooperatives or state-owned enterprises, making tax concessions to private investment, or prohibiting trade union activity.[16]

An excellent recent study of California law makes the point cogently.[17] When water was diverted from the Colorado River to the Colorado Desert of California it changed a desert into one of the most fertile agricultural regions of the world, a region aptly renamed the "Imperial Valley." In the initial legislation, hard fought for and lobbied for by land speculators from California, there was a provision that no farm in excess of 160 acres had water rights. Over the years since the original legislation the average farm size in the Imperial Valley steadily increased as agribusiness replaced farming to the point where in 1979 the average acreage per farm in the valley was 700 acres. Clearly most of the farms in the area were not legally entitled to use the water on which the entire enterprise depended. Years of lawsuits tried to enforce the 160-acre maximum to no avail. The state, the courts, and local practice coalesced to give large landowners and monopoly capital agribusinesses water for as many acres as they could buy, beg, borrow, or steal—all in clear and open violation of the law. Protests and lawsuits against the large landowners forced a change: not in the use of water by farms over 160 acres but in the law. Today, as a result of the effort to restrict the power of large landowners in the Imperial Valley, the law has changed to allow owners of large farms access to water. Monopolies continue to prosper in agriculture as they do in oil, automobiles, and banking.

The history of racist laws in pre-Civil War America is a history of contradictions and people's struggles against them. To legitimize slavery as an institution, white Americans defined people with black skin as nonhuman. They were not supposed to possess souls, human intelligence, or the capacity for civilized conduct. On the other hand, the institution of slavery demanded that black people as well as white people perform human tasks: building shelter, forming communities, raising children, working. Without work, shelter, and procreation the slave population was of no economic value. The work done was not the work nonhumans could do or there would have been no necessity for slaves. This contradiction, as Genovese has brilliantly pointed out, led to the creation of laws trying to make logical sense out of what was inherently illogical.[18] Slaves could not testify against whites, even if the whites were accused of formenting revolution among the slaves, because slaves were not human and only human beings had the right to appear as witnesses in court. Thus we have the bizarre example of an abolitionist white being set free in a trial because the only witnesses who could testify that he had incited the slaves on a plantation to rebel were the slaves themselves, who because they were not "human" could not testify in court.

A similar set of contradictions characterizes law and the legal order with respect to women. Women, like slaves, were denied the vote and the right to work. The U.S. Supreme Court in 1867 held that a woman who had successfully completed law school and passed the bar in Illinois had no right to practice law. The Court's opinion was as follows:

The claim that [under the Fourteenth Amendment of the Constitution] the statute law of Illinois . . . can no longer be set up as a barrier against the right of females to pursue any lawful employment for a livelihood (the practice of law included), assumes that it is one of the privileges and immunities of women as citizens to engage in any and every profession, occupation, or employment in civil life. It certainly cannot be affirmed, as an historical fact, that this has ever been established as one of the fundamental privileges and immunities of the sex. On the contrary, the civil law, as well as nature herself, has always recognized a wide difference in the respective spheres and destinies of man and woman. Man is, or should be, woman's protector and defender. The natural and proper timidity and delicacy which belongs to the female sex evidently unfits it for many of the occupations of civil life. . . .

It is true that many women are unmarried and not affected by any of the duties, complications, and incapacities arising out of the married state, but these are exceptions to the general rule. The paramount destiny and mission of women are to fulfill the noble and benign offices of wife and mother. This is the law of the Creator. And the rules of civil society must be adapted to the general constitution of things, and cannot be based upon exceptional cases.[19]

Garfinkle, Lefcourt, and Schulder point out:

Not only were women totally excluded from the practice of law as lawyers until the present century, but they were also excluded from the whole legal apparatus—as judges, jurors, and litigants—by the same rationale. The rule of common law was that juries consisted of "twelve good men." One exception was made: when a pregnant woman faced execution, a jury of twelve women was convened to decide whether she should be executed before or after giving birth to her child.[20]

In 1869 Sophia Jex-Blake and six other women sought admission to medical school at the University of Edinburgh. In the midst of great controversy, threats of physical harm, and concerted opposition by male professors and students the seven women were allowed to attend segregated classes, for awhile. The university refused, however, to award the chemistry prize to the student with the highest marks, as was traditionally the case, because that year the student with the highest marks was a woman. The controversy grew so heated that the university ultimately reneged on its willingness to allow the women to attend. The women went to court for satisfaction. They received none. The court ruled that the university had the right to discriminate against women even though they could not discriminate against people because of their religion or race.[21]

Sexism at Edinburgh was not an isolated event. Women in the 1800s could not vote, attend law school, be admitted to practice law, serve in Parliament or city councils. By law women were not considered "persons" and therefore were not eligible for or covered by laws applied to "persons"—only men were people in England in the 1800s so far as the law was concerned.

That this changed is well recognized. What is not so well recognized is that it changed when and only when women violently and consistently opposed the oppression and exploitation institutionalized in the law. The view that the law gradually changed as customs and beliefs changed, or that the law became more fair and tolerant

　　　　LAWMAKING: THE DIALECTICS OF PROBLEM-SOLVING

as the logic of a democratic and free society for all slowly worked its magic through legal reasoning, is simply mythical. It was the consequence of women willing to undergo humiliation, torment, imprisonment, and even death in the struggle for equality in law and in society that wrought what changes have occurred. In the 1800s as in the 1900s the institutions perpetuated themselves with their built-in biases and blatant sexism so long as they were not challenged. Even when challenged the changes were slow and piecemeal.

One hundred and fifty years of women's struggle for equality in law have brought changes but not equality. One authority estimates that there are in the United States today over 800 pieces of blatantly sex discriminatory laws currently on the statute books: in Wisconsin a wife can be disinherited by her husband; in most states women cannot co-sign for a loan but their husbands can even though technically the property is "communal"; in some states a man can still legally kill his wife if he catches her having sexual relations with another man; in rape cases courts allow as admissible evidence the woman's "reputation"—a woman with prior sexual experience is less likely to be believed if she claims she was raped; in most of the United States it is not a crime for a man to rape his wife or a woman with whom he is living.[22] Delaware law, for example, provides explicitly: "It is not rape for a man to have sexual intercourse with his wife without her consent. It is not rape for a man to force intercourse with a woman who is living with him as his wife."[23] And in rape cases, "evidence of good reputation as well as bad, is admissible."[24] In England a husband cannot be charged with rape of his wife though he may be charged with assault.[25] A man who kills his wife for adultery stands a reasonably good chance of being excused his "understandable" reaction; a woman committing the same act under the same circumstances stands a good chance of being convicted of murder. A black man raping a white woman is much more likely to be convicted of murder and executed than a white man accused of raping a black woman. Women continue to be seen in law and in practice as "property" to be owned and controlled by men.[26] As recently as 1961 the U.S. Supreme Court denied a woman's appeal from conviction by an all-male jury:

At the core of appellant's argument is the claim that the nature of the crime of which she was convicted peculiarly demanded the inclusion of persons of her own sex on the jury. She was charged with killing her husband by assaulting him with a baseball bat. . . . The affair occurred in the context of a marital upheaval involving, among other things, the suspected infidelity of appellant's husband, and culminating in the final rejection of his wife's efforts at reconciliation. It is claimed, in substance, that women jurors would have been more understanding or compassionate than men in assessing the quality of appellant's act and her defense.[27]

Women's rights movements and struggles effectively change the law. Changing the law, however, does not guarantee changing patterns of social relations. The superstructure's effect on the base requires more than changing statutes and appellate court decisions. In 1954 the U.S. Supreme Court decided in *Brown* v. *Board of Education* that segregated schooling was illegal. Since 1954, as David Freeman shows, the most measurable impact of the decision has been as a source of legitimacy for

continued racial discrimination in schooling.[28] Similarly, changes in criminal procedure demanded by Supreme Court decisions from Miranda to Gideon to Gault have
often had little effect on actual practice.

Schematically we can summarize the theoretical argument consistent with these
cases of lawmaking as shown in Fig. 6.1.

In classical Marxist theories the most basic contradiction under a capitalist
economic system is between capital and labor, as we pointed out earlier. If the workers
and capitalists both persistently and consistently pursue their own interests as defined
by the logic of capitalism then the relationship between workers and capitalists, indeed
the entire system of production, will eventually be destroyed. This contradiction, and
others inherent in any historical period, produce, in our schema, a wide range of
dilemmas and conflicts. The attempt by workers to organize and demand higher wages
(the consequence of which was reflected legally in the Wagner Act, as discussed
above), better working conditions, and tenure of employment is a result of the basic
contradiction. The attempt by owners to resist these demands creates conflicts. The
dilemma for capital, the state, and the government is how to resolve the conflicts: how
to maintain the capitalist system without fomenting a revolution or destroying capital's
right to ownership and control.

Note that it is the conflicts that create the dilemmas; and it is the conflicts toward
which state intervention is directed. Rarely, except in revolutionary circumstances, are
the basic contradictions addressed. The contradictions create conflicts and dilemmas
which people try to resolve. In the resolution of conflicts and dilemmas other
contradictions are revealed and created, other conflicts generated, and a multitude of
dilemmas and struggles ensured.

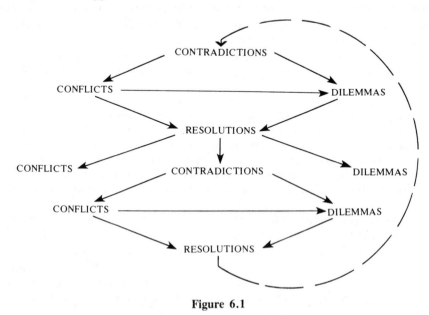

Figure 6.1

LAWMAKING: THE DIALECTICS OF PROBLEM-SOLVING

We have touched on sexist and racist legislation, conflicts, dilemmas, and attempted resolutions thereof in the preceding section. Let us turn now to some more specific illustrations of legislation designed to resolve conflicts created by contradictions in the extant political economy of a particular historical period.

The Special Areas Acts in Britain

Between 1934-37 Great Britain passed a series of acts designed to alleviate the economic crisis experienced throughout the capitalist world during the Great Depression. The legislation consisted of three separate enactments: the Special Areas (Development and Improvement) Act of 1934; the Special Areas Reconstruction (Agreement) Act of 1936; and the Special Areas (Amendment) Act of 1937.

The basic contradiction to which these laws were a response is this: under capitalism it is part of the logic and ideology of the system that industry (and therefore employment opportunities) will develop in those areas of the country which provide the best opportunities for industrial and economic expansion. There is also the belief that allowing private entrepreneurs the freedom to locate industries and business wherever they wish will in the long run provide the best economic growth and highest possible standard of living for the workers. Unfortunately this does not always happen. Capitalism is subject to economic crises (slumps and peaks) which follow from certain fundamental features (and contradictions) of capitalist economic forms. As a result it will happen from time to time (and to some extent at all times) that there are large parts of any capitalist country which suffer from periodic or permanent economic depression.

During times of general economic recession the number of depressed areas as well as the extent to which these areas suffer from unemployment will be vastly increased. This creates conflicts and dilemmas. The very manifestation of the conflict will be labor unrest, sometimes violence, and an attendant growth of militant and radical political movements. The dilemma for the state and the government is how to resolve these conflicts while protecting the capitalist system. Needless to say, how to resolve the basic contradictions will *not* be part of the discussion. The discussion will focus instead on the wisdom of intervening to counteract what is a "natural consequence" of the capitalist economic system and if intervention is to take place what form it should have.

During the 1930s in Great Britain (and elsewhere) this was precisely what happened. The economy generally declined precipitously and large geographical areas suffered inordinately high rates of unemployment and economic stagnation. Workers became increasingly vocal in demanding state intervention to reduce the high rate of unemployment. Members of Parliament elected from these constituencies were pressed to call for national initiatives to alleviate the growing crisis. At first the response of the government (that is, the elected officials and their appointees) was, to use a politically popularized phrase from several generations later, "to tough it out": "The initial reaction to the crisis was to pursue strict financial orthodoxy, that is, balanced budgets and reduced government expenditure. . . ."[29]

The ideology of capitalism, the logic of this economic form, precluded intervention by the state. Alan Page quotes Lord Eustace Percy's pertinent remark:

Because I saw the facts, I did take a somewhat defeatist view of the possible solutions to the problem. There were basically only two possible solutions: new industry or migration. Not that I was alone in my defeatism. It is difficult to realize how slowly their prewar predecessors of all political complexions rid themselves of the assumption that the movements of industry must necessarily be determined by solid economic motives and the "artificial attraction" of new industries to depressed areas must therefore run counter to fundamental laws.[30]

Another government spokesperson echoed this sentiment and even suggested that intervention ran counter to the laws of nature:

It is quite clear that the normal economic process which we have learned to expect has been working, and that, as labor is relieved by the easier production of, and reduced demand for, the commoner necessities of life, so that labor has been absorbed by the more intricate requirements of a more advanced civilization. . . . Although, of course, that change-over may create, and does create, in certain areas and in certain industries, very grave problems and very heavy stresses, yet I do not think one is entitled to regard it as an unhealthy symptom of a developing civilization; and I am sure it would be not only unwise but impossible, for any government to attempt to fight against an economic tide of that kind and try to standardize at any time the prosperity of this or that industry.[31]

The high sounding oratory and the call, waiting for the inexorable wisdom of capitalist development to fulfill the promise of inevitable progress, did not unfortunately alter the course of history. Nor did the oratory solve the contradictions nor diminish the conflicts. "The demands that something be done steadily increased throughout 1933 and into the early months of 1934." The *London Times* ran several articles and reported a survey which said in part: "There are parts of Durham whre one feels strongly, sometimes angrily, that London still has no conception of the troubles that affect the industrial North."[32]

The increasing disaffection and criticism made some sort of action by government imperative. A committee was established which, after considerable floundering, rendered a report. On October 24, 1934, the Interim Report of the Committee was approved by cabinet. Then came the attempt to use the legislation principally for its symbolic value: "Subsequent deliberations were entirely devoted to the public presentation of the proposals, it being agreed that the experimental nature of the measures should be emphasized to preclude their extension to other areas [other than those carefully delimited in the report] which regarded themselves as depressed."[33] Page summarizes the results of his study in a way that catches quite nicely the fit between his research findings and the general model of contradictions-conflicts-dilemmas-resolutions that we are proposing:

In the subsequent process of conflict and amendment the legislation and its meaning emerged from the interactional sequence between the demands of the economy, the proponents of change and the actions of politicians and bureaucrats. Its meaning was thus an emergent property of this political process. What had been originally viewed in terms of existing norms and institutions, became successively reconceptualized as, a problem of severe localized unemployment and depressed areas, a problem of the adequacy of legislative intervention and finally, with the setting up in 1937 of a Royal Commission on the Distribution of the Industrial Population, as one of the locations of industry.[34]

We see quite clearly the workings of the law creation process as an effort to resolve conflicts and dilemmas posed by fundamental contradictions of the economy being manifested, in extreme form, by the normal workings of economic change. The response to the conflicts is both ideological (at first resistance, then rationalization for intervention) and structural (involving changing economic patterns and modification of heretofore predominant economic policy). Finally, Page also considers in his analysis the end product of this process, i.e., the creation of new conflicts reflecting other contradictions revealed by the attempted resolution:

The Act of 1934 was in many ways to become the vehicle for the promotion of the cause of the depressed areas through the exposure of its inadequacies rather than, as had been intended, the means to their political suppression.[35]

It may help to grasp the argument if we reiterate briefly why the model we are proposing stands as a solution to the shortcomings of the major alternative of law creation.

Taking the creation of the Special Areas Acts in Britain as our data, how might we argue that consensus theory accounted for this legislative innovation? Presumably the argument would have to be made that it was the general ideology of the people which was the moving force behind the creation of these laws. The problem, of course, is that as we have seen the prevailing ideology of at least a majority of the legislators was diametrically opposed to such legislation. It was antithetical to the logic, ideology, and belief in capitalism to attempt to create industry in depressed areas. It was in fact only in the context of ''political realism,'' which is to say in view of the persisting conflicts and threats to the established political (and perhaps economic) order, that legislation was effectively passed.

Nor does the theory that the law inevitably reflects the interests of the ruling class fare much better. Clearly the ideology and the perceived interests of the ruling class were hostile to the government's intervention in the location of industry. One could argue, of course, that this view was shortsighted; that unless something drastic was done the entire ruling class might have been overthrown by a revolution and therefore that the new laws were part of a stopgap measure which preserved the ruling class with the least amount of sacrifice. Such a view is untenable logically because it is tautological and teleological. It is tautological because *any* solution to a problem can be interpreted as protecting ruling class interests if the ruling class survives the change. It is teleological because it attributes some kind of rationality to the system that is independent of the people making decisions. It is more accurate, and better scientific theory, to see the relationship between the larger social, economic, and political forces and the decisions being made by those who shape and create the legislation. This is what is intended by our model.

It may also be pertinent at this juncture to point out the extent to which other less general theories fit in with and round out the model being proposed. As we have seen from the analysis of the Special Areas Acts, to a very real extent the passage of these acts was a symbolic gesture consciously designed to placate a critical force which could not be ignored. This reflects what Edelman has called "the symbolic use of politics" and what Gusfield found as a crucial factor in the creation of prohibition laws.[36] It would be a mistake, however, to argue that these laws were *only* symbolic or that all laws are created for purely symbolic purposes. The intention of the legislators and the presumed effect of the legislation are rarely carried forth in a unilateral way between the formulation of law and its implementation; but it would be erroneous to suppose for that reason that the entire process is merely symbolic. It has symbolic elements and its symbolic character should not be overlooked any more than its legitimating function (that is, the extent to which it helps to legitimize the existence of the entire system) can be ignored. But these functions alone cannot explain the creation of law. The social forces that produce law are a more dynamic process than can be tucked away easily into a simplistic causal relationship such as is assumed by theories that focus solely on the symbolic quality of laws.

Pollution and Law

In recent years we have witnessed a rapid growth in the passage of public law relating to the environment and to consumer protection. For the most part processes by which these laws have developed have not been the subject of systematic attention. One exception to this void, however, is the recent study of pollution laws conducted by Neil Gunningham. This area of legislation is particularly pertinent for our inquiry because it highlights the conflicts between public interest representatives (what Becker called "moral entrepreneurs") and those who own the industries which are largely responsible for the pollution.

Gunningham begins by pointing out the growth in recent years of concern over pollution. He singles out the publication of Rachel Carson's *Silent Spring* and the extent to which the media generally have brought the problem of pollution to public attention. But, he adds, "to explain the growth of environmental concern and the demand for legislation is not necessarily to explain the emergence of legislation. Only some legislative campaigns are successful, others fail."[37] The author goes on to point out that, although public awareness about pollution problems increased in the years preceding passage of new laws, there was certainly nothing approaching consensus. "At one extreme are those who regard pollution as a minor problem and who deny that the environment is being threatened, while at the other, it is suggested that over-population, exploitation of natural resources and pollution will cause eco-catastrophe if present policies are not drastically amended."[38]

In his search for a plausible explanation for the emergence of pollution laws Gunningham also dismisses a simplistic "class conflict" explanation. He argues that the "working class" has not been particularly active or well organized in the campaign for antipollution laws. He acknowledges, however, that the most important groups opposing pollution control are "capitalists with strong economic interests in maintaining the status quo."[39] Gunningham also notes that some government agencies (bureaucracies) develop a vested interest in opposing certain forms of environmental laws and come out strongly trying to influence legislation:

In the pollution campaign, the clearest example of an agency engaged in status politics is the U.S. Department of Agriculture (U.S.D.A.) whose irresponsible attitude towards pesticides has been severely criticized. Why U.S.D.A. went overboard on new pesticides can be understood within an organization perspective. The department found its power and responsibilities diminishing in comparison with several other departments. Graham notes how the twentieth century has reached the farm, and the successful farmer-businessman, with his vast acreage, college degree and modern machinery was less dependent on the U.S.D.A. than the poorly educated struggling farmer with his scanty crop a decade or two earlier.[40]

Under these circumstances the U.S.D.A. found itself

in the tradition of all bureaucracies which feel their position threatened by shrinking responsibilities. The department's impulse to fabricate programs which gave it the illusion of "business" has been especially apparent . . . in the business of promoting pesticides, springing to arms at the first whisper of a pest.[41]

The position taken by the U.S.D.A. and the negative reflex action of capitalist owners to any pollution legislation were, however, shortsighted for they failed to realize a fundamental contradiction between industrialization and the quality of the environment. Though short-term profits will be maximized by spewing forth industrial waste into rivers and oceans, "it has become apparent with dramatic suddenness that, at the present more or less uncontrolled rate of industrial and urban development, the major rivers and lakes of the country will become incapable of supporting marine life and unsuitable for humans."[42] In the long run it is apparent that the maximization of profits by ignoring environmental pollution will not be in the interests of capital.

Furthermore one of the most effective long-term profit maximization guarantees is the development of a monopoly. The law has often been used as a subtle means of increasing monopoly by creating law which gives an advantage to the largest firms in a particular industry. Thus the meat inspection laws in the United States were lobbied for and praised by large meat processing firms precisely because the added expense of meat inspection meant that the larger firms could more easily distribute the added expenses with a minimal loss of immediate profits; smaller firms would be forced out of business, thus increasing monopoly for the larger companies.

The same process is apparent vis-à-vis pollution legislation. "In 1956 when the Clean Air Act was passed, industry was predominantly hostile to effective antipollution legislation inasmuch as this represented increased costs without any direct dividend . . .''[43] However, by 1968 when another Clean Air Act was passed this met with little industry opposition.[44]

Gunningham explains this shift as occurring in part because of the change in the importance of management as contrasted with owner control over major corporations in the modern capitalist countries. More importantly, however, Gunningham observes: ''Thus, where a firm can afford to implement pollution controls and still make a sufficient profit to maintain expansion, research, etc., we may expect it to do so if it perceives it to be in its own long-term interests.''[45]

Again we see the fit between our model and the reality of the legislative process culminating the passage of law. The contradiction between exploiting the physical environment for maximum profit and destroying that environment to the eventual demise of the system (not to mention the people) creates conflicts between interest groups demanding change and owners attempting to maintain maximum profits and control. Ideology enters into justifying and protecting interests by arguing for the inherent morality of private ownership and private control of the profits derived therefrom.[46] A resolution to the conflict emerges in the form of legislation that is in fact in the interests of the profit structure of the largest industrial firms and simultaneously placates the demand of those minority groups seeking state intervention in the industrial process. These laws, however, reveal other contradictions in the form of increased monopoly which itself will lead to further conflicts and dilemmas resulting in yet other legislative innovations. And so the world (at least the world of law) turns.

It is important to note at this point that contradictions are not limited to those that exist between social classes. There are contradictions within particular classes as well. A recent study of the politics of public transportation in California by Alan Whitt is informative in this regard.[47] Whitt, focusing on the relative utility of what he calls the ''pluralist, elitist and class-dialectical models,'' analyzes the forces behind five separate (but interrelated) referendums on public transportation which were voted on by the people of California. In California, as in many other states, voters are sometimes asked to approve or disapprove a particular piece of legislation. The five campaigns studied by Whitt were (1) the issue of whether or not to approve the construction of a mass transit system in San Francisco (BART); (2) Proposition A (1968) to establish rail and bus service public transportation in Los Angeles; (3) Proposition 18 which affected all of California and diverted revenues heretofore used for highway construction to public transportation; (4) Proposition 5 which was similar to 18; and (5) Proposition A which was a 1974 version of Proposition A above.

Each of the campaigns followed some typical patterns: groups mobilized to protect their own interests and support their values. They did not, however, mobilize in a vacuum. Some groups, downtown businessmen for example, favored mass transit measures and would have supported them but were under pressure from the highway construction and oil industries to oppose them. What support was forthcoming was thus sometimes rather half-hearted. Opposition was often conspiratorially organized with contributions from various banks and industries being virtually ''on demand'': even to the point where each industry-financial institution contributed according to a predetermined percentage of the size of the market they controlled.

In some cases massive expenditures by large industry successfully defeated the referendums through advertising and political campaigns. But money was not always victorious. Furthermore, the "elite" or the "ruling class' was not only divided, it changed over time, opposing mass transit proposals at first but later coming to accept and support them (presumably because they discovered it was not all that inimical to their economic interests). In short, Whitt's study reveals quite forcefully the shortcomings of both "pluralist" and "elitist" models—models in the tradition of the "interest group" and "ruling class" perspectives outlined above. Whitt's study also supports the explanatory power of a dialectical paradigm:

It is this broader context which allows us to more fully appreciate the political events herein analyzed. Now we see more of the motivation behind such campaigns, the contradictions and conflicts manifested therein, and the reasons for the previously difficult-to-explain patter of political contributions. We can see these political events in the context of the contradictions which the dominant class must face: 1) the market economy *versus* the need for planning, 2) selling transportation as a private good *versus* the requirement for public services, 3) the competition among cities and among capitalists for growth-generating developments *versus* coherent structure and regularity in urban development, 4) the need to construct new urban transit systems *versus* the budget crisis and occasional mass resistance, 5) the desire for class hegemony *versus* the requirements of legitimacy and mass persuasion, and 6) the desire for class unity *versus* the divisive tendencies of intracapitalist class differences and conflicts. . . . Rather than seeing [the political events in the five campaigns] as simply a clash of organized interest groups pursuing their own goals as the pluralist model would hold, or as the reflection of an elite working its will, we see that the situation is more complex than either of these models would lead us to believe. There is both competition and cohesion here, but that is not the real point. It is most important to understand that the capitalist class must respond to contradictions and crises in the economy, in the cities, and in the polity.[48]

Furthermore, and this point is essential, neither the "polity" nor the working class is impotent. The ruling class must respond somehow to forceful demands made by organized groups or risk losing not just the ideological legitimacy of the system but the ability to control its own destiny. In a word, the process is dialectical, it avoids "both the determinism of a completely materialist science, and the voluntarism of idealist philosophy."[49]

Profits, Markets, Law, and Labor

One of the contradictions inherent in capitalist economic systems is that between profit and markets. If the owners pay workers very low wages then profits will be high but the workers will not be able to purchase the goods produced by the owners. If, however, the owners pay the workers very high wages there will be a heavy demand for products but less profit. One solution to this contradiction is to legalize slavery: keeping some workers at forced labor on subsistence wages while allowing others a higher standard of living and relying on them to purchase the products. Slavery was a solution to this contradiction which was ideologically defended and legally institutionalized for over a hundred years while the Industrial Revolution was taking place in Europe and America.

Another tack to resolve this contradiction is to seek external sources of labor and external markets. This resolution was also institutionalized as capitalism developed in Europe by way of expansion into colonies in Asia, Africa, America—in fact to almost every area of the world where technological development was slowed, thus making the people of these parts of the world more easily conquerable.

Simply appearing on the scene, however, was not sufficient to guarantee that the people would work or buy products from Europe. In most areas of the world touched by European ships and settlers the indigenous peoples had little interest in working for wages. These areas of the world were dominated either by tribal or by feudal economies within which the idea of working for wages made little sense. Furthermore, except for an initial interest in some oddities the Europeans had on board their ships, European manufacturing and industry had few products which appealed to the peoples of these worlds sufficiently to entice them into working long and arduously for the Europeans. Thus a problem of some magnitude arose for the would-be European profiteers: how to induce the people to work and to purchase goods. The resolution of this problem took many different forms and varied from one part of the world to another depending on the cooperativeness of local governments, the degree to which local areas were governed by a central authority, the extent to which Europeans could quickly subjugate the people, and so forth. In America, for example, the native American populations generally resisted the attempts at using them for labor and as markets so successfully that the settlers relied on a constant stream of immigration from the criminal and impoverished classes of Europe. In Africa, however, quite a different situation led to substantially different solutions.

The Africans were understandably reticent to work for European settlers. As mentioned, their way of life and the material conditions of their existence were uncongenial to working for wages as laborers under the direction and control of foreigners. The Europeans, however, were able to establish control over substantial African territories and set up large plantations for raising crops that were salable on the European market. The problem was to induce laborers to work on these plantations. Significantly, the passage of laws to accomplish this purpose was shrouded with the highest moral pronouncements by lawmakers who tried to justify the laws in terms of the contribution they made to the well-being of the Africans themselves by helping them to learn to take "a share in life's labor which no human being should avoid." The fact that the Africans had "shared in life's labor" sufficiently to create a thriving culture was conveniently ignored in the one-sided rhetoric of the settlers.

One major institutional innovation to create an abundance of labor for the settlers was the passage of a law requiring that all Africans pay a poll tax to the colonial government. A supporting legal innovation to the poll tax law was a law requiring that all Africans register with the colonial government. Failure to pay the poll tax or to register was punishable as a criminal offense, by the imposition of fines, imprisonment, or corporal punishment. The reasons for the law were quite clearly stated. Sir Harry Johnston, a colonial administrator, observed:

Given abundance of cheap labour, the financial security of the Protectorate is established. . . . All that needs to be done is for the Administration to act as friends of both sides, and introduce the native labourer to the European capitalist. A gentle insistence that the native should contribute his fair share to the revenue of the country by paying his tax is all that is necessary on our part to ensure his taking a share in life's labour which no human being should avoid.[50]

The reason this procedure worked so effectively was simple: the only possible source of money for paying the poll tax was to work for wages on the plantations. The only way to pay fines imposed for failing to register was to earn wages on plantations. The only way to survive without being subjected to corporal punishment and imprisonment, in other words, was to work at least part of the year for the European settlers:

We consider that taxation is the only possible method of compelling the native to leave his Reserve for the purpose of seeking work . . . it is on this [taxation] that the supply of labour and the price of labour depends. To raise the rate of wages would not increase but would diminish the supply of labour. A rise in the rate of wages would enable the hut or poll tax of a family, sub-tribe or tribe to be earned by fewer external workers.[51]

The poll tax alone did not solve the entire labor problem. Many laborers worked only long enough to raise the money for the poll tax and then deserted, sometimes in the middle of a harvest, thus jeopardizing the entire crop. To resolve this dilemma the colonial governments enforced registration laws:

Labourers who deserted as soon as they had earned enough to pay their taxes were no use to the settlers. To meet their [the settlers'] demands, the government in 1919 put into effect a native registration ordinance which compelled all Africans over the age of sixteen to register by giving a set of fingerprint impressions, which were then forwarded to a central fingerprint bureau. By this method, nearly all deserters could be traced and returned to their employers if they broke a contract. Fines (up to $75.00) and imprisonment (up to 90 days) were imposed for a host of minor labour offenses. Another form of compulsion took shape in vagrancy laws which operated against Africans who left the reserves without becoming wage earners.[52]

In Papua, New Guinea, Australia institutionalized indentured servitude to secure a labor supply for its colonies:

The indenture system was inherited from the Germans in New Guinea and from the British in Papua; the Australians did not make any basic changes in its legal provisions or in its operation but initially they did modify the system in the interests of planters. There were two main aspects of the system. First it was recognized that the "native" had to be forced to work: he was seen by planters and officials as "lazy" but even apologists for the system now acknowledge to an extent that force was needed because Papua New Guineans generally preferred village life to working on plantations or at mining sites. In any case, the result was that the worker in the indenture system was subject to criminal penalties if, among other things, he "deserted" his employer or failed to work diligently.[53]

These instances of the creation and use of law to secure a labor force are interesting also for the light they shed on the relative influence of ideology and economic interests. In New Guinea, for example, ideology was important in two respects. First, the law limited the number of working hours and stipulated minimal dietary and sanitation conditions of work. Second, ideological pronouncements served as a rationale for the system of indentured servitude sanctioned by law:

The provisions themselves were not always beneficient and humane. For much of the colonial period the minimum wage (which was in practice a maximum wage) was five shillings a month in New Guinea and ten shillings in Papua. To take only one more of many possible instances, the death rate among labourers, especially in the gold fields, was frequently extremely high and this was mainly because of the inadequate dietary standards; despite official recognition of this, little was done to correct the situation. More generally, the "native" must be "raised eventually to the highest civilization of which he is capable" but the process must not be rushed. It was believed by the colonists (ostensibly anyway) that requiring the "native" to work on plantations and at mines was part of the "sacred trust" because to so work was a civilizing influence and the best sort of education the "native" could get.[54]

The anthropologist Lucy Mair makes a similar point with respect to the importance of ideological commitments when they conflicted with economic interests in New Guinea:

Where conditions of work were concerned the pressure of economic demand was stronger than humanitarian considerations. Rapid development, it was argued, was in the interests of the whole country, and therefore of course in those of the native population: It must not be hampered by pedantic insistence on the letter of the law. The plantation had had to encounter every kind of difficulty, and should not have their burdens increased beyond what they could bear. Inspection was in any case inadequate, and officers who were anxious to enforce the prescribed conditions felt that they could not count on support from headquarters.[55]

The same process, with slightly different resolutions, took place in Brazil at the time of the breakup of slavery.[56] With the abolition of slavery landowners were left without an adequate work force. Increasing wages, cooperative farming, better work conditions, workers' control of the product of their labor were all logically possible solutions to the labor problem. The one that emerged, however, was not so enlightened: the police were enlisted on the side of landowners to enforce nonexistent "vagrancy" laws against people who refused to work for the wages offered by the landowners. The alternative was simple: work for the wages offered or go to jail. Thus was the contradiction in yet another way.

All these resolutions have this in common: they serve the interests of those who own the means of production at the expense of those who must sell their labor to survive.

Our model of lawmaking differs from models that give law and society a life of their own which is independent of the decisions people make. A recent treatise on law by Donald Black attempts to construct a theoretical paradigm in which law moves, spreads, goes up and down, is higher and lower.[57] We shall not dwell on the utility of such conceptions here but the point is that in Black's model people are not resolving problems, settling disputes, or struggling to survive. Social forces are moving automatically and inexorably toward some unknown (and probably unknowable) end. The model we are suggesting takes quite the opposite starting point: rather than law or society or even history determining the content of the law it is people in a particular historical context who are determining the content of the law. To paraphrase Marx, people make their own history but they do not make it out of whole cloth.

Thus what is a solution to a contradiction in one place and time need not be the solution in another. The use of force to create a labor supply in Africa and New Guinea was not identically replicated in the same form wherever colonies were created. In Southeast Asia opium addiction was an important ingredient in creating a labor supply,[58] while indentured servitude helped to build railroads in the United States.

Work Conditions and Law

The advent of industrialization unleashed a veritable Pandora's box of contradictions onto societies. Owners of factories single-mindedly pursuing the logic of capital accumulation, profit maximization, and industrial expansion demanded eighteen-hour work days, paid a bare minimum of wages necessary for the survival of an adequate work force, and permitted unsanitary and unsafe conditions at work so long as these did not materially reduce profitability. As we have seen, these conditions prevailed in the colonies. They persist today in countries such as South Africa where the labor force is thus far relatively impotent against a totalitarian government, and for some workers (farm laborers in the United States) they exist everywhere. As measured by the sands of time, it was not long after the advent of industrialization and manufacturing that workers began struggling against owners for shorter work hours, better work conditions, and higher wages. "At the dawn of the industrial revolution . . . the human consequences of that technological change were unforeseeable."[59]

So too were some of the problems that would emerge with the development of population concentration. In the middle of the fourteenth century the fact that people moved increasingly into more concentrated living conditions was an important factor in the spread of the Black Death which decimated the population of most European countries. In England at least half the population died before the pestilence had run its course. As a result of this plague, the supply of labor was severely reduced for all sectors of the economy. Workers were in a position to bargain, at least minimally, for the sale of their labor. As a result "the difficulty of getting men to work on reasonable terms [from the standpoint of owners] grew to such a height as to be quite intolerable."[60] The Statute of Labourers (23 Edward 111, 1349) set a maximum limit on the working day and limitations on wages as well. It is significant, and pertinent to the theory being proposed, that the effect of the Statute of Labourers lasted only as long as the work force was limited. As the population grew, even though wages increased the effect of inflation in fact reduced the real wages of the workers to such an extent that four hundred years later the historian, J. Wade, remarked that there had been "a greater degree of independence among the working classes than prevails at present; for the board, both of artifficers and labourers, would now be reckoned at a much higher proportion of their wages."[61]

More generally, "in the history of capitalist production, the determination of what is a working day presents itself as the result of a struggle, a struggle between collective capital, i.e., the class of capitalists, and collective labour, i.e., the working class."[62] The law reflects and contributes to that struggle in the endless effort to resolve the contradictions inherent in a system in which the production of commodities is a public process requiring participation and cooperation of diverse persons while the product of the process is privately owned.

A more recent study of the development of the law of industrial accidents furnishes more evidence of the essential character of this process. Friedman and Ladinsky state: "By the last quarter of the nineteenth century, the number of industrial accidents had grown enormously. After 1900, it is estimated, 35,000 deaths and 2,000,000 injuries occurred every year in the United States."[63]

In the early days of industrialization in the United States there was scant legal attention paid to the plight of the worker. The atmosphere and the attitude of lawmakers reflected the logic of capitalism at its barest: owners' responsibilities were narrowly circumscribed. It was argued by lawmakers and in courts that the "free-market economy" would automatically adjust to the fact that some jobs were more dangerous than others. Commenting on one of the precedent-setting cases in the early history of law concerned with compensation for industrial accidents, Friedman and Ladinsky note that the judge's opinion

spoke the language of contract, and employed the stern logic of nineteenth century economic thought. Some occupations are more dangerous than others. Other things being equal, a worker will choose the least dangerous occupation available. Hence, to get workers an employer will have to pay an additional wage for dangerous work. The market, therefore, has already made an adjustment in the wage rate to compensate for the possibility of accident, and a cost somewhat similar to an insurance cost has been allocated to the company.[64]

The application of this logic to industrial accidents was accomplished through the extension by the courts of the "fellow-servant rule" to industrial accidents. This rule was applied in the case of *Priestly* v. *Fowler* decided in 1837. In that case an employee was injured when an overloaded coach he was driving, on instructions from his employer, broke down. The court decided that the employer was not responsible because employers generally were not responsible for acts committed by their employees. The reasons cited by the judge were obscure and "perhaps irrelevant to the case at hand" but nonetheless this decision was the ruling case in industrial accidents for almost a half of a century.

The logic, or lack of it, might appeal to capitalists but was unconvincing to workers forced to accept work wherever it was available at whatever wages were prevailing. Thus, as labor organized and became more militant in its demands not only for higher wages and shorter working hours but for protection against disabling and murderous working conditions, the law gradually changed.

The late 1800s and early 1900s began a period of heretofore unprecedented conflict between the working class and the capitalist class in the United States. "Following the Civil War, workingmen attempting to organize for collective action engaged in more than a half century of violent warfare with industrialists, their private armies, and unemployed workers used to break strikes."[65] The railroad workers strike in 1877 that crippled the railroad industry across the United States, the Haymarket Square Bombing in 1866, the Homestead strike at Carnegie Steel, the Pullman strike in 1894 in which federal troops were used to force the workers back to work, the bombing of the *Los Angeles Times* in 1910, and the I.W.W. strike in Massachusetts in 1912 are but a small sampling of the number and intensity of labor-capital conflict throughout this sixty-year period.[66]

The issues were many, of course, but foremost among them were wages, hours of work, safety and worker participation in management. In resolving these overt conflicts the law was used in a variety of ways: to suppress the strikes, to ameliorate conditions, to force owners to pay higher wages and shorten work days, to make unions illegal, and later to recognize their legality.

With the increasing militancy and organization of labor it was inevitable that the law would change. One such change appeared in the form of judicial opinion and court decisions that moved away from the narrow interpretation of *Priestly* v. *Fowler*. In *Parker* v. *Hannibal* (1891) the judge said:

In the progress of society, and the general substitution of ideal and invisible masters and employers for the actual and visible ones of former times, in the forms of corporations engaged in varied, detached and widespread operations . . . it has been seen and felt that the universal application of the [fellow-servant] rule often resulted in hardship and injustice. Accordingly, the tendency of the more modern authorities appears to be in the direction of such a modification and limitation of the rule as shall eventually devolve upon the employer under these circumstances a due and just share of the responsibility for the lives and limbs of the persons in its employ.[67]

In the years following, the fellow-servant rule was steadily undermined. "By 1911, twenty-five states had laws modifying or abrogating the fellow-servant doctrine for railroads. . . . The Federal Employer's Liability Act of 1908 . . . abolished the fellow-servant rule for railroads and greatly reduced the strength of contributory negligence and assumption of risk as defenses."[68]

A Wisconsin judge went a long way in expressing the change in law and judicial attitude when he said in the case of *Driscoll* v. *Allis-Chalmers* (1911):

When [the faithful labourer] . . . has yielded up life, or limb or health in the service of that marvelous industrialism which is our boast, shall not the great public . . . be charged with the duty of securing from want the laborer himself, if he survive, as well as his helpless and dependent ones? Shall these latter alone pay the fearful price of the luxuries and comforts which modern machinery brings within the reach of all?[69]

In the face of changing judicial opinion and continued labor struggle and conflict, even the National Association of Manufacturers became convinced that some sort of worker compensation plan was inevitable: "By 1911 the NAM appeared convinced that a compensation system was inevitable and that prudence dictated that business play a positive role in shaping the design of the law—otherwise the law would be settled for us by the demagogue, and agitator and the socialist with a vengeance."[70] Thus it came to pass that between 1910—1920 the method of compensating employees injured on the job was fundamentally altered in the United States. In brief, workmen's compensation statutes eliminated . . . the process of fixing civil liability for industrial accidents through litigation in common law courts. Under the [new] statutes compensation was based on statutory schedules, and the responsibility for initial determination of employee claims was taken from the courts and given to an administrative agency. Finally, the statutes abolished the fellow-servant rule and the defenses of assumption of risk and contributory negligence. Wisconsin's law, passed in 1911, was the first general compensation set to survive a court test. Mississippi, the last state in the Union to adopt a compensation law, did so in 1948.[71]

As Friedman and Ladinsky point out in their analysis of industrial accident laws: "The history of industrial accident law is much too complicated to be viewed as merely a struggle of capital against labor, with law as a handmaid of the rich."[72] Clearly, the law of industrial accidents reflects the struggle of capital and labor. Indeed, it is practically the test case of the theory that the law reflects this (and other) struggles between social classes. It is certainly true, however, that this history stands as a clear exception to the theory that the law is simply a reflection of the interests and ideologies of the ruling class. The law reflects the contradictions and attempts to deal with conflicts generated by those contradictions. In capitalist economic systems, worker-capitalist contradictions are among the more important forces shaping the law.

Friedman and Ladinsky, it must be noted, do *not* analyze the development of worker compensation laws with reference to the efforts of workers to organize and to rebel against a system of labor not of their making. Rather, as a direct result of the lenses (the theory) they use to look at the issue, they seek "needs of society" which give rise to "solutions to problems." In their words: "Whether (a particular legal rule) . . . would find a place in the law relative to industrial accidents depended upon needs felt and expressed by legal institutions in response to societal demands."[73]

Lost in this interpretation is the very real, undeniable class struggle between workers and capitalists that took place during the time that worker compensation laws were formed. It is astounding, albeit not unique to Friedman and Ladinsky, that an analysis of worker compensation laws could almost completely ignore the riots, rebellions, and incipient revolutions which gave rise to the "needs felt and expressed by legal institutions in response to societal demands." It was not some mystical, reified "society" demanding legal changes; it was people organized, brutalized, and struggling. It was not "societal demands" that led to the initial interpretation of workers' accidents as risks rightfully taken by the workers and magically compensated for by the "free market"; it was the struggle of capitalists to maximize profits.

Though the reinterpretation of historical events according to a predetermined theoretical position is not unusual in science (see, for example, Hanson's superb analysis of physicists observing the same phenomenon with different lenses),[74] it is nevertheless incumbent on us to recognize what is left out of such an analysis. Furthermore, it is imperative that we understand the implications of the analysis as well. For if we see the law as shaped through struggle and conflict in relation to fundamental contradictions, then the engine of social change becomes conflict, not harmony and equilibrium. The forces that are important to understand, then, are *not* the interstices of legal institutions (judges' reasoning, prosecutors' discretion) but the social forces of power, conflict, contradictions, and dilemmas which create the "necessity" for legal institutions to respond, for law to change.

The more general point is that the creation of law reflects a dialectical process, a process through which people struggle and in so doing create the world in which they live. The history of law in capitalist countries indicates that in the long run the capitalists fare considerably better than do the working classes in the struggle for having their interests and views represented in the law. But the shape and content of the law are nonetheless a reflection of the struggle and not simply a mirror image of the short-run interests and ideologies of "the ruling class" or of "the people."

6.2 LAW CREATION AND CONTRADICTION IN SOCIALIST SOCIETIES

The media stereotype. of socialist law as dictates coming down from a bureaucracy completely removed from people is doubtless a gross distortion. As with the perspective that sees the ruling class in capitalist societies as the beginning and end of lawmaking, so the view of the centralized bureaucracy as the only force of any consequence in socialist societies is likewise fallacious.

Actually existing socialist societies, however, such as the Soviet Union and the eastern European countries, can be understood in terms of the same theoretical framework we have used to analyze capitalist societies. Rudolph Bahro, an East German social scientist, points out the basic contradiction in actually existing socialist societies. The contradiction is between the productive forces of modern-day socialist societies and the human social relations that have resulted from the socialist organization of production:

The abolition of private property in the means of production has in no way meant their immediate transformation into the property of the people. Rather, the whole society stands property-less against its state machine. The monopoly of disposal over the apparatus of production, over the lion's share of the surplus product, over the proportions of the reproduction process, over distribution and consumption, has led to a bureaucratic mechanism with the tendency to kill off or privatise any subjective initiative. The obsolete political organisation of the new society, which cuts deep into the economic process itself, blunts its social driving forces.[75]

One consequence of the reality created by this socialist contradiction is the proliferation of criminal law and a criminal justice system paralleling in many important ways the law creation processes under capitalism analyzed in this chapter.

A recent inquiry by James Brady indicates the extent to which contradictions inherent in socialist societies are a moving force in the law creation process:

[In China] the central struggle is fundamentally a conflict between competing ideas for economic development . . . the Ethic of Social Revolution and the Ethic of Bureaucratic Centralization. The two ethics and their conflicts result from a contradiction between social and economic necessities for China. . . . China must have a closely coordinated economy to organize labor and marshal scarce material and technological resources for industrial growth. At the same time, the Maoist leadership remains committed to decentralized popular participation and ongoing social change. In brief, the economy demands social discipline and the politics call for social change.[76]

That contradiction, according to Brady, is responsible for the creation of a criminal justice bureaucracy which is in conflict with local collectives attempting to determine their own destiny. At times these conflicts, as with similar conflicts in capitalist countries, culminate in violent attacks on representatives and symbols of the various institutions which stand for one or the other of the possible directions the resolution of the contradiction may take. These attacks, as well as the constant dialogue and debate, in turn create other laws, other resolutions, and so forth.

A fundamental contradiction inheres in a society committed to rapid industrialization and to social equality (that is, equality of power, wealth, privilege, and prestige) in that these two goals cannot simultaneously be maximized. At least in the short run during the transformation from an individualistic capitalist economy to a collectivistic socialist economy there will be a reduction in productivity as workers and peasants take control of the means of production. One resolution of this *dilemma* is to create a large state bureaucracy which is presumably controlled by and acting in the interests of ''the people.'' The bureaucracy, then, can serve to plan and organize productivity at least as efficiently as, and probably more so than, the previous system, capitalism, had. However, as Max Weber so rightly showed us, bureaucracies create their own interests and their own self-serving rules. To avoid this in the People's Republic, some of the communist party leaders advocated ''perpetual revolution'' to cleanse the bureaucracies of self-serving people and to maintain control over the bureaucracies by the people.

The resolution proposed by Mao was not universally accepted, however:

There were some traces of tension between the supporters of the two great political ethics, even in the first years after Liberation (1949). The more radical (social change oriented) party members noted that rule by a paternalistic bureaucrat-technocrat elite in the Soviet Union was accompanied by low popular morale and despite advanced machinery, production rates among Russian workers were quite low. Such doubts and differences were first confined to inside debates within the Chinese Communist Party. However, as industrialization progressed and social inequalities persisted both the party radicals and the general public became increasingly impatient.[77]

This inside debate exploded into sweeping national argument in the ''rectification'' crises of 1956-57 (100 Flowers/Anti-Rightist) and 1966-68 (Cultural Revolution).

These great events and countless lesser struggles show the marks of a shifting conflict between the competing ideas of bureaucratic centralization and popular revolution.

The energetic participation of the people can only be ensured by continuing revolution in opportunity and social relations, and this is best accomplished by decentralization, flexibility, and local sensitivity in decision-making. On the other hand, the need to coordinate carefully the allocation of technical resources points to a highly centralized economy and a stabilized bureaucratic society. At the same time, the party and state officials base their very legitimacy on the ideals of social revolution, and the leadership draws its political strength from the voluntary support of unpaid citizen activists. The country does not have the money, resources, or ideology to resolve this contradiction.

The history of Chinese justice provides an especially clear "window" on this dialectic conflict of political economic perspectives. The supporters of the two ethics have each advanced an ideology of justice and a set of complementary justice institutions. The radical supporters of the Social Revolution Ethic have created and defended a popular justice system operated by the mass organizations and explicitly committed to social reform. The advocates of the more conservative Bureaucratic Ethic have established and maintained a more regular set of justice bureaucracies guided by law and routine procedures and less concerned with ongoing social change. There is considerable cooperation between the two justice systems in routine peace-keeping work, but in times of political crises there have been open conflicts between bureaucratic and popular justice.[78]

The Chinese resolution to dilemmas posed by fundamental contradictions in the political economy was to establish two systems of criminal justice which existed side by side. This solution in turn produced conflicts and other contradictions. Struggles over which system should dominate continue and doubtless will go on for the foreseeable future.

6.3 CONCLUSION

People occupying roles and influencing law differ in the precise nature of the resolutions forged in response to structurally induced contradictions. The Soviet Union opted early for the development of a legal system committed to bureaucratic centralization. The conflicts this has generated are legion and are exploited by the western media and politicians just as the Soviet media and political leadership exploit labor strife in the United States, both claiming that these conflicts are evidence of the oppressive, undemocratic, and exploitative nature of the other's economy.

In this chapter we have presented a model for explaining the larger social forces behind the creation of law. This model stresses the overriding importance of basic contradictions in the political economy as the starting point for a sociological understanding of law creation. It puts people squarely in the middle of these contradictions as some struggle to resolve the contradictions by fighting against existing law (laws supporting colonialism, wage discrimination, or racism for example) while others are creating new laws. In the process, ideological justifications develop, shift, and change; these ideologies, in turn, become a force of their own influencing the development of legal institutions which reflect the interplay between material conditions and ideology.

We have analyzed several laws in some detail by way of demonstrating both the utility of the theory and the kinds of data for which the theory is relevant. We have intentionally focused in this chapter primarily on civil law. The theoretical findings and trends applicable to criminal law we pursue in the next chapter.

NOTES

1. Jerome Hall, *Theft, Law and Society*, 2nd ed. (Indianapolis: Bobbs-Merrill, 1952) pp. 3-4.

2. L. Friedman, *Law and Society: An Introduction* (Englewood Cliffs, N.J.: Prentice-Hall, 1977), p. 99.

3. Richard Quinney, *Critique of Legal Order: Crime Control in Capitalist Society* (Boston: Little, Brown & Co., 1974), p. 138.

4. G. Kolko, *The Triumph of Conservatism* (New York: Free Press, 1963). See also Albert E. McCormick, Jr., "Dominant Class Interests and the Emergence of Anti-Trust Legislation," *Contemporary Crises* 3(1979):399-417.

5. Kolko, *Triumph of Conservatism*, p. 106.

6. *Ibid.*, p. 108.

7. *Ibid.*, p. 109.

8. K. Calavita, "A Sociological Analysis of the U.S. Immigration Law," Ph.D. dissertation, Department of Sociology, University of Delaware, 1980.

9. K. Klare, "Judicial Deradicalization of the Wagner Act and the Origins of Modern Legal Consciousness, 1937-1941," *Minnesota Law Review* 62(1978):265-339.

10. *Ibid.*, p. 266.

11. *Ibid.*, p. 267.

12. A. Hunt, "Perspectives in the Sociology of Law," in P. Carlen, ed., *The Sociology of Law* (Keele, Staffordshire, England: University of Keele Press, 1976), pp. 33-43. See also C. Sumner, *Reading Ideologies* (London: Academic Press, 1979).

13. A. L. Morton, *A People's History of England* (London: Lawrence and Wishart, 1938); W. J. Chambliss, "A Sociological Analysis of the Law of Vagrancy," *Social Problems* 12(1964):46-67; Hall, *Theft, Law and Society*.

14. See, for example, Jack Anderson's column on the asbestos industry in the *Philadelphia Evening Bulletin*, October 5, 1979, p. 72; J. M. Graham, "Amphetamine Politics on Capitol Hill," *Society* 9(1972):14-23; and Kolko, *Triumph of Conservatism*.

15. Karl Marx, "So-called Primitive Accumulation," *Capital*, vol. 1 (New York: Vintage Books, 1977), pp. 873-943.

16. R. B. Seidman, *State Law and Development* (New York: St. Martin's Press, 1978), p. 10.

LAWMAKING: THE DIALECTICS OF PROBLEM-SOLVING

7. B. Barclay, J. Schmidt, and D. Hill, "State, Capital and Legitimation Crisis: Land and Water in California's Imperial Valley," *Contemporary Crises* 4(1980):1-26.

18. E. Genovesse, *Roll Jordan Roll: The World the Slaves Made* (New York: Pantheon Books, 1974).

19. R. Lefcourt, ed., *Law against the People* (New York: Random House, 1971), pp. 105-123.

20. A. M. Garfinkle, C. Lefcourt, and D. B. Schulder, "Women's Servitude under Law," in *ibid.*, pp. 105-123. As quoted in Elaine Wood, "Causal Analysis of the Passage of Gender Equality Laws," unpublished manuscript, University of Delaware, 1980.

21. Albie Sachs and Joan Hoff Wilson, *Sexism and the Law* (London: Martin Robertson, 1978).

22. Garfinkle *et al.*, "Women's Servitude."

23. Wood, "Gender Equality Laws."

24. Delaware State Code 772.

25. R. V. Miller [1954] 2 QB 282.

26. S. Griffin, "Rape: The All-American Crime," *Ramparts* 10(1971):26-35. Reprinted in W. J. Chambliss, *Criminal Law in Action* (New York: John Wiley & Sons, 1975), p. 107.

27. *Hoyt* v. *Florida,* as cited in Lefcourt, *Law Against the People,* p. 107.

28. A. D. Freeman, "Legitimizing Racial Discrimination through Anti-Discrimination Law: A Critical Review of Supreme Court Doctrine," *Minnesota Law Review* 62(1978):1049-1119.

29. Alan Page, "State Intervention in the Inter-War Period: The Special Area Acts 1934-1937," *British Journal of Law and Society* 3(1976):189.

30. *Ibid.,* p. 195.

31. *Ibid.,* p. 193.

32. *Ibid.,* p. 195.

33. *Ibid.,* p. 198.

34. *Ibid.,* p. 200.

35. *Ibid.,* p. 202.

36. M. Edelman, *The Symbolic Use of Politics* (Urbana: University of Illinois Press, 1970). J. Gusfield, *Symbolic Crusade: Status Politics and the American Temperance Movement* (Urbana: University of Illinois Press, 1963).

37. N. Gunningham, *Pollution, Social Interest and the Law* (London: Martin Robertson, 1974), p. 35.

38. *Ibid.*

39. *Ibid.,* p. 39.

40. *Ibid.,* p. 40.

41. F. Graham, Jr., *Since Silent Spring* (London: Hamish Hamilton, 1970), p. 225.

42. W. Friedman, *Law in a Changing Society* (Harmondsworth, England: Penguin Books, 1972), p. 521.

43. Gunningham, *Pollution, Social Interest and the Law,* p. 42.

44. *Ibid.*

45. *Ibid.,* p. 46.

46. See Colin Sumner, *Reading Ideologies: An Investigation into the Marxist Theory of Ideology and Law* (London: Academic Press, 1979).

47. Alan A. Whitt, "Toward a Class-Dialectical Model of Political Power: An Empirical Assessment of Three Competing Models," *American Sociological Review* 44(1979):81-100.

48. *Ibid.,* pp. 97-98.

49. R. P. Appelbaum, "Marxist Method: Structural Constraints and Social Praxis," *American Sociologist* 13(1978):78. R. P. Appelbaum, "Marx's Theory of the Falling Rate of Profit: Towards a Dialectical Analysis of Structural Social Change," *American Sociological Review* 43(1978):67-80.

50. Sir H. Johnston, *Trade and General Conditions Report* (Nyasaland, 1895), p. 11.

51. Sir Percy Girovord and N. Lees, *Kenya* (London: Leonard and Virginia Wolff, 1924), p. 186.

52. S. Aaronovitch and K. Aaronovitch, *Crisis in Kenya* (London: Lawrence and Withrop, 1947), pp. 99-100.

53. P. Fitzpatrick, "Really Rather Like Slavery: Law and Labour in the Colonial Economy in Papua, New Guinea," *Contemporary Crises* (forthcoming).

54. *Ibid.*

55. Lucy P. Mair, *Australia in New Guinea* (Carlton: Melbourne University Press, 1970), p. 184.

56. Martha Huggins, "Social Change, Crime and Social Control: The Case of Pernambuco Brazil, 1865-1915," mimeographed, Ibadan, Nigeria, 1980.

57. D. Black, *The Behaviour of Law* (New York: Academic Press, 1977).

58. W. J. Chambliss, "Markets, Profits, Labor and Smack," *Contemporary Crises* 1(1977):53-76.

59. L. Friedman and J. Ladinsky, "Social Change and the Law of Industrial Accidents," *Columbia Law Review* 67(1967):50-52.

60. Karl Marx, *Capital,* vol. 1 (New York: International Publishers, 1967), p. 272.

61. J. Wade, *History of the Middle and Working Classes,* 3d ed. (London, 1835), pp. 24-25.

62. Marx, *Capital,* p. 235.

63. Friedman and Ladinsky, "Social Change," p. 60.

64. *Ibid.,* p. 55.

65. R. E. Rubenstein, *Rebels in Eden: Mass Political Violence in the United States* (Boston: Little, Brown & Co., 1970), p. 29.

66. W. A. Williams, *The Contours of American History* (Cleveland: World, 1961); W. A. Williams, *The Roots of the Modern American Empire* (New York: Random House, 1969).

67. Friedman and Ladinsky, "Social Change," p. 59.

68. *Ibid.*, p. 64.

69. *Ibid.*, p. 67.

70. *Ibid.*, p. 69.

71. *Ibid.*, p. 70.

72. *Ibid.*, p. 54.

73. *Ibid.*, p. 55.

74. Norwood Russell Hanson, *Patterns of Discovery* (Cambridge: At the University Press, 1958).

75. R. Bahro, *The Alternative in Eastern Europe* (New York: Schocken Books, 1978).

76. J. P. Brady, "Political Contradictions and Justice Policy in People's China," *Contemporary Crises* 2(1977):128-129.

77. *Ibid.*, pp. 130-131.

78. *Ibid.*

7

Crime and punishment

The vocabulary, theory and methodology we propose as suitable for the study of law and society begin not with vast impersonal forces sweeping across empty heads and determining human action but with thinking, choosing, creating human beings. Society is a collection of human beings, not an entity with its own needs, force, and consciousness. It consists of people acting together in repetitive patterns shaped but not determined by the constraints and resources of a particular historical period. Among the constraints and resources inherited economic relations and political organization constitute two key elements.

All this suggests the critical importance of the dialectic, a methodolgy that takes the interaction of people and institutions as the starting point for an understanding of social relations. Thus we stand in opposition to theories, whether based on Marx, Weber, Durkheim, Dicey, Bentham, or Hart, that argue that the social structure (the mode of production), societal norms (religious beliefs or shared values), or "societal needs" determine the content of law. It seems absurd to speak of the law as "behaving." Law does not behave. People behave, and in their behavior make, interpret, and apply law. Though they do not write on an unmarked slate, people write their own law as surely as they write their own history.

Some argue that, although corporation, property, tort, and labor law reflect the dialectics of people struggling to control their lives, criminal law reflects more basic shared values and societal needs. Emile Durkheim established a theoretical perspective that guided generations of social scientists in their study of law when he said:

The only common characteristic of crimes is that they consist . . . in acts universally disapproved of by members of each society. . . . Crime shocks sentiments which, for a given social system, are found in all healthy consciences.[1]

The collective sentiments to which crime corresponds must, therefore, singularize themselves from others by some distinctive property; they must have a certain average intensity. Not only are they engraven in all consciences, but they are strongly engraven.[2]

The wayward son, however, and even the most hardened egotist are not treated as criminals. It is not sufficient, then, that the sentiments be strong; they must be precise.[3]

An act is criminal when it offends strong and defined states of the collective conscience.[4]

Those acts, to offend the common conscience, need not relate "to vital interests of society nor to a minimum of justice."[5]

Durkheim went on to suggest two grand hypotheses that have played a central role in studies of law and society ever since. He postulated that:

1   Criminal law represents the synthesizing of the essential morality of a people based on religious and customary values shared by "all healthy consciences" and reflecting societal needs.

2   Criminal behavior is created by society in its effort to establish moral boundaries, the violation of which threatens the fabric of social order.

We shall consider each of these hypotheses in the light of extant empirical data.

7.1 CRIMINAL LAW AS A SYNTHESIS OF SHARED VALUES AND A REFLECTION OF SOCIETAL NEEDS

We must distinguish at the outset between the origins of law and the degree to which particular laws reflect societal consensus at a particular point in time. The political scientist Ted Robert Gurr in the following passage demonstrates the confusion that sometimes arises from a failure to make this distinction:

There are two contending academic interpretations of the societal origins of criminal law. . . . From an empirical point of view the accuracy and fruitfulness of the two interpretations surely varies among types of crime and among societies. . . .

Murder can threaten simultaneously the securtiy of elites and the moral sensibilities of virtually everyone in society.[6]

Professor Gurr makes two very common errors. First he confuses the origins of law with its present circumstance. That most people might agree today that murder, rape, vagrancy, and theft constitute socially abhorrent behavior does *not* mean that the law making them crimes arose out of shared values. As we shall see they did not.

Second, Professor Gurr errs in believing that the response to a questionnaire in fact reflects a person's view of appropriate behavior. Real-life circumstances rarely coincide with abstract statements. Take for example the "generally agreed-upon" dictum "Thou shalt not kill." Killing often has its justifications. Not long ago, some courts exonerated a man who killed his wife after discovering her in an adulterous act. Even today, in some jurisdictions a person may kill someone who enters her home to steal something. The law protects us if we kill someone who threatens us with serious bodily harm. A policeman may kill someone fleeing from a felony even when the suspected felony consists of nothing more serious than a hubcap. In actual practice police possess de facto immunity from legal restrictions which gives them license to kill suspected offenders. Executioners may kill people condemned to die by a court; soldiers may kill if ordered to. Only if the side they fight for loses will their action usually come before a court. In Germany from 1931 to 1945 government bureaucrats, police, and army personnel killed thousands of Jews, communists, socialists, people from countries other than Germany, and political dissidents. At the time the laws sanctioned these killings; they only became criminal after Germany lost the war. Had Germany won the war, no doubt U.S. soldiers would have been tried for murder.[7]

The same principle applies to all sacred values. Rape, theft, assault, drunkenness: when analyzed situationally the presumed agreement on the value rapidly dissolves into conflicting points of view. If she has no other means of feeding them, may a woman steal for her starving children? Whatever you answer, others disagree. No consensus exists. As the German sociologist Karl Schumann observed:

While the consensus on "Thou shall not kill" may be empirically valid, criminal laws allow killing during war, killing by unsafe automobiles, killing by making sufficient health services unavailable for the poor, killing by unsafe working conditions and so forth. . . . If there is a general moral consensus not to harm the health of other persons, criminal laws do not reflect this consensus. Hazardous work conditions, low piece wages which force individuals to work overtime and destroy their health, and injuries caused by police and prison guards, to name a few of many exceptions, are not criminalized at all.[8]

How much consensus presently exists on whether or what criminal acts are right or wrong remains an open question. That issue, however, begs the more important one. That murder threatens both the security of elites and everyone's moral senses may have absolutely nothing to do with the *origins* of laws prohibiting murder. Professor Gurr assumes rather than tests or develops a theory of the origins of law. Logic does not require us to assume that because today an act "threatens the security of elites and offends the moral sensibilities of everyone" that people created these laws for these reasons.

The question we must answer is, Why does the law define some acts as criminal, and not others? An answer requires us to look at specific instances of criminal law and discern the forces responsible for their creation. When we do this we find universally a conspicuous lack of consensus in the origins of law. Different people in different eras have not even defined murder as it is today. Before the Norman conquest in England a killing was "first of all an offense against the victim or his family and was therefore to be settled by suitable payment to the sufferers."[9] It was only with the conquest of England by the Normans and the subsequent attempt by William and his heirs to unite the country under one kingdom did killing someone become a matter of state concern.

The early kings of England were involved in a struggle for political power and control of economic resources against both the Catholic Church and the feudal landlords who controlled various parts of England and who commanded what military might existed. To centralize power in his hands the king established murder, theft, trespassing, poaching, and robbery as acts against the king's peace.[10] These became crimes against the state not because of a moral consensus, but as part of a political struggle between the Crown, the Church and the great feudal nobles.

C. Ray Jeffrey also noted the change from the customary practice where families shared responsibility for members' behavior to the state's assumption of responsibility and the definition of crime as an individual act:

State law and crime came into existence during the time of Henry II as a result of this separation of State and Church, and as a result of the emergence of a central authority in England which replaced the authority of the feudal lords. Henry replaced feudal justice with state justice by means of justices in eyre, the king's peace, a system of royal courts, and a system of royal writs. Common law emerged as the law of the Crown available to all men. The myth that the common law of England is the law of the Anglo-Saxons is without historical foundation. The family was no longer involved in law and justice. The State was the offended social unit, and the State was the proper prosecutor in every case of crime. Justice was now the sole prerogative of the State. "Custom passes into law." This shift occurred historically when a political community separate from the kinship group emerged as a part of the social organization. A comparison of tribal law and state law reveals these basic differences.

Tribal Law	State Law
Blood-tie	Territorial-tie
Collective responsibility	Individual responsibility
Family as unit of justice and order	State as unit of justice
Feud or compensation	Punishment[11]

The transformation of law from familial-centered responsibility to state control resulted from the struggle for political power and economic resources taking place between the king and the towns on one side and the feudal nobles and the church on the other. In the end the kings won the battle. The law was one of the mechanisms used by the kings that made them victorious.

In the centuries following the Norman conquest (1066) the entire body of criminal law we live under today developed. Out of the struggles between feudal landlords, towns, peasants, kings, barons, mercantilists, capitalists, and workers criminal law was created, altered, adopted to different proposals, and ultimately erroneously sanctified as the culmination of "shared values." The examples are legion. We shall describe the history of theft, vagrancy, and drug laws as illustrative of the process.

Theft, Law, and Society

During feudal times, when landowners became the undisputed masters of the economic resources of the society, laws conerning theft lacked sophistication and subtlety and were narrowly defined. Only with the advent of commerce and trade in Europe did the laws of theft take the broad outlines of their present form. As the feudal landowners lost control over the resources of the society and over the lawmaking machinery, laws of theft emerged to protect the interests of the developing economic elites. This process has been studied by Jerome Hall and reported in his classic work *Theft, Law and Society.*[12]

A turning point in the law of theft came in the *Carrier* case, decided in England in 1473:

The facts are simple enough: the defendant was hired to carry certain bales to Southampton. Instead of fulfilling his obligation, he carried the goods to another place, broke open the bales and took the contents. He was apprehended and charged with felony.[13]

At the time of the defendant's arrest and trial for felony no law in England made it a crime for a person to convert to his own use goods which he acquired legally. An earlier rule applied to servants, but prior to the *Carrier* case the courts had disallowed it. Yet despite this lack of prevailing common law or legislative enactment a tribunal of the most learned judges in England decided against the defendant and found him guilty of larceny. By so doing they established a new law, one central to the well-being of the emergent class of capitalist traders and industrialists.

The judges hotly debated the decision, as did legal scholars. Nobody could justify the new law as logically required by existing laws. It was possible, however, for the judges to create legal fictions that justified the decision. In this way they protected the interests of the new mercantile class, not through their direct involvement in law creation but through the "perceived need" of the judges sitting on the highest courts of the time. The "perceived need," of course, represented the mobilization of a bias which favored the interests of the not yet dominant, but soaring new economic class.

Following the *Carrier* case in 1473, the law of theft expanded and developed throughout the sixteenth, seventeenth, and eighteenth centuries with the decisions in the eighteenth century playing the major role. "Larceny by servant" became established in the sixteenth century. Over time, the courts' interpreted cases expanded the legal definition of "possession of the master" to include instances where the master had never seen the goods, so long as the servant placed goods received by him in a receptacle of his master. The courts also broadened the interpretation of "servant" to include cashiers, clerks, and persons hired to transport goods from place to place.

The fullest development of the law of theft took place in the eighteenth century:

Growth in the eighteenth century is so accelerated that it protrudes conspicuously from the pattern of the whole course of the criminal law. . . . It is in this century that one comes upon the law of receiving stolen property, larceny by trick, obtaining goods by false pretenses, and embezzlement.[14]

Hall's analysis of why these laws emerged when they did, and why they had not been formulated earlier, is instructive:

Beginning in 1607, advancing rapidly with the emigration consequent on the civil disturbances, the colonial expansion followed, 1640-1664 presenting a peak.

Immediately the colonies served a double purpose. They supplied raw materials. They also furnished a market for the sale of goods manufactured at home; and the home manufacturers were prompt to protect that market. The tremendous change in the organization of industry is the first development of major importance which closely touches the law of the eighteenth century. Trade became increasingly impersonal and free from supervision. . . . In the Middle Ages goods were produced by individuals, their families and neighbors, for local consumption. Next came regulation and close supervision by crafts and guilds in villages and small towns. . . . And, finally with the Industrial Revolution came large-scale production.

All this was accompanied by changes in the economic organization of society . . . the transition from an agricultural economy toward a dominantly manufacturing system.

There was another eighteenth century development of the greatest importance, namely, the rise of credit and banking facilities and the use of modern instruments to facilitate trade. . . .

This growth in banking and the use of paper currency and instruments of credit affected the law of theft in several important respects. The effect upon the law of embezzlement was direct and sharply marked. . . . The Act of 1742, the first true embezzlement statute passed by a Whig parliament, anxious to protect the greatest Whig mercantile institution in the country . . . applied only to officers and servants of the Bank of England. . . . The second embezzlement statute, enacted in 1751, applied to officers and employees of the South Sea Company, and the third (1763) extended only to employees of the Post Office. . . . In 1799 . . . the first general embezzlement statute [was enacted].[15]

What Hall has been describing in these passages is of course the emergence of a law required to protect capitalists and capitalism. The interests which the laws of theft were designed to protect were the interests of the capitalists:

The pattern of conditions which gave rise to embezzlement may therefore be delineated as follows: (1) the expansion of mercantile and banking credit and the use of credit mechanisms, paper money, and securities; (2) the employment of clerks in important positions with reference to dealing with and, in particular, receiving valuables from third persons; (3) the interests of the commercial classes and their representation in parliament; (4) a change in attitude regarding the public importance of what could formerly be dismissed as merely a private breach of trust; and (5) a series of sensational cases of very serious defalcation which set the pattern into motion and produced immediate action.[16]

The transition from feudal economy to capitalist economy; the victory of capitalists over feudal landlords in a series of wars and contests for control of the state;

the representation by capitalists of their interests in Parliament; and the changing social relations (the emergence of clerks, for example, who took money and other negotiable instruments in the name of their employer) coalesced to bring about a whole gaggle of new laws, among them, today's laws of theft.

There is an interesting footnote to this investigation by Hall which is pertinent to our discussion for it illuminates how the theoretical perspective (what Twining and Miers call "standpoint")[17] with which we approach our inquiry colors the interpretation we give to the data.

When Hall conducted his study, Legal Realism, a school of jurisprudence that took its inspiration from Oliver Wendell Holmes, had just begun to convince legal scholars that the courts as well as legislatures did in fact "make law" and not merely interpret it. Hall's study, conducted within the perspective of the Realists, supplied solid empirical evidence in support of the Realists' claim. His work, as that of many others, laid a groundwork for a sociology of law. Hall himself, however, swerved from his ground-breaking study to attempt to revitalize natural law theory, the very opposite of Legal Realism.[18] His understanding of how society created the law of theft became a general theory that the criminal law reflected "society's" values and needs. His data, however, speak louder than his words. In explaining the development of the law of theft the data forced Hall to adopt a conflict perspective of society. He consistently shows how "social and economic conditions" shaped the law. The forces of production changed social conditions, which led to laws enacted "in the interests of the commercial classes and their representation in parliament."[19] In summing up, however, Hall sought an explanation based not on a conflict perspective, but societal consensus. He wrote that his study shows how "the functioning of courts is significantly related to concomitant cultural needs."[20] And that "the chronological order of the principal phases of legal change is (1) a lag between the substantive law and social needs, (2) spontaneous efforts ('practices') of judges, other officials, and laymen to make successful adaptations, and (3) legislation."[21] In his summing up, he argues that the laws of theft from the *Carrier* case in the fifteenth century to the fully developed laws of theft in the eighteenth century fulfilled a "need" of the society, not the "needs" of the classes whose special interests they served. Because this interpretation of law is so common it is worth careful scrutiny.

Cui bono. We must always ask a simple but searching question: For the good of whom? (Cui bono?) The laws of theft do not directly serve the interests of those who work for the owners of the property. If workers convert owners' property to their own use, those laws subject them to harsh punishment. Prior to these laws a worker who converted an employer's property to his own use became liable only to civil sanctions: having to repay the amount of property stolen, loss of job, etc. The legislature and the court could have decided, quite logically and with just as much legal precedent, that these conflicts between employee and employer should remain a matter of civil law. Whole schools of philosophy (philosophical anarchism, for example) argue that in the name of fairness and equity the law should allow workers, if they can manage it, to convert the property of capitalists to their own use. At first blush, that suggestion seems outlandish. The courts and legislatures, however, did make just that kind of decision when they developed the principle of *caveat emptor* (let the buyer beware). They refused to pass legislation or make law in the courts to protect consumers from misrepresentations and deceptions of capitalists *selling* goods. There seems precious little moral difference between workers pilfering from capitalists and capitalists pilfering from consumers. But the one became a crime, the other became "good business." Capitalists needed or at least benefited greatly from the new theft laws. To argue that "society" needed or benefited from them amounts to little more than an unsubstantiated platitude. To assume a consensus assumes that only the ideology of the ruling class counts.

Whigs and Hunters

The same proposition emerges from E. P. Thompson's study of "The Black Act." As we have seen (see Chapter 5), in 1723 England passed a law making it a capital offense punishable by death to engage in a wide range of activities—poaching, wearing a disguise while in an area where deer or horses were kept, damaging fish ponds, wounding or killing cattle, etc. Under feudalism peasants living on manorial land had the right to hunt, fish, and gather wood on the lord's property. The emergence of capitalism, however, changed the serf to a wage earner and the lord's manor to a private estate:

The historical movement which changes the producers into wage-workers, appears, on the one hand, as their emancipation from serfdom and from the fetters of the guilds. . . . But, on the other hand, these new freed men became sellers of themselves only after they had been robbed of all their own means of production, and of all the guarantees of existence afforded by the old feudal arrangements. And the history of this, their expropriation, is written in the annals of mankind in letters of blood and fire.[22]

To effect the transition to capitalism and alter the people's use of communal land, Parliament enacted criminal laws imposing severe sanctions—including death—for "poachers and wood stealers." Despite these laws, however, people continued to exercise what they considered their "natural rights" to hunt, fish, and gather wood in the only available space: the lord's land.[23]

The Black Act greatly increased the number of offenses for which courts could impose the death penalty. This led some social and legal historians to conclude that some overwhelming problem must have elicited the Black Act as a response.[24] If one reasons from the perspective that the law responds to social needs, the sudden sharp increase in harsh penalties for criminal acts suggested that the Black Act responded to some increase in the incidence and severity of poaching. E. P. Thompson tested this theory by examining the records available from courts and local sheriffs and the discussions within government. His research shows that the Whig party, which controlled the government at the time, responded to changing economic and political

CRIME AND PUNISHMENT

conditions brought about by the shift from feudal to capitalist social relations. Under feudalism people had had the right to kill some of the animals on local estates and to fish in the streams. The law dealt with violations of the rules as civil matters—i.e., wrongs by one person against another. With the development of capitalism, however, came a different ideology of private property, and a changed set of class relations.

The act registered the long decline in the effectiveness of old methods of class control and discipline and their replacement by one standard recourse of authority: the example of terror. In place of the whipping-post and the stocks, manorial and corporate controls and the physical harrying of vagabonds, economists advocated the discipline of low wages and starvation, and lawyers the sanctions of death. Both indicated an increasing impersonality in the mediation of class relations, and a change, not so much in the "facts" of crime as in the category— "crime"—itself, as it was defined by the propertied. What was now to be punished was not an offense between men (a breach of fealty or deference, a "waste" of agrarian use-values, an offense to one's own corporate community and its ethos, a violation of trust and function) but an offense against property. Since property was a thing, it became possible to define offenses as crimes against things, rather than as injuries to men.[25]

The functions of the severe penalties went beyond the mere threat of punishment, however. As Douglas Hay points out:

The rulers of eighteenth-century England cherished the death sentence. The oratory we remember now is the parliamentary speech, the Roman periods of Fox or Burke, that stirred the gentry and the merchants. But outside Parliament were the labouring poor, and twice a year, in most countries in England, the scarlet-robed judge of assize put the black cap of death on top of his full-bottomed wig to expound the law of the properties and to execute their will.[26]

Hay notes further the sanctification of private property during this period:

Once property had been officially deified, it became the measure of all things. Even human life was weighed in the scales of wealth and status: "the execution of a needy decrepit assassin," wrote Blackstone, "is a poor satisfaction for the murder of a nobleman in the bloom of his youth, and full enjoyment of his friends, his honours, and his fortune." Again and again the voices of money and power declared the sacredness of property in terms hitherto reserved for human life. Banks were credited with souls, and the circulation of gold likened to that of blood. Forgers, for example, were almost invariably hanged, and gentlemen knew why: "Forgery is a stab to commerce, and only to be tolerated in a commercial nation when the foul crime of murder is pardoned." In a mood of unrivaled assurance and complacency, Parliament over the century created one of the bloodiest criminal codes in Europe. Few of the new penalties were the product of hysteria, or ferocious reaction; they were part of the conventional wisdom of England's governors. Locke himself defined political power as the right to create the penalty of death, and hence all lesser ones. And Shaftesbury, the enlightened rationalist who attacked both Hobbes and the Church for making fear the cement of the social order, at the same time accepted that the "mere Vulgar of Mankind" might perhaps "often stand in need of such a rectifying Object as *the Gallows* before their Eyes."[27]

Yet for all the passage of statutes authorizing the death penalty, relatively few people actually hung. Intriguingly, the same people who advocated severe penalties supported in actual practice alternative sanctions. Radzinowicz argues that this reflected a conflict between the judiciary and the legislature.[28] But, as Hay points out, other data of the period suggest harmony between the two.

Eighteenth-century England had an aristocratic ruling class whose long struggle with the newly emergent capitalist class had already begun. By articulating criminal laws with severe sanctions, the state helped establish the ideology of the purported classes; buttressing landed classes and capitalists alike. By showing mercy in the actual application of the sanction, however, the aristocracy gathered adherents. It established its legitimacy not as justice, but as mercy. Patronage became a key bulwark of aristocratic privilege.

A ruling class organizes its power in the state. The sanction of the state is force, but it is force that is legitimized, however imperfectly, and therefore the state deals also in ideologies. Loyalties do not grow simply in complex societies: they are twisted, invoked and often consciously created. Eighteenth-century England was not a free market of patronage relations. It was a society with a bloody penal code, an astute ruling class who manipulated it to their advantage, and a people schooled in the lessons of Justice, Terror and Mercy. The benevolence of rich men to poor, and all the ramifications of patronage, were upheld by the sanction of the gallows and the rhetoric of the death sentence.[29]

Rather than societal needs of consensus we propose a dialectical model which holds that changing social relations resulting from changes in legal, political, and economic forms ineluctably change law and the legal order. Law, born in society's womb, in turn changes society. Social and legal relations shaped by a feudal economic system and a political organization that shared out power among feudal barons could not survive the transformation to monarchy in control of the economy. Sixteenth-century law could not survive the emergence of mercantilism. Mercantilist law fell before capitalism. Law is a living institution, created by people occupying roles and positions in a social structure. It does not, however, arise automatically in response to "social needs." It reflects the fundamental contradictions and conflicts of the time. The shape of monarchial law, of mercantile law, of capitalist law responds not only to the demands of the ruling class, but the historically derived matrix of ideas and class forces of the particular epoch.

People coping with the contradictions and conflicts of western capitalist political economies produced our system of criminal justice. As we have seen in the studies of theft and in the emergence of the Black Act the long transition from feudalism to capitalism involved struggles which culminated in a set of criminal laws. In each period, the criminal law buttressed the logic and ideology of the then-prevailing system. Society embodied deepseated contradictions: between owners and workers, between peasants and landowners, between traditionally granted public access to land and the private ownership of property. These contradictions rather than consensus or societal needs, became the wellspring of British and American criminal law.

Schematically we can depict the theory we have been developing as follows:

Political economy ——➤ contradictions in the social and economic demands of different classes.

Contradictions in demands ——➤ dilemmas and conflicts between those classes.

Contradictions-dilemmas-conflicts ——➤ resolutions in terms of the form of the state and the legal order.

Resolutions ——➤ contradictions-dilemmas-conflicts.

And so on without end.

These forces and this process constitute the limits within which the state defines acts as criminal and from which the criminal law gets its form and its content.

Labor and Criminal Law

Industrial societies must produce a surplus. If producers consumed everything produced by human labor industrialization becomes impossible. Those who produce the goods through their labor must give up some proportion of the product to generate a surplus. Some of that surplus becomes new capital investment. So does the system recreate itself continuously; so does industrialization become possible. To accomplish this the state everywhere uses the legal order to coerce and cajole people into working at jobs they would otherwise avoid and giving up products they otherwise would keep for themselves.

Even before the surplus is expropriated from the workers, the state must create an adequate work force. At times this raises formidable problems. In the fourteenth century, the resistance of feudal landlords and the Black Death, (a cholera plague that reduced the population of Europe by 50 percent) generated a severe labor shortage. To better themselves, laborers left the landed estates to take advantage of the increased relative demand for their services. The state introduced vagrancy laws to resolve the conflict between feudal landlord and laborers. The early vagrancy statutes reflect the Crown's siding with the landowners:

Every man and woman, of what condition he be, free or bond, able in body, and within the age of three-score years, not living in merchandise nor exercising any craft, nor having of his own whereon to live, nor proper land whereon to occupy himself, and not serving any other, if he in convenient service (his estate considered) be required to serve, shall be bounded to serve him which shall him require. . . . And if any refuse, he shall on conviction by two true men . . . be committed to gaol till he find surety to serve.

And if any workman or servant, of what estate or condition he be, retained in any man's service, do depart from the said service without reasonable cause or license, before the term agreed on, he shall have pain of imprisonment.[30]

In 1351 this statute was strengthened by the stipulation: "And none shall go out of the town where he dwelled in winter, to serve the summer, if he may serve in the same town."[31] These laws were "an attempt to make the vagrancy statutes a substitute for serfdom."[32]

Gradually feudalism disappeared. In 1575 Queen Elizabeth granted freedom to the last serfs in England. After that, the state acted first in the interests of the new landed gentry, and later of the manufacturing classes. Changes in vagrancy laws reflected this transition. The breakup of feudalism coincided with increased commerce and trade. The commercial emphasis in England at the turn of the sixteenth century had particular importance in the development of vagrancy laws. With commercialism came considerable traffic bearing valuable goods. In the middle of the fourteenth century 169 important merchants plied their trade. At the beginning of the sixteenth century 3000 merchants engaged in foreign trade alone. England became highly dependent upon commerce for its economic surplus. Italians conducted a great deal of the commerce of England during this early period. The populace despised them. Citizens attacked and robbed them of their goods. "The general insecurity of the times made any transportation hazardous. The specal risks to which the alien merchant was subjected gave rise to the royal practice of issuing formally executed covenants of safe conduct through the realm."[33]

The new focal concern continued in 1 Edw. 6 c.3 (1547), and was even more general in its scope:

Whoever man or woman, being not lame, impotent, or so aged or diseased that he or she cannot work, not having whereon to live, shall be lurking in any house, or loitering or idle wandering by the highway side, or in streets, cities, towns, or villages, not applying themselves to some honest labour, and so continuing for three days; or running away from their work; every such person shall be taken for a vagabond. And . . . upon conviction of two witnesses . . . the same loiterer [shall] be marked with a hot iron in the breast with the letter V, and adjudged him to the person bringing him, to be his slave for two years.[34]

In sum, the vagrancy laws constituted a legislative innovation designed to provide an abundance of cheap labor to England's ruling class of landowners during a period when serfdom was breaking down and when the pool of available labor was depleted. They hit at the "idle" and "those refusing to labour." With the breakup of feudalism the utility of these laws disappeared. The increased dependence of the economy upon commerce and trade made irrelevant the former use of the vagrancy statutes. After the turn of the sixteenth century the emphasis turned to "rogues," "vagabonds," and others suspected of criminal activities. During this period, the statutes embraced "roadmen" who preyed upon citizens who transported goods from one place to another. The increased importance of commerce to England during this period brought forth laws to protect it. The vagrancy statutes originally aimed at providing serfs for feudal landlords became a weapon in this new enterprise.[35]

In the United States during the latter nineteenth and early twentieth centuries, vagrancy statutes again came to serve the interests of the propertied classes. During times of harvest, agricultural states enforced vagrancy statutes as a means of pushing the indigent into agricultural labour. In depressions, analogous statutes served to keep the unemployed from entering the state.

Vagrancy statutes also came to serve the police as a catch-all to permit the police to deal with the poor in their discretion. Vagrancy statutes inherently swim in vagueness. The Jacksonville, Florida ordinance at issue in *Papachristou* v. *City of Jacksonville*, 405 U.S. 156 (1972), for example, reads as follows:

Rogues and vagabonds, or dissolute persons who go about begging, common gamblers, persons who use juggling or unlawful games or plays, common drunkards, common night walkers, thieves, pilferers or pickpockets, traders in stolen property, lewd, wanton and lascivious persons, keepers of gambling places, common railers and brawlers, persons wandering or strolling about from place to place without any lawful purpose or object, habitual loafers, disorderly persons, persons neglecting all lawful business and habitually spending their time by frequenting houses of ill fame, gaming houses, or places where alcoholic beverages are sold or served, persons able to work but habitually living upon the earnings of their wives or minor children shall be deemed vagrants and upon conviction in the Municipal Court shall be punished [by 90 days imprisonment, $500 fine, or both].''[36]

(Parenthetically, one could hardly formulate a better statement of the early twentieth-century middle-class American Protestant ethic.)

Everywhere, the police must respond to dual demands. On the one hand, they must obey the law. They have no general authority to arrest. They may only arrest for breach of a law. On the other hand, they must prevent crime before it happens. Nobody has a scientific way of identifying potential criminals before they commit a crime, although all people have their prejudices. The police, therefore, must simultaneously scrupulously refrain from arresting a person until she has breached the law, and arrest a person likely to commit a crime before she has breached the law.

Police escape this dilemma by seizing upon vague laws, like the Jacksonville ordinance. The statute gives them the opportunity to arrest practically anybody they suspect will likely commit a crime, and then claim that the accused violated the ordinance. In *Papachristou*, five consolidated cases concerned ten individuals. Four had been driving in an automobile in the small hours—two black men and two white women. One was a part-time organizer for a black political group. The police arrested one because, they claim, he had a reputation as a thief. (The police arrested his companion for "loitering" after they had ordered him to stand in the driveway of a house.) The police stopped one for speeding, but charged him as a "common thief." Another had a bad record. A policeman saw him on the street and called him to the police car, intending to arrest him unless he had a good explanation for being on the street.

In short, vagrancy statutes became an important weapon in police hands to enforce a kind of order based on policeman's suspicions, rather than due process of law.

The contradiction between the uses to which the police put vagrancy statutes and the U.S. Constitution's Due Process Clause finally did in vagrancy statutes in this country. In *Papachristou*, a case supported by the American Civil Liberties Union, the Supreme Court struck down the Jacksonville ordinance as a violation of due process (they held it unconstitutionally vague). Justice Douglas said that

here the net is cast large, not to give the courts the power to pick and choose, but to increase the arsenal of the police. . . . Where the list of crimes is so all-inclusive and generalized as the one in this ordinance, those convicted may be punished for no more than vindicating affronts to police authority. . . . Another aspect of the ordinance's vagueness appears when we focus, not on the lack of notice given a potential offender, but on the efficacy of the unfettered discretion it places in the hands of the Jacksonville police. Caleb Foote . . . has called the vagrancy-type law as offering "punishment by analogy." . . . Such crimes . . . are not compatible with our constitutional system. . . . Arresting a person on suspicion, like arresting a person for investigation, is foreign to our system, even when the arrest is for past criminality. Future criminality, however, is the common justiffication for the presence of vagrancy statutes. . . . The Jacksonville ordinance cannot be squared with our constitutional standards and is plainly unconstitutional.[37]

As a practical matter, so ended the long, disreputable history of vagrancy statutes.

Criminal Law and Criminal Response

People are not machines. The state may pass laws to change consciousness, establish legitimacy or coerce compliance. The people whom the law addresses may not, however, accept the commands. Villagers continued to poach, clerks continued to "liberate" goods and funds from their employers. In the eighteenth and early nineteenth centuries in England, workers were faced with the advent of manufacturing. Concomitantly, as manufacturers tried to move the production of goods from village homes to manufacturing plants, the workers confronted a decline in their control over their labor. They rebelled:

The hours of work were fourteen, fifteen, or even sixteen a day, six days a week throughout the year except for Christmas Day and Good Friday. That was the ideal timetable of the industrialists. It was rarely achieved, for the human animal broke down under the burden; and he squandered his time in palliatives—drink, lechery, bloodsports. Or he revolted, burned down the factory, or broke up the machinery, in a pointless, frenzied, industrial "jacquerie."[38]

As Pearson points out, nobody can construe the workers' reaction to the advent of machine manufacturing replacing village crafts as "pointless." They sought to arrest the inhuman process of manufacturing that demanded long hours at routinized, boring tasks away from the home.

During the seventeen and eighteen hundreds "machine smashing" periodically ripped through the land:

Attacks on machines took place from the 1760s when Hargreaves' spinning jenny was repeatedly smashed, and mills which used the jenny were turned over. According to traditional accounts, Hargreaves was chased out of the neighbourhood, and his promotor, the factory owner, "Parsley" Peel, retreated from North East Lancashire in disgust, taking his capital to another area where he hoped the work force would be more sensible. Peel's mills near Blackburn and Accrington were completely destroyed, one having been already rebuilt after attacks by machine-smashers only a few years before.

There were many more attacks on machines. One of the most famous periods of disturbance was during the War in Europe when from 1811 to 1813 various kinds of new machines were attacked in Nottinghamshire, Yorkshire and Lancashire. The attackers were known as the "Luddites," and they claimed leadership from a probably fictitious "General

Ludd.'' To mention one more instance, there was a great uprising against the machine in North East Lancashire in 1826 when power-looms were destroyed in the cotton towns. Machine-smashing was not restricted to the textile industry, of course. In 1830 there was an explosion of popular discontent throughout southern and eastern England when the rural poor attacked the hated threshing machines and set fire to hay ricks. Known as the Swing Riots, these rioters attacked the machines in the name of ''Captain Swing.''[39]

Machine smashing was also employed by workers as a means of obtaining higher wages and better working conditions, what Pearson refers to as ''strike by rioting.'' These acts were quite consistent with eighteenth-century English culture:

The ''crowd'' or the ''mob'' could take as its object the defense of any number of rights and customs—the fair price of food, fair access to the common lands, or smuggling which was so common in England, as in most parts of Europe, to be thought of as a ''right'' rather than a ''crime.''[40]

Along the coasts, local residents also engaged in the systematic wrecking of ships. In response to the demands of the mercantile classes, government put teeth into the laws forbidding the activity. So too did the government intervene against the machine smashers. Whatever motivations, they experienced the law ''as the lash of the whip, the threat of transportation, the gallows at Tyburn, and the awful sight of the bodies of convicts swinging in chains.''[41]

Child-Saving

In the modern world, we have come to define ''juvenile delinquency'' as an important social problem. Ironically, the issue of recalcitrant and uncontrolled youth has existed as long as time. How did the legal system select youth for special treatment? In two separate analyses of the emergence of ''child welfare'' and ''delinquency'' laws Tove Stang Dahl[42] and Anthony Platt[43] provide us with some answers. Summarizing the results of his research into the child-saving movement in the United States Platt concludes:

The child-saving movement had far-reaching consequences for the organization and administration of the juvenile justice system. Its overall impact was conservative in both spirit and achievement. The child-savers' reforms were generally aimed at imposing sanctions on conduct unbecoming ''youth'' and disqualifying youth from the benefit of adult privileges. The child-savers were prohibitionists, in a general sense, who believed that social progress depended on efficient law enforcement, strict supervision of children's leisure and recreation, and enforced education. They were more concerned with restriction than with liberation, eliminating ''foreign'' and radical ideologies, and preparing youth as a disciplined and devoted work force. The austerity of the criminal law and penal institutions was only of incidental concern; their central interest was in the normative outlook of youth and they were most successful in their efforts to extend governmental control over a whole range of youthful activities which had previously been handled locally and informally. In this sense, their reforms were aimed at defining, rationalizing and regulating the dependent status of youth. Although the child-savers' attitudes to youth were often paternalistic and romantic, their commands were backed up by force and an abiding faith in the benevolence of government.

The child-saving movement had its most direct impact on the children of the urban poor. The fact that "troublesome" adolescents were depicted as "sick" or "pathological," imprisoned "for their own good," addressed in paternalistic vocabulary, and exempted from criminal law processes, did not alter the subjective experiences of control, restraint and punishment. It is ironic, as Philippe Aries observed in his historical study of European family life, that the obsessive solicitude of family, church, moralists and administrators for child welfare served to deprive children of the freedoms which they had previously shared with adults and to deny their capacity for initiative, responsibility and autonomy.

The child-savers' rhetoric of benevolence should not be mistaken for popular, democratic programs. Paternalism was a typical ingredient of most reforms in the Progressive era, legitimizing imperialism in foreign policy and extensive state control at home. Even the corporate rich, "revealed a strikingly firm conception of a benevolent feudal approach to the firm and its workers" and "were willing to extend—to provide in the manner of traditional beneficence—such things as new housing, old age pensions, death payments, wage and job schedules, and bureaus charged with responsibility for welfare, safety, and sanitation. But when benevolence failed—in domestic institutions such as schools and courts or in economic policies abroad—government officials and industrial leaders were quick to resort to massive and overwhelming force.[44]

This does not suggest that the child-savers and other Progressive movements did not achieve significant reforms. They created major changes. In the arena of criminal justice they developed new institutions that transformed juvenile justice. These reforms, however, to use Andre Gorz's distinctions, were "reformist" rather than "structural":

Structural reform . . . does not mean a reform which rationalizes the existing system while leaving intact the existing distribution of powers; this does not mean to delegate to the (capitalist) State the task of improving the system.

Structural reform is by definition a reform implemented or controlled by those who demand it. Be it in agriculture, the university, property relations, the region, the administration, the economy, etc., a structural reform *always* requires the creation of new centers of democratic power.

Whether it be at the level of companies, schools, municipalities, regions, or of the national Plan, etc., structural reform always requires a *decentralization* of the decision making power, a *restriction on the powers of State or Capital*, an *extension of popular power*, that is to say, a victory of democracy over the dictatorship of profit.[45]

By this definition, then, the child-saving movement constituted a "reformist" change. Those whom it proposed to benefit did not control it. It did not create new centers of democratic power. It extended and consolidated state power. It helped to preserve existing economic and political relationships.

This interpretation of the child-saving movement resonates with those revisionist histories of the Progressive era that argue that in part Progressivism became a businessmen's movement, and that big business became an integral part of the

Progressive coalition. Gabriel Kolko points out that large corporations and business leaders supported federal regulation of the ecomomy in order to protect their own investments and stabilize the marketplace.[46] Business leaders and political spokesmen at bottom agreed about fundamental economic issues. "There was no conspiracy during the Progressive Era," notes Kolko. "There was a basic consensus among political and business leaders as to what was the public good, and no one had to be cajoled in a sinister manner."[47] In his analysis of liberal ideology in the Progressive era, James Weinstein similarly argues that "few reforms were enacted without the tacit approval, if not the guidance, of the large corporate interests." For the corporation executive, liberalism meant "the responsibility of all classes to maintain and increase the efficiency of the existing social order."[48]

An examination of other areas of reform during the Progressive era reveals that, like in the child-saving movement, those programs which enjoyed business support generally had conservative consequences, despite their sometimes revolutionary rhetoric. For example, upper-class businessmen who did not need cheap child labor supported child labor reform. According to Jeremy Felt's history of that movement, "the abolition of child labor could be viewed as a means of driving out marginal manufacturers and tenement operators, hence increasing the consolidation and efficiency of business."[49] Educational reforms also enjoyed big-business support. Charles Loring Brace, writing in the mid-nineteenth century, recommended, "in the interests of public order, of liberty, of property, for the sake of our own safety and the endurance of free institutions here, a strict and careful law, which shall compel every minor to learn to read and write, under severe penalties in case of disobedience."[50] By the close of the century, a sterile and authoritarian educational system had been imposed upon an ungrateful and hostile working class.

In her studies of child welfare in England and Norway, Dahl confirms these general conclusions.[51]

Public Indignation

Part of the mythology that surrounds the law holds that a change in the values of "the people" creates new law. This perspective, which social scientists as well as lawyers often espouse, sees an assumed "value-consensus" of the community as the root of all law. Such a view does injustice to the realities of legislation. Nevertheless, a substantial body of data indicates that public views on morality *do* affect legislation—especially those views of segments of the public which are represented by groups of moral entrepreneurs. These consist of groups organized to influence lawmaking and law enforcement according to their view of morality.

Some of the earliest systematic work on the issue of public indignation and criminal law legislation was done by the Danish sociologist Svend Ranulf in the two classical studies *The Jealousy of the Gods* and *Moral Indignation and Middle Class Psychology*.[52] By careful historical analysis Ranulf shows that in both Greece and Europe the "disinterested tendency to punish" for moral breaches emerges with the development of a lower middle class.[53] Ranulf explains this phenomenon. Moral indignation stems from a basic tendency of the lower middle class to envy the position of the more affluent classes. This psychological interpretation seems less than enlightening but, as Ranulf notes, accepting the historical sequence of events does not necessitate the acceptance of his explanation.

Evidence of the role of moral entrepreneurs as a force creating changes in the criminal law is provided by Joseph Gusfield's study of the emergence of prohibition laws.[54] Gusfield argues persuasively that the moving force behind the emergence of prohibition laws consisted of an organized effort by those segments of the middle class who saw their economic and social position threatened by changing economic forces. The decline of small-town society with its middle-class, rural background created a constituency anxious to assert its importance through law. This threatened, downwardly mobile class managed to bring sufficient political pressure that politicals passed law in order to placate them.[55]

An examination of the role of groups also demonstrates the effect of public indignation on the emergence and shape of the law organized to protect the ''public interest.'' In the United States, much of the law governing criminal procedure has taken its shape from the do-good efforts of groups of moral entrepreneurs, especially the American Civil Liberties Union and the National Association for the Advancement of Colored People. The ACLU has litigated many criminal law cases concerned with police procedures. The ACLU provided funds and legal counsel for a series of landmark cases in which the U.S. Supreme Court virtually rewrote the laws governing police behavior. Although they defend the rights of the lower classes, the members of these moral entrepreneurial groups consist mainly of middle-class members of the community, and rest upon financial contributions from these same people.

The moral indignation of the middle class by itself does not guarantee that a legislature will enact a criminal law or that an appellate court will in effect do the same thing. In general it appears that middle-class indignation most likely culminates in the creation of new law when the indignation coalesces into a working organization with specific roles and financial backing.

Middle-class organizations, for the most part, cannot combat or counteract the forces of the classes which control the economic resources of the society. As we saw earlier in our consideration of the history of criminal law legislation, the economic elites' interests find protection in the elite ability to influence legislation directly and in their capacity to mobilize bias. This ability flows from their position in society. During the discussion of the Drug Abuse, Prevention and Control Act of 1970, for example, the interests of the law-enforcement bureaucracies and the drug industry had such ample representation that the moral indignation of the middle class, ostensibly the basis for the law's enactment, became a mere excuse to legitimize the new act.

The groups of moral entrepreneurs who represent the indignation of at least some segment of the middle class fare best when they engage forces less potent than the economic elites. In particular, they most affect criminal law legislation when they engage the law-enforcement bureaucracies or small businesses only.

Such was the case in a recent debate in New York over revision of the laws concerning prostitution.[56] The issue arose over Article 230 of the 1965 New York State Penal Law. Sections 230.00, 230.05, and 230.10 of the code read as follows:

Sec. 230.00 Prostitution
A person is guilty of prostitution when such person engages or agrees or offers to engage in sexual conduct with another person in return for a fee.
Prostitution is a violation. L. 1965, c. 1030, eff. Sept. 1, 1967.

Sec. 230.05 Patronizing a prostitute
A person is guilty of patronizing a prostitute when:

1 Pursuant to a prior understanding, he pays a fee to another person as compensation for such person or a third person having engaged in sexual conduct with him; or

2 He pays or agrees to pay a fee to another person pursuant to an understanding that in return therefore such person or a third person will engage in sexual conduct with him; or

3 He solicits or requests another person to engage in sexual conduct with him in return for a fee.

Patronizing a prostitute is a violation. L. 1965, c. 1030, eff. Sept. 1, 1967.

Sec. 230.10 Prostitution and patronizing a prostitute; no defense
In any prosecution for prostitution or patronizing a prostitute, the sex of the two parties or prospective parties to the sexual conduct engaged in, contemplated, or solicited is immaterial, and it is no defense that:

1 Such persons were of the same sex; or

2 The person who received, agreed to receive or solicited a fee was a male and the person who paid or agreed or offered to pay such fee was a female. L. 1965, c. 1030, eff. Sept. 1, 1967.

At the time its proponents put forward this revised code, the statute provided for prostitution a penalty of up to three years in a reformatory or a year in jail. Until 1960, court decisions defined prostitution as an act that only a female could commit. A 1960 court decision drew homosexuality under the statute's umbrella.[57]

The new code on prostitution made two significant changes: First, it included as a violation patronizing a prostitute and, second, it greatly reduced the penalty for prostitution by making the act a "violation" rather than a crime. The maximum sentence for a violation is fifteen days rather than a year in jail.

In 1961 the governor of New York appointed a commission to recommend needed revisions of the Penal Law and the Code of Criminal Procedure. The commission staff relied heavily on the advice of Chief Justice John M. Murtagh, a judge nationally known for his concern with criminal procedures in dealing with prostitution. The commission members also relied on England's *Wolfenden Report* (1957), the model penal codes of the American Bar Association, and procedures in other states.

After four years of work the commission held "public" hearings on the proposed penal code revision. The "public" probably did not know of them. Some special interest groups did. Of the 520 articles in the Penal Code, as a result of these hearings the legislature revised only the one dealing with prostitution. Its major change added "patronizing a prostitute" as a violation, something *not* included in the commission's original proposed code. Including "patronizing" had as its major proponent the American Social Health Association. It argued that to control the spread of disease effectively required the patron's punishment. The association buttressed its view by arguments from Dorris Clarke, attorney and retired chief probation officer of the New York City Magistrates Court. Further support came from testimony of an independent doctor who argued that since both customer and prostitute engaged in the forbidden activity, both should receive punishment.

Judge Murtagh and a few spokesmen for the police combatted this position. They argued that the police needed to have the confidence of customers to get testimony against prostitutes. That opposition, however, could not in number or organization match the patron clause's proponents. That clause entered the law.

On the eve of the new law becoming effective the police relaxed their enforcement policies. Subsequently a rumor circulated that prostitutes had engulfed the city. The source of the rumor does not appear, but "New York politicians, businessmen, and the police may have begun to talk about an influx of prostitutes and the need for a 'cleanup' because they were dissatisfied with the law becoming 'soft' on prostitutes."[58] During this time police department representatives began telling newsmen of increases in prostitution.

The commission that had drafted the new law denied these allegations. In any event, in August 1967 midtown businessmen and the New York Hotel Association, along with politicians and government officials, pressured the police to get rid of the prostitutes in the area of Times Square. Approximately two weeks before the new law became effective the police made a series of raids around Times Square and arrested suspected prostitutes by the score. On August 20 alone on Times Square alone they arrested 121. Between August and September 23, they arrested 1300. After the date when the new law became effective (September 1), they charged most of these arrested not with prostitution, but with loitering or disorderly conduct.

The New York Civil Liberties Union, the Legal Aid Society, and a New York judge all made vociferous protests over the mass arrest of persons for disorderly conduct and loitering when even the police knew that these charges would not stand up in court. The *New York Times* reported on September 22, 1967:

In a press release, the New York Civil Liberties Union protested police practices in the "Times Square cleanup campaign." The NYCLU reported, "Literally hundreds of women have been arrested and charged with disorderly conduct during the summer months, and the situation still continues." "There is a conspiracy on the part of the police to deprive these women of their civil rights by arresting them on insubstantial charges." "Women are being arrested in a dragnet and charged with disorderly conduct and loitering in order to raise the number of arrests." "Many innocent girls are undoubtedly being caught in the net and the entire practice is an outrageous perversion of the judicial process. Furthermore, women who refuse to submit to the unlawful practices of the police have been manhandled."

The Union reported Judge Basel saying, "I don't doubt that most of them are prostitutes, but it is a violation of the civil liberties of these girls. Even streetwalkers are entitled to their Constitutional rights. The District Attorney moved in all these cases to have the charges thrown out, but in every case the girls were arrested after it was too late for night court, so they were kept over night with no substantial charges pending against them."[59]

The police roundup continued. From September 23 to September 30 another 1100 arrests were made. These arrests brought the total from August 20 to September 30 to 2400, only 200 fewer arrests in six weeks than had been reported during the preceding six months. Significantly, only 61 percent of the arrests for violation of the prostitution ordinance involved the arrest of patrons—even though a policeman could only legally arrest a prostitute if he observed a patron offering and a prostitute accepting a fee.

This began a campaign by the police department, in cooperation with the hotel association and businessmen in the area, to change those parts of the new penal code that liberalized the prostitution laws. In September 1967 the police department prefiled amendments for conservation in the 1968 legislature. These amendments, in effect, would have given the police almost complete discretion in the arrest of suspected prostitutes. They would have returned prostitution to the status of a crime, thus increasing the penalties. These amendments would have effectively enabled the police to avoid the application of the law to patrons without formally changing this part of the penal code.

The mayor of New York City created a committee to look into the new law and the problem of prostitution. The committee in the end recommended that the law reclassify prostitution as a crime instead of its present status as a "violation" (thus increasing the maximum penalty from fifteen days to one year in jail). But the committee did *not* recommend adopting any of the other changes advocated by the police and the hotel association. When they presented this proposal to the state legislature, it went to a Senate committee. The committee voted *against* sending the bill back to the Senate. In the end, the welfare, civil liberties, and bar association interests dominated over the interests of the police and the businessmen with respect to the severity of the sanctions and the criteria for making an arrest. The police and businessmen controlled enforcement policies, but no immediate change in the law ensued. The New York Bar Association, NYCLU, and Legal Aid Society, along with some prominent public figures, proved more potent forces in shaping the formal law than did the police and the hotel owners association.

The analysis of the New York controversy over prostitution demonstrates this. For the most part the controversy over the new law engaged only different groups of moral entrepreneurs from the middle class, civil liberties and welfare groups on the one side, police and small businessmen on the other. The issue did not touch the interests of the state's economic elite or even the bulk of the city population. They stood on the sidelines. To the extent that the upper classes entered the debate at all, they tacitly supported the new legislation (or so one judges from the support given by the bar associations and commissions in their suggested revisions). This case also illustrates how discretion by the police, prosecutors, and judges can subvert the law. The 1965 revision made patrons, who doubtless represented the entire spectrum of social classes, equally culpable. The police, however, through selective enforcement, rendered this aspect of the law virtually meaningless and forced reconsideration by the lawmakers.

Law-enforcement agencies become vested interest groups with considerable influence over legal norms. Their influence flows in part from the ignorance of people and legislatures about the relevant facts and explanations for criminality. Most people assume that law-enforcement personnel have real expertise in this area. Law enforcement agencies can therefore often define what constitutes the "best" rules for them to enforce. Not surprisingly, these people rarely advocate laws likely to create enforcement problems. On the whole, they seek the enactment of laws prohibiting acts which they feel deserve criminal sanctions and which will permit enforcement with a minimum of organizational strain.

The emergence of antidrug laws in the United States illustrates the important role of law-enforcement agencies in shaping legal norms. The United States first enacted an antidrug law in 1914.[60] The legislature ostensibly had the purpose to better collect tax revenues on drugs brought into the country. The statute did not propose to punish drug users or to restrict the physicians' freedom in administering drugs to drug addicts. Subsequently, however, as a consequence of the efforts of federal law-enforcement agencies responsible for enforcing the drug laws, the courts broadened the interpretation of the Harrison Act to prevent the administering of drugs to addicts by physicians and the possession and taking of drugs by addicts. In addition, the Federal Narcotics Bureau waged an intensive propaganda and lobbying campaign in state as well as federal governmental agencies. Consequently most states now have antidrug laws that make it criminal to possess or distribute drugs, or give them to addicts.

Court decisions have not always coincided with the intention of the Federal Narcotics Bureau. There exists today substantial legal precedent for permitting physicians under certain circumstances to administer drugs to addicts. The bureau, however, can select for prosecution only those cases that the higher courts will not likely overturn. They rarely prosecute cases where appeals to higher courts may occur. Some of the earlier decisions have, therefore, remained on the books. As a consequence, many physicians are ignorant about the freedom they in fact enjoy in the treatment of drug addicts. The medical profession's treatment of drug addiction thus became a function not of medical wisdom, but of pressures generated by the Federal Narcotics Bureau, partly on legislatures and partly through the threat of prosecution.

More recently, the efforts of the Federal Narcotics Bureau and local police agencies have supported the expansion of the antidrug laws to include marijuana and LSD. For years the enforcement of drug laws concentrated on the lower classes. Marijuana originally became a "problem" among the Mexican-American population. Other drugs prevailed in the ghettos. "Respectable" members of the community could generally maintain their drug habits with the help of their physicians or other sources of drugs (including at times enforcement agents themselves) which ran little risk of arrest. In their own bureaucratic interests, the law-enforcement agencies expanded these laws, which did not at the time appear to commit them to a program that would involve arresting persons who could cause them "trouble."

The situation did not turn out exactly as anticipated. As part of their lifestyle, students in colleges and high schools adopted marijuana and a host of other drugs. As a consequence, the police frequently used entrapment and general harassment of student "drug users." Since they used these techniques against the children of the middle and upper classes, their parents became strongly critical of the police—a criticism the police would normally have avoided.

Today, there has come into being a strong movement to eliminate marijuana and some other drugs from the list of harmful drugs prohibited by law. Although originally opposed by the law enforcers, they increasingly favor it. The enforcement of these laws against middle- and upper-class youths has not brought forth praise and rewards for the enforcement agencies. On the contrary, it has exposed them to a great deal of criticism. In the last analysis it seems likely that this fact, and not scientific evidence demonstrating that marijuana causes less injury than alcohol, will bring about changes in the laws in question. The harmful effects of an action have little relevance to the decision to define it as criminal.

Significantly, law-enforcement agencies rarely lobby or propagandize to obtain laws which might require them to arrest persons of high social standing. For example, law enforcement agencies rarely concern themselves with illegal business practices. To insist on stringent enforcement of such laws would only make life difficult for the agencies.

The Mobilization of Bias

An understanding of the legal order requires that we examine how the legal order excludes issues as well as how it brings them under its umbrella. People, social classes, and groups with sufficient organization, money, and interest affect legislation not only by getting laws enacted that favor their interests and views, but also by preventing the enactment of laws that will interfere with them. In this process, special economic interests have particular importance. In 1970 the pharmaceutical industry lobbied for and participated in the writing of legislation that protected vital interests of the industry by excluding certain drugs from the category of "dangerous drugs."[61]

The Comprehensive Drug Abuse, Prevention and Control Act of 1970 is intended to control the distribution and use of "dangerous drugs." The bill includes the controversial provision that law-enforcement agents can legally enter private dwellings without even having to knock on the door (thus contradicting the sacrosanct value that "a man's home is his castle") to search and investigate for the presence of drugs. The bill was introduced to the Congress by President Richard Nixon with the strong support of two of his major law-enforcement officers, Attorney General John Mitchell and the director of the Bureau of Narcotics and Dangerous Drugs, John Ingersoll.

As drafted by the Nixon administration with consultation from representatives of the drug industry, the bill granted heretofore unheard-of powers to the bureaucracies of the state and federal governments whose duty it was to enforce the laws controlling the distribution and possession of "drugs." Significantly, the bill placed greatest emphasis on imported drugs, and drugs produced easily by individuals (principally heroin, marijuana, and LSD). Drugs that the pharmaceutical manufacturers produced, even though they frequently sold illegally, the bill left virtually uncontrolled. This came about not by accident but through the concerted efforts of the pharmaceutical industry to protect its economic interests.

So far as the pharmacists were concerned. the issue centered on the manufacture of amphetamines, metaphetamines ("speed"), and two drugs closely related to these, Librium and Valium. A series of hearings before various congressional committees and in the two houses brought the following facts to light. Each year in the United States the pharmaceutical industry produces between *eight and ten billion* amphetamine pills, consumed mainly by white, middle-class American housewives, businessmen, students, physicians, and athletes. Doctors testified that many of these consumers become psychologically dependent upon them. Two of the drugs—Librium and Valium—according to testimony before the Congress, may lead to depression and suicide. Dr. Stanley Cohen of the National Institute of Mental Health testified that many use these drugs for prolonged periods, which can result in malnutrition, prolonged psychotic states, heart irregularities, convulsions, hepatitis, and sustained brain damage.[62]

The Bureau of Narcotics and Dangerous Drugs provided the Congress with a report that two drugs, Valium and Librium, were involved in 36 suicides and 750 attempted suicides. Dr. John D. Griffith of the Vanderbilt Medical School stated: "Amphetamine addiction is more widespread, more incapacitating, more dangerous and socially disrupting than narcotic addiction." He further testified that "making these drugs available for obesity and depression has proved to be quite harmful to the public."[63] The director of Student Health Services at the University of Utah testified:

Amphetamines provide one of the major ironies of the whole field of drug abuse. We continue to insist that they are good drugs when used under medical supervision, but their greatest use turns out to be frivolous, illegal and highly destructive to the user.[64]

These statements about amphetamines' threat to public health, and the accompanying addiction, suicide, and the like, have at least the same probability as the evidence provided on the horrors and dangers of other drugs such as LSD, marijuana, and heroin. These, however, do not make large profits for the pharmaceutical companies.

Congress's failure to include these drugs in the same category as the more widely publicized ones did not result from the presentation of evidence contradicting the findings mentioned above. It resulted from a willingness to ignore evidence that pointed towards a law inimical to the interests of the drug industry. The hearings also documented that the drug industry profits greatly from the current freedom to manufacture and distribute these drugs. On these two drugs alone Hoffman-LaRoche Laboratories, producers of Valium and Librium, earned a profit in one year of over four million dollars.[65]

Drugstores sold most of the eight billion pills legally through prescriptions provided by doctors. These firms produced many pills that got diverted into the illegal market. The Bureau of Narcotics and Dangerous Drugs estimated that American drug companies produced legally between 75 and 90 percent of the amphetamines on the illegal market. Some of these pills enter the illegal market through forged prescriptions, theft, and fraud. But the drug industry plays a willing and cooperative victim of some of these practices. Narcotics bureau officers reported that one could write some drug companies, using a fake address and stationery, and obtain massive quantities of the drugs. One agent reported that he obtained twenty-five thousand pills by sending a letter to a drug company and signing his name as a medical doctor. Prescriptions on amphetamines and related drugs also invite misuse. One can write a prescription for an indefinite supply, enabling the prescription holder to return to the drugstore at will to have the prescription refilled.

Experts also testified that the real medical needs of society required, at most, the production of only a few thousand (instead of eight or ten billion) pills a year. Dr. Griffith testified that "a few thousand tablets would supply the whole medical needs of the country."[66] Some doctors even testified that the amphetamines were of almost no medical use whatsoever. Congressman Claude Pepper of Florida reported that his Select Committee on Crime had, in the fall of 1969, distributed questionnaires to medical deans and health organizations throughout the United States. Of fifty-three responses received by his committee only one suggested that the drug had any use whatsoever and this one suggested only that it might have some use in "the early stages of a diet program." Dr. Cohen estimated that 99 percent of the prescriptions supposedly served dietary purposes. Obesity thus becomes a legitimate excuse to get high on speed.

The testimony and reports of medical experts did not constitute, of course, the only side presented at the congressional hearings. At every stage in the history of the bill the pharmaceutical interests had strong representation. The director of the Bureau of Narcotics and Dangerous Drugs admitted, under questioning, that in drafting the bill the administration had involved representation from the drug industry.

During the hearings drug industry lobbyists testified, as did leading industry figures. The testimony invariably emphasized the danger of "speed freaks" but denied that the industry had any responsibility for the problems. Further, the industry apologists stressed the medicinal value of amphetamines, a value largely contradicted by independent testimony. Finally, the industry spokesmen insisted that present controls met the problem, and that government intervention would violate the freedom of the industry necessary for it to serve the public interest.

In the end the Congress simply swept under the rug all testimony and facts contrary to the drug industry's view. The pharmaceutical companies employed lobbyists, the national pharmaceutical associations sent representatives, and the Congress passed the bill without controlling the manufacture and distribution of any of the drugs from which the drug industry profits. In this way Congress avoided two problems: On the one hand, it did not provide legislation that would have angered the drug industry; on the other hand, they did pass a law which made it possible to arrest, prosecute, and convict more readily those powerless members of society who engage in the taking of drugs, the profits of which do not go to the established industries. One cannot interpret this legislation as a sincere attempt to do something about drug abuse. In consequence and by design it exemplifies how the laws reflect the interests of those in power at the expense (both financial and psychological) of those who lack the economic, and therefore the political, power to influence the legislative process. The Comprehensive Drug Abuse, Prevention and Control Act of 1970, strongly supported by Nixon and Mitchell, became an important weapon in the arsenal of the drug industry to reduce competition from unorganized entrepreneurs.

Worker Safety and Health

The failure of the criminal law to protect workers against unsafe and unhealthy work conditions constitutes another striking example of our thesis. For centuries, society has known of the extent and seriousness of the problem. Legal remedies, however, have emerged very slowly. On logical and moral grounds, this would seem a useful arena for criminal sanctions. The law here, however, rarely employs them.

As early as 1713 an Italian medical doctor wrote a book entitled *Diseases of Workers,* which documented the diseases and dangers found in work sites affecting significant portions of the work force in Europe.[67] The medical profession, however, did not pursue the implications of Dr. Ramazzini's pioneering work. Not until the mid-1800s did a French doctor discover the dangers inherent to workers in the sulphur industry. In 1897, the dangers to people working with benzol first became recognized. Before chemicals were recognized as dangerous, however, the mining industry was singled out as a particularly dangerous work site. 1489 people were killed working in mines in 1900. Railroads were also cited. In 1890, 2451 workers were killed and more than 22,000 injured in railroad accidents. The rate of fatalities per thousand employees in 1890 was 3.27 and the rate of injuries was 30.00 per thousand.[68]

The situation today has hardly become better. The coal mining industry in 1977 saw 139 miners killed and 14,933 became permanently disabled.[69] These figures do not include workers who suffer from black lung disease (pneumoconiosis). A recent federal government report on the coal industry estimates that with the increasing price of oil and the concomitant increased pressure to produce more coal the fatalities and injuries in the mining industry will rise annually by 35 and 39 percent, respectively, raising the number of people killed in 1985 to 370 and the number suffering disabling injuries to 42,000.[70]

Overall in the United States by conservative estimates over two and a half million people each year have their health severely affected by work-related illness and injury. Over 100,000 people die each year in accidents or from illnesses directly resulting from work. By comparison in 1976, according to the FBI, 20,505 people were murdered. The number of victims of all violent crimes (assault, robbery, etc.) amounted to just over one million.[71] Five times the number of people murdered died due to work. The number of people injured or suffering serious health problems as a result of work conditions is more than double the number of people victimized by violent crimes.

For several hundred years, people have known of the enormous toll of work-related accidents. Nevertheless, the attention directed toward "crimes of violence" and the need for "law and order"—indeed the very creation of large police forces in the world's nations and cities—evidences the mobilization of bias toward crimes of property and personal injury and away from the problems of worker safety and health.

Predictably, what attention the legal order has paid to the problem of worker safety and health has risen in periods of worker agitation and strikes. In Sweden, for example, a new set of laws establishing a large state bureaucracy to enforce factory safety and health arose on the heels of the country's largest strike.[72] Workers in recent years themselves became more conscious of the dangers they face in mining, agricultural, and chemical industries. This consciousness in turn led to the disruption of work, strikes, slowdowns, and demands by labor unions for more effective laws and law enforcement to protect workers.[73] As a result, legislatures enacted laws protecting workers from some health and safety hazards have been passed. The outcome, however, does not seem impressive.

The laws do not provide for effective enforcement. There suffices neither the size nor the organization of the enforcement agencies nor are the sanctions available to them sufficient to force business to comply with safety standards. Indeed, two recent studies in the United States and one in Sweden demonstrate that, because of the links existing between the enforcement bureaucracies and the industries they supposedly supervise, the law induced not increased worker safety so much as a burgeoning bureaucracy, with frequent "consultations" and "meetings," infrequent inspection of work sites, and even less frequent imposition of sanctions that might force a change in established practices.[74]

7.2 MORAL BOUNDARIES OR CLASS CONFLICT

We noted earlier the importance of Durkheim's two grand hypotheses on the study of criminal law. The first, which we have discussed, concerns the function of societal needs and shared values on the law creation process. The second hypothesis, which we now take up, is the proposition that societies create deviance and crime as a way of establishing its moral boundaries. Durkheim only suggested this hypothesis; it was almost seventy years later that Kai Erikson set out to test Durkheim's assertion.[75]

Using as his data the creation of the crime of witchcraft among the Puritans of New England, Erikson investigated the hypothesis that

crime (and by extension other forms of deviation) may actually perform a needed service to society by drawing people together in a common posture of anger and indignation. The deviant individual violates rules of conduct which the rest of the community holds in high respect; and when these people come together to express their outrage over the offense and to bear witness against the offender, they develop a tighter bond of solidarity than existed earlier.[76]

From his study of deviance among the Puritans, Erikson concludes that the community in effect created several "crime waves" in order to help to establish the moral boundaries of the settlement. Yet his data hardly supports his conclusion. During the relatively short period of some sixty years, this small community had three major crime waves: the antinomian controversy of 1636, the Quaker prosecutions of the late 1650s, and the witchcraft hysteria of 1692.[77] This suggests, at the very least, that each crime wave failed miserably as a source of community consensus and cohesion; otherwise so small a group of people could not have needed so many serious crime waves in so short a period of time.

As Erikson describes the Puritan settlement and these three "crime waves," crises of community morality did not precipitate them. Power struggles did, between the rulers and the ruled. As Erikson points out:

The use of the Bible as a source of law was [a problem in that] many thoughtful people in the colony soon became apprehensive because so many discretionary powers were held by the leading clique . . . "the people" themselves (which in this instance really means the enfranchised stockholders) were anxious to obtain an official code of law; and so a constitutional battle opened which had a deep impact on the political life of the Bay. On one side stood the people, soon to be represented in the General Court by elected Deputies, who felt that the Bible would supply a clearer and safer guide to law if the elders would declare at the outset how they intended to interpret its more ambiguous passages. On the other side stood the ruling cadre of the community, the ministers and magistrates, who felt that the whole enterprise would be jeopardized if they were no longer able to interpret the Word as they saw fit.[78]

Anne Hutchinson, a particularly sharp-witted and articulate woman of the community, provided an interpretation of the Bible at odds with that of the "ruling cadre" of the community. At first her activities seemed merely bizarre. In time, however, her home became a center for interpreting the Bible and began in fact to threaten the hegemony of the settlement's established authority.

Anne's talent for stirring up discussion and provoking controversy was widely respected in Boston. It must be remembered that religious activities were almost the only entertainment known in the Bay, and since the Hutchinson home always rang with the sound of religious conversation, it soon became an important community center—a kind of theological salon. As many as eighty people might gather in the parlor to talk about the sermon of the last Sabbath, and in these discussions the most prominent voice almost always belonged to Mrs. Hutchinson herself. John Winthrop [who when he died in 1649 was the "unquestioned leader of his people and in every respect entitled to be remembered as the founder of Massachusetts"] thought her "a woman of haughty and fierce carriage, of nimble wit and active spirit, and a very voluble tongue," but visitors to her home might have added that she could debate a point of theology so compellingly that at time she seemed almost inspired. Before long, the household seminars in Mrs. Hutchinson's parlor were far more popular than the sermons of John Wilson. *Not only did most of the Boston congregation turn to her for religious counsel, but many of the ranking magistrates, including the young Governor, appeared at her meetings regularly* (emphasis added).[79]

Such appeal did not go unnoticed by the "ruling cadre." John Winthrop wrote, "It was a wonder upon what a sudden the whole church of Boston (some few excepted) were become her converts."[80] Faced with such a threat to their authority, the established church leaders responded in a time-honored fashion. They sought to undermine her influence by labeling the source of the threat. The label they chose had a long history in the church as a source of heresy. They called Anne Hutchinson an "antinomian." With effort, the label stuck and in the end Anne Hutchinson and a few of her followers who in the beginning only "thought they were engaged in a local argument about church affairs . . . found themselves banished as criminals, disarmed as potential revolutionaries, or asked to recant crimes they had never known they were committing."[81]

Anne Hutchinson and her influence over the "young Governor from England" clearly threatened the establishment. A power struggle ensued. In the end victory fell to the establishment. As Erikson says, "Sainthood in New England had become a political responsibility as well as a spiritual condition." The case against Mrs. Hutchinson and her followers had a political cast. The arguments that emerged from the Hutchinson parlor used the language of theology, but (to the extent that seventeenth-century thought distinguished them) the charge against them constituted not heresy but sedition. Once the leading men of the colony began to notice the effect Mrs. Hutchinson's crusade had upon the settlers of the Bay, they moved heartily to the attack.[82]

Neither the "community" nor its search for "moral boundaries" labeled Anne Hutchinson and her followers as criminals. She posed a threat to the authority, power, and economic well-being of the ruling class. That threat undid her.

Some twenty years after the antinomian crisis the Quakers entered the colony and another outbreak of criminality resulted. The situation hardly differed from the earlier one:

The elders of Massachusetts were confronted by an elusive group of adversaries who seldom stated their case with calm reasoning but often acted as if they possessed some special insight into the mind of God. The Antinomians spoke hazily about the "covenant of grace" and the Quakers spoke in equally vague terms about an "inner light," but both were suggesting roughly the same thing; that men should engineer their own relations with God and need not submit their religious experience to the review of any church official.[83]

At first, the Quakers hardly threatened Massachusetts' power structure. Two women arrived by boat but their arrival coincided with "a worldwide reaction against the very kind of orthodoxy the settlers were trying to establish."[84] The Quaker movement, like the Hutchinsonian movement before it, gathered converts and became a threat. By the time the General Court met in October of 1658 there were "perhaps two dozen foreigners traveling around the countryside in an effort to stir up dissension and a hundred or more local converts who met together for religious meetings." In early 1658 "the constables raided a house in Salem and arrested nineteen inhabitants of the town who had met there with two foreign missionaries.'' Subsequent records of the county court indicate that this cell continued to meet in one fashion or another for many years and soon grew to a membership of over fifty people—quite a considerable number in so small a town.[85]

The courts responded to the threat in typical Puritan fashion. The General Court enacted laws that punished Quakers more severely than had heretofore been possible. There was, subsequently, a show of force against the Quakers that included the public execution of two of their members. Local constables performed ''prodigious feats of persecution and in the months that followed, the number of confiscations, household raids, public floggings, and the like were greatly increased.''[86]

For all the reaction against the Quakers, the conflict had minimal *ideological* context.[87] The authorities formally accused the Quakers of little more than wearing hats in front of magistrates and using words like ''thee'' and ''thou.'' Yet because the movement increased its popularity among some of the people of Massachusetts, it posed a threat to the authority of ministers and magistrates. They therefore defined as criminal to be a Quaker and meted out the most severe punishments in order to stop the potential revolution.

The outbreak of witchcraft, the Puritan settlement's last crime wave, differed somewhat: there, the ruling class responded not to a threat posed by those chosen as deviant (i.e., the alleged witches) but rather to more general conflicts in the community that threatened the authority and control of its leaders.

In 1670 . . . a series of harsh arguments occurred between groups of magistrates and clergymen, threatening the alliance which had been the very cornerstone of the New England Way. In 1675 a brutal and costly war broke out with a confederacy of Indian tribes led by a wily chief called King Phillip. In 1676 Charles II began to review the claims of other persons to lands within the jurisdiction of Massachusetts, and it became increasingly clear that the old charter might be revoked altogether. In 1679 Charles specifically ordered Massachusetts to permit the establishment of an Anglican church in Boston, and in 1684 the people of the Bay had become so pessimistic about the fate of the colony that several towns simply neglected to send Deputies to the General Court. The sense of impending doom reached its peak in 1686. To begin with, the charter which had given the colony its only legal protection for over half a century was vacated by a stroke of the royal pen, and in addition the King sent a Royal Governor to represent his interests in the Bay who was both an Anglican and a man actively hostile to the larger goals of New England.[88]

Erikson also points out that during this period there threatened ''an even darker cloud'' in the form of land disputes and personal feuds. Not being able to attack the king of England and accuse him of being a criminal (though at one point they did arrest the royal governor), the potential diversion of witchcraft served to give at least the appearance of a reaffirmation of authority to those who ruled. So long as the special assistants of the courts who had the power to point out witches complied with the interests of the ruling class by accusing underlings as witches (and carefully avoided accusing any of the ruling elites), the courts followed their ''testimony'' and imposed criminal sanctions on the supposed witches. However, as will happen when functionaries are not directly answerable to the state, in time the witch-hunters

were beginning to display an ambition which far exceeded their credit. It was bad enough that they should accuse the likes of John Alden and Nathaniel Cary, but when they brought up the name of Samuel Willard, who doubled as pastor of Boston's First Church and President of Harvard College, the magistrates flatly told them they were mistaken. Not long afterwards, a brazen finger was pointed directly at the executive mansion in Boston, where Lady Phips awaited her husband's return from an expedition to Canada, and one tradition even has it that Cotton Mather's mother was eventually accused.[89]

As Erikson says, under these circumstances "the leading men of the Bay began to reconsider the whole question." They soon decided that new rules of evidence should apply in witchcraft trials. In December when the magistrates brought fifty-two persons to trial, they immediately acquitted forty-nine, sentenced to death three (two of whom were "the most senseless and ignorant creatures that could be found") and five others who were earlier condemned received their death warrants. The governor eventually reprieved all eight. Witchcraft trials ended one year after the witches first came to Salem Village.

In Massachusetts, of course people labeled particular behavior and people as "criminal" because of the consequences of that characterization. The consequences, however, did not "establish moral boundaries" but rather aided those in power to maintain their position. That in so short a time several crises led to deviant outbreaks suggests the conflict inherent in the Puritan social structure and the inability of any one group to permanently establish "moral boundaries" that would provide a permanent harmony. Furthermore, Erikson gives no evidence that any of these crime waves actually increased social solidarity except through the elimination of alternative centers of authority or power. The branding of others as criminal, heretic, or witch served to reduce conflict with them, but this hardly qualifies as evidence that process established "moral boundaries." Puritan leaders created crime waves to help the ruling stratum to maintain control of the community. Nothing evidences that these crime waves increased moral solidarity, nor can one conclude from this study that crime would serve the same function in another historical period. Purporting to identify universal needs of all societies, Durkheim's model overlooks the role crime plays in the dialectics of social change and class struggle.

Law Creation, Legitimation, and the Ruling Class

From the studies discussed thus far, one might be tempted to characterize all law as merely reflective of ruling class interests. In the end, workers did succumb to the automated mass-production factory; early vagrancy laws did coerce people into working on landed estates, and later the lineal descendants of those laws coerced people to work in urban industry; under the guise of saving the children, juvenile delinquency became institutionalized as a social problem, in reality in the interests of the ruling class. We can hardly overstate the importance of the ruling class in the creation of law. That very existence of today's ruling class, however, resulted from struggles that occurred earlier, as the result of which one set of social relations replaced another. Feudalism's ruling class lost out to the mercantilists and capitalists in the struggle for power to define crime. The capitalists in the Soviet Union lost out to the socialists; the feudal landlords and capitalists in China lost out to the communists.

Furthermore, even when wholesale changes in the political economy do not result from struggles sparked by contradictions, laws change to reflect the struggles. Workers secured an eight-hour workday; women secured the vote; organized groups of "moral entrepreneurs" succeed in changing law and the legal order in significant ways. That existing elites greatly influence law seems unarguable. Equally unarguable, however, those they seek to control often insist on limiting the power of those who rule.

7.3 CONCLUSION

Understanding consists of dividing the world into abstract units which we then use to order our observations. Too early, however, we become enamored of our observations and reify them. "Society"—an observation of some use in helping us to understand what is going on—has become an entity for many otherwise perfectly intelligent social scientists. When this happens we cease asking the right questions and become mired in abstract disputes rather than carrying on with the *sine qua non* of social scientific inquiry: the description and explanation of social reality.

People lie at the root of the social science enterprise. Their decisions make up our data. People construct worlds, create conflicts, adjudicate disputes, and make law. This chapter is about how people go about making criminal laws.

But people do not create their reality on a clean canvas. They, like the painter, must fit their creative efforts to the size and shape of their canvas, the paints they have, and the way they have come to see the world they wish to depict. All these things, and more, result from personal experiences (things like social class background, socialization in school, family, and peers), but in the long train of history they also result from larger forces that shape our lives.

An impressive number of studies in recent years focus on the creation of criminal laws. We have summarized the results of some of these studies. We have also criticized with contradictory evidence the more common theories of law creation; theories, for example, that see the law as a reflection of value-consensus, societal needs, public opinion, moral indignation, or increasing rationalization. Where then can we turn for a useful model?

It does not suffice to say that the law reflects conflicts, power, and interests. A theory must stipulate a process by which the events to be explained (in this case the creation of criminal law) come about.

The starting point for our theory is the observation that every historical era and every economic system contain certain basic *contradictions*. Contradictions inhere in the structure of the political organization, the economic system, and the ideological structure. We define a contradiction as a set of relations that contain elements that cannot coexist and which by their incompatible nature undermine basic features of the society.

The existence of contradictions creates dilemmas and conflicts which the people in positions to influence and create law try to resolve. Since they generally limit their efforts to manipulating the symptoms of the contradictions (i.e., resolving conflicts and dilemmas) the resolutions generate further contradictions, conflicts, and dilemmas. Thus does the process of law creation become ongoing and dialectical.

NOTES

1. Emile Durkheim, *The Division of Labor in Society* (New York: Free Press, 1933), p. 73. (Originally published, 1893.)

2. *Ibid.*, p. 77.

3. *Ibid.*, p. 79.

4. *Ibid.*, p. 80.

5. *Ibid.*, p. 81.

6. Ted Robert Gurr *et al.*, *The Politics of Crime and Conflict: A Comparative History of Four Cities* (Beverly Hills, CA: Sage, 1977).

7. Mark Kennedy, *Beyond Incrimination,* New York: Warner Modular Publications, 1967.

8. Karl F. Schumann, "Approaching Crime and Deviance," paper presented at European Group for the Study of Deviance, Amsterdam, 1975.

9. A. L. Morton, *A People's History of England* (London: Lawrence-Wisehart, 1938), p. 70.

10. *Ibid.*, p. 90.

11. C. Ray Jeffrey, "The Development of Crime in Early English Society," *Journal of Criminal Law, Criminology and Police Science* 47(1957):666.

12. Jerome Hall, *Theft, Law and Society*, 2nd ed. (Indianapolis: Bobbs-Merrill, 1952). See also George Fletcher, *Rethinking Criminal Law* (Boston: Little, Brown & Co., 1978).

13. *Ibid.*, p. 4.

14. *Ibid.*, pp. 34-35.

15. *Ibid.*, pp. 63-66.

16. *Ibid.*, p. 66.

17. W. Twining and D. Miers, *How to Do Things with Rules* (London: Weidenfeld and Nicholson, 1976).

18. Jerome Hall, *Living Law in a Democratic Society* (Indianapolis: Bobbs-Merrill, 1949).

19. Hall, *Theft, Law and Society,* p. 3.

20. *Ibid.*

21. *Ibid.*, p. 2.

22. Karl Marx, *Capital: The Process of Capitalist Production,* vol. 1, taken from the 3rd German ed. by Samuel Moore and Edward Aveling, and ed. by Frederick Engels (New York: Humbolt Publishing Co., 1890), p. 715.

23. E. P. Thompson, *Whigs and Hunters: The Origin of the Black Act* (New York: Pantheon Books, 1976).

24. L. Radzinowicz, *History of English Criminal Law and Its Administration from 1750,* 4 volumes (London: Stevens, 1948-68).

25. Thompson, *Whigs and Hunters.*

26. D. Hay, "Property, Authority and Criminal Law" in D. Hay, P. Linebough, J. Rule, E. P. Thompson, and C. Winslow, *Albions Fatal Free: Crime and Society in Eighteenth Century England* (London: Allen Lane, Penguin Books, 1975), p. 27.

27. *Ibid.,* p. 28.

28. Radzinowicz, *English Criminal Law.*

29. D. Hay, "Property," p. 27.

30. 23 Ed. 3 (1348).

31. 25 Ed. 3 (1351).

32. C. Foote, "Vagrancy-Type Law and Its Administration," *University of Pennsylvania Law Review* 104(1956):615.

33. F. Bradshaw, *A Social History of England* (London: University of London Press, 1915), p. 54.

34. 1 Edw. 6.C.3. (1547).

35. W. J. Chambliss, "A Sociological Analysis of the Law of Vagrancy," *Social Problems* 12(1964):45-69.

36. *Papachristou* v. *City of Jacksonville,* 405 U.S. 156 (1972).

37. *Ibid.*

38. Geoffrey Pearson, "Goths and Vandals—Crime in History," *Contemporary Crises* 2(1978):119-139.

39. *Ibid.,* p. 121.

40. *Ibid.,* p. 128.

41. *Ibid.,* pp. 129-130.

42. T. S. Dahl, "State Intervention and Social Control in Nineteenth Century Europe," *Contemporary Crises* 1(1977):163-187.

43. A. Platt, *The Child-Savers: The Invention of Delinquency* (Chicago: University of Chicago Press, 1969).

44. *Ibid.,* pp. 36-39.

45. As quoted in *ibid.,* p. 39.

46. G. Kolko, *Railroads and Regulation, 1877-1916* (Princeton: Princeton University Press, 1965).

47. *Ibid.,* p. 12.

48. James Weinstein, *The Corporate Ideal in the Liberal State 1900-1918* (Boston: Beacon Press, 1969), pp. ix, xi. As quoted in A. Platt, *The Child Savers,* p. xxi.

49. Jeremy P. Felt, *Hostages of Fortune* (Syracuse: Syracuse University Press, 1965).

50. C. L. Brace, *The Dangerous Classes of New York and Twenty Years Work among Them* (New York: Wynkoop and Hallenbeck, 1872), p. 352.

51. Dahl, "State Intervention."

52. S. Ranulf, *The Jealousy of the Gods and Criminal Law at Athens,* trans. Annie I. Fausball (New York: Arno Press, 1974).

53. S. Ranulf, *Moral Indignaton and Middle Class Psychology: A Sociological Study* (Copenhagen: Levin & Munksgaard, 1938).

54. J. Gusfield, *Symbolic Crusade: Status Politics and the American Temperance Movement* (Urbana: University of Illinois Press, 1963).

55. *Ibid.*

56. P. Roby, "Politics and Criminal Law: Revision of the New York State Penal Law on Prostitution," *Social Problems* 17(1969):83-109.

57. *Ibid.,* p. 87.

58. *Ibid.,* p. 94.

59. *Ibid.,* p. 95.

60. Alfred R. Lindesmith, *The Addict and the Law* (Bloomington: Indiana University Press, 1965). D. Dickson, "Bureaucracy and Morality: An Organizational Perspective on a Moral Crusade," *Social Problems* 16(1968):143-156. H. Becker, *Outsiders* (New York: Free Press, 1963). T. Duster, *The Legislation of Morality: Law, Drugs and Moral Judgment* (New York: Free Press, 1970). C. Reinarman, "Moral Entrepreneurs and Political Economy: Historical and Ethnographic Notes on the Construction of the Cocaine Menace," *Contemporary Crises* 3(1979):225-254.

61. J. M. Graham, "Amphetamine Politics on Capitol Hill," *Society* 9(1972):14-23.

62. U.S. House of Representatives, House Hearings, Feb. 1970, pp. 606, 607, 610, as quoted in Graham, *ibid.*

63. *Ibid.,* pp. 616, 618.

64. *Ibid.,* pp. 636, 641.

65. Graham, "Amphetamine Politics," p. 19.

66. House Hearings, Feb. 1970, p. 458.

67. Patrick Donnelly, "OSHA: The Sociology of Worker Health and Safety," Ph.D. dissertation, University of Delaware, 1980.

68. *Ibid.,* Chapter 3, p. 2.

69. Daniel Curran, "Dead Laws for Dead Men: The Case of Federal Coal Mine Health and Safety Legislation," Ph.D. dissertation, University of Delaware, 1980, p. 5.

70. *Ibid.,* p. 5.

71. Donnelly, "OSHA," Chapter 3, p. 3.

72. L. R. Stearns, "Fact and Fiction of a Model Enforcement Bureaucracy: The Labour Inspectorate of Sweden," *British Journal of Law and Society* 6(1979):1-23.

73. *Ibid*. See also Donnelly, "OSHA," and Curran, "Dead Laws."

74. Stearns, "Fact and Fiction," and Curran, "Dead Laws."

75. Kai T. Erikson, *Wayward Puritans: A Study in the Sociology of Deviance* (New York: John Wiley & Sons, 1966).

76. *Ibid.*, p. 4.

77. *Ibid.*, p. 67.

78. *Ibid.*, p. 59.

79. *Ibid.*, pp. 77-78.

80. *Ibid.*, p. 78.

81. *Ibid.*, p. 71.

82. *Ibid.*, p. 87.

83. *Ibid.*, p. 108.

84. *Ibid.*, p. 109.

85. *Ibid.*, p. 118.

86. *Ibid.*, pp. 121-122.

87. *Ibid.*, pp. 126-127.

88. *Ibid.*, pp. 137-138.

89. *Ibid.*, pp. 179-180.

8

Appellate courts and law creation

While legislative bodies grind out legislation, courts interpret the meanings of the words contained in the law. In a common-law system such as prevails in the United States, Canada, Australia, England, and most countries of Africa, court decisions add new law to legislation. We must therefore understand the court system and how laws are created in that corner of the legal order.

8.1 THE COURT STRUCTURE

The judicial process depends on two distinct levels: the trial court and the appellate court. The functions of the two types of courts, while to some degree overlapping, are in most respects quite different.

A plaintiff having a cause of action against another (or a prosecutor with a criminal action against a defendant) initiates the action in a trial court. He does this by reciting the facts which he believes to be true and which he believes add up to a right for a judgment in his behalf. The paper in which he recites these facts and his claim for judgment, called the complaint, is served upon the opponent together with a summons.

The opponent now has two alternatives open to him. He may move to dismiss the complaint for failure to state a cause of action. Such a motion is, in a sense, a "so what?" motion. It means that even if everything said in the complaint is true, so what?

The argument implied is that there is no rule of law that subsumes the alleged facts. Or he can answer the complaint by asserting that some or all of the factual allegations are untrue. (In some jurisdictions he can do both simultaneously.)

The motion to dismiss the complaint for failure to state a cause of action raises one sort of issue of law. The answer raises issues of fact. If the defendant does not move to dismiss the complaint or if the motion is denied, then the case goes to trial. The trial proper is concerned only with the resolution of the issues of fact. In the course of the trial, the judge will have to make a variety of rulings, on evidence and on various procedural motions. These motions, too, raise issues of law. Ultimately the trial results in a judgment for or against the plaintiff.

These events take place in "lower" courts, usually municipal and superior courts. The losing party then has a right to appeal. An appeal in most instances in this country brings before the appellate court only questions of law. It asks the appellate court to review not whether the judge or jury correctly resolved the factual issues, but whether the judge properly decided the various questions of law raised by a motion for dismissal or by the various motions made in the course of the trial.

The role of trial courts is therefore quite different from the role of appellate courts. Trial courts are engaged most of the time in trying issues of fact: listening to witnesses, examining documents, or directing juries in their consideration of these matters. In addition, trial courts engage in a whole group of ancillary activities—the appointment of administrators for decedents' estates and receivers in bankruptcies, the sentencing of convicted criminals, and a host of others.

Of all these variegated activities of the court, only questions involving issues of law come before appellate courts. Every issue of law arises because a litigant has asked the trial judge to do something. In response, the judge either acts or declines to act in accordance with the request. If the aggrieved party believes that the judge has acted wrongly, he may appeal.

To say that the trial judge acted wrongly is to say that he adopted a wrong rule, or norm, to guide his action. What is at issue in the appellate court is the correct statement of the norm or rule which ought to guide the trial judge. The statement of the rule by the appellate court, under the case-law system of precedents, becomes the rule for a host of similar cases thereafter.

When we discuss the appellate courts and their work, therefore, we are concerned with their rule-defining function. As we shall see, to define a rule in genuine dispute in fact requires the court to create a new one. We are concerned, therefore, with the scope of discretion of the appellate courts in their rule-creating function.

Whether appellate courts are value-neutral depends in part on whether their role is merely to subsume logically the relevant facts under a preexisting norm, or whether the process of judging on the appellate level requires the exercise of discretion. Before we investigate this general problem, we shall examine two models of government, the one asserting that the rule of law denies official discretion, the other asserting its inevitability.

8.2 THE PERVASIVENESS OF OFFICIAL DISCRETION

Ever since Dicey, it has popularly been supposed that the rule of law requires the absence of discretion in the rule-applying authorities. More modern models, especially those of Hans Kelsen and H.L.A. Hart, yield precisely the opposite conclusion.

Dicey and the Rule of Law

A. V. Dicey (1835-1922) in 1885 write an extraordinarily influential book, *The Law of the Constitution*,[1] in which he asserted that law consisted in a body of fixed and ascertainable rules, and by the "rule of law"

we mean . . . that no man is punishable or can be lawfully made to suffer in body or goods except for a distinct breach of law established in the ordinary legal manner before the ordinary courts of the land. In this sense the rule of law is contrasted with every system of government based on the exercise by persons in authority of wide, arbitrary, or discretionary powers of constraint.[2]

Dicey's proposition was a vigorous statement in opposition to the trend of state intervention in economic processes. Inevitably, where the state must make decisions concerning economic affairs, it must exercise some power of choice. Dicey's most influential twentieth-century disciple, Friedrich von Hayek,[3] has gone so far as to assert that, since planning implies official discretion impossible for citizens to foresee, it is inconsistent with the rule of law. Hayek defines the rule of law in a radical, Diceyian way: it means "that government in all its actions is bound by rules fixed and announced beforehand—rules which make it possible to foresee with fair certainty which authority will use its coercive powers in given circumstances and to plan one's individual affairs on the basis of this knowledge."[4]

While most jurisprudents and social scientists today would probably deny the Dicey-Hayek notions of what ought to be the case with respect to economic affairs, there is nevertheless a shared sentiment that the rule of law as defined by them surely should apply to at least the courts and the police. Two modern authors, Hans Kelsen and H.L.A. Hart, however, have developed models of law and the legal system based on different principles. These models are worth examining.

Hans Kelsen and the Hierarchy of Norms

Hans Kelsen was an Austrian jurist whose work has had a major impact on modern jurisprudence. A positivist, he apparently began his work in ignorance of Austin's contribution,[5] and his intellectual roots were in neo-Kantianism. Neo-Kantian idealism, drawing its inspiration from Kant himself, viewed the natural and the cultural sciences as being dominated by different governing principles. The governing principle of the natural sciences was said to be causality, the governing principle of the cultural sciences, volition.

Kelsen fastened on the notion of volition as the essential characteristic of law. A pure theory of law, therefore, must build on this single principle, carefully cleansed of notions of justice, politics, ethics, or sociology. Since human volition is expressed primarily in norms of conduct, the pure science of law must be concerned with the relationship between norms of conduct. Natural science is concerned with what *is* the case, and how what is the case can be predicted from what came before. Law, in Kelsen's view, is concerned only with what *ought* to be the case.

The effort, therefore, is one of reduction: to reduce the analysis of law to the single irreducible principle of volition. This principle can be explicated only in terms of how it works its way through the legal order; hence what is required is an examination of the formal relationship between norms.

Kelsen thus arrived at the same position as the English positivists, albeit by a totally different route. Just as Austin disregarded what the law ought to be and concentrated his attention on the norms themselves, so did Kelsen. A norm, to be effective, must be sanctioned by an authority. The central formal problem with respect to a legal norm, therefore, is its source. Each norm must find its authority in some higher authority, who in turn must be acting in accordance with a norm. Thus, by a regressive series, one discovers that the source of the norms must be some Original Source, which Kelsen calls the *Grundnorm,* or constitution. The *Grundnorm* possesses the original power to issue norms to subordinate authorities by hypothesis. It cannot be explained without invoking the other social sciences which Kelsen has excluded from his ken. Thus Kelsen, by a consideration only of the inherent characteristics of volition, ends with a hierarchical structure of norms issuing from an Original Source, which resembles Austin's Sovereign in many ways.

The legal order, therefore, in Kelsen's view can be perceived as a hierarchy of norms. The act of a jailer in incarcerating a convicted criminal derives its justification from the convicting judgment of the judge, which in turn derives its validity from statutes enacted by the legislators, who in turn derive their authority from the Constitution itself.

Now the state, as traditionally conceived and, indeed, as conceived by Austin, is an entity distinct from the legal order. Kelsen asserts that this dualistic view of state and law has an essentially ideological function. The essence of the state is popularly thought to be power; the essence of law is order. By conceiving of the state and law as distinct entities, "the state is transformed from a bare fact of power to a legal institution justifying itself as a community governed by law (Rechtsstaat).''[6] Thus, the dualistic view of the state ends by asserting the primacy of order over power—in popular terms, as the rule of law. It ends, therefore, by justifying and strengthening the state's authority, by inducing the layman to view the state as controlled not by power, but by the values which most men perceive in order—by law.

Kelsen denies that the state and law are different entities. To be a state, says Kelsen, "the legal order must have the character of an organization in the narrower and specific sense of this word, that is, it must establish organs who, in the manner of division of labor, create and apply norms that constitute the legal order; it must display a certain degree of centralization."[7] In sociological language, the state is a set of positions defined by norms, whose function is to create, modify, and sanction the breach of norms. The hierarchy of norms thus is simultaneously the legal order and the state itself.

The hierarchical order of norms is based on a successive concretization of their content. The Constitution lays down norms of the broadest sort for the conduct of the legislators. Legislators lay down rather more concrete, but still very general, laws for the conduct of judges. Judges, in turn, must make these general rules concrete in individual cases. Statutes which delegate power to policemen to make arrests necessarily give them discretion, for they must make determinations about when to apply the general rule. *Thus at every stage in the legal order, there is discretion in the officials who occupy the various positions in it.*

The discretion granted to officials at every level of course is not the same in scope. Legislators have very different roles to play from those of judges, and judges from those of policemen. In every case, however, there is necessarily room for discretion—a discretion bounded by norms which explicate its limits, but nevertheless a discretionary power.

What Kelsen's model suggests, therefore, is that logically the central characteristic of a legal system cannot be the inflexibility of its rules, but the pervasive existence of discretion. His model suggests that the ideal of a government of law (i.e., in which norms govern every sort of activity in society) rather than of men (in which there exists significant areas of discretion in officials) is a myth properly relegated (at best) to high school textbooks on civics. It tells us to expect that the normative system within which officials operate endows them with wide areas of discretionary activity.

That this is so can be seen in the very nature of modern government. A complex government is a bureaucratic government. As Weber has said, such a government requires the specialization and differentiation of functions. The activities of the persons in different positions are then controlled by a central decision-making structure through rules which lay down general standards for the behavior of the rule-applying bodies.

Hart and the Concept of Law

H.L.A. Hart, like Hans Kelsen and John Austin, is a positivist. He directs our attention to three recurrent issues in jurisprudence: "How does law differ from and how is it related to orders backed by threats? How does legal obligation differ from, and how is it related to, moral obligation? What are rules and to what extent is law an affair of rules?"[8] He first proceeds to demolish Austin's rather simplistic notion that laws are commands to citizens, mainly on the grounds that whatever effect a law may have upon the citizen, it is only rarely a coercive "order" in the sense that the command by an army officer to a subordinate is an "order." Kelsen urged that rules of law had best be considered as hypothetical judgments. The rule "Thou shalt not kill," according to Kelsen, is best understood as a fragment of a hypothetical judgment addressed to the judge: "If it appears before you that the defendant has killed, then you shall order a sanction to be visited upon the defendant.''[9] Hart urges that to so understand the rules of law is to obscure their effect as a form of social control. The rule is the ''internal'' reason why the citizen does not kill in the first place; only when the norm is breached does it come into play in its second sense.

The fact is that some rules of law are norms in a double sense. In the first place, they are addressed to the ordinary citizen and they describe society's role-expectation for him, under pain of sanction. In the second place, they are role-defining norms for the judge, for they describe the action expected of him if certain conditions come to pass. Such rules may be called (as Hart calls them) ''primary'' rules.

The dual aspect of the primary rules of law, that they are addressed simultaneously to citizen and judge, is an essential element of the legal order.[10] It is a necessary feature that derives from the fact that rules of law are distinguished from custom primarily in that there are separate enforcement agencies to adjudicate whether most rules of law have been violated and to assess and enforce the sanction. The dual aspect of the primary rules is indeed expressive of this fact. Custom, on the other hand, which is enforced not by a special agency, but by the persons affected or by the mass of citizens without official sanction, can be thought of as being a primary norm *simpliciter,* addressed to the citizens and sanctioned directly by the persons or collectivities who believe that the custom has been breached.

Parenthetically, it may be noted that this dual aspect of primary rules of law is the source of many of the problems posed in the sociology of law. Where the norm that the citizen actually regards as controlling his conduct is different from that regarded by the judge as controlling, the judge is called upon to sanction a norm that is rejected by the citizen. In areas where it is deemed desirable to permit citizens to determine their own norms of conduct, e.g., in much of the business and commercial world, the primary rules as invoked by the judges ought to conform to the norms defined by the relevant groups themselves. In other areas of law, where the lawmakers regard the rejected legal norms as proper and the privately defined norms as improper, e.g., in the subculture of the homosexual, the disagreement points up the necessity of devising ways to institutionalize the authoritatively approved substantive norms embodied in the primary rules.

Hart then distinguishes a completely different set of rules which can hardly be deemed ''commands'' in any sense. These are rules typically addressed only to officials. They define the scope of the official's power to create law; they purport to describe to him where he shall look to determine which primary rules are authoritative; and they describe the procedures which the official is to follow in exercising his powers. Usually these rules are supported by sanctions much more diffuse than those which support the primary rules; in many cases, formal sanctions are in fact nonexistent.

The rules defining these sorts of official conduct Hart has labeled ''secondary'' rules. Most often they are power-conferring rules, which purport to define only the outer limits of official discretion. Hart concludes that the ''heart'' of a legal system is a ''complex union of primary and secondary rules.''[11] Obviously, he means by this a legal system which contains institutions with the specialized functions of creating, adjudicating, and enforcing norms. A "legal system" has at its heart the conjunction of the two sets of rules only if by "legal system" one means a system of norms enforced by such specialized institutions. Hart's concept of law is thus ultimately dependent on a definition which reflects the sort of society in which Hart lives.

Hart goes on to point out that the effectiveness of a system of law depends on the "unified or shared official acceptance" of the secondary rules. He says:

What makes "obedience" misleading as a description of what legislators do in conforming to the rules conferring their powers, and of what courts do in applying an accepted ultimate rule of recognition (which defines which primary rules are authoritative), is that obeying a (primary) rule (or an order) *need* involve no thought on the part of the person obeying that what he does is the right thing both for himself and for others to do: he need have no view of what he does as a fulfillment of a standard of behaviour for others of the social group. He need not think of his conforming behaviour as "right," "correct," or "obligatory." . . . Instead, he may think of the rule only as something demanding action from *him* under threat of penalty; he may obey it out of fear of the consequences, or from inertia, without thinking of himself or others as having an obligation to do so and without being disposed to criticize either himself or others for deviations. But this merely personal concern with the rules, which is all the ordinary citizen *may* have in obeying them, cannot characterize the attitude of the courts to the rules with which they operate as courts (and, one might add, most other officials in the law-enforcement system). This is most patently the case with the ultimate rule of recognition in terms of which the validity of other rules is assessed. This, if it is to exist at all, must be regarded from the internal point of view as a public common standard of correct judicial decision, and not as something which each judge merely obeys for his part only.[12]

Hart then makes a point seemingly unrelated but which, as we shall see, goes to the heart of the matter. He points out that the nature of language, in which all norms must be cast, is that it has an "open" texture. If one uses the word "table," for example, most people would have little difficulty in identifying with that word a four-legged article of furniture with a flat top standing about thirty inches high and without built-in drawers or cabinets. This meaning of the word Hart calls its "core" meaning. But what happens when we start sawing off the legs, an inch at a time? At some indeterminate point we shall start wondering whether the article of furniture is a "table" or a "bench." This indeterminate area Hart refers to as the "penumbra" of the word.

Lon Fuller has added a significant gloss to Hart's linguistic analysis. He demonstrates that in fact even the core meaning of words varies, depending on the context. Suppose, for example, that an ordinance reads, "Any person who sleeps in a public waiting room of a bus system or railroad shall be convicted of loitering and fined not more than $5.00." That a drunk, sprawling over a bench asleep in a way that offends standards of public decency, is within the core meaning of the offense defined by this ordinance is self-evident. But what of the middle-class commuter who missed his midnight train and perforce must wait for the milk train four hours later, who sits upright, respectable, but dozing? That his case is at best in the penumbra is likewise self-evident. Yet his conduct is within the "core" meaning of "sleeps," viewed as a word abstracted from the context. Thus, Fuller urges, the core meaning of statutes cannot be determined from the words alone, but must be considered in terms of context and purposes.

That there is a "core" meaning, however, seems clear; that there is also a "penumbra" is likewise clear. In any event, there must be a necessarily vague area for the application of any rule. It is evident that every level of the law-application and law-enforcing apparatus must be endowed with discretion to determine the purposes of rules, and whether a given set of facts lies within or without the core meaning of the rules. When a policeman sees our middle-class commuter dozing on the bench, he necessarily must exercise discretion to arrest or not to arrest the man. The discretion which Kelsen thought must exist on every level of the legal order thus arises, not merely through the logical characteristics of a system whose sole principle is volition, but inevitably from the very nature of language and symbols.

In practice, there are additional reasons for the existence of wide discretion on the part of law-applying authorities of which two especially may be identified. First, many of the norms controlling conduct, both primary and secondary, are vague, ambiguous, and contradictory. To a large extent, this is a result of our commitment to a system of laws which finds its roots in the common law. Many of the norms of conduct both for citizens and for officials find their origins, not in statutes, but in case law. The very nature of a case-law system (as opposed to the systems found in many countries where there are systematic codifications of various areas of law) is that the selection of issues to be actually decided follows a hit-or-miss pattern, depending on whether individual litigants choose to initiate a case raising the question. Moreover, the determination of each case is made on the basis of the facts of that particular case, as litigated by particular litigants in a particular lawsuit. The facts of the particular case and the way in which private litigants have chosen to raise them frequently determine the shape of the ruling which emerges. This rule may or may not be the one which a wise legislator would have selected had he had in hand adequate empirical studies of the possible effect of potential alternative rules before deciding the case. The existence of vagueness, ambiguity, and contradiction in the pertinent norms gives the law-applying official a wide discretion in selective enforcement.

A second reason is related especially to the secondary rules. The value-acceptances of those classes who are in control of state power tends to presuppose order, not merely as one of the desirable objectives of a polity, but as the essential value to be achieved. It is only natural for people with that kind of value-set to want to see the law-enforcement agencies hemmed in by the fewest and most relaxed norms possible. For example, one might refer to the storm of protest that has arisen against the *Miranda* decision, on the ground that it will permit more criminals to go free than otherwise might have done. This decision, as we shall see below, requires the police to notify a suspect of his right to counsel and excludes confessions obtained in violation of that rule. To emphasize the objective of punishing criminals means, to these protesters, refraining from defining sharply the permissible scope of police action in searching out, arresting, and interrogating the suspects. It is only to be expected, then, that the very norms defining the scope of power of enforcement agencies will in many, probably most, cases be couched in deliberately vague terms.

The limitations on the use of violence by police in effectuating arrest, for example, are ordinarily defined as the use of "reasonable" force, i.e., the force required by a reasonable man to effectuate the arrest. But the word "reasonable" in this context has no determinate meaning; it is a normative construct made by the judge or jury *ex post facto*. In practice, judges and juries are loath to constrain police in their activities against criminal or dissident elements. Thus the norm which purports to limit police to "reasonable" force in fact gives them a discretion whose boundaries are found to exist rather more in law review articles than in practice.

The Hart model qualifies, but fundamentally is consistent with, what is predicted by the Kelsen model. We can expect to find great areas for discretionary action by law-enforcement officials and, indeed, by officials of the state structure generally. Even those norms which define the limits of discretion we can expect to find cast in vague terms. Finally, we can expect to find that there are very few, if any, sanctions for much of official action. In short, we can expect to find a normative structure that defines the action of law-applying agencies very vaguely indeed, and whose limits depend on sanctions enforced, not by other agencies, but by self-limitation on the part of the agencies themselves, which are supposedly limited by these norms.

8.3 FROM DISPUTE-SETTLEMENT TO RULE CREATION; THE NORMS OF JUDICIAL DECISION-MAKING; PRIMARY RULES AND SECONDARY RULES

A lawsuit charges that a citizen violated a rule of law. When such a case is brought before a judge, the latter's action is supposedly guided by two different kinds of norms. As we have seen, there are primary rules which may be regarded in one aspect as norms for the conduct of the citizen and in another respect as norms for the conduct of the judge.[13] A primary rule instructs a judge that if it appears to him that a certain kind of violation was committed by someone, then he shall direct that a sanction of a certain sort be applied.

But there is a vast collection of such primary rules. The mere statement of the statutes of the United States, let alone the tremendous number of decisions construing them and the administrative decisions making them more concrete, occupies thousands of pages of small print. Citizens and judges alike must determine which of this host of primary rules ought to govern conduct in a specific case.

Citizens and judges make this determination in different ways. Citizens usually know the rules relevant to most of their day-to-day actions. Businessmen know business law. Drivers know the traffic rules. They are aware of these norms because at some point they have been told what they are. When in doubt, the citizen ordinarily asks someone whom he believes to be knowledgeable about the rules. For the more affluent members of society, it is the lawyers in the community who advise them on the law; for the less affluent, it is likely to be a "prison-house lawyer" or some counterpart in the local community.

When a lawyer advises a citizen what the law is in a given case, he is aware that his advice may ultimately be tested before a judge. In this sense, therefore, his statement of what the law is can be viewed, as Holmes suggested,[14] as a prophecy of what a judge will do if such a case is presented in court.

The lawyer can only make such a prophecy if he is reasonably confident that the judge will act in an ascertainable manner in determining which primary rule should govern a specific case. That is to say, a lawyer must be able to assume that the judge will follow a norm of conduct of which the lawyer is aware, in the selection of a primary rule. This set of norms Hart has named "rules of recognition." It is on these norms that lawyers rely in advising the citizenry and on which citizens rely in their daily life. They therefore constitute a most important statement of society's role-expectation of judges.

8.4 CLEAR CASE AND TROUBLE CASE

When a petitioner—the state in a criminal case, the plaintiff in a civil suit—brings an action, he recites a set of facts which he believes entitles him to an order of the court ordaining that a particular state sanction be imposed. In a criminal action, the prosecutor asks for a verdict of guilty of the crime charged, on the basis of which specific sanctions flow: imprisonment, fine, etc. In a civil action, the plaintiff asks for a judgment which (in most cases) states that the defendant ought to pay a sum of money to the plaintiff.

It is up to the judge to determine the primary norm which controls the case. There are secondary rules which are supposed to guide him under these circumstances. The paradox is that, although there are two different kinds of cases that come to be decided, there is only one legitimate set of secondary rules.

Cases that come to be decided are of two sorts, which we may call "clear" cases and "trouble" cases. In the clear case, the large majority of the cases that come to court, there is really no issue of law. Every time a defense lawyer and the plaintiff's attorney can agree on the question, whether the defendant is liable in law to the plaintiff, they must be in agreement about the governing norm of law. If the defendant's counsel in a criminal case honestly believes that defendant has no defense in law, he must be in agreement with the prosecution as to the appropriate norm to apply to the case.

But there are also a relatively few cases in which this unanimity of counsel is lacking. In these cases, the parties are sharply at odds about which rule of law ought to be applicable and its proper content. It is these cases, the "trouble" cases, which make up the grist of the work for the appellate courts.

The "clear" case does not pose an issue of law because two conditions are met. In the first place, there is a preexisting primary rule of law which can be accurately discovered by following the norms of judicial behavior embodied in the secondary rules. The primary rule may be statutory or it may be embodied in the common law. Not only must the form of words that symbolize the rule be agreed upon, but the concepts to which the words refer, their meaning, must be commonly understood.

More often than not the meaning of words in a rule of law can be understood only in terms of the policy which the rule is designed to promote. The clear case then depends not merely on the discovery of the form of words in which the primary rule is embodied, but also on a common understanding among lawyers and judges of their contextual meaning. In the second place, as we have seen, every primary rule can be rewritten as though it were a hypothetical judgment, in the form "if thus-and-so appear to the court to be the case, then the judge shall give judgment for plaintiff." The second condition for a "clear" case is that the facts of the case at hand must so clearly be specific instances of the generalized categories of the primary rule as to be beyond question, i.e., they must lie within the "core" meaning of the rule.[15]

Each of the two conditions for a case to be a "clear" one has been said by some writers of the American realist school of jurisprudence to be illusory. The radical realists argue that, at least in a system of case law depending on precedents, a precedent cannot establish a rule of any ascertainable content. Therefore, it is said that any earlier case can have *any* meaning which the judge assigns to it.[16] We shall discuss this objection below when we discuss the role of precedents in our system of judicial decision-making. The second objection grants that there are "relatively precise" rules of law established by precedents which the judge can apply. However, it is argued that these rules

can only be applied once the case has been characterized as being a member of the class controlled by a given rule. Thus, the decision reached in any particular case will depend not upon the particular rules of the legal system but rather upon the characterization which the judge makes of the particular fact situation. And ... since this process of characterization is not a logical or deductive process, it follows that the judge can characterize the fact situation any way he wishes in order to produce the desired result.[17]

Which of these arguments is true—Hart's linguistic theory that there are "core" cases which are unquestionably within the meaning of a given rule, or the radical realists' claim that every case requires the judge to characterize it as within or without the rule, a process which permits the judge complete freedom to decide the case either way as he chooses—is an empirical question. If there are in fact cases in which every trained lawyer would agree that the case is plainly within the meaning of the rule, then the radical realists' view cannot be accurate.

As we saw earlier, there indeed are such cases. Moreover, any complex society must be run by rules. Lawrence Friedman has stated the case persuasively:

If most of the operating ... rules of the legal system were not well settled ... many of the normal processes and activities of life that people carry on with reference to legal rules would be profoundly altered. In a complex social and economic system, a legal system on the model of law school appellate cases would be insupportable. There are strong needs to know what is lawful, for example, whether we are validly married if we go through certain forms.... We need to know the permissible ranges of speed. Moreover, in business affairs, we need to know that a deed in a certain form executed in a standard manner truly passes title to a piece of land. If every such transaction had to be channeled through a discretionary agency, the economic system could not survive in its present form. A market economy and a free society both impose upon the legal system a high demand for operational certainty in parts of the law which regulate important aspects of the conduct of everyday life and everyday business.... [D]iscretionary rules are tolerable as operational realities only in those areas of law where the social order or the economy can afford the luxury of slow, individuated justice. If there is a social interest in the mass handling of transactions, a clear-cut framework of nondiscretionary rules is vital.[18]

"Trouble" cases arise because either of the two conditions defining a "clear" case is missing. In the first place, there may be disagreement about the formulation of the rule of law. This disagreement may arise for a variety of reasons. It may arise because the applicable legal norm contains a word which is inherently vague, such as the statutes creating criminal negligence. In *Commonwealth* v. *Pierce*,[19] for example, the accused was a physician. Being called to attend a sick woman, he, with her consent, kept her in flannels soaked in kerosene for three days, as a result of which she died. The defendant honestly believed that the prescribed cure would be efficacious. Was he guilty of homicide by negligence? That depended on whether the construction of the word "negligence" which the court adopted required that the accused perceive that he was running a risk; and on that question, there was no clear precedent. (Judge O. W. Holmes held that there ought to be no such requirement and held Pierce guilty.)

Dispute over the applicable norm may also arise because, while the act at issue is plainly within the "core" meaning of the words used, the particular act appears to be outside the rationale of the rule. In *People* v. *Roberts*,[20] for example, the defendant's wife was incurably sick, suffering from multiple sclerosis. She was in great anguish and desired to end her life. Defendant admitted that, at her request, he mixed a poison and placed it within her reach. She drank it and died. The statute classified murder by poison as murder in the first degree. Ought he be included within the statutory definition? (He was convicted of murder in the first degree and sentenced to life imprisonment.)

Another kind of trouble case arises when the content of the applicable rule is subject to doubt. In *Regina* v. *Kemp*,[21] for example, three doctors, from both sides, agreed that the accused had killed his wife while he was in a fit of melancholia during a temporary loss of consciousness arising from a physical disease, arteriosclerosis. The applicable common-law rule affecting insanity, which was formulated in *M'Naghten's Case*[22] in 1843, permits defense of insanity only on the ground that the accused was suffering from a "disease of the mind." Was a physical disease affecting the brain a "disease of the mind"? (The court held that it was.) In *Hotema* v. *United States*,[23] the accused believed in witches and that the Bible taught that one should not suffer a witch to live. He believed that the party he slew was a witch. The applicable common-law rule (also based on *M'Naghten's Case*) held that the defense of insanity was available if the accused was suffering from an insane delusion at the time of the killing. Was the belief in witches an "insane delusion"? (The court held that if the belief were the result of investigation and belief in the Scriptures, and that he knew it was a violation of human law to kill witches, accused would be guilty; but if the belief were the product of a diseased mind, he would be not guilty by reason of insanity.)

The circumstances in which the rules themselves are vague may be cited almost unendingly. In addition to cases in which the rules themselves lack definition or clarity, however, are cases in which there is doubt whether a particular action falls within or without the "core" meaning of the words used. In *McBoyle* v. *United States*[24] the petitioner was convicted of transporting in interstate commerce an airplane that he knew had been stolen, and he appealed. The statute under which he was convicted, the National Motor Vehicle Theft Act of October 1919, provided in part: "That when used in this Act: (a) the term 'motor vehicle' shall include any automobile, automobile truck, automobile wagon, motor cycle, or any other self-propelled vehicle not designed for running on rails." Was the stolen airplane included in the phrase "any other self-propelled vehicle not designed for running on rails"? (The Supreme Court held that it was not.) By comparison, in *Taylor* v. *Goodwin*,[25] the accused was charged under a statute forbidding "furiously" driving a bicycle. Was the bicycle included in the word "carriage"? (The court held that it was.) Judge Lush[26] concurred in the result. In the following year, Judge Lush held that for purposes of a taxing statute a bicycle was not a "carriage."[27] In these cases, the facts at issue fall within the penumbra of the words used, and a court must resolve whether to extend the core meaning of the word to include the facts at issue.

In any such "trouble" case, there is *ex hypothesi* no preexisting primary rule of law covering the case at hand. Instead, there is a dispute about what the appropriate rule may be. If there is no clearly applicable primary rule, the court is necessarily faced with the problem of choice: it must determine what the appropriate form and content of the rule is to be. Instead of discovering a preexisting norm, the court must actually create a norm. Its range of choice as to what the norm shall contain will usually be limited by the legal materials with which the court must work. Whatever the limitations, however, the choice of law in such a case is a creative act. It is in fact a legislative, i.e., lawmaking, act.

The same sort of judicial creativity occurs when a court has discovered that there exists a clearly articulated and well-understood legal rule, which arguably but not clearly subsumes the facts of the case at hand—the "penumbra" case. The choice which then faces the court may be viewed as one of whether the facts of the case are to be brought under the rule; that is, it is a characterization problem. In such a case, the court is actually required to redefine the rule, for by determining that a particular state of facts is *clearly* within the rule, the court is enlarging the scope of the rule's core meaning. By enlarging its meaning, the court is in fact refashioning the rule. Thus, just as in the case where the rule itself is vague or ambiguous, the determination that the rule subsumes a particular set of facts within its penumbra requires the court to create a new rule of law. Again, although the scope of judicial creativity is limited by the received techniques, nevertheless the court is faced with the necessity of making a choice between alternative possible rules of law.[28]

That the court in any "trouble" case must fashion a new rule of law to govern the case at hand suggests an important truth: in every trouble case, the norm to which the actors are being held is formulated *after they have acted*. It is an *ex post facto* norm.[29]

The "clear" case and the "trouble" case therefore present very different problems to the judge. In the clear case, the judge must first discover some preexisting articulated legal rule, within whose core meaning fall the facts of the given case. In the trouble case, on the other hand, the judge must fashion a new rule *ex post facto,* which will simultaneously determine the cause at hand and govern future cases of similar nature.

We can now explain why it is that the process of *applying* rules necessarily involves courts in the process of *making* rules. So long as a case meets the conditions of a "clear" case, the court is indeed only applying the rules; that is, it determines whether the facts of the case meet the conditions for the invocation of a sanction. If, however, the rule is not clear, or if the facts are not plainly within its core meaning, the court in deciding the case must devise a rule which will include the facts at hand within its core meaning.

8.5 APPELLATE COURTS AS A RULE-MAKING SYSTEM

A variety of materials go into a court decision: the legal material with which the court must work, the values it must take into account, the personality and background of the judge, etc. The court takes all the "raw" materials and converts them by more or less determinate processes into rules or norms of law.

Thus viewed, appellate courts may be thought of as a rule-making system. Each court has certain inputs, which then go through a conversion process—the judge does something with them. The outputs are the rules that become the norms for the future conduct of citizens and judges. (See Fig. 8.1.) We shall examine in turn the inputs, the conversion processes, and the outputs of appellate courts.

The traditional myth is that the only significant input into the rule-making process is "the law." In fact, however, as we have already seen, appellate judges are in the business of formulating rules about how men ought to act in certain circumstances; indeed, they articulate the most formal and the most heavily sanctioned norms in society. What a decision-maker decides ought to be the case obviously depends not

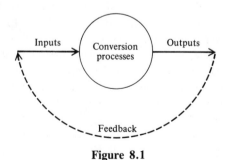

Figure 8.1

only on the various notions of law and policy which are called to his attention, but on a variety of different influences, of which we mention seven: (1) the way in which the issues are presented, (2) the sources of theory, (3) the personal attributes of the judge, (4) the professional socialization of the judge, (5) situational pressures on the judge, (6) organizational pressures on him, and (7) the alternative permissible rules of law.

Inputs: Issues

It is self-evident that most issues that call for decision by appellate courts are raised as a result of the choices made by individual litigants to bring the cases before the courts. Judges do not determine those choices. The result is that, on the whole, courts have been particularly active in rule-making in those areas of law which affect litigants who are sufficiently wealthy to be able to activate legal processes. For example, law books are full of cases detailing the rules with regard to the law of trusts. Trusts are a device by which wealthy people place money or property in charge of a responsible person (or, more frequently nowadays, a corporation) to be managed for the benefit of children, widows, or for charitable purposes. The corpus of trust law concerns the norms of conduct for trustees: what investments they may or may not make, what kinds of accounts they must keep, with whom they may deal, the exact line that demarcates fair dealing by trustees from frauds on their part on the beneficiaries, and so on. There are hundreds of appellate cases which define these rules with great detail and relative precision. Yet these cases affect numerically only the tiniest fraction of the population.

By contrast, there are many legal problems affecting the poor which never reach the courts, although the number of persons affected may be very large. Consider, for example, the problem of industrial insurance. As life insurance became an important element in our economic and social life, cases concerning it have come before the courts rather frequently, since most life insurance is carried by relatively affluent persons. Moreover, the amounts of money involved in these cases frequently are relatively substantial, making litigation concerning them economically worthwhile. There is, however, a kind of life insurance called "industrial insurance," which is written in small principal amounts ($100 to $500). No medical examination is required. The premiums are likewise small, and since they are collected weekly, they frequently amount to no more than a few cents a week.

Because the amounts at issue are so small, very few cases concerning industrial insurance have ever reached appellate courts. As a result, the insurance policies tend to favor the insurance companies over those insured most unfairly. In 1934, Fuller wrote that there were warranties concerning the health of the insured

sufficiently inclusive to make most of the policies issued void if these warranties were taken literally. . . . Many of the policies are so worded as to bind the companies to practically nothing. Not infrequently a large portion of the premium is paid for disability insurance *which is cancellable at any time by the company.*[30]

Nevertheless, these abuses have arisen, and, except in those rare intances where the legislature has intervened, they remain as widespread today as they were in 1934.

Cases concerning them have simply not been in litigation. As a result, appellate courts have never had an opportunity to lay down rules to control the relationships created by insurance contracts of this sort. The insurance companies, the economically most powerful party to the contracts, largely remain in a position to determine unilaterally the conditions of the contracts.

Perhaps nowhere has the effect of economic constraint on the issues posed to courts for decision and clarification been more significant than in the area of criminal law. One example may suffice: the norms controlling the actions of police in the course of making arrests and interrogating criminal suspects. Proportionately, far more poor people than middle-class people are arrested or interrogated by police. Moreover, the police generally feel fewer restraints in treating the poor, for the poor tend to be politically powerless and hence are usually less capable of exerting unpleasant pressures on a policeman, if he treats them in ways not warranted by the norms which are supposed to guide a policeman or if he exercises his discretion in a way adverse to their interests.

As a result, most instances of police malpractice occur with respect to the poor. Only in very, very rare instances are these malpractices brought to the attention of the courts by poor people, for they lack the money to hire lawyers. As a result, if the definition of the norms regulating police conduct vis-à-vis persons suspected of crime depended solely on rules articulated by appellate courts in cases initiated and litigated to the appellate stage by poor persons themselves, the norms would remain vague and ill-defined.

There is one important ameliorating factor in this matter with respect (in recent years) to civil rights and civil liberties. A few private associations, nationwide in scope, have interested themselves in these areas, acting as moral entrepreneurs. The National Association for the Advancement of Colored People for many years supported litigation affecting the civil rights of black citizens, no one of whom was likely to have been wealthy enough to finance the litigations. The roster of issues which the NAACP has litigated is very long indeed: the white primaries in the South, the provision of equal facilities for higher education, the requirement that juries be selected in a nondiscriminatory manner, the prevention of racial discrimination in interstate commerce, and, most far-reaching of all, the school desegregation cases.[31]

With respect to police practices, the American Civil Liberties Union has been particularly active. Indeed, it is not too much to say that the entire law of police practice has been created through the cases supported by the ACLU.

In recent years a large proportion (perhaps most) of the significant cases that have brought innovations in criminal law have been the result of interested groups serving as moral entrepreneurs to bring about changes in the law. In the preceding chapter we pointed out how law-enforcement agencies act in this capacity. More often than not, however, it is independent groups which have provided the necessary financial backing in bringing a case from lower courts to appellate courts. The important features of the processes are nonetheless the same: the law gets shaped by the efforts of moral entrepreneurs who for whatever reason (personal gain, high moral principle, etc.) are willing to expend the energy and money necessary to seek a change in the law.

APPELLATE COURTS AND LAW CREATION

This is not to say that appellate courts are altogether powerless to influence the kind of cases which come before them. One important formal exception is the U.S. Suprme Court's discretionary appellate jurisdiction, defined by means of the exercise of the ancient *writ of certiorari*. Since 1926 the Supreme Court has had the power to decide whether or not to accept most appeals. The statute extending this power to the Supreme Court was enacted because the docket of the Court was becoming seriously overloaded. It was believed that the Court's chief function was not to ensure that justice was done in individual disputes, but to resolve issues of law. As a consequence of *certiorari,* the Court has at least a veto power over the selection of issues for determination. While it still cannot determine which issues will arise, it can prevent itself from deciding issues which in its opinion ought not be heard at the moment.

Appellate courts can also exercise significant influence over the sort of cases brought before them by the content of their opinions—which is a somewhat less formal, but nevertheless important procedure. The dissenting opinion may play a particularly important function in pointing out a legal path which might win a majority in the court. Such an opinion practically invites new litigation aimed at the point suggested by the dissent.

Inputs: Policy

Whence come the arguments which influence the decision of judges of the appellate courts? Here one must be careful not to assume that the arguments in question are the "real" or "true" determinant of judicial behavior. No doubt they are the overriding determinant in some cases; but many other elements also enter into the conversion process that transforms the inputs of problems, policies, personality, training, and social pressures into specific decisions, and among these elements the policies and the arguments of the counsel supporting them are of course not insignificant.

One example of the importance of policies and the arguments in support of them may suffice. In 1860, the first case involving the so-called fellow-servant rule came to the Supreme Court of Wisconsin. The fellow-servant rule was an exception carved by the English common-law courts into the general rule that an employer is liable for the torts (negligent or intentional wrongs) of his employees acting in the course of their employment. For example, when an employee runs over someone in a truck on his employer's business, the employer is liable in damages, although he may be thousands of miles away from the scene. If, however, the person injured is also an employee of the employer, then the fellow-servant rule (in general) barred recovery. When this rule first came to the Wisconsin court, the judges refused to follow precedents from other states, on the ground that the rule lacked sound policy.[32] Two judges voted in favor of the rule, one judge abstained on jurisdictional grounds.

In the very next year, a similar case came before the Wisconsin Supreme Court.[33] Now the court reversed itself. The judge who had earlier abstained and one of the two judges who had voted with the majority not to be bound by the fellow-servant rule now voted to adhere to it. In reversing his position, Judge Dixon said in part:

In coming to this conclusion [i.e., that his vote ought to be changed] I have no words of apology to offer, and but few observations. . . . I recede more from that deference and respect which is always due to the enlightened and well considered opinions of others, than from any actual change in my own views. The judgment of a majority in [the first Wisconsin case on the fellow-servant rule] is sustained by weighty and powerful reasons. Like reasons are not wanting on the other side, and that side is sustained by the almost unanimous judgments of all the courts both of England and this country. I think I am bound to yield to this unbroken current of judicial opinion.[34]

The judge who changed his position, therefore, based this shift on deference to the opinions of other judges. This was a policy judgment. To the extent that judges pay deference to the opinions of other judges merely because of the weight of numbers arrayed against a given position, to that extent are idiosyncratic or arbitrary decisions avoided.

The source of this shift in the Wisconsin case can be traced quite distinctly in the brief of the counsel. In the earlier case, counsel for the railroad said only that "if repeated decisions arising under almost every variety of circumstances can settle and determine the law, then the principle [the fellow-servant rule] cannot be disputed. It has been decided by the highest courts of England, New York, Pennsylvania, Illinois and South Carolina, and the decisions have been numerous. . . ."[35] In the later case, however, the same counsel for the railroad argued far more vigorously and at much greater length. We quote only a very small portion of the brief:

The decision in [the earlier Wisconsin case on the fellow-servant rule] has the merit of standing alone. . . . We have supposed that when a question had been repeatedly before the Courts, and as often and as repeatedly decided, and the same principle affirmed, not only was it prima facie evidence of the law, but *conclusive*. . . . In every case in this country, or in England, where the question has been raised, the decision has been directly the reverse of the decision made by this Court! [Citing seven English and twenty-nine American decisions.]

. . . we submit that where there is found to be such a unanimous and unvarying amount of authority, that this Court ought to hesitate and ponder well before placing itself on record in opposition to all these Courts. . . . We do ask this Court . . . to adhere to the maxim of the law, *stare decisis* [i.e., that precedent should be followed]. And we insist that even if the "reasoning" of some of the judges in giving their opinions is not entirely satisfactory to every member of this Court, that it is more in accordance with the maxims of the law for this Court to abide by former precedents *stare decisis* where the same points come again in litigation, as well to keep the sale of justice even and steady and not liable to waver with every new Judge's opinion, as also because the law in that case, being solemnly declared and determined, what before was uncertain and perhaps indifferent, is not become a permanent rule, which *it is not in the breast of any subsequent Judge to alter or swerve from, according to his own private judgment, but according to the known laws and customs of the land*,—NOT DELEGATED TO PRONOUNCE A NEW LAW, BUT TO MAINTAIN AND EXPOUND THE OLD ONE.[36]

The arguments of the counsel in a case are, as the Wisconsin cases suggest, a principal source of the policy arguments used by appellate courts.

Not every lawyer, however, carries as much weight with a court as every other. In every court there are counsel who appear before it time and again, usually representing substantial clients. Judges come to respect some of these men and not others. It is predictable that the arguments of some well-known counsel will be accorded weight that will not be accorded to the arguments of lesser known lawyers.

Not only are lawyers more or less well known and more or less persuasive, but the lower courts from which the cases come are more or less well respected. So also are the appellate courts whose decisions may be precedents for the cause at hand. In a classic study, Rodney L. Mott received ratings of the various state appellate courts from 259 law school professors. He also determined the relative frequency of cases from the several appellate courts which appeared in law school case-books. In addition, indices were constructed of the number of times the opinions of the several state appellate courts were cited by other state courts, by the U.S. Supreme Court, and with approval by the U.S. Supreme Court. From these various indices he constructed a rank order of state supreme courts, which ranged from 25.18 for New York down to 2.12 for New Mexico.[37] Schubert points out that occasionally a higher court will even try to legitimize its opinion by trading on the reputation of a lower court judge,

as did Chief Justice Vinson in a politically conservative opinion supporting a decision approving the conspiracy convictions... of the leaders of the American Communist Party.[38] Vinson attempted to advertise the position of the majority of the Court (for whom he spoke) as being really not illiberal, since the Supreme Court (as he pointed out) merely was approving the decision and supporting rationale that had been adopted in this very case by the Court of Appeals for the Second Circuit. That court had spoken, in turn, through no less august a personage than the great Learned Hand, author of *The Bill of Rights* and (both off and on the bench) of other reputedly liberal writings, and a federal judge whom most lawyers considered to be of much greater ability than all but a handful of the justices who have sat on the Supreme Court during the twentieth century.[39]

The opinions of other lower courts and the arguments of counsel are, of course, the formal inputs of policy arguments. There are a host of informal ones, however, of which the comments of law school professors are perhaps the most important. The relationship between leading law schools and appellate courts is close. Many justices, both of the federal and state appellate courts, choose their clerks from able young members of the graduating class of either their own law school or, if there is only one major law school in the state, from that. Most important of all are the law reviews. These journals constitute a unique institution, being the only major professional journals whose editors are students. In the cases of the major law reviews—those of Harvard, Yale, Columbia, Michigan, Wisconsin, and a few others—faculty control is literally nil. These reviews are the major forum for publishing the results of legal research, and their impact on the courts can be very great. For example, the arguments which justified the "one man, one vote" Supreme Court decision in the legislative redistricting case, *Baker* v. *Carr*, was first put forward in an article in the *Harvard Law Review*.[40]

The policy input deriving from the law schools is unique, for besides the personal attitudes of the judges themselves, it is the only important policy input which is independent both of the institution of the courts themselves and of the economic, moral, or personal interests of the litigants. Moreover, as we have seen, pragmatic decision-making requires empirical studies of the actual effect of the rules. Such studies, to the extent that they are in fact made, appear in the law reviews. The importance of these reviews is attested by the frequency with which they are cited as authority in appellate opinions.

Inputs: The Personal Characteristics of the Judges

Since in many of the trouble cases, the issue turns upon questions of value, it would seem that the personal characteristics of the judges are relevant. To understand properly why judges make the policy choices they do, it is necessary to examine these characteristics in three dimensions: first, their background as individuals; second, their background as lawyers; and third, their situation as appellate judges.

There are judges on many appellate levels in the United States. Our attention here is directed only toward the highest state and federal appellate judges. We shall direct our attention first at the characteristics of judges appointed to the Supreme Court of the United States in the period 1933-57. Some of these characteristics are suggested by Table 8.1. From this table (and further data of the same sort concerning all the Supreme Court justices in our history), Schmidhauser concludes that "throughout American history there has been an overwhelming tendency for presidents to choose nominees for the Supreme Court from the socially advantaged families."[41]

The degree to which these personal attributes condition judicial decision-making is rather more difficult to ascertain than the characteristics themselves. Statistically significant relationships have been established between certain personal characteristics and voting tendencies. For example, one investigation established that

democratic judges were more prone to favor (1) the defense in criminal case, (2) administrative agencies in business regulation cases, (3) the private parties in cases involving the regulation of nonbusiness entities, (4) the claimants in unemployment compensation cases, (5) the libertarian position in free speech cases, (6) the finding of constitutional violation in criminal cases, (7) the government in tax cases, (8) the divorce seeker in divorce cases, (9) the wife in divorce settlement cases, (10) the tenant in landlord-tenant disputes, (11) the labor union in union-management cases, (12) the debtor in debt collection cases, (13) the consumer in sales of goods cases, (14) the injured party in motor vehicle accident cases, and (15) the employee in employee injury cases. Nine of these findings (1, 2, 4, 6, 7, 10, 13, 14, and 15) proved to be statistically significant relationships.[42]

Whether these results can be construed to mean that a judge reaches his conclusions *because* he is a Democrat is, of course, subject to serious question. Grossman reports Bowen's finding that none of the variables most significantly associated with judicial decisions explains more than a fraction of the total variance among judges.[43] Grossman concludes that "mere tests of association are inadequate, though useful, and more powerful measures indicate the presence of other intervening variables, between the case and the ultimate decision."[44]

TABLE 8.1   The personal attributes of the Justices appointed to the United States Supreme Court, 1933-57*

Occupations of fathers	
High social status (proprietors, wealthy farmers, professional men)	13 (81%)
Low social status (mechanics and laborers, small farmers)	3 (19%)
Setting of birth	
United States	
Urban	6 (37.5%)
Small town	8 (50%)
Rural	1 (6.2%)
Europe (Austria)	1 (6.2%)
Ethnic origins	
Western European derivation	15 (93.7%)
Central, eastern, or southern European derivation	1 (6.3%)
Religious Affiliations	
High social status religious affiliations (Episcopalian, Presbyterian,	
Unitarian)	8 (50%)
Intermediate social status affiliations (Roman Catholic, Jewish)	3 (19%)
Low social status affiliations (Methodist, Baptist)	3 (19%)
"Protestant" (no other information available)	2 (13%)
Nonlegal educational background	
College or university of high standing	10 (61%)
College or university of average standing	4 (26%)
Academy or school of average standing (public or private)	2 (13%)
Legal education	
Law school of high standing	10 (61%)
Private apprenticeship and study under prominent lawyer or judge	1 (6%)
Law school of average standing	5 (32%)
Prior legal or professional experience	
Lawyers who were primarily politicians	10 (62%)
Lawyers who were primarily state or federal judges	1 (6%)
Corporation (primarily) lawyers	2 (13%)
Lawyers by education primarily engaged in academic pursuits	3 (19%)

*   J. A. Schmidhauser, "The Justices of the Supreme Court: A Collective Portrait," *Midwest Journal of Political Science* 3(1959): 2-37, 40-49.

Inputs: The Socialization of Judges

The socialization of appellate judges can best be regarded as involving three stages: that of law student, that of practicing attorney, and that of lower court judge—the usual steps in a judicial career.

The American law school education is a classic example of an education in which the subject matter formally studied is ridiculously simple, but the process of socialization into the profession very difficult. Thurman Arnold once remarked of jurisprudence what is in many respects true as well of the formal part of the study of law. He said that jurisprudence is a tedious subject, tedious not in the way studying a difficult discipline like physics is tedious, but in the way tossing feathers into the air, hour after hour, is tedious. To the extent that the study of law is a study of the universe of norms alone, there is precious little about the law which would challenge a bright junior high school student. By their last year in law school, the better students, those on the law reviews for example, are getting reasonably good grades on the basis of a couple of days' study prior to end-of-term examinations.

The key to an understanding of the socialization of American lawyers in law school is best found through an examination of the outstanding aspect of their educational method, the case method of instruction.[45] Initiated by Langdell at Harvard in 1871, the case method has long since become the dominant form of instruction in every American law school.

This method, in its classic form, has two aspects that are important for our purposes. First, it purports to teach the norms of law by presenting the students, not with textbooks stating in black-letter type what the rules are, but with appellate opinions giving the facts of the cases, the decisions of the court, and the reasons it gave to justify its opinions. Second, the case-study method is, at least in theory, teaching in the Socratic style.[46]

There can be no doubt that the case method is a thoroughly inefficient way to teach and to learn the rules of substantive law. Its functions are quite different. Two of these functions are especially important in connection with socialization. First, the constant dialogue between professor and students trains most students very rapidly to be tough-minded and independent in thought. At the beginning of the first year, if the professor said that black was white, most law students would carefully make a note of that proposition. By the end of the year, it sometimes seems that if the professor said that "one and one make two," somebody would ask, "Are there no exceptions?" That kind of hard-nosed, sharp questioning of everything is obviously the first essential both to competent counseling and to competent trial practice.

The second function of the case method as originally conceived is perhaps more subtle. The use of decided cases as the basic teaching materials and the concomitant exclusion of an examination of the law in action confines the questions asked to those raised in the cases. Questions that challenge the basis of the system as it exists are thus excluded, except insofar as an imaginative professor raises them. In the latter case, the very use of case materials demonstrates that he is raising an academic question, not an issue with which a hard-nosed, practical lawyer need be concerned.

For example, in times long ago, before automobiles, accidents between horse-drawn vehicles or between vehicles and pedestrians were decided on the basis of which rider or driver acted without due care. The care and skill of the rider of a horse, or that of the man who holds the reins of a stagecoach, plainly are the principle element in determining whether an accident occurs. When the vehicle involved no longer is so simple, but is an enormously complex automobile, traveling at speeds that convert it from an inert mass of metal into a highly dangerous projectile, the original design of the automobile and the design and condition of the roadway probably play an even greater part in determining accident occurrence than the skill of the drivers. Dominated by the perception of the problems derived from earlier cases, however, lawyers and judges have not until very recently begun to question the ancient way of defining the issue.

Hard-nosed independence is necessary if the system is to generate legal advisers who can advise competently, i.e., independently. More important, perhaps, is the necessity, for the continuance of the system, that lawyers and judges define the problems presented within the framework of the existing system. So long as they so define the problems, whether they take a ''liberal'' or ''conservative'' tack is relatively unimportant. The early socialization of judges and lawyers, thus, tends paradoxically to make them intellectually independent, but to restrain them from looking for radical solutions, for throughout their law school education they are taught to define problems in the way they have always been defined.[47]

The seeming paradox of intellectual independence combined with acceptance of the existing definition of the situation persists in later practice. The successful lawyer constantly sharpens his wits in situations of conflict. His whole professional career, however, necessarily requires him to take the institutions of American society at any moment as given. One advises a client to act in a particular way because he believes that the system as it is now structured requires him so to do.

Nevertheless, the successful lawyer tends to adopt conservative solutions for a second reason. If he is to be financially successful, his clients must be able to pay fees. In general, rich people and businessmen pay larger fees than poor people and wage earners. Successful lawyers represent successful clients. Inevitably, the successful lawyer, if not already attuned to the value-sets of his client, tends to adopt them.

The successful lawyer who becomes a judge tends to avoid advocating radical solutions for still a third reason. In America, one becomes a judge, in all except a tiny minority of instances, in part because he has been a political animal. The appointee to judgeship more likely than not has already served, as a young lawyer, in the capacity of prosecutor, city councilman, or the like. He probably is a member on the local political club executive committee or its analogue. He cannot successfully play the political game by rocking the boat.

The final stage in the socialization of the appellate judge is in most cases a period of time as a trial judge. Judges of all sorts, and trial judges even more than appellate judges, tend to be tied to the existing institutional structure by a myriad of strands of interest and interaction. On their favor turns the careers of many lawyers with whom they were schoolmates and have been professional colleagues, fellow soldiers in political wars, and friends, frequently for many years. It is a rare judge who adopts a value-set markedly different from those of his reference group.

The socialization of lawyers and judges in the past has, therefore, tended to make appellate judges tough-minded and independent people who define situations in ways conformable to the existing institutional structure. In addition, the reference group of most judges can be expected to induce him to select relatively conservative answers to the issues raised.

Inputs: Situational Factors

We recall that H.L.A. Hart asserts that the success of a legal system depends on the fact that judges have internalized the secondary rules which define their positions. Whether this assertion is completely true may be seriously questioned. Hart can make this assumption, however, because there are few, if any, formal court-enforced sanctions to support the secondary rules. That is, of course, largely true. There are nevertheless a host of informal sanctions that tend to coerce the appellate judge not only to conform to the secondary rules, but generally not to challenge the conservative values.

Judges, like everyone else, want increased status, power, and privilege. The appellate judiciary is itself a career. The judge who is promoted to an intermediate state appellate bench may yet be promoted to the highest state court. The judge of a federal district court may hope some day to be elevated to the Supreme Court of the United States. Judges cannot but be aware that their decisions will be a principal index used in their promotion. When Judge Burger of the United States Court of Appeals for the District of Columbia was promoted to Chief Justice of the United States, it was quite clear that his conservative stance in judging was a principal consideration in his promotion. Mr. Dooley long ago wrote that "the Supreme Court reads the election returns."[48]

Even apart from the potential reward of promotion, there are more immediate situational pressures which tend to make judges more, rather than less, conservative. Judges, especially appellate judges, hold possibly the highest status positions in society. They are invited to join the clubs of the highest elites, they socialize with the powerful and the rich, they meet political leaders at cocktail parties, at political rallies, and in clubhouses. Their power to influence events through informal but critical conversations is enormous. That power bears a direct relationship to their personal prestige among those with whom they socialize. A judge who is anxious to maintain his power in these informal groups cannot permit his opinions to deviate very far from the value-sets held by those with whom his web of life is so closely interwoven.

Finally, it is important to realize that there are other, illicit pressures operating on relatively wide scale on the trial court level, and they are not unknown on the appellate level. Occasionally charges of open corruption are made and sustained against judges. Even more pervasive is the effect of friendship, power, and influence. The young attorney who has tried cases in a local court against older, more established counsel, with a long history of close personal contacts with the trial judge, soon learns that where there is discretion to be exercised—and how pervasive is that discretionary power we have already suggested—it will not often be exercised in his favor.

All the ordinary situational factors tend to operate to ensure that judges will not be radicals. Still a different kind of pressure on the courts is the obvious, but often ignored, bureaucratic pressure of resource allocation.

Inputs: Organizational Interests

A salient characteristic of organizational behavior is that the ongoing policies and activities of organization are those designed to maximize rewards to and minimize strains on the organization. The system of courts is an organization, and it acts in accordance with the general principles applicable to all organizations. Leon Green has said:

> The policies which the courts most clearly articulate are those which concern the administration of the courts themselves. They hesitate to modify the law if the decision will "open the door to a flood of litigation," make it difficult to define limits of liability, require an investigation of factual details for which their processes are not well designed, make the re-examination of corollary or subsidiary principles necessary, or threaten to upset an established equilibrium in social conventions, trade practices or property transactions.[49]

We shall discuss two significant organizational pressures to which courts have responded: the volume of litigation and "crises."

The principal source of strain on the courts has been the constantly rising volume of litigation. In the early and middle nineteenth century, this tendency reflected the rising commercial activity of the country. Just as the courts were getting this matter under control through a variety of devices which we shall shortly discuss, there came a wave of litigation by employees against employers arising out of industrial accidents. Ultimately, this problem was largely taken out of the courts by the development of workmen's compensation commissions in the 1910s—just in time to clear a few dockets for the enormous flood of automobile accident cases that engulfed the courts in the 1920s and which have remained the most frequent causes of legal action today.

Yet courts cannot increase their personnel or their physical plant easily. A court cannot expand out of "profits" or by adding a subsidiary or two to meet new problems. It does not control its own purse strings, and those who do have been notably slow in responding to its increased work loads.[50]

The contradiction between a rising volume of litigation and the lag in expanding court structures has been met in a variety of ways.[51] Outside the courtroom, businessmen found it in their interests to adopt form contracts and routine procedures to handle the mass of run-of-the-mill transactions. Once construed by a court, such routine transactions became less likely to require judicial scrutiny soon again.

The principal response, however, was that of the courts themselves. Repetitive, routine sorts of cases, for example, are handled in repetitive, routine ways that obviate formal hearings in most instances on the trial court level, and rarely raise issues for appeal. Most traffic fines are paid by mail, without even the formality of a court appearance.

The courts in fact approve real sanctions against those litigants who do not desire to take advantage of the routine responses. It is a rare parking or speeding offender who will litigate a case, even if he is convinced that he is not guilty, so time-consuming are the court appearances required to determine the issues. As a result, only a miniscule percentage of the routine summonses issued ever give rise to any event which consumes a court's time.

Appellate courts have been quick to approve techniques which lower the pressure exerted by the volume of business. In most judicial systems, the chief justice is not only the chairman of the appellate bench, but also the chief administrative officer of the court system. Frequently he and his fellow judges have instituted formalized pretrial conferences, which, although nominally designed to identify the issues, obtain agreement on exhibits, etc., before the trial, in fact are primarily glorified bargaining sessions between plaintiff and defense attorneys. In Connecticut, for example, pretrial sessions are held formally for one or two weeks twice a year. During this period all other work of the trial courts stops, and the judges engage in a massive effort to settle every lawsuit on the calendar awaiting trial. Insurance adjusters in automobile accident cases and plaintiffs themselves must be in attendance, so that if a settlement is reached between attorneys, the parties themselves can approve it.

In criminal matters also, appellate courts have been eager to sanction devices designed to reduce the load on the court system. They have frequently placed a stamp of approval on the negotiated plea, asserting that because it saves the state time and money (read: lessens the pressure of business on court dockets) it is a wise and useful device. As a consequence of this approval, over 90 percent of the cases handled in criminal courts are settled by negotiated pleas of guilty by the defendant. In a typical case, the defendant is charged with an offense but agrees to plead guilty to a less serious one to avoid a court trial and the possibility of being found guilty of the more serious charges. Courts encourage such negotiations in part by agreeing to "go along with" the recommended sentence of the prosecuting attorney, the sentence often being an integral part of the negotiation which has previously taken place.

The changing judicial attitude toward arbitration is largely a reflection of the increased volume of judicial business. The earliest cases of arbitration were frowned on as attempts by private parties by contract to "oust the jurisdiction of the court." Responding to the demands of businessmen for quicker and cheaper forms of litigation, as well as to their own desires to reduce the impact of litigation upon the courts as a system, the courts have changed the rules so that today not only is arbitration judicially favored, but as a matter of fact there are many more commercial arbitrations than there are commercial lawsuits.

The cost of litigation also has probably been a major factor in cutting down the volume of judicial business. The court fees themselves are relatively low. In many states, they have not changed for nearly a century, so that as little as fifty cents or a dollar may be all that is required in some cases. In other jurisdictions, however, fees may be substantial. Courts have been especially quick to raise the fees for jury trials in noncriminal cases, because that is a particularly slow method of adjudication. In some states, for example, the fee for a jury trial may be as much as sixty dollars or more.

The principal cost of litigation, however, is the cost of paying lawyers. First-class trial lawyers today receive five hundred dollars a day or even more for trial work; and trials can consume an unconscionable amount of time, for procedures are frequently complex, the methods of examining witnesses are slow and cumbersome, and the court calendar is shot with innumerable delays. Appeals are even more expensive, for there are substantial printing bills for briefs to be submitted to the court, and expensive research and writing to be done by counsel. Even so, however, the American system of costs is not so burdensome as the British system. In America, win, lose, or draw, each side usually pays its own counsel (there are a few exceptions). In England, on the other hand, the losing party must pay the fees, not only of his own lawyer, but of the opponent's lawyer as well—a most substantial disincentive to litigation and appeal.

The cost of litigation in commercial matters is, of course, only in part stated in the actual out-of-pocket expenses of court and counsel fees. Litigation is viewed by most businessmen as a hostile act. If a lawsuit is instituted, almost invariably the parties will not continue to do business. A businessman, therefore, will bring an action against a customer or supplier only when he believes that the benefits to be derived from the action will outweigh any hope of future business relationships.[52]

While cost sanctions effectively limit the use of legal process in most cases to those able to afford them, these sanctions typically do not operate very effectively with respect to the largest category of litigation today: automobile accident cases. This is so for two reasons. In the first place, the plaintiff and defendant in automobile accident cases only in the most rare instances have ever had any previous relationship and do not usually perceive any benefit in maintaining future conditions of amity. The bringing of a lawsuit is not regarded by either as necessarily a hostile act; it is indifferent. The nominal defendant is rarely concerned, since the real defendant, who must pay the judgment, if any, is almost always an insurance company. So the sanction which probably more than any other reason inhibits litigation between businessmen and their customers rarely obtains.

Secondly, there has developed by lawyers' custom over the years a widely used device for paying the fees of a plaintiff's lawyer: the contingency fee. The lawyer agrees to render all the necessary services in a particular piece of potential or actual litigation in return for a portion of the ultimate return, whether by settlement or judgment. Fees run (as in New York) as high as 40 percent of the total recovery. If the case is unsuccessful, the lawyer gets nothing and indeed may be out of pocket for court costs. On the other hand, the potential return in most automobile accident cases is sufficiently certain to warrant lawyers who specialize in such claims to take the case of almost any person injured in an automobile accident.

Besides personal injury cases, however, poor people are frequently unable to pay for counsel and for litigation. In some areas, this has meant that the legal remedies theoretically available to everyone have remained a middle-class luxury. Divorce is one example. The standard legal fee for an uncontested divorce in most states is on the order of three hundred dollars. A poor person cannot afford it. If he or she leaves the spouse, the situation usually remains ambiguous, cloudy, with one or both partners frequently living in adultery (with corresponding insecurity for potential children and susceptibility to criminal arrest) rather than regularizing the relationship with a divorce and a new marriage.

Various devices have been tried to make legal services available to the poor. The small-claims court was designed theoretically to provide a quick and cheap forum in which court processes would be made available, without the need for counsel, to persons making very small claims, which ordinarily would not warrant the cost of a lawyer. In fact, such courts have been used far more frequently by unsecured creditors such as doctors, lawyers, or businessmen to press charges *against* the poor rather than *for* them.[53]

A second method that has been devised is to make available to the poor legal services of certain particular agencies of the government that specialize in certain recurring sorts of claims. For example, a wage claim by an employee is in most states prosecuted not by the employee himself, but by the state's Department of Labor. The department first attempts to obtain the wages due by negotiation with the employer. This failing, the department will most frequently bring a criminal prosecution against the employer for the offense of failing to pay wages when due, a statutory crime in most jurisdictions. Such criminal prosecutions are almost invariably settled by the employer paying the claims under threat of imprisonment if he does not. Similarly, state departments of welfare will frequently prosecute claims against husbands and fathers for the benfit of poor or destitute wives and children.

A third device has been the creation of new tribunals, entirely separate from the courts, to service the poor. The outstanding example in this regard, of course, is the Workmen's Compensation Commission, to which has been turned over the great bulk of industrial accident litigation.

The remaining major area in which the poor are entangled in the law without real legal protection for reasons of costs in hiring attorneys has been the criminal law. Although courts are required to appoint attorneys for those who cannot afford them the quality of legal defense available is generally very low. Furthermore, most criminal cases are decided by pleas of guilty and the defendant is often ignorant of his or her rights.

In addition to these five general responses to the pressures of litigation, appellate courts have devised (or have been given by legislation) certain discretionary powers to decline to accept certain appeals. As we pointed out earlier, this power is most notable in the Supreme Court of the United States. That Court has the power to decide for itself, on the whole, which appeals to accept for decision, and which to reject, by the granting of a *writ of certiorari*. Only if four justices affirmatively vote to grant the writ will the Court hear an appeal. In this way, the Court can limit its decision-making to matters calling for significant rule-making: constitutional issues, matters in which there is a conflict between the rules announced by different courts of appeal in the federal system, problems of statutory construction, and the like.

The increasing volume of litigation, therefore, has probably been the single most important variable in determining judicial responses. A second significant variable has been the court's recognition of "crisis" cases. Some cases present issues which are highly charged with political or moral significance. Like all decision-makers, in such instances courts tend to perceive a potential threat to their own legitimacy, for if their decision is not in fact enforced, their whole structure of authority may be undermined.

Such a situation was brought about by the question of legislative apportionment. Some states had for many years increasingly weighted the representation of urban dwellers against rural residency. Instances of complex and absurd gerrymandering were not infrequent. Numerous challenges were made to such imbalances by the initiation of lawsuits directed to the question, whether the equal protection clause of the U.S. Constitution forbade such gross discrimination. The Supreme Court for many years persistently declined to consider such cases, either by exercise of *certiorari* powers or by labeling the issue "political" and not "judicial." Finally, it did accept such a case (*Baker* v. *Carr*) and, by deciding it in favor of the plaintiff, worked a major political realignment in the state governments whose effect is only just beginning to be felt.

Crisis cases, as Friedman has suggested,[54] are of two different kinds. Some, like the great Steel Seizure case,[55] are plainly nonrecurrent. Such crisis cases are not nearly so threatening to a court as cases involving deep-seated social conflicts, in which the court *must* in its decision advantage one side or the other. Courts tend to avoid such cases—the reapportionment cases are an excellent example—for as long as they can. When they do face up to the problem, they try to be unanimous (as the Supreme Court was in *Brown* v. *Board of Education*)[56] in order to legitimize the decision as heavily as possible. The rule is likely to be one whose administration can be delegated to other agencies. It will be as objective and as quantitative as possible, in an effort to end constant probing by litigants for its outermost boundaries. Since the simplest of all rules to administer is one which rejects the case and others like it completely, there is perhaps some tendency to solve crisis cases by rejecting any form of judicial interference.

Inputs: Permissible Rules of Law

As we have seen, the critical question in any trouble case is to formulate a controlling rule of law to govern the case at hand. Yet a court is sharply limited in the range of choice of potential major premises.

The leading—and all-important—rule limiting the range of choice by appellate courts of potential major premises to resolve the trouble case brought before them is that any premise which they adopt (and which therefore becomes a rule of law to control all similar cases in the future) must be "permissible." *It must be arguably consistent with some existing rule of law.*

Consider, for example, a Sudanese case, *Khartoum Municipal Council* v. *Cotran*.[57] The facts were as follows: In the exercise of powers granted under the Local Government Ordinance 1951 the defendant had dug a drain between 4½ and 5 meters from the side of an unlit road in a residential area in Khartoum. The drain was uncovered, unlit, and unguarded, but on the night in question, there was some dim light shed on it from nearby. The plaintiff, a district judge, and his companions arrived in the road by car to attend a party at a nearby embassy and were obligated to leave the car about 150 yards from their destination. The plaintiff left the road in order to avoid a traffic jam and, in attempting to take a short-cut, fell into the drain. As a result he suffered serious injuries to his left foot, involving surgery and considerable pain and suffering. In the event, he was left with a stiff painful foot amounting to a 70 percent loss of the use of the foot.

Under the English common law (which for these purposes we may assume was received in the Sudan), the court held that the defendant was under a duty to take reasonable care to protect the users of the street from the drain it had dug. (In so finding, the court relied upon a whole gaggle of English precedents, ranging in time from 1842 to 1955). The court then went on to discuss the standard of care required and held that the municipality did not take reasonable care to protect the public. It made a judgment of about $5500 in favor of the plaintiff.

The problem before the Sudanese court was really whether it was wise to expend $5500 for a single individual who was injured by the local council's negligence. For example, if the money had been spent to hire two nursing sisters for a year, who might have saved the lives of a number of children who otherwise might have died, might it not be a more sensible use of the money? Yet the Sudanese court could not within the limits of the judicial process adopt such a solution. The existing law held that municipalities were under a duty to take reasonable care to protect the users of its streets. Any major premises adopted by the court had to be consistent with this rule. So long as the English precedents were deemed applicable, it could not have held, for example, that municipalities were immune from such actions at law, even if in the African circumstance that had been the more sensible and socially useful rule.

Why this sharp limitation upon the creativity of a court in devising solutions to emergent problems? Courts in modern, complex, stratified societies have the primary function of settling disputes by winner-takes-all, i.e., by rule application. They are not primarily rule-creating organizations. The legislature is the primary formal lawmaker in every modern country. A court's power to create law arises only incidentally out of its dispute-settling function. It can create law only when it *must* do so in the course of determining the major premise for the lawsuit, an inevitable (if relatively infrequent) consequence of dispute-settling by way of norm enforcement. That is to say, society's role-expectations for judges is that, in the first instance, they will decide clear cases according to rules of law, and only when that is impossible will they be forced to create a rule of law to cover the case at hand. In a clear case, there is a norm, in its primary and secondary forms, which clearly subsumes the facts at hand. The court is expected to settle the dispute by applying the norm on a winner-takes-all basis. The court is not expected to determine new law to resolve the dispute.

Moreover, the court's legitimacy depends to a great degree upon its ability to maintain the position that it is not creating law, but only applying it. One can accept the decision of an umpire far more easily if his decision appears to be *compelled* by rules over which he has no discretionary control.

In a trouble case, however, the position of a court is ambiguous. It still is a rule-applier. But it is also a lawmaker, for any rule established in this case will be a rule for other similar cases in the future. It must act as a lawmaker, while generally appearing to be only a law-applier.

Courts have historically resolved this ambiguity by limiting the scope of their lawmaking to that which they are *required* to do, and no more. They have achieved this limitation by restricting the range of potential major premises to those which arguably are consistent with existing rules of law. It is a limitation that arises not from choice, but from the imperatives of the court's ambiguous position in a trouble case as a dispute-settler in a system that settles disputes on the basis of winner-takes-all and norm enforcement but where the applicable rule is not clear.

What we can expect, therefore, is a set of rules of two sorts. First, there must be rules which tell a judge that a given rule is in fact an authoritative rule of law. Secondly, there must be rules which tell a judge in a trouble case that a proposed alternative major premise is in fact "permissible," i.e., that it is arguably consistent with an authoritative rule of law. Since in a trouble case there are invariably at least two such permissible major premises, we must expect the rules in this second category to run at least in pairs, and still be equally authoritative.

In fact, the very nature of precedent suggests that the rules which control the use of a *single* case are susceptible of validating not a single rule, but several rules.[58] The rules of statutory construction run in contradictory pairs.[59] That they do is the best evidence that their function is not to decide cases, but to demonstrate that either of the potential rules of law urged by the opposing parties in a trouble case is at least arguably consistent with existing law. Their function is to demonstrate that the case is indeed a trouble case.

8.6 CONCLUSION

The principal inputs into the lawmaking processes of the appellate courts are issues, policies, the personal attributes of judges, their socialization, situational pressures, the organizational interests of the courts, and the permissible rules of law. It is intriguing how these various inputs are necessarily biased in favor of ensuring that courts as institutions are more available to the wealthy than to the poor and tend to produce solutions in the interests of the wealthy. The single most important variable would seem to be the high cost of litigation, for that one factor alone tends to have the consequences that the issues brought up for decision will be those in which the more advantaged in the community are interested and that the policies urged will be those urged by the more competent or better known and respected counsel. There are, however, other significant factors pointing in the same direction. The recruitment policies for judges have historically resulted in selection from a thin upper slice of American society. Although this factor is not conclusive in determining the outcome of individual cases, it does seem to make the overall policy output of courts politically conservative. The techniques of socialization of judges tend to have the same effect, and their educational and professional experience tend to ensure that judges are loyal adherents to the status quo. The organizational interests of the courts, especially that of restricting the amount of litigation, also tend to restrict litigation to the well-to-do. Perhaps most important of all, the system of precedents and statutory construction limits the choice of judges to relatively small changes in the existing system. We can generalize our argument in a set of propositions:

1 Every decision-making structure necessarily limits the range of potential inputs with respect to the problems to be considered, the potential hypotheses for their solution, and the data to be examined.

2 By these limitations, decision-making structures necessarily predetermine the range of potential outputs.

3 Every decision-making structure is therefore necessarily biased against a particular set of potential outputs and in favor of another set of potential outputs.

4 Therefore, every decision-making structure is necessarily value-loaded; it cannot be value-neutral.

These are the inputs for the appellate judges who must respond to the issues by formulating new rules to solve the problems posed. We turn in the next chapter to a consideration of how, given the inputs, the judges and the courts proceed with the "conversion processes," that is, the processes which characterize the manipulation of the inputs and which culminate in decisions.

NOTES

1. A. V. Dicey, *Introduction to the Study of the Law of the Constitution* (London: MacMillan, 1959).

2. *Ibid.*, p. 188.

3. Friedrich von Hayek, *The Road to Serfdom* (Chicago: University of Chicago Press, 1944).

4. *Ibid.*, p. 72.

5. Wolfgang Friedmann, *Legal Theory* (London: Stevens, 1967), p. 228.

6. Hans Kelsen, *The Pure Theory of Law*, trans. M. Knight (Berkeley: University of California Press, 1967), p. 285; translated from the first edition, 1930. Originally published by the University of California Press; reprinted by permission of The Regents of the University of California.

7. *Ibid.*, p. 286. Reprinted by permission.

8. H.L.A. Hart, *The Concept of Law* (Oxford: Clarendon Press, 1961), p. 13. Reprinted by permission of the Clarendon Press. See also Ronald Dworkin, *Taking Rights Seriously* (London: Duckworth, 1977).

9. Kelsen, *Pure Theory of Law*, p. 7. Reprinted by permission.

10. See Chapter 1.

11. Hart, *Concept of Law*, p. 111. Reprinted by permission.

12. *Ibid.*, p. 112. Reprinted by permission.

13. See Chapter 3.

14. O. W. Holmes, "The Path of the Law," *Harvard Law Review* 10(1897): 457, 458.

15. Cf. Hart, *Concept of Law,* pp. 120-132.

16. H. Oliphant, "A Return to Stare Decisis," *American Bar Association Journal* 14(1928): 71-73.

17. Richard A. Wasserstrom, *The Judicial Decision: Toward a Theory of Logical Justification* (Palo Alto, Calif.: Stanford University Press, 1961), p. 19. Reprinted by permission. See also Max Radin, *Law as Logic and Experience* (New Haven: Yale University Press, 1940), p. 51; Oliphant, "Stare Decisis," pp. 72-73; Jerome Frank, *Law and the Modern Mind* (New York: Tudor, 1936), p. 268n ("in a profound sense, the unique circumstances of almost any case make it an 'unprovided' case").

18. L. Friedman, "Legal Rules and the Process of Social Change," *Stanford Law Review* 19(1967): 786-840 at 792. Reprinted by permission.

19. 138 Mass. 165, 52 Am. Rep. 264 (1884).

20. 211 Mich. 187, 178 N.W. 690 (1920).

21. [1957] 1 Q.B. 399, England.

22. 10 C.L.&F. 200 (1843); 8 E.R. 718, House of Lords, England.

23. 186 U.S. 413, 22 S. Ct. 895, 46 L. Ed. 1225 (1901).

24. 283 U.S. 25, 51 S. Ct. 340, 75 L. Ed. 816 (1931).

25. 4 Q.B.D. 228, England (1879).

26. This is *not* a pseudonym.

27. *William* v. *Ellis,* 5 Q.B.D. 175, England (1880).

28. See R. B. Seidman, "The Judicial Process Reconsidered in Light of Role Theory," *Modern Law Review,* 32(1969): 516.

29. *Ibid.,* p. 523.

30. Lon Fuller, "American Legal Realism," *University of Pennsylvania Law Review* 82(1934):429, 439n.

31. *Brown* v. *Board of Education,* 347 U.S. 483 (1954). This was the monumental Supreme Court decision stating that separate or segregated schools were not and could not be equal.

32. *Chamberlain* v. *Milwaukee and Mississippi Railroad Co.,* 11 Wis. 248 (1860).

33. *Moseley* v. *Chamberlain,* 18 Wis. 700 (1861).

34. Quoted in C. Auerbach, L. K. Garrison, W. Hurst, and S. Mermin, *The Legal Process: An Introduction to Decision-Making by Judicial, Legislative, Executive, and Administrative Agencies* (San Francisco: Chandler, 1961), pp. 159-161.

35. *Ibid.*

36. *Ibid.*

37. Rodney L. Mott, "Judicial Influence," *American Political Science Review* 30(1936): 295-315.

38. *Dennis* v. *United States,* 341 U.S. 494, 510 (1951).

39. From *Judicial Policy Making* by Glendon Schubert, p. 110. Copyright © 1965 by Scott, Foresman and Company. Used by permission.

40. A. Lewis, "Legislative Apportionment and the Federal Courts," *Harvard Law Review* 71(1959): 1057-98.

41. J. A. Schmidhauser, "The Justices of the Supreme Court: A Collective Portrait," *Midwest Journal of Political Science* 3(1959): 2-27, 40-49.

42. J. Grossman, "Political Party Affiliation and the Selection: Judges' Decisions," *American Political Science Review* 55(1961):843. Reprinted by permission.

43. R. Bowen, "The Explanation of Judicial Voting Behavior from Sociological Characteristics of Judges," Ph.D. dissertation, Yale University, 1965.

44. J. Grossman, "Social Backgrounds and Judicial Decision-Making," *Harvard Law Review* 79(1966): 1551-63.

45. See J. W. Hurst, *The Growth of American Law: The Law Makers* (Boston: Little, Brown & Co., 1950), pp. 256-276.

46. A. P. Blaustein and C. O. Porter, *The American Lawyer* (Chicago: University of Chicago Press, 1954), p. 167.

47. We shall see later that a strange sea change, originated by the American realists, is afoot in the legal world. The essence of the realist movement is to examine, not only the law-in-the-books, but also the law-in-action—the way in which the role-occupant actually performs, as well as the way in which he is expected to perform. The confrontation of the pious hopes of American law, with all its high-flown phrases, by the gross reality of the poor, the black, and the Vietnam war has tended to force many American law students to define the situation in terms of reality rather than the categories received from the conventional wisdom expressed in decided cases. What effect this change will have on the average practicing lawyer remains to be seen. It is sufficient to note here that American law students, in numbers which seem to increase geometrically from year to year, are opting for service programs for their first employment after law school rather than more lucrative private practice.

48. "Mr. Dooley" was the pseudonym of Finley Peter Dunne, a newspaper columnist. E. J. Brander, ed., *Mr. Dooley and the Choice of Law* (Charlottesville, Va.: Michie, 1963), p. 52.

49. Leon Green, "The Study and Teaching of Tort Law," *Texas Law Review* 34(1956): 16. Reprinted by permission.

50. Friedman, "Legal Rules," pp. 786, 798-799.

51. See generally *ibid., passim,* from which this dicussion is drawn.

52. See S. Macauley, "Non-Contractual Relations in Business: A Preliminary Study," *American Sociological Review* 28(1963): 55.

53. See I. J. Rapson, "The Dane County Small Claims Court," unpublished thesis in the University of Wisconsin library, 1961.

54. Friedman, "Legal Rules," p. 808.

55. *Youngstown Sheet and Tube Co.* v. *Sawyer,* 343 U.S. 579 (1952).

56. 347 U.S. 483 (1954).

57. *Sudanese Law Journal Review* 85(1958).

58. See Chapter 9.

59. See Chapter 5.

9

Appellate court decisions

Every rule which is formulated and announced by an appellate court comes into existence because somebody has conceived that she was aggrieved by the action of somebody else and so instituted a lawsuit of some sort. While the rule articulated by an appellate court must be a generalized rule applicable to all other parties in similar situations, it must also resolve the instant litigation. Moreover, since judges are sworn to uphold the law, they cannot (or ought not) create new laws which are completely unrelated to the existing framework of rules. As we have seen, the law-creating functions of appellate courts are not something they search out, but which inevitably they must fulfill. Nevertheless, theirs is not a law-creating function de novo. Their primary job is dispute-settling. This limits the scope of their creativity as rule-makers. Several constraints, all arising out of the fact that appellate courts do their rule-making in the immediate context of dispute-settlement, account for some of the peculiar characteristics of the rules which they create.

The vast proportion of the rule output of appellate courts is inducive of incremental, rather than radical, change; it aims at overall solutions which are relatively conservative, and it is dominated by the courts' own institutional interests over all other interests in society. To the first two of these generalizations, however, a sharp exception must be made for the present Supreme Court of the United States, for reasons which are peculiar to it. We discuss first the output of appellate courts other than the Supreme Court.

9.1 APPELLATE COURTS GENERALLY

Long ago Roscoe Pound said that the great paradox of the law is between the need for stability and the need for change. People need and demand predictability in their jural relationships. They want to know that when they act in certain specified ways there will be certain specified consequences. Actors want a world in which at least their most important actions are governed by ascertainable, predictable norms. At the same time, however, the world moves, and not only in the physical way that Galileo had in mind. Constant flux in social relations is the human condition. The power of the state expressed through law can no more than Canute hold back the tide. If the law tries to cast society in a rigid mold, the stresses and strains become so great that tension, anomie, incoherence, and violence inevitably result.

But to say that the law must always strike a balance between stability and change is to say nothing very helpful. The choice posed at any given moment to the rule-maker is only very rarely one whose resolution, one way or the other, will result in immediate, deeply rooted unrest. The nature of the institutional constraints on appellate courts dictates that their choice in general will lead only to incremental change; they favor a return to equilibrium without changing existing institutions more than is required to maintain existing power relations.

Interstitial Rules

Most lawsuits are "clear" cases. They call for the application of preexisting norms. In "trouble" cases, in which the rules themselves are at issue, the traditional conversion process requires that each party must demonstrate that his claimed rule of law is based on at least one possible reading of existing rules which are accepted as such; that is, as we have seen, one must start with the clear-case rules. Bound by norms defining such conversion processes, the court's choice is inevitably a narrow one. In a leading New York case on the definition of insanity, for example, the defendant (Schmidt) cut the throat of a woman after, he claimed, he had heard the voice of God calling upon him to kill her as a sacrifice and atonement; after having killed her, he believed that he was in the visible presence of God.[1] The rules then in force in New York provided that a person could plead insanity as a defense to a criminal charge only if he could prove that "at the time of the committing of the act, the party accused was laboring under such defect of reason, from disease of the mind, as not to know the nature or quality of the act he was doing; or if he did know it, that he did not know what he was doing was wrong." That rule was laid down in the M'Naghten case in 1843.[2] In the New York case, the defendant Schmidt admitted that he knew what he was doing was illegal when he cut the woman's throat, but he believed that he was obeying a higher law. The narrow issue in the case was whether the word "wrong" meant "illegal" or "morally wrong," for Schmidt claimed that he did not know that what he was doing was morally wrong. The court decided that the proper construction of the term "wrong" was "morally wrong." But the court was not called upon to consider whether the entire standard of insanity, based as it was on the rule laid down in 1843, ought to be maintained. A legislature would at least have considered that issue. The institutional role and structure of the courts, arising from their original purpose of dispute-settlement, forbade them to take so radical a step.

The character of appellate courts as small groups probably also contributes to this inhibition. As we have seen, the decisions of these courts are frequently based on compromises, on the bargaining between members of the courts themselves. The usual result of such bargaining is to ensure that the opinion will justify the decision on grounds that can command the widest agreement among the various members of the court. The narrower the rule is, the more people can agree with it.

Incapacity for Planning

A corollary to the built-in limitation that appellate courts can induce only incremental rather than radical changes is that courts are incapable of laying out an entire area of law in order to plan a total, integrated response to the challenges posed to them. They cannot take on the "big picture." For example, litigation over water rights in the southwestern United States frequently takes the form of disputes between upstream and downstream owners, each of whom claims the right to divert a certain percentage of the river's flow into his own drainage ditches. As might be expected, many such disputes can flare up along a river. There have been cases in which, as a result of a number of such individual actions, the judicial system made a series of judgments with the brilliant result that they allocated far more than 100 percent of the river's flowage.

There are those who have urged that the rules devised by appellate courts, despite the apparently fortuitous way in which cases arise, nevertheless do tend to form a complete and harmonious system. Llewellyn argued that since disputes arise out of conflict, and since conflict is most likely in developing or growing areas of social activity, the development of rules is apt to match the dynamics of society itself. As Fuller has pointed out, this is a sort of classical free-market theory of legal rule-making.[3] Nevertheless, Fuller has shown that a whole field of law may be permanently influenced and biased by the special factors present in the first case raising the question. (It is an old principle that widow's and orphan's cases make bad law.) Moreover, the order in which cases arise may shape the law in a way that a lawmaker who could assess the entire program would perceive to be unwise. The movement for the establishment of law revision commissions is in part aimed at rectifying such mistakes; the commissions are to be specialized agencies with the function of overviewing entire fields of law.

Inability to Create New Organizations

The most pressing social problems of our time can only rarely be solved by general rules alone. There has thus been an increasing reliance on specially created organizations, each presumably dedicated to the execution of certain areas of public policy, for solutions to emergent tensions. Witness the astounding growth of acronymed agencies in the past half century.

In the school desegregation case, for example, the Supreme Court recognized that the social problem to which its decision was directed could not be solved by laying down universal norms of conduct. Instead, the Court in the *Brown* decision articulated a policy. Ideally, there would have been created an agency empowered to use a whole bag of sanctions—education of public officials, increased school aid for comforming school districts, punishment for obdurate school districts, technical assistance in solving specific local questions, etc.—for the institution of that policy. But its institutional structure imposed a sharp limitation on what the Court could do. The best that it was able to do was to send the case back to individual district courts for the latter to use their equity power to bring about desegregation "with all deliberate speed." The absence of adequate specialized agencies to deal with the problem continued for a whole decade after *Brown,* until the Department of Health, Education, and Welfare was given limited authority in the area in the Civil Rights Act of 1964.

Inability to Determine Potential Consequences

The more the proposed change varies from what presently is the case, the greater is the risk that unforeseen consequences will intervene. Dahl and Lindblom expanded this notion into a whole theory which claims that only incremental change is completely rational.[4] The greater the change, therefore, the more risky it is to proceed in the absence of competent empirical data anticipating what the consequences will be. Conversely, the less empirical information is available, the more likely it is that the change-agent will abstain from instituting comprehensive change in favor of incremental change.

Courts suffer from an institutional disability that prevents them from making the sort of empirical studies that might permit them to make comprehensive changes with even a minimum amount of confidence in the result.

Courts depend on the adversary system for the kind of fact-gathering required to determine whether a particular state of affairs occurred at a particular time and place.[5] Legislative-like rule-making, however, requires different kinds of facts, such as are collected, analyzed, and reported by the several social science disciplines. For the purposes of obtaining these types of facts the usual procedures in the courts are largely irrelevant. Occasionally, as in *Brown,* such evidence may be introduced on the trial court level through expert witnesses. Sometimes the social science data are submitted to the appellate court in the form of a "Brandeis brief" (so called because it was first used by Louis Brandeis when he was an attorney). Both these devices, however, are useful only within severe limitations. The expert is hampered by limits imposed by the rules of evidence, which are designed to guard against various sorts of problems that arise when experts testify in cases involving insanity, medical issues, and the like, and which are ill-adapted to the admission and exclusion of social science data. The Brandeis brief is not subject to close scrutiny by the opposing parties. In neither case is there opportunity for persons affected by the potential ruling, but not parties to the lawsuit, to be represented except as they may be able to argue as an *amicus curiae* (''friend of the court'').

Increasing Concern with Trivia in Private Law

As Friedman has demonstrated,[6] in the mid-nineteenth century appellate courts were central to the formulation of universalistic rules of contract law—and, one might add, in other areas of private law as well. The market reigned, largely without restraint; the people saw in the release of individual energy the engine of economic development.[7] Disputes between individuals were readily perceived by courts as specific examples of universal rules which ordered the operations of the market, and they were decided in those terms. By the middle of the twentieth century, however, everything was *toto caelo* different.

Mid-twentieth century society, taken in general, was middle-of-the-road. It believed in the sanctity of majority rule and majority opinion; it did not really believe that men held irreconcilable economic goals, but believed rather in the possibilities and values of teamwork and compromise; it believed that nobody gained if the farmer suffered, that strong unions and clean employee cafeterias were good for business, and that it would be morally wrong for labor to lack a voice in running an industry. It was fashionable in 1955 to see (and decry) ''conformity'' in American society; certainly developments in mass communications and transport made cultural and moral homogeneity possible. The use of ''fairness'' as a criterion for settling contract disputes meant the replacement of inherited legal concepts with current concepts of what was right. Particular disputes were to be judged in terms of current ethical standards. It meant foreswearing the use of general principles applied absolutely; it meant that courts were dispute-settlers, not agencies creating general norms at the impulse of particular occasions.[8]

The search for particularity and fairness impelled the creation of many government agencies concerned with contract performance of various sorts. As Friedman concludes,

In part, the activism of government (in the middle of the twentieth century) was a judgment that the market was a failure; in another sense, it was a judgment that the economy consisted not of a market, but of many markets, each with its appropriate modality of control. In such a context, the law of contract remained alive, not however, as the organic law of the state's economic system—a kind of constitution for business transactions—but as one among many. It was the system of rules applicable to marginal, novel, as yet unregulated, residual and peripheral business, and quasi-business transactions, transactions which might, in exceptional cases, call for problem-solving and dispute-settling. ''Contract'' stepped in where no other body of law and no agency of law other than the court was appropriate or available.[9]

The sharp diminution in the rule-making output of appellate courts in contract cases was, ultimately, the result of their primary commitment to dispute-settlement. Since the rule-making processes of appellate courts are never placed in motion unless there is a dispute to settle, so long as other agencies have original jurisdiction in contract cases, the contract rule-making output of appellate courts is bound to decline and become more and more restricted to trivia.

The same thing has happened in most other areas of private law. Workmen's compensation commissions have drained off all but an infinitesimal fraction of industrial accident cases. Better methods of land registration and a wide use of title insurance have reduced the number of litigations arising from real estate transactions. Standardized lease forms have sharply cut down the number of landlord-tenant litigations, and in many places rent-control agencies have superseded even the use of the standardized lease form. Insurance contracts have their forms laid down by insurance commissioners. When businessmen litigate, they tend to appeal, more often than not, to governmental agencies of all sorts: local planning and zoning commissions with respect to real estate problems, licensing boards, regulating agencies, tax agents, and specialized tax courts.

Only in one area has the courts' rule-making output in private law proliferated: automobile accidents. In the nineteenth century, tort law—the law that purports to regulate disparate activities within a basically nonregulated society—contained an important component which adjusted the relationships between industry and those affected by its activities. The inadequacy of tort law for regulating such activities led in time to its replacement by other sets of rules: zoning, which tried to prevent incompatible land uses from too close contact, food and drug administrations, public utility commissions, and the like. Only with respect to automobiles have the courts retained their control over practically the entire area—a control whose demise is being heralded by the development of national and state legislation laying down safety standards for automobiles, and whose death-knell will be sounded when the states enact legislation assimilating automobile accidents under the absolute liability imposed in workmen's compensation cases.

9.2 THE CONSEQUENCES OF INCREMENTAL CHANGE

The institutional constraints upon appellate courts, according to which they can undertake rule-making only in response to particular disputes between particular parties, and cannot plan large areas of law systematically or create new organizations, have combined with the sorts of conversion processes which courts traditionally employ to limit the scope of choice available to appellate courts in their rule-making efforts. Added to this is the fact (which may be a result rather than a cause of the courts' limitations) that increasingly they have been concerned with trivia in the rule-making role. Consequently, they have been unable to bring about radical institutional changes (again excepting the Supreme Court of the United States). Whatever the position of a particular bench in the conservative-radical political continuum, its rule output has necessarily been reflective of the blinders of institution, the conversion processes, and attention to trivia.

The examples are legion. The solution of many of our most pressing social problems today requires a radical redistribution of income. Courts, even if they are so inclined, can do only very little about this. No matter how lenient a court may be when a dispute between a wealthy landlord and a poverty-stricken inhabitant of the ghetto comes before it, the rule it articulates must assume the fact that by and large tenants must pay rent to landlords. Courts have no way of subsidizing the rent or of constructing public low-rent housing for the poor. Another example can be found in our system of compensation for injuries in automobile accidents. Such accidents are as much a concomitant of a highly mobile society in which automobiles are very widely owned, as industrial accidents are in an industrial society. Just as the cost of industrial accidents ultimately became regarded as part of the costs of production, which ought to be borne largely by the ultimate consumer as part of the price of the product, so ought we at least to consider whether part of the general social cost of a highly mobile society is not the cost of automobile accidents. We have no difficulty in seeing that roads are part of the general social cost; the cost of automobile accidents might well be regarded in the same way. By reason of the several constraints we mentioned, however, courts are incapable of adopting so radical a position even if they wanted to do so.

The actual narrowness of the courts' vision precisely matches the narrowness of vision that can be predicted for Chin's systems model. Appellate courts only make rules in response to stresses arising in existing institutions. The changes they can conceivably make are incremental, designed to make the existing structures function smoothly once again, i.e., to return to an equilibrium in which the institution can operate without further intervention by governmental agencies.

When the restricted scope of choice which is available to judges is considered, not from their point of view, but from the point of view according to which society is based on conflict between its various groups and strata, a radical vision results. In the words of Harold Laski,

Every society is the theatre of a conflict between economic classes for a larger material benefit, for, that is, a larger share in the results to be distributed from the productive process. Since the power to produce within any society is dependent upon peace, the state must maintain law and order to that end. But, in so doing, it is necessarily maintaining the law and order implied in the particular system of class relations of which it is the expression. In a feudal society, that is, the law and order which the state maintains is the law and order necessary to the preservation of feudal principles. In a capitalist society, the state maintains the law and order necessary to maintain capitalist principles.[10]

It seems improbable that courts will ever be able to accomplish, save by miniscule changes moving with glacial slowness, the sort of revolutionary shifts in power which would be necessary to change the system entirely. It would even seem highly unlikely that any court could accomplish anything more than incremental change.

Yet the fact is that, although most appellate courts in most decisions do no more than make incremental changes, the Supreme Court of the United States has made decisions which have brought about thoroughgoing changes in particular institutions, accompanied by significant shifts in power relations with respect to those institutions. How can we account for this paradox?

9.3 COMPREHENSIVE CHANGE AND THE SUPREME COURT

It is an intriguing fact that in the 1960s a radical trend arose in the Supreme Court of the United States. In case after case, the Court quite decisively disconfirmed what we just stated to be the necessary character of court decisions. In *Miranda* v. *Arizona,*[11] for example, the Court laid down a whole manual delineating the permissible scope of police interrogation on arrests. In *Matter of Gault,*[12] it outlined the required procedures for juvenile courts. In *Baker* v. *Carr*[13] it ordered far-reaching changes in state electoral laws. In *Brown* v. *Board of Education,*[14] it laid down a broad rule which has had profound effects on the entire social fabric of most parts of the country. In none of these cases can it fairly be said that the rules laid down were "interstitial" or "molecular." Why this sharp divergence from the traditional form of rule output of appellate courts? The reasons seem to lie in the unique institutional position of the Supreme Court, the role of moral entrepreneurs in constitutional litigation, and the pragmatic decision-making methods which the court has come more and more to employ.

Its Institutional Position

The Supreme Court's power of judicial review of legislation or actions by any governmental body in the country to determine if laws or governmental actions square with constitutional norms in effect gives it a limited veto power over every other branch of government. As a result, it is frequently called upon to decide the direction of the central thrust of entire institutions, as our four examples demonstrate. The Court's first duty is to uphold the Constitution, a notoriously ambiguous document which speaks frequently, not to peripheral matters, but to the most important values of government: fairness, protection of the individual from hostile action by the state, the openness of our society, its potential for peaceful social change, the protection of minority interest from majority will. To resolve ambiguities in most statutes requires a court to forge a new rule which effects only interstitial change. To resolve ambiguities in the Constitution frequently requires the Supreme Court to forge new rules which radically change the essence of existing institutions.

In recent years, the Supreme Court has been called upon to answer just such far-ranging questions at a time when other branches of government were deadlocked on the issues involved. For many years the Court had been making small, molecular attempts to solve the problems as they arose in narrow terms. It had tried on a case-by-case basis to curb police interrogations by limiting their admissibility, but to no avail. Legislatures seemed incapable or unwilling to move into the premises.

Petitioners had been knocking at the Supreme Court door for years claiming discrimination in representation in the states, and the Court had responded only that the matter was "political" and therefore not justifiable. But the "political" bodies which ought to have remedied the situation, the Congress and the state legislatures, showed no sign of moving to resolve the problems. Similarly, desegregation in public education was regarded by all the members of the Court as a denial of the promise of the American dream, and yet Congress patently did not propose to interfere.

The Court's institutional position and the facts of history therefore determined that many of the constitutional cases that would reach it would call into question not only the operations of specific public institutions, but the general direction in which the institution was moving. The constitutional position of the Court has required it to test the institutions in question against the values which it perceives to be expressed in the Constitution itself, at a time when it seemed useless to rely upon some other, perhaps more appropriate, agency to reform these institutions. Moreover, a mechanism existed whose operation ensured that even issues primarily of interest to the poor would come up in contexts in which the policy inputs of at least the petitioners would be directed at deep-seated change.

Rules Important to Special Interest Groups

That courts can only consider issues arising in specific disputes is ordinarily a sharp constraint on their rule output. By the same token, however, the courts are almost the only branch of government whose rule-making capacities can be put into motion at the instance of an individual. Legislatures are under no requirement to move at individuals' requests. Administrative agencies in most cases, too, need not respond to the petition of isolated individuals. The courts alone must respond.

As a result, where the issuance of a rule is important to a particular interest group, it is relatively easy (albeit expensive) for a case to be taken to the highest rule-making levels even when the intrinsic importance of the case would not justify such an investment. In state as well as federal courts, tax cases have abounded precisely for this reason. Many states have in the past levied taxes on businesses with only transient interests within the states in question. More frequently than not, the amount involved for any particular business in any particular state has been insufficiently large to warrant the costs of appeals through a multitude of administrative agencies and state and federal courts. Since, however, a favorable ruling would have an impact far beyond the particular case, business associations of various sorts have litigated such cases in a continuing effort to persuade the appellate courts to announce rules favorable to their interests.

The peculiar position of the Supreme Court of the United States in constitutional matters has made it the special target of such "test cases." Probably no single individual would have litigated the question of prayers by six-year-old children in public schools before the Supreme Court, at a cost of many thousands of dollars. Yet such cases have repeatedly come before the Court. In these cases the litigations are often carried on in the name of particular individuals, but the real interested party is an organization such as the American Civil Liberties Union. *Brown* v. *Board of Education*, the school desegregation case, whose impact upon the American society has probably been more widespread than any other case in American legal history, was conceived, tried, and appealed by the NAACP. Most of our current rules governing criminal procedure were created upon litigation by civil liberties groups, as were most of the cases involving freedom of expression, loyalty oaths, and the like. Many, perhaps most, of these cases arose in areas where it was plainly hopeless even to try to persuade the Congress to move. Indeed, in many of these cases there have been congressional efforts to reverse the Court's ruling by statute.

The existence of moral entrepreneurs has been of great significance in alleviating the built-in bias of the appellate court system, and especially of the most expensive of the courts, the Supreme Court, to select issues for decision which are of primary interest to the well-to-do. But the constitutional position of the Supreme Court, and the fact that there exist moral entrepreneurs to carry the cases to it, would not alone explain why the Court has abandoned incremental change as the core of the judicial technique in so many cases. These factors at best provide the opportunity for more wide-ranging decision-making. It also needs an entirely different method to guide its decision, and this method the court has found in the pragmatic, realist mode of deciding cases which has dominated Supreme Court constitutional decisional techniques since the late 1930s.

Pragmatic Decision-Making

We have already seen that as a result of historical progression, the Supreme Court, since the judicial "revolution" of 1937, has adopted as its most usual form of deciding cases the pragmatic method which is associated with the realist school of jurisprudence.[15] In *Miranda*, for example, even the dissenting justices agreed that the general technique of decision-making adopted by the majority was proper, although they disagreed sharply with the results:

That the Court's holding today is neither compelled nor even strongly suggested by the language of the Fifth Amendment is at odds with American and English legal history and involves a departure from a long line of precedent does not prove either that the Court is wrong or unwise in its present reinterpretation of the Fifth Amendment. It does, however, underscore the obvious—that the Court has not discovered or found the law in making today's decision, nor has it derived it from some irrefutable sources; what it has done is make new law and new public policy in much the same way that it has in the course of interpreting other great clauses of the Constitution. That is what the Court historically has done. Indeed, it is what it must do and will continue to do until and unless there is some fundamental change in the constitutional distribution of governmental powers. . . . Decisions like these cannot rest alone on syllogism, metaphysics or some ill-defined notions of natural justice, although each will perhaps play its part. In proceeding to such constructions as it now announces, the Court should also duly consider all the factors and interests bearing upon the cases, at least insofar as the relevant materials are available; and if the necessary considerations are not treated in the record or obtainable from some other reliable source, the Court should not proceed to formulate fundamental policies based on speculation alone.[16]

Endowed as it is with constitutional power to make decisions controlling the direction of institutions, dominated by a philosophy which no longer conceives of the Court's role in decision-making as limited to considering existing legal materials, but feeling free to go to many other "nonlegal" sources for empirical data and even for value-judgments; bound only by the broad language and frequently ambiguous history of the Constitution; and now confronted by situations, presented with increasing insistence by moral entrepreneurs, which the Court regards as blocking the substantial achievement of values it deems important and therefore constitutionally enthroned, and which the passage of years demonstrated were not about to be resolved by the legislature, the Court would naturally try to remove those obstructions entirely and in one blow. The alternative was to permit them to continue and then await the cumbersome, slow, and expensive process of case-by-case litigation to resolve the problems over time. The Supreme Court has acted decisively.

This is not to say, however, that there are no limitations on decision-making by the Supreme Court. The Court's institutional role requires that it make decisions in constitutional cases only insofar as it can shore up its decision on some plausible reading of the Constitution. It can only consider solutions which can be accomplished through formulating a universal rule, applicable to all persons in similar situations. Most important of all, it cannot create a new organization to resolve problems, no matter how plainly the solution requires it.

The *Gault* case is an interesting example of this last and perhaps most important constraint on the Court. In that case, a juvenile had been committed as a delinquent to the State Industrial School by an Arizona juvenile court, on the ground that he had violated a state statute in using lewd language over the telephone to a woman neighbor. The commitment was accomplished without notice of hearing, confrontation of witnesses, counsel, or cross-examination; and it was made on the basis of a confession, which under *Miranda* was inadmissible because it violated the privilege against self-incrimination. The traditional justification for permitting such seeming violations of constitutional standards in juvenile cases was that the state stood *in parens patriae* and that, in the exercise of its fatherly care for juveniles, it could quite properly help them to develop into well-adjusted, law-abiding citizens. Since these, rather than "punishment," were the purposes of commitment, it was believed that no "rights" were being violated by doing what was thought to be in the child's interest.

The Court swept all these rationalizations aside in large part by undercutting their factual premises. The classification "delinquent" "has come to involve only slightly less stigma than the term 'criminal' applied to adults." The claim of secrecy of records (invoked to justify the denial of procedural protections) "is more rhetoric than reality." The benevolent, fatherly approach in the interests of the child is not in the best interests of the child after all; modern research suggests that "the essentials of due process may be a more impressive and more therapeutic attitude so far as the juvenile is concerned." The very fact of incarceration is enough; "it is of no constitutional importance—and of limited practical meaning—that the institution to which he was committed is called an Industrial School."[17]

In this instance, the Court articulated major new rules of procedure for juvenile courts across the nation, in a far-reaching opinion that went well beyond the decisional demands of the case before it. But there were other options, not open to the Court, which might have been used to resolve the problem of the juvenile courts without introducing the very rigidities of procedure against which the juvenile court movement had initially rebelled. Justice Stewart stated, dissenting:

In the past 70 years many dedicated men and women have devoted their professional lives to the enlightened task of bringing us out of the dark world of Charles Dickens in meeting our responsibilities to the child in our society. The result has been the creation of a system of juvenile and family courts in each of the 50 states. There can be no denying that in many areas the performance of these agencies has fallen disappointingly short of the hopes and dreams of the courageous pioneers who first conceived them. For a variety of reasons, the reality has sometimes not even approached the ideal, and much remains to be accomplished in the administration of public juvenile and family agencies—in personnel, in planning, in financing, perhaps in the formulation of wholly new approaches.

I possess neither the specialized experience nor the expert knowledge to predict with certainty where may lie the brightest hope for progress in dealing with the specialized problems of juvenile delinquency. But I am certain that the answer does not lie in the Court's opinion in this case, which serves to convert a juvenile proceeding into a criminal prosecution.[18]

Justice Stewart was stating that he disagreed with the decision in *Gault* because there were undoubtedly other, better solutions available: more money, more personnel, and greater legislative and administrative attention might and probably would find solutions which did not so clearly abandon the desiderata of informality and a sense of paternal care.

The Supreme Court and the Developmental (or Tension-Management) Model

Just as the ordinary appellate court in most cases finds that its position, inputs, and conversion processes require its role as change-agent be similar to that demanded by the structural-functionalist model, so also the same factors require that the Supreme Court in constitutional cases define its role as change-agent in terms of Chin's "developmental" (or Moore's "tension-management") model. As in the ideal case, the Court conceives of its position as change-agent in much broader terms than most appellate courts. It believes that it can and should sweep away the obstructions to the continuous growth and development of the institutions in question. Its attitude toward precedent in constitutional law reflects the view that institutions are constantly changing, and therefore it should not mechanically apply old precedents to the new situations. On the other hand, its inability to create new structures means that it must in the main accept and rely on the existing institutions. It could not strike down the juvenile court system, for it could not supply some other organization to meet the problem of juvenile delinquency. It could not even contemplate striking down the whole system of state education and substituting for it a federal, nonsegregated system, even though the desirability of such an alternative should at least be discussed by a change-agent who perceived the entire range of alternatives. But it could and did decree comprehensive changes in these institutions.

The Court could not examine the widest range of possible alternatives. Just as the ordinary appellate court is in most cases bound to find a solution tenable within the meaning of the statute or case-law authorities, so the Supreme Court must find a solution in constitutional cases tenable under the Constitution. The comparatively large scope available to the Supreme Court is a function, in the final analysis, of the fact that the Constitution really is the basic document of the government. The restraints on the Court's scope for choice likewise are a function of the Constitution. Insofar as the Constitution defines the basic institutions of American government, the Court must fit its decisions within the limits defined by the goals of those institutions.

9.4 APPELLATE COURTS: LIBERAL OR CONSERVATIVE CHOICES

We have tried to demonstrate that the institutional position of appellate courts sharply limits their range of choice of a potential rule. They are forced by their position and function to confine their role as change-agent to one similar to that suggested by Chin's system model—i.e., to the introduction of incremental changes with the aim of reducing emergent tensions within a particular institution. Willy-nilly they are forced to accept the goals for the institution already set by society. In the result, their overall function is inevitably conservative: the appellate courts' law-creating powers are used to maintain the ongoing system, with only the adjustments necessary to accommodate to the new pressures thrown up as society changes. (The Supreme Court of the United States, in constitutional cases at least, may be an exception to this rule, a matter which we discuss below.)

The overall conservative cast of appellate court decisions is therefore built into the institution itself, regardless of the personal biases of the individual judges. The most flaming radical activist, as an appellate judge, could never in his role as appellate judge fashion any of the agencies of the Welfare State—social security, pure food and drug administrations, workmen's compensation, licensing of radio and television stations, and the like—let alone bring about revolutionary changes.

Even within these tight institutional restrictions, however, judges must make choices. Every rule *does* embody a choice. Can it be said that even within their limited scope courts generally make choices agreeable to the economically and politically dominant classes in the community?

It is perhaps useful to recapitulate the various inputs into the system which suggest that the rule output would be warped in favor of the wealthy. The issues which arise for decision are determined by those who bring the lawsuits and in light of the expenses involved in litigation, obviously the well-to-do will invoke the judicial machinery rather more frequently than most citizens. The major source of policy inputs is the lawyers, and typically the wealthy can employ the prestigious lawyers whose fees they can afford. The general tendency among lawyers employed by the wealthy is to conform to the values and specific views of their clients. The personal attributes of the judges suggest that they are recruited from a very narrow, educated, and well-to-do slice of the total population.

From all these considerations Laski concluded that the actual output of the rule-making system was bound to favor the wealthy even within the range permitted by the institution.[19] On this point he was sharply challenged by Roscoe Pound, who said:

With an economic interpretation of the general course of history and so of legal history one can have no quarrel. Nor within limits can one quarrel with such an interpretation of certain types of events in legal history. What must give us pause is making it the sole weapon in the jurist's armory or the sole instrument in his tool chest; the reference of every item in the judicial process, of every single decision and every working out of a legal precept by applying the technique of the law to the received materials of decision, to the operation, conscious or unconscious, of the desires and self-interest of an economically dominant class.[20]

Pound asserted that "what stands out in the history of Anglo-American law is the resistance of the taught tradition in the hands of judges drawn from any class you like, so they have been trained in the tradition, against all manner of economically or politically powerful interests."[21]

What Pound suggested is that the socialization of lawyers and judges is such that they make their choices in each case in accordance with the received rules of recognition and received values. "The strongest single influence born in determining single decisions and in guiding a course of decision is a taught tradition of logically interdependent precepts and of referring cases to principles."[22] He recognized that so legalistic a judicial process could not resolve the issue in trouble cases. But he believed that there was a common set of values, taught to judges and lawyers, which served as standard for resolving ambiguities: "It is here that the ideal element in law comes into play, since the results of choosing one starting point rather than another are measured by the received social ideal, as it has been taught to judges and lawyers. The effect of economic changes upon this ideal is for the most part gradual and slow, no matter what class is affected. The business man and the leader of industry have had quite as much cause for complaint in this respect as the labor leader; and the farmer, long dominant in American politics, no less than either. As Maitland puts it, 'taught law is tough law.' "[23]

Pound's contention, if true, plainly seems to demonstrate not his thesis so much as Laski's. If there is a "received social ideal" in the law, it must be immanent in its vast panoply. The law at any given moment, viewed in its entirety, could not in the nature of things lay down prescriptive rules adapted to the world that is to be. At its very best it might describe as well as prescribe the world that is. Considering the creaks and lack of fit in most human institutions, it is even more likely to include rules mainly adapted to the world that was. By the very nature of law, the social ideal embodied in it tends to look backward to the past and not forward into the future; it must always retain a strong scent of the nostalgic. Businessmen and leaders of industry do have cause for complaint about much of our body of laws, for even today it contains remnants of feudalism altogether dysfunctional with respect to the demands of contemporary American society, whether viewed from the perspective of the entrepreneur or the working classes.

For all these reasons, it is not surprising that if one is asked to characterize the central thrust of most appellate opinions, the answer will no doubt be that the values expressed are relatively conservative. What is perhaps a more interesting fact, however, is that a substantial number of appellate decisions are not so backward-looking, that often judges have decided in favor of the disinherited. For example, given the rigid framework of the fellow-servant rule in the nineteenth century, judges were adroit in carving exceptions to it to protect widows and orphans whose breadwinners had been injured or killed in industrial accidents. Most notably of all, the Supreme Court of the United States since about 1937 has been consistently more liberal than the Congress, at least in certain kinds of cases, especially in tax cases, cases involving freedom of speech, of press, or of religion, and criminal procedure. How is it possible to reconcile such choices with what would seem to be overwhelming bias in inputs toward conservative rulings?

The answer is complex. We shall discuss first the problem of the state appellate courts and secondly the special problem of the Supreme Court of the United States.

In the first place, all predictions about human activity as a function of class position, socialization, and the like are based upon probabilities. The verification of such predictions is not that *individuals* will act as forecast, but that the central tendency of the *group* will be as predicted.

Judging is an intensely individual matter. Each judge must, finally, vote for himself. That one predicts that the overall tendency of appellate judging even within the narrow range of choice presented will be relatively conservative therefore does not exclude the probability that there will be a minority of liberal decisions as well. In the same way, to predict that in throwing dice, numbers one through five will show on five-sixths of the rolls, implies that the six spot will appear one-sixth of the time.

Chief Justice Stone offers a remarkable example of the danger in predicting that a man from a conservative background will invariably be a conservative judge. Stone was primarily a Wall Street lawyer before going to the bench, although he had served in the academic world as well. His appointment was bitterly opposed by trade unions and some others who claimed to speak for ''the masses,'' on the ground that given his background he could only be expected to let his ingrained class biases intrude upon his judgment. His opponents, however, were very wrong, for Stone distinguished himself as one of the strongest champions of civil liberties, of the poor and underprivileged, that ever sat on the bench. Other examples could be cited.

Also, there has always been a strong tendency among judges and lawyers, fostered by the adherence to precedents, toward placing a high value on consistency and coherence in laying down legal norms. During the period in which the formal style of opinion-writing prevailed, these considerations became the sole criteria of legitimacy. Even the most ardent realist must give some consideration to them. When a sufficient emphasis is put on consistency and coherence in law, there is a tendency for individual value-preferences to be overridden by the urge to conform to already existing laws.

The existing corpus of the law is not colored a monochromatic conservative. It contains elements, the product of historical forces long since deceased, which remain to serve interests other than those for which they were originally intended. For example, the earliest written assertion of the right to trial by a jury of one's peers was made at Runnymede by the feudal barons, asserting their aristocratic interests against the centripetal forces of the Crown. Trial by jury has come through many a sea change from Magna Charta to its present form. Whatever its contemporary utility, it seems clear enough that its function no longer is to serve the needs of a particularistic feudal class.

The tendency toward coherence in the law favors the continuation of rights already in the corpus of norms. To the extent that these rights exist, conservative judges by remaining faithful to the law as it was may nevertheless in particular cases make choices that are not unfavorable to interests other than those already possessing power and privilege.

In the United States, a third factor has been of importance in procuring "liberal" court rulings, and that is the overarching influence of the U.S. Supreme Court. The opinions of this Court, especially in constitutional matters, cannot readily be ignored by state appellate courts, and even less by lower appellate courts in the federal system. Since 1937 the Supreme Court has, with remarkable if not complete consistency, tended to make libertarian rather than conservative decisions in civil rights and civil liberties cases; it has regularly decided in favor of government control of business in cases concerning economic regulations and in favor of the government in tax cases.

Courts which adhere to the formal style of judicial opinions suppress, as we have seen, the reasons for their choice of major premise on which they base their decisions. Given the conservative single-breasted gray in which the inputs to the decision processes are clothed, the fact that the decisional output is not invariably so clothed testifies to the Court's response to the ameliorating factors which we have suggested may be operative.

The Supreme Court of the United States poses a special problem. Its judges come from a remarkably select slice of American society. Their values, in terms of naked class interest and socialization, one might think, should have given the Court a more conservative bias than it has in fact displayed. Why this seeming paradox? Why should the Supreme Court have had, since 1937, a remarkably uniform liberal complexion?

The United States Supreme Court and Political Values

If Pound's notion that judges look to the "received social ideal," i.e., the ideal taught to judges and lawyers, be true, then it would be impossible to explain the Court's liberal tendencies, unless the received social ideal of the justices of the Supreme Court was different from that of the judges of other appellate courts. What does seem quite clear is that apparently the social ideal of the majority of the Supreme Court justices changed markedly between the early 1930s and the early 1940s, a change strikingly demonstrated by the shift in the presumption of constitutionality.

Prior to 1938, it was well established that every statute was presumably constitutional and would be declared unconstitutional only if the unconstitutionality could be clearly demonstrated. Prior to that date, the Court held unconstitutional as violating the due process clause many statutes purporting to limit the use of property, but only a tiny handful as violating the freedoms expressed in the First Amendment—freedom of speech, press, association, and religion. It had, over the years, held the income tax laws unconstitutional, not because they levied a tax on earned income, but because they levied a tax on the rents and profits of property; it had held unconstitutional a statute setting maximum hours for women, a child labor law, and much of the New Deal legislation aimed at curbing what the Roosevelt administration regarded as abuses of big business. On the other hand, it had upheld convictions for waving a red flag, for stating that the United States' entry into the First World War was a mistake, for drafting a call for a dictatorship of the proletariat.

The "social ideal" implicit in these cases seems clear. The Constitution (in the words of Holmes) was seen as the embodiment of Herbert Spencer's social statics. Property rights were held to have a higher value than human rights. The contract clause and the due process clause were seen as major protections not for individuals, but for corporations.

If the Court's basic value premises had remained unchanged from those embalmed in these cases, what has happened since 1943 would have been impossible. In that year, Chief Justice Stone, in a famous footnote, said that it might be that the freedoms embodied in the First Amendment—of speech, press, and religion—were so important that legislation abridging any of them was not entitled to the usual presumption of constitutionality.[24] Since then, it has become a decided rarity for the Court to declare unconstitutional a statute involving a limitation on property rights. The "great, the indispensable freedoms secured by the First Amendment,"[25] on the other hand, have been protected from state infringement over and over again. Far from using its position to defend the economic status quo against attacks by the disadvantaged, the Court has come to see its most important function as the final protector of the channels by which minorities can try to bring about peaceful social change.

If Pound were correct, so radical a shift of position could not have occurred; the idea of "received social ideal" cannot account for so quick a change in the Court from being a protector of the status quo to being the protector of the challengers of the status quo. The new judges who came to the Court after 1937 obviously had a different sort of social ideal than had those whom they replaced.

This historical shift demonstrates that Pound's notion of a *single* "received social ideal" is not empirically valid. There are as many "social ideals" in American life as there are antagonistic interest groups. These contradictory ideals are all simultaneously enshrined in different areas of American law. Our law imposes granite-like protections for private property against state expropriation. In many other areas it favors property rights over human rights. At the same time, in still other segments it elevates human rights and the democratic process to the highest level. Plainly, the judges who came to the Court after 1937 took their received social ideal from the latter tradition.

That they did so was in part a result of the political processes by which judges are selected for the Court. But they were also the product of the new pragmatic methods of decision-making which the Court had increasingly adopted and institutionalized. The judges who since 1937 have represented the majority have tended to believe that their notions of justice are better served by looking to the consequences of the rule in society and making pragmatic choice based on these investigations, rather than by determining the major premise inarticulately, without express regard for its effects on the polity, and justified mainly by a purported logical or elegant relationship to the existing corpus of rules of law.

The more recent judges, therefore, have resorted to a system of justification of the realist type, for the realists see the world in terms of process, not of ideal models. They are in the pragmatic tradition. Dewey held that the only statements about what ought to be the case that were valid were those that could be empirically verified, i.e., those which could be determined to be useful in resolving problems by empirical data. Dewey's philosophy was sharply oriented toward facts; it was scornful of large abstractions and denied the utility of *summa bona* or ideal models as measures of value.

The pragmatic view of decision-making seems to allow alternative conceptions of the role of values. On the one hand, it is sometimes asserted that problems arise from fact situations alone and admit of but a single "best" solution; this is a sort of natural law conception. Even Llewellyn seems to have believed that there is a "right" or "just" solution for every problem. He subscribed to a statement by the German jurist Goldschmidt that "every fact-pattern of common life, so far as the legal order can take it, carries within itself its appropriate, natural rules, its right law. . . . The highest task of law-giving consists in uncovering and implementing this immanent law."[26] Dewey at times seems to have adhered to much the same view.[27]

On the other hand, at times it seems that Dewey's pragmatism and its legal analogue, realism, lead necessarily to a sort of aimless expediency. Expediency, it is then claimed, permits each justice's idiosyncratic value-sets full play. Alexander Bickle describes the ultimate result of this viewpoint:

The final fruit of neo-realism—perhaps either arrested realism or surrealism would be more accurate—is a genial, nihilistic attitude of co-existence with the Court and its work, along with a complete lack of interest in the process by which the work is achieved, or in the proper role of that process in a democratic society. The Court itself is interesting as a mountain is said to be to a climber, because it is there. If there is any judgement to be exercised about it, it is a factional, predilectional one about results. The rest is *elegantia juris,* and it couldn't matter less.[28]

Both these positions deny any function to the generalized aims, usually culturally acquired, of the decision-maker. At least in constitutional litigations, the Constitution itself supplies such generalized objectives: due process, equal protection, free speech and assembly, freedom of religion, right to counsel, the privilege against self-incrimination. All these are generalized objectives which the Court is institutionally required to adopt.

If the system of decision-making follows the formal style, how these generalized objectives become ends in view depends not on any assessment of reality, but on the arid requirements of syllogisms. It is equally logical to assert that "separate but equal" facilities in education will help to achieve the generalized aim of equal protection, as to assert that only integrated facilities will move education toward that generalized aim.

Syllogistic reasoning denies the assignment of values to the alternative means, for those values could only be determined by empirical data.

Empirical evidence showing the various consequences of the utilization of different means makes it impossible to ignore the values of the means used in pursuing specific ends in view. If empirical data show that the consequences of "separate but equal" educational facilities include identifiable psychological bruises inflicted upon the minorities discriminated against, then the decision-makers cannot ignore that fact. The dilemma posed by the exclusive use of syllogistic reasoning is resolved by empirical data.

So long as judges refrain from examining the actual consequences of the means chosen for certain ends, it is possible to assert that the high-flown generalized objectives of the Constitution are achieved by whatever means are logically compatible with them. "Separate but equal" treatment is logically compatible with the equal-protection clause. The test of voluntariness of a confession is logically compatible with the privilege against self-incrimination. Judicial abstinence in requiring equal weighting of votes in state representative assemblies is logically compatible with the notion that a republican form of government requires representative assemblies to determine electoral matters. Entrusting young persons to the uncontrolled discretion of juvenile courts is compatible with a major premise that "we want to do what's good for Johnny." Only when one is confronted with the actual empirical consequences of the means used does he have to place in the balance the values to be assigned to those means.

To articulate the rhetoric of constitutional protection, but to infer through syllogistic reasoning alone the means to be used to promote certain ends, ensures that, save for chance serendipity, the constitutional phraseology will become a mere legitimizing myth that does not reflect the reality of the situation. Only when the empirical consequences of the means used is examined, and the values involved weighed alongside the generalized ends of the constitutional guarantees, is it possible to bring about the concrete realization of the constitutional objectives in the form of specific ends in view. The realist formula for judicial decision-making requires not the relative weighing of a set of prizings, but a process of valuation in which means and ends become analytically indistinguishable.

If the conjunction of commonly accepted values and empirical data invariably points in only one direction, then one should expect the Court to be always unanimous in its decisions. This is far from the case, however; more frequently than not the Court speaks with a divided voice. That divided voice may reflect differing values held by the justices, which values, however, should not be construed as different notions of the *summum bonum*, or "received social ideal" as postulated by Pound.

In the first place, the justices may come to differing opinions because of different assessments of the empirical data. In *Miranda*, for example, the majority found the evidence sufficient to show that the police engaged in improper activity in pretrial questioning. That evidence, we recall, was based entirely on the contents of police manuals. Justice Clark dissented from the majority in rejecting the empirical data as "merely writing in the field by professors and some police officers. Not one is shown by the record here to be the official manual of any police department, much less in universal use in crime detection."[29] Why the justices take such different views of the data may have nothing whatever to do with values of "liberty" as against "authority"; that is, it is without reference to a received social ideal. In *Miranda* it may have resulted from differing assessments of the weight to be given to manuals against more concrete evidence.

Secondly, the difference may result from the judges' having different ideas as to the proper role of the Court. Justice Frankfurter was noted for the fact that, despite his politically liberal views, his strong adherence to doctrines of judicial self-restraint frequently led him to vote for antilibertarian positions.

Thirdly, even though the justices may accept the same set of values, they may differ, as reasonable men will, with respect to the solution. Justice Stewart's dissent in *Gault* was based on the same concern for the welfare of the juvenile defendant as was the majority's. He disagreed only with the method of protection adopted by the majority.

Finally, however, there is a group of cases in which the constitutional doctrine itself, as construed, requires the Court to weigh conflicting goals that are both constitutionally protected: freedom versus security; individual rights versus community protection; the national interest versus "state's rights." All these are recurrent problems. In such cases, it is difficult to avoid the conclusion that the judges are, indeed, required to invoke their own value-sets in making the ultimate decision. That the Court has in the past three decades rather consistently chosen to pursue a libertarian path with regard to human rights can probably only be attributed to the political processes by which the justices have been selected.

9.5 SUMMARY

To understand why any role-occupant acts as he does, one must examine the norms defining his position, the social, personal, and other forces operating upon him, and the activities of sanctioning agents. There are no formal sanctioning agents controlling appellate courts (except, in some instances, higher appellate courts).

Courts, more than any other institution in society, are ordinarily regarded as value-neutral institutional frameworks within which conflict can be resolved. The adjudicative function in a winner-takes-all system of justice requires the court in every case to determine the relevant norm. In trouble cases, a court must create that norm. Law creation inevitably requires a value-choice. By making that choice, an appellate court ceases to be a merely value-free, neutral framework for the resolution of conflicts. It becomes involved in that conflict; it and its decisions become tools in the social struggle.

To view the courts in this way, however, decidedly is not equivalent to adopting the radical realist viewpoint—what Bickle called "a genial, nihilistic attitude." While appellate courts do have discretion, and they do exercise choice, it is a choice made in the context of the legal process. That process is defined by its inputs and the norms of judicial decision-making. The received norms, based on the assumption that judges do not create law, end up by permitting the widest scope to the unexpressed value-choices of the judges, under the mask of adherence to precedent and statutory language. More modern norms for judicial decision-making require judges to look not to logical, but to empirical justification of their choice of rule. The judges must therefore consider not only the values involved in the generalized objectives, but also those that are implicated in the means. By transforming the question of value-choice from one of the relative priority to be given to specific prizings to one of valuation in which generalized objectives are to be translated into specific ends in view, judges are unable so easily to mask their value-choices behind an impenetrable fog of syllogistic rhetoric.

We observe that in analyzing the work of the appellate courts we have given the major emphasis to the effects of norms and roles, and only a relatively minor emphasis to the impact on the judges of their paticipation in a bureaucratic structure. This relative emphasis, as we shall see, is in marked contrast to the relative emphasis that seems to be operative in determining the activities of the people. Appellate judges are as formally removed as possible from the grubby pressures that coerce other men to respond to social forces. What pressures there are, tend to force the judges to follow the norms laid down for their positions, and to ensure that men selected for judgeships have deeply internalized the rules defining their positions.

To say that appellate courts are not a value-free, neutral framework, therefore, is not to say that appellate judges are free to do what they choose. How they exercise their discretion, and in whose favor, depends on the entire social complex in which they act, which selects issues for their examination, which recruits them for their roles, which defines the small-group interaction of judges, which in turn defines the limits of their choice. This social complex ensures that appellate courts would in the main limit their choices to enhancing incremental changes, occasionally to promoting comprehensive changes, but never to bringing about revolutionary changes. They can never make rules which will bring about sweeping changes in the allocation of power that will alter the entire structure of society. By invoking the power state within a framework that so limits their choices, they become willy-nilly a bastion of the status quo.

NOTES

1. *People* v. *Schmidt,* 216 N.Y. 324, 110 N.E. 945 (1915).

2. 10 Cl. and F. 200 (1843); 8 E.R. 718 (H.L.).

3. Lon Fuller, "American Legal Realism," *University of Pennsylvania Law Review* 82(1934): 428-438.

4. R. Dahl and C. Lindblom, *Politics, Economics, and Welfare: Planning and Politico-economic Systems Resolved into Basic Social Processes* (New York: Harper, 1953).

5. The sufficiency of the processes to gather even these sorts of facts has been vigorously attacked. See, e.g., Jerome Frank, *Courts on Trial: Myth and Reality in American Justice* (Princeton: Princeton University Press, 1950).

6. L. Friedman, *Contract Law in America* (Madison: University of Wisconsin Press; © 1967 by the Regents of the University of Wisconsin).

7. See J. W. Hurst, *Law and Conditions of Freedom* (Madison: University of Wisconsin Press, 1956).

8. Friedman, *Contract Law,* pp. 191-192. Reprinted by permission.

9. *Ibid.,* p. 193. Reprinted by permission.

10. Harold Laski, *The State in Theory and Practice* (London: Allen and Unwin, 1935), p. 162. Reprinted by permission.

11. 382 U.S. 436 (1965).

12. 387 U.S. 1 (1967).

13. 369 U.S. 186 (1962).

14. 347 U.S. 483 (1954).

15. See Chapter 3.

16. Justice White, dissenting in *Miranda* v. *Arizona,* 384 U.S. 436 (1965), pp. 531-532.

17. 387 U.S. 1, 27 (1967).

18. 387 U.S. 1, 78 (1967).

19. Laski, *The State,* p. 151.

20. Roscoe Pound, "The Economic Interpretation and the Law of Torts," *Harvard Law Review* 53(1940): 365, 366. Reprinted by permission.

21. *Ibid.,* p. 366.

22. *Ibid.,* p. 367.

23. *Ibid.*

24. *Thomas* v. *Collins,* 323 U.S. 624 (1945).

25. *United States* v. *Caroline Products,* 304 U.S. 144 (1938).

26. K. N. Llewellyn, *The Common Law Tradition: Deciding Appeals* (Boston: Little, Brown & Co., 1960), p. 122. Quoted in S. Mermin, "Concerning the Ways of Courts: Reflections Induced by the Wisconsin 'Internal Improvement' and 'Public Purpose' Cases," *Wisconsin Law Review* (1963): 192-252. See also V. J. Wilson and T. G. Russell, "Common Law and Common Sense," *Harvard Law Review* 41(1939): 301.

27. J. Dewey, *Theory of Valuation* (Chicago: University of Chicago Press, 1939).

28. From *The Least Dangerous Branch* by Alexander M. Bickle, p. 81. Copyright © 1962 by the Bobbs-Merrill Company, Inc.; reprinted by permission of the publisher.

29. 384 U.S. at 499.

10

Obedience to law

Why do people obey the law? Sociology rarely poses that question. Mainstream criminology focuses on the issue of *deviance*. The question usually asked is, Why is it that some people violate the law? Asking that question leads criminologists to make an number of questionable assumptions.[1] First it assumes that most people obey the law. Second it assumes a high degree (if not complete) of consensus on what is right and wrong behavior. Third it assumes that "the law"—particularly judges and prosecutors who administer criminal law—determines efficacy by applying the customs of the community or society. Fourth it assumes that people do not "make choices" but react rather in an automatic fashion depending on their socialization experiences and their instincts.

Given these assumptions obedience to law can never become an issue. Everyone will obey positive law except a few rare recalcitrants. When the problem is posed in this fashion the answer inevitably is a psychological one: the search is on for social and psychological experiences which differentiate deviants from nondeviants.[2] The relationship between deviance and institutions or social structures is thereby ignored.

Research destroyed this criminological model. It became apparent that most people violate the law sometimes and many people violate the law in the course of their daily lives.[3] Very few people, research showed, unfailingly obey the law. The

American legal realists discovered the systematic difference between the law-in-the-books and the law-in-action. Examining behavior not merely of officials, but also of nonofficial addressees of the law, anthropologists found a great buzzing beehive of variegated activity, much of it only peripherally related to the formal norms that presumably defined behavior. Sally Falk Moore wrote that "the social reality is a peculiar mix of action congruent with rules (and there may be numerous conflicting or competing rule-orders) and other action that is choice-making, discretionary, manipulative, sometimes inconsistent, and sometimes conflictual."[4] Not conformity but deviance became the expected mode of behavior: society again transformed itself from clockwork to cloud.

During the 1960s a competing model arose, a part of a far-reaching paradigm change in sociology. This model denies the notion that society and law base themselves on consensus:

We could no longer accept the idea presented by Michael and Adler forty years ago that most of the people in any community would probably agree that most of the behavior which is proscribed by their criminal law is socially undesirable. According to the emerging "critical criminology," criminal law should not be viewed as the collective moral judgment of society promulgated by a government defined by almost everyone as legitimate. Instead critical criminology argued that our society was best seen as a *Gebeitsverband*, "a territorial group living under a regime imposed by a ruling few in the manner of a conquered province."[5]

In a *Gebeitsverband*, no one expresses surprise that individuals occasionally disobey, but rather that anybody obeys.

That model rejected the notion that all but a tiny few have their minds programmed to follow the law. Instead, it focused on the question of choice. How and why do people choose to act as they do?

Many argued that the ordinary functioning of society shows that we do not make conscious choices to obey or disobey most law. Most people go about their jobs, return to their home, engage in their ordinary activities without consciously "choosing" to do so. People do not calculate their advantage by the minute. Even criminals do not do so.

That observation correctly describes obedience to some law. We give the name "society" to a group of people living together because of their repetitive patterns of behavior. Existing social relations persist over time and the total set of norm roles, statuses, value-sets, rewards, and penalties, in short, the entire culture, form a more or less integral whole. If they did not, the society would become an anarchy. Laws more or less consistent with the existing social order need not always rely upon the threat of legal sanction to induce obedience. The surrounding institutional matrix structures social relations, rewards and punishments, constraints and resources so that the role-occupant usually makes a personally advantageous decision—at least in the short run—when he chooses to conform. So obvious is the choice that he probably does not make it consciously, that is, his behavior has become institutionalized.

Nevertheless, even in highly institutionalized societies, choice does occur. Businesses calculate the consequences of tax and antitrust law. A decision about where to park a car frequently depends on the chances of getting a ticket.[6] As Lemert put it, "The captured position of individuals in modern pluralistic society sheds light on the choice of means and ends. One general consequence of this position is the increase of calculational behaviour and a heightened awareness of alternatives, a necessary willingness to consider a wide variety of values and norms as functional alternatives to ends."[7] Many legal rules require or permit doing what one ordinarily would not do if the rules did not exist. Since these rules either cause a great deal of nuisance or offer great advantages, most people calculate extensively.[8]

Before anyone can choose to obey or not, they must know what the law requires of them. That calls, first, for a rule or policy that defines and prescribes the required activity. If rule or policy wallows in ambiguity or vagueness, its addressees must behave as they think best; that is, ambiguity amplifies the influence of training, socialization, considerations of personal advantage, and subjective factors. Secondly, the role-occupant must receive notice of the rule in a way that will spark obedient behavior.

In addition, the role-occupant must have opportunity and capacity to obey the law. "Ought" presupposes "can." Unless one *can* obey, she *will* not. Anglo-American law recognizes this by allowing physical impossibility as a complete defense to a charge of crime. Want of opportunity or capacity also prevents obedience to noncriminal rules. Opportunity sometimes depends upon factors that others should supply. For example, in 1973 Massachusetts enacted a statute requiring a building inspector who found a violation of the Building Code to send to the tenant of the building a notice of the violation together with a letter outlining the tenant's remedies—to bring a lawsuit, to withhold the rent, to repair the violation herself and charge it against the rent, and so forth. By 1975, two years later, not a single building inspector in the entire state had sent such a letter. Everyone of them disobeyed the law. The cause did not lie in their prejudices or attitudes. The statute failed to prescribe who ought to supply the necessary form letter to the building inspectors and they did not have the expertise to draft it. Programs frequently fail because the officials do not receive sufficient resources to do the job required. Commissions against discrimination in employment have so little money that they cannot prosecute offenders; commissions on factory safety in 1976 averaged only 40 *cents* per worker per year to carry out an inspection program. The range of monies allocated was from 2 cents per worker in Texas and Oklahoma to $2.20 in Oregon. Many officials disobeyed the law addressed to them for want of opportunity or capacity.[9]

Conversely, opportunity and capacity to disobey increase the potential for violation. Laws prohibit the possession of burglary tools in part because they have a high potential for burglary: bankers commit embezzlement more frequently than do bricklayers.

Besides creating the necessity for choice, lawmakers must ensure that role-occupants will choose to obey. To do that, addressees must perceive the desired behavior to be in their interest, taking into account not only the legal sanctions but all the rewards and punishments of the larger environment. Four elements bear upon this perception: (1) the rewards or punishments the role-occupant will earn as a result of obedience or disobedience; (2) the opportunity to disobey; (3) the way in which the domain (value) assumptions of role-occupants filter reality; and (4) the process by which role-occupants decide to obey. Do they choose publicly or in secret? By consulting an oracle or the local party leadership? By authoritarian command or by participatory discussion?

The legal order necessarily commands its targets to do what otherwise they might not. Because we live in a conflict society with some holding vastly more power than do others, the legal order always prescribes behavior that goes against what some people would do if the law did not exist. The critical question is, Why do people obey such laws? We propose the following guidelines. People are most likely to obey the law when:

1   Its prescriptions are precise and defined by rule or policy.

2   The rule or policy is communicated to addressees.

3   The addressees—be they organizations, role-incumbents, or people in general— have an opportunity to obey the law.

4   The addressees—whether organizations, role-incumbents, or people in general— have the capacity to obey the law.

5   It is in the addressees' interests to obey the law.

6   Addressees perceive that it is in their interests to obey the law.

7   The process by which addressees come to decide whether or not they obey involves their participation in decisions and conduces toward obedience.

Ambiguity still shrouds these categories. We try to give them greater specificity in the following sections by using concrete examples from researches that have looked at the ability of laws to change people's behavior. Specifically we look in some detail at the impact of safety and health at work laws and at laws designed to control the size of a country's population.

10.1 FACTORY SAFETY AND HEALTH

There is a fundamental contradiction between worker safety and corporate profits. An immediate affect of improving safety and health conditions may be a reduction in profits unless prices can be raised. Raising prices, however, creates other problems for owners: competition from other countries may reduce their sales or consumers may opt to purchase other commodities instead of those produced. In the overall economy this raising of prices creates inflation, underproduction, and economic crises.

The fact remains, however, that many occupations are exceedingly hazardous. Lumbering, mining, agriculture, construction, assorted forms of manufacturing, and even unlikely occupations such as nursing contain within them a multitude of health and safety hazards that leave workers maimed, ill, and dead every year.[10] In the United States, for example, every year over 100 thousand workers die from work-related accidents and illnesses. Another 2.5 million people are injured or become ill.[11]

Workers are not pieces of clay to be molded solely in the interests of profits. From the inception of the Industrial Revolution workers expressed their concern for job safety through organized and spontaneous efforts. At a certain point the conflict reaches a level which can no longer be ignored by employers or the state. Laws are then passed which command relevant role-occupants to change their behavior. Owners are commanded to change certain features of the work environment. Agents of the state are commanded to inspect, report, and if necessary impose sanctions on owners who fail to comply with legally prescribed safety and health standards. Courts are commanded to impose fines or imprisonment on owners who refuse to comply. Workers are commanded to conduct themselves on the job in a safe fashion (to wear safety glasses or to use protective shields on machinery, for example). All of this is ostensibly accomplished through the creation by law of a bureaucratic organization which is given the responsibility to implement and enforce the law.

In Sweden, the task of implementing factory safety and health legislation falls to the Swedish Labor Inspectorate. This agency was born in response to worker demands buttressed by strikes and industrial conflict. Funds were allocated to the inspectorate to enable it to conduct inspections, make reports, keep records, file complaints with the court, and see that the recommendations of the inspectors and the courts are carried through by employers and employees. This is to be accomplished through the basic procedure of periodic inspections carried out by state employees trained in factory safety and health. Inspectors are to visit workplaces and check existing safety and health procedures to see that they comply with the law. Where violations are found the inspectors are commanded by law to take appropriate steps to have the situation rectified. The steps are as follows:

First there is an inspection. Then, if a violation is found that cannot be solved on the spot or is too serious to handle with an informal request, a written notice is sent to the company of what should be put right, and requesting that the Inspectorate be informed of the action being taken. If this letter is not answered, usually another letter is sent requiring that the necessary change be made by a particular date; this is a formal direction. If the employer then replies that the direction gives inadequate time or he thinks it is wrong or in any other way protests, inspectors may make another visit to the site. If, in the end, the employer still does not comply, then another letter is written warning the company that if they do not comply, the case will be taken up with the Board of Labour Inspectorate which includes employer, union, and inspectorate representatives. This board can decide to attach a fine to the direction, it can decide to prohibit the employer from working with the machine or in the place in question until the change is made, or it can decide to rewrite the direction. If, at the end of the time the employer has been given—and sometimes this can be two or three years if the change is a substantial one like a new ventilation system—the changes still are not made, the Board of the Labour Inspectorate will notify the courts and they will proceed to levy criminal sanctions for non-compliance.[12]

Resource Allocation

How resources are distributed is always a key issue in the effectiveness of an organization. A law providing for police protection or airline and factory inspections will be more or less implemented depending on the organizational procedures adopted by the implementing agencies. The people who occupy organizational roles in bureaucracies are often caught in difficult dilemmas. Police required to enforce laws against drunkenness, for example, may find themselves severely criticized if they enforce antidrunk laws in upper-class areas of the city but praised for their diligence if they enforce those laws in the slums.[13] Stearns discovered that the inspectorate was caught in a bind between the law and the reality of political power and the law.[14] Conscientious inspections coupled with the imposition of effective sanctions brought criticism and political pressure to the inspectors and the inspectorate. On the other hand, worker demands that the state intervene and provide safer and healthier working conditions could not be ignored in the face of strikes and political pressure. Meanwhile ever more far-reaching health and safety legislation increased the demands made on the bureaucracy. The resolution to this dilemma encouraged symbolic law enforcement coupled with systematic avoidance of trouble by reducing actual inspections. (See Fig. 10.1.)

The resolution of the dilemma was for the inspectorate to *increase* substantially the number of conferences and consultations of the organization, while at the same time actually *reducing* the number of work sites inspected. All the while the government's budget to the inspectorate increased; between 1949 and 1976 the number of persons employed by the inspectorate increased from 170 to over 400.[15] Thus the size and scope of the inspectorate increased year by year with a corresponding decline in the number of inspections. Thus was the problem ''solved'' bureaucratically by pursuing the line of least resistance among the bureaucratic alternatives available. In response to workers' demands, the number of meetings, conferences, layers of bureaucratic experts, etc., increased with the increased budget but the effectiveness of the organization declined in response to employer demands.

Implications

The implications of Stearns's research on the Swedish factory inspectorate are far-reaching. It is a story written over and over. Fundamental contradictions lead to conflicts which are resolved through laws creating or enhancing bureaucratic control over the *symptoms* of the contradiction. The hierarchical, one-way communicating bureaucracy attempts to resolve the dilemmas produced by promulgating rules and regulations enforced and overseen by ''experts.'' In these circumstances the theory we have developed would anticipate that the affect of the law would be close to zero, which it is, because:

1   The contradictions giving rise to the conflict are untouched. (There is no effort to resolve the contradiction between safe work conditions and profits.)

2   The communication of the law is one way and does *not* involve the participation of workers and owners in the construction of rules on policies for implementing the law.

3   The law is ambiguous rather than clear and precise. What constitutes a ''violation,'' what constitutes a ''dangerous'' or ''unhealthy'' condition is left to the discretion of the inspector.

OBEDIENCE TO LAW

Fig. 10.1 Number of Work Sites Visited (1965-75) Compared with the Number of Conferences, Consultations, and Lectures (1965-75).[16]

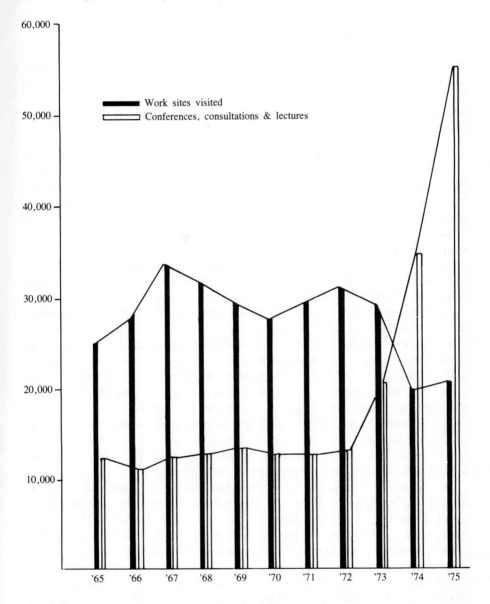

From L. R. Stearns, "Fact and Fiction of a Model Enforcement Bureaucracy: The Labour Inspectorate of Sweden," *British Journal of Law and Society* 6 (1979): 10. Reprinted by permission of the author and publisher.

4   The ability and opportunity of the bureaucracy to change the conditions within the competitive, free-market economy are greatly restricted. They are, in fact, nonexistent in most cases.

5   It is not in the interest of the employer to change company priorities, of the inspector to enforce the law, or often of the worker to obey the law. If the employer changes, her profits decline. If the inspector enforces the law, his agency is subject to criticism from the business community. If the workers obey the law, they may find themselves in suffocating masks which hinder work as much as help to reduce dust exposure, or using machine guards which slow down their pace of production and thus cut into their wage packets.

These characteristics of factory safety and health law in Sweden apply with equal force to other industrialized nations. Donnelly found the same lack of successful enforcement of safety and health laws through the Office of Safety and Health Administration in the United States;[17] Curran's study of Mining Safety and Health (M.S.H.A.) came to the same conclusion.[18] W.G.O. Carson's study in Great Britain of the factory inspectorate and his recent study of safety on oil rigs in the North Sea also support this conclusion.[19]

The failure of the bureaucracy to carry through adequately the ostensible intention of the law is not solely attributable to bureaucratic characteristics, as Carson's study of safety on the North Sea oil rigs demonstrates. Great Britain's decision to lease the oil exploration rights in the North Sea to private companies was dictated by the simple economic fact that large multinational oil companies possessed the necessary capital to undertake the enterprise while Great Britain did not. Once leased to private capital, the revenues from the oil were crucial for the survival of the government and the nation's economy. Thus to insist on a high level of safety precautions for workers not only meant facing all the contradictions and problems of obedience detailed above; it also threatened the revenues on which the government so desperately depended.

It is tempting to interpret these findings as overwhelming evidence that *in effect* the state and the bureaucracies of which it is made up are simply powerless to combat the interests of capitalists. This, however, is only part of the story. The passage of the laws themselves flies in the face of so simplistic an explanation.

Furthermore there are relative success stories. The British mining industry at the end of World War II was an appallingly dangerous source of employment: by 1943 the rate of deaths and injuries in underground coal mines had climbed to 287 per 1000 miners and the incidence of occupational diseases was so high that men were loath to return to the pits after war service.[20] Today, the British coal mining industry has one of the best safety records in the world.[21]

The success in effecting this change is not without caveat but both the relative achievement of the British legislation on health and safety in the mines, and its degree of failure to ensure the continued maximization of health and safety priorities for miners can be understood by judging the legislation according to the criteria we have set out:

1 The contradiction between safety and profits which gives rise to difficulties in enforcing safety legislation effectively was tackled by Britain after World War II by nationalization of the mining industry.

2 Communication of the law was facilitated by giving an important place to workmen inspectors, workmen site observers, and union consultation in the maintenance of health and safety in the mines.

3 Health and safety legislation usually contains a clause that the procedures should be implemented to the degree that they are reasonably practicable. The Mines and Quarries Act of 1952 was drafted without the ambiguous phrase "reasonably practicable" qualifying the obligations which the act placed on the management of the nationalized industry. These words frequently appear in the sections on health and safety statutes which impose duties that might prove onerous to employers if they were demanded under all circumstances, e.g., when they necessitate large expenditure by the company.

There was nothing fortuitous about these words not appearing in the Mines and Quarries Act. The first draft of the bill used them liberally. The National Union of Mineworkers and sympathetic Labour party politicians, however, recognized their potential to undermine the value of a clear and precise health and safety law. Through the coordinated struggle of these representatives of the miners the words "so far as is reasonably practicable" were deleted from the 1952 act.

4 The ability of the national mines inspectorate, the union safety inspectorate, and the worker inspectors to continue to ensure the improvement of work conditions for British miners is restrained to the degree that nationalization and progressive legal enactments cannot create a perpetual shift in priorities within the demands of an otherwise orientated economy. An enclave of change comes under great strain when its priorities are at odds with those of the surrounding marketplace. A nationalized industry within a free market may minimize the profit motive but it cannot ignore considerations of competition as long as it is involved in trade with mining industries where cost-cutting and hazard-increasing production practices are still employed. Today, hazard-producing bonus schemes and cost efficient rather than saftey-maximizing investment programs are being pursued.

5 Similarly, if workers' jobs are under threat production is money and hope of security, even at the risk of injury. Under such conditions learned safety priorities will slide and participation will mean less. The National Coal Board of Britain, once holding to the position that the production of coal should be for the benefit of the miners, not for the profit of owners or investors, now waves the banner of a profit competitiveness. As a consequence the capability of the addressees of the legislation—mine managers, safety inspectors, and coal miners—to comply with the command is greatly reduced and the hazards of working in the mines in Britain are once again on the increase.[22]

10.2 THE CONTROL OF POPULATION GROWTH: A CASE STUDY OF OBEDIENCE TO LAW

During recent years many governments used some state power and the legal order ostensibly in an effort to eradicate age-old miseries of poverty and oppression. One of their strategies sought to control demographic variables—rates of population growth and population movements. Stable rates of population growth, however, eluded most developing countries. The poor remained with us, the rich and powerful controlled their lives, and most population rates roared on, unabated.

The effort to use the legal order to control population growth must constitute one of the more bizarre attempts to use law to induce changed behavior. Intuition tells us that no segment of human experience seems as impervious as reproductive behavior to the commands and sanctions of law. Here we attempt an explanation for the relative success and lack of success of various efforts in the Third World to use the legal order to affect population change, concentrating on efforts to change gross or crude birthrates (i.e., the number of live births per 1000 in the population). We do not argue here the desirability of those efforts. Practically every Third World country adopted an antinatalist policy, either explicitly or more frequently under the euphemism of family planning. Some reached that conclusion from conservative economic premises. They assumed that the state cannot by changing economic institutions expand production, and therefore concluded that only a decrease in population could achieve increased per capita product. Others, more radical, planned to change economic institutions. That requires the accumulation of surpluses for investment. If the population keeps growing, those surpluses go instead for consumption, to feed the new mouths that keep coming along. Thus, the relatively radical states also reached the conclusion that, at least at the start of the development effort, an antinatalist policy was desirable.

No state attempted by a foolish fiat to order couples on pain of serious criminal sanction not to have more than a given number of children. On the other hand, unless a nation had a population policy, it could not expect couples consciously to change their fertility behavior pursuant to it.

Singapore in 1965 set a goal to reduce the crude birthrate from over 30 per 1000 to around 20 per 1000. Jamaica set its target at 35 per 1000 in 1976. A few other countries also prescribed more or less concrete fertility goals in their national plans. Probably China most clearly articulated specific population goals, resulting in a policy in favor of population planning:

China pursues a policy of developing its national economy in a planned way, including the policy of planned population growth. We do not approve of anarchy either in material production or in human production.[23]

More frequently, influenced by human rights arguments extolling free choice, however, governments had no explicit population policy or one that merely asserted the general desirability of family planning. In the Phillipines, the president declared that "the population problem must be reorganized as a principal element in long-range national planning if governments are to achieve the aspirations of their people.''[24] The actual population policy, however, stated only that ''a national program of family planning which respects religious beliefs of the individual involved shall be undertaken.''[25] The 1965 Turkish Law concerning Population Planning declared that ''Population Planning means that individuals can have as many children as they wish, whenever they want to. This can be ensured through preventive measures taken against pregnancy.''[26]

Two consequences ensued. In the first place, government often adopted development programs without ever consciously assessing their consequences for population control. Sometimes, laws with antinatalist and laws wtih pronatalist consequences coexisted. In the second place absent any norm explicitly directed to the population, the state effectively delegated family-planning decisions to individuals. That ineluctably subjected those decisions to individual discretion and hence gave the most effect to their existing arenas of choice. Since those very arenas of choice led couples to have relatively large families, such a population policy in fact accomplished nothing.

In a few places, however—eastern Europe, China, Korea, Thailand, Turkey, Columbia, Egypt, Jamaica, Singapore, and the United States[27]—population expansion slowed noticeably and in some places even reversed its upward thrust. In eastern Europe by 1969 it had generally dropped below 1 percent per annum,[28] the United States had practically achieved Zero Population Growth by 1975.[29] Within a single country, too, gross birthrates frequently fluctuated markedly with time. In Jamaica, they fell from 42.4 per 1000 in 1960 to 34.4 per 1000 in 1970.[30] Population growth in Singapore fell from 4 percent per annum in 1959 to 1.17 percent per annum in 1979.[31] In most of the Third World, urban people had lower birthrates than rural, educated lower than uneducated, elites lower than the masses. Rates of growth in European population during the past two centuries suddenly bloomed, then faded.[32]

We have argued that no one will likely obey laws looking toward new behavior unless the laws exist and become communicated, opportunity and capacity to obey exist, addressees' interests favor obedience, and they perceive that it does. Bringing new information about these matters to the people's attention is most effective when the people solve the problem that the law purports to address, discover for themselves that the opportunity and capacity exist, and that their interests accord with obedience. That is most likely to occur when the people participate in a problem-solving process under the tutelage of a change-agent.

China made great strides in population control mainly by utilizing such a process. ''Barefoot doctors and party cadres received considerable training in the policies and technologies of population control. Public meetings discussed fertility controls. Individual couples made their decisions in a group, participatory, problem-solving context. The consequences boggle the minds of those who have never traveled to China: apparently small communities collectively decided who ought to have children in a given year, and the couples in the community abided by the group decision.[33]

It is evident that China's success in controlling population does not depend upon a particular gimmick that other countries might duplicate. It profoundly reflects the organization of Chinese society, the mutual interdependence of its members, the improvement in the status of women, widespread information about contraception and the availability of hardware for its practice, ideologies conducive to fertility limitation, and a political organization in which the population regularly participates not only in fertility decisions, but in a host of other decisions about matters that affect their lives.

A number of other countries experienced less dramatic but significant declines in population growth through a combination of communication of law, opportunity to obey, shifting economic interests of the population, etc. Two variables that accompany declines in family size are increased education and social class: the higher the educational and social class levels the smaller is the size of the family.[34] High economic class generally accompanies education, availability of contraceptive devices or abortion, relatively liberated roles for women, children viewed as a net economic loss, reasonable old-age security, nonexpandable housing, and an appropriate reference group, together with subjective factors that ordinarily coincide with these. Urban dwellers are far more likely than rural people to possess these several characteristics; so do the highly educated. Thus, most generally, fertility depends upon the mode of production. For lowered birthrates to occur a society must have the characteristics of a developed society dependent not upon subsistence agriculture but manufacturing industry in the cities and industrially organized agriculture in the countryside, with a relatively high standard of living, old-age security, and general education for all, in which government has a markedly participatory style. "Development" efforts that focus narrowly on the modern industrial sector, or on enclave type plantations and mines, probably will not reduce fertility as effectively as policies which bring the benefits of development to the bulk of the population in traditional sectors.[35] In this broad sense, high fertility and underdevelopment accompany each other.

If underdevelopment and high fertility hunt together, then the neo-Malthusian hypothesis cannot stand. That hypothesis argues that governments cannot control production or make distribution more equitable for short and even medium term; therefore, it can increase per capita incomes only by reducing the number of heads. Kingsley Davis sarcastically suggested a government truly dedicated to antinatalism must adopt monstrously barbaric measures:

In countries where contraception is used, a realistic proposal for a government policy of lowering the birth rate reads like a catalogue of horrors: squeeze consumers through taxation and inflation; make housing scarce by limiting construction; force wives and mothers to work outside the home to offset the inadequacy of male wages, yet provide few childcare facilities; encourage immigration to the city by paying low wages in the country and the transit system; increase personal insecurity by encouraging conditions that produce unemployment and by haphazard political arrests.[36]

On the contrary; antinatalist behavior in the long run cannot likely obtain until the political, social, and economic institutions of the less developed countries change radically. At the same time, these countries will find their institutions desperately difficult to change until they acquire some control over the population variable.

Neo-Malthusian theory fails not merely because it seems immoral to accept the Third World's poverty as a given, but because it cannot lead to workable solutions for the population problem. It fails because it implies attempts to use the legal order to change behavior in ways that lie beyond the limits of law.

In this example of the attempt to use law to control the number of children people have we see both the influence of law and its limitations. "Obedience to law" is not a one-way street. Even the most repressive societies find it impossible to pass down and effectively implement laws that go against the interests of the people. It is possible, however, to change effectively even so personal a decision as whether or not to have children by making that decision part of a broader set of social, political, and economic changes whereby small families serve the interests of the people, where the reason and importance of the law are directly communicated, where the targets of the law are themselves involved in the law creation process, where the people are provided an opportunity to obey, and where countervailing forces against obedience are minimized. Then and only then is the likelihood of obedience to the law greatly advanced.

By contrast, where these factors are absent then disobedience is almost guaranteed. In our next example, as we shall see, practically all of these factors are absent and compliance with the law is correspondingly minimal.

Responding to Crime

The law commands police officers to arrest *all* suspected offenders. The law in Wisconsin, like practically every other jurisdiction, says: "The chief [of police] and every policeman... shall arrest with or without process and with reasonable diligence... every person found in the city... violating any law of the state or ordinance of the city." In the vocabulary we have developed for analyzing the law, this is a command to a role-occupant (police officers). Failure to comply with the command is disobedience. A moment's reflection, of course, tells us that this is a command that police officers disobey daily. There is a saving phrase in the law, "reasonable diligence," which gives the police discretion. But what does reasonable diligence mean in actual practice? A study of organized crime in Seattle, Washington, is instructive. This study documents in some detail the degree to which police in at least one American city systematically failed to "arrest every person in the city found violating the law."

It is prohibited by state law in Washington to engage in gambling, prostitution, usury (the loaning of money without a state license or at interest rates above legally prescribed limits), the sale of illegal drugs, the sale or distribution of pornography, the sale of lottery tickets, bookmaking, pinball machines, and a host of other activities generally referred to as "the vices" or the "rackets."

Yet there is a thriving business in all of these illegal activities.[37] "The vices available in Seattle are varied and tantalizing. Gambling ranges from bookmaking to open poker games, bingo parlours, off-track betting, casinos, roulettes and dice games.... Prostitution covers the usual range of ethnic groups, age, shape and size.... It is found in houses... on the streets, through pimps, or in suburban apartment buildings and hotels.... High interest loans are easy to arrange through stores that advertise 'your signature is worth $5,000.'... Pinball machines are readily available throughout the city, most of them paying off in cash.... Gambling, prostitution, drug distribution, pornography and usury flourish in the lower class center of the city."[38] And the author adds that these vices flourish "with the compliance, encouragement and co-operation of the major political and law enforcement officials in the city."[39]

What is true of Seattle is and has been true of every major American city (and most European cities as well) since the turn of the century. Writing in the early 1900s the muckraking journalist Lincoln Steffens observed, "the startling truth... that corruption was not merely political—it was financial, commercial, social—the ramifications of boodle were so complex, so various and far-reaching, that our mind could hardly grasp them."[40] In 1931 the National Commission on Law Observance and Enforcement concluded that "'nearly all of the large cities [of the United States] suffer from an alliance between politicians and criminals."[41] The Keefauver Committee in 1951 concluded that illegal gambling, drugs, and assorted other vices had grown to gigantic proportions throughout the United States and had international connections; the same results were repeated by the McClelland Committee and numerous state and national committees since then. In 1972 the Knapp Commission in New York City

found corruption to be widespread. It took various forms depending on the activity involved, appearing at its most sophisticated among plainclothesmen assigned to enforcing gambling laws.... Plainclothesmen collected regular biweekly or monthly payments amounting to as much as $3,500 from each of the gambling establishments in the area under their jurisdiction and divided the take in equal shares. The monthly share per man ranged from $300.00 to $400.00 in midtown Manhattan to $1,500 in Harlem.... Corruption in narcotics enforcement lacked the organization of the gambling pads, but individual payments... were commonly received and could be staggering in amount.... Corrupt officers customarily collected scores in substantial amounts from narcotic violators.... They ranged from minor shakedowns to payments of many thousands of dollars, the largest narcotics payoff uncovered in our investigations having been $80,000.... The size of this score (payoff) was by no means unique.[42]

National scandals have become so commonplace that they no longer attract much attention. Former Governor Marvin Mandel of Maryland was recently found guilty of fraud and racketeering; Senator Barry Goldwater has been accused of investing in businesses known to be owned and controlled by organized crime figures; former vice-president of the United States Spiro Agnew pleaded "nollo contendre" to charges of soliciting and accepting kickbacks from contractors; former governor of Pennsylvania Milton Shapp admitted that he accepted $10 thousand in cash for his campaign and later could not account for how that money was spent. Richard Nixon's campaign funding was the subject of endless unanswered questions about the propriety of the contributions. Innumerable businessmen and corporations contributed illegally to Nixon's campaigns and huge amounts of cash were stashed away in safes with no one to account for its expenditure.

The Federal Bureau of Investigation in 1978, 1979, and 1980 created a temporary sensation by charging several senators and congressmen with soliciting and accepting bribes from FBI agents posing as representatives of Arab business interests, and so it goes.

Recent research on the relationship between the vices, rackets, and the police in America comes to the same conclusion: in practically every city of the United States illegal gambling, drugs, pornography, prostitution, usury, etc., are readily available and are known to be prevalent among the police, politicians, and other "community leaders."[43]

Why do the police flagrantly disobey the law that commands them to arrest anyone known to them to be violating the law? Why do they become partners in the activities of organized crime? We believe the answer lies in the theory we have constructed. On the political and economic level the police are responding to contradictions inherent in capitalist democracy. Capitalism demands contradictory things. On the one hand, the accumulation of capital and the creation of profits are extolled as virtues and the *sine qua non* of power, privilege, prestige, and success. On the other hand, certain kinds of behavior that are officially illegal are matters of great dispute in this world of pluralistic moralities. Gambling, prostitution, the use of drugs, loaning and borrowing money illegally, using inside information to buy and sell property, etc., are activities that are condoned by many, admired by some, and condemned by others. The police are placed squarely in the middle of an irresolvable contradiction. If they enforce the law as they are commanded, the business community will be aroused beyond control. For one thing, a city without vice will be a city without tourists; hotels and restaurants as well as all the local businesses that depend on conventions (conventions that sometimes bring 50 to 100 thousand visitors to the city) and tourists are well aware that without the vices tourism will precipitously decline. The government itself is caught in the bind: without tourism taxes and money for schools, roads, salaries for police and government officials, and so forth will decline. And of course all the politicians who depend on those who profit from the rackets for campaign contributions will be up in arms if the law is enforced. Thus, the enforcement of vice laws and ultimately the management of the vices by a network of politicians, law-enforcement agents, businessmen, and professionals are the most rational solution to the conflicts and dilemmas posed. In the words of our theory: there is no capability of complying with the law for any of the role-occupants.

Since discretionary decision-making is recognized as inevitable, in effect, all bureaucratic decisions become subect to the discretionary will of the officeholder. Moreover, if one has a reason to look, vagueness and ambiguity can be found in any rule, no matter how carefully stipulated. And if ambiguity and vagueness are not sufficient to justify particularistic criteria being applied, contradictory rules or implications of rules can be readily located which have the same effect of justifying the decisions which, for whatever reason the officeholder wishes, can be used to enforce his position. Finally, since organizations characteristically develop their own set of common practices which take on the status of rules (whether written or unwritten), the entire process of applying rules is almost totally dependent on the discretion of the officeholder. The bureaucracy thus develops its own set of precedents which can be invoked in cases where the articulated rules do not provide precisely the decision desired by the officeholder.

Ultimately, the officeholder has license to apply rules derived from a practically bottomless set of choices. Individual self-interest then depends on one's ability to ingratiate himself to officeholders at all levels in order to ensure that the rules most useful to him are applied. This is precisely the consequence of the organizational response to the dilemma created by laws prohibiting the vices. Hence, the bureaucratic nature of law-enforcement and political organization makes possible the corruption of the legal-political bureaucracy.

How do these findings fit our theory of obedience to law? It is clear from the description that the constraints and resources available to the police, politicians, and businessmen who provide and protect the vices in Seattle and elsewhere in the United States make it virtually certain that corruption will become institutionalized. A policeman will simply not find it in his interests to enforce laws against the vices. Suppose, for example, that a police chief in Seattle, Chicago, New Orleans, or Detroit decided to "clean up the city." Suppose to do this he met with his police captains, lieutenants, sergeants, and patrolmen and communicated very clearly to them his decision. He could, within the reach of his office, also provide sanctions if they did not enforce vice laws. He could, in fact, create a situation in which antivice laws would be enforced. The chief would not be in office six weeks. Businessmen who depended on tourism and large conventions (restaurants, hotels, motels) not to mention those who profit directly from racketeering would organize a campaign against the chief of police. Law enforcement in all other areas—all those areas where informants who sell narcotics or organize the vices provide crucial information—would suddenly come to a standstill. Furthermore, the enforcement of these laws would clearly not be in the interests of many if not most of the police officers and politicians in the city. Campaign contributions for politicians would dry up. Even contributions for the governor and the national political campaigns that had formerly come from the profits from illegal businesses in the city would cease coming and pressure from national and state politicians would be brought to bear on the local political party organizations. The chief would simply have to go.[44]

The law exists in a social context. It can and does affect this context. It can and does create compliance under some circumstances. In China after the Communist party came to power in 1949 virtually all the vices described above as ubiquitous in American cities were eliminated: prostitution, drug trafficking, gambling, usury, etc., were for all intents and purposes eliminated by a government that communicated the law, established procedures and practices in which it was in the interests of bureaucrats or bureaucracies to obey, systematically eliminated all political and business operations dependent on profits from such enterprises, and gave communities an opportunity to work out their own procedures for compliance.[45]

10.3 CONCLUSION

Historically, lawyers and sociologists concerned with law have focused on the official behavior of judges, police, and bureaucrats. They devoted much less attention to the behavior under law of nonofficials. In this chapter we have proposed a general theory of behavior under law and have used it to generate explanations for the behavior of couples in the face of antinatalist laws and policies, factory safety and health enforcement, and political corruption. Lawyers frequently assume that most people obey the law because of the laws' inherent persuasiveness. Sociologists frequently argue that people obey the law because of "values and attitudes." We argue that these explanations cannot explain behavior in the face of law; that behavior is best understood as resulting from a set of choices that actors make within their milieu; that arena of choice consists of a great deal more than the rules of law and their threats, or what goes on inside the actor's head. As these examples suggest, to understand behavior in the face of law we must look at the world through the eyes of the addressee of the law, whether the actor or the official. When we begin to do that, we see the world does not resemble the ordered patterns that both the lawyers' and the sociologists' models demand. People do not follow the laws with great rigor; disobedience becomes as normal as obedience. Some laws most people obey most of the time; some laws most people disobey. Most people hug the right side of a blind curve; most American males at some time commit serious felonies. Obedience to law becomes a matter of choice. That choice does not arise in a vacuum; past history determines the milieu, and the milieu constrains our choices. We choose, but in a world not of our choosing.

NOTES

1. M. Phillipson, *Understanding Crime and Delinquency: A Sociological Introduction* (Chicago: Aldine, 1974). Also see R. Brown, E. Kamenka, eds., *Law and Society* (New York: St. Martin's Press, 1978).

2. W. J. Chambliss, *Criminal Law in Action* (New York: John Wiley & Sons, 1975).

3. R. Quinney, *The Social Reality of Crime* (Boston: Little, Brown & Co., 1970). Also see Ian Taylor, P. Walton, and J. Young, *The New Criminology: For a Social Theory of Deviance* (London: Routledge & Kegan Paul, 1973), and A. Turk, *Criminality and Legal Order* (Chicago: Rand McNally, 1969).

4. S. Falk Moore, *Law as Process* (London: Routledge & Kegan Paul, 1978), p. 3.

5. Quinney, *Social Reality of Crime*, p. 11.

6. W. J. Chambliss, "The Influence of Punishment as a Deterrent," *Crime and Delinquency* 12(1966): 70-75; see also W. J. Chambliss, "Types of Deviance and the Effectiveness of Legal Sanctions," *Wisconsin Law Review* (1967): 703-719.

7. E. Lemert, *Human Deviance, Social Problems and Special Control* (Englewood Cliffs, NJ: Prentice-Hall, 1967), p. 10.

8. *Ibid.*

9. Daniel M. Berman, *Death on the Job: Occupational Health and Safety Struggles in the United States* (New York: Monthly Review Press 4(1980): 239-266. See also P. Stangeland, *Condeep: A Platform Construction Site in Stavagner* (Stavagner Norway: *Rogalands Forskning,* Rapport No. 1, 1977).

10. L. R. Stearns, "Fact and Fiction of a Model Enforcement Bureaucracy: The Labour Inspectorate of Sweden," *British Journal of Law and Society* 6(1979): 1-23.

11. Berman, *Death on the Job,* pp. 47-48. See also P. Donnelly, "Social Problems versus Social Issues: The Case of Worker Safety and Health," Ph.D. dissertation, Department of Sociology, University of Delaware, 1980.

12. Stearns, "Fact and Fiction," pp. 18-20.

13. W. J. Chambliss, "Vice, Corruption, Bureaucracy and Power," *Wisconsin Law Review* (1971): 1130-1155.

14. Stearns, "Fact and Fiction."

15. *Ibid.,* p. 9.

16. *Ibid.,* p. 4.

17. Donnelly, "Social Problems versus Social Issues."

18. D. Curran, "Dead Laws for Dead Men: The Case of Federal Coal Mine Health and Safety Legislation," Ph.D. dissertation, Department of Sociology, University of Delaware, 1980.

19. W.G.O. Carson, "White Collar Crime and the Enforcement of Factory Legislation," *British Journal of Criminology* 10(1970): 383-398. W.G.O. Carson, "Some Sociological Aspects of Strict Liability and the Enforcement of Factory Legislation," *Modern Law Review* 33(1970): 396-417. W.G.O. Carson, "The Other Price of Britain's Oil: Regulating Safety on Offshore Oil Installations in the British Sector of the North Sea," *Contemporary Crises* 4(1980): 239-266. See also P. Stangeland, *Condeep: A Platform Construction Site in Stavagner* (Stavagner, Norway: *Rogalands Forskning,* Rapport No. 1, 1977).

20. L. R. Stearns, "Crimes against Workers: Nationalization as a Strategy of Control," *Contemporary Crises,* forthcoming.

21. Donnelly, "Social Problems versus Social Issues," p. 104.

22. Stearns, "Crimes against Workers," p. 17.

23. Quoted in I. Chen, "Planned Population Growth in China," cyclostyle, n.d.

24. Ex. O. N. 233, May 15, 1970, 66. O. G. 5187 (May 26, 1970), quoted in I. R. Cortes, "Population and Law: The Fundamental Rights Aspect in the Phillipine Setting," in *Law and Population Growth in the Phillipines,* Law and Population Growth Book Series no. 9, (Medford, Mass: Fletcher School of Law and Diplomacy, 1974), p. 6.

25. Presidential Decree No. 79, Dec. 8, 1972 O. G. 9896 (Dec. 18, 1972), quoted in Cortes, "Population and Law," p. 6.

26. *Official Gazette,* April 15, 1965, quoted in K. Davis, "Population Policy: Will Current Programs Succeed?" in M. Micklin, ed., *Population, Environment and Social Organizations: Current Issues in Human Ecology* (Hinsdale, Ill.: Drysdale Press, 1973), p. 352.

27. R. S. McNamara, "Accelerating Population Stabilization through Social and Economic Progress" (Washington, D.C.: Overseas Development Council Paper No. 24, 1977).

28. I. Bowen, *Economics and Demography* (New York: Crane, Russak, 1976), p. 149.

29. N. Keyfite, "Do We Know the Facts of Demography?" *Population and Development Review* 1(1975): 269.

30. R. C. Rosen, *Law and Population Growth in Jamaica,* Law and Population Monograph Series no. 10, (Medford, Mass: Fletcher School of Law and Diplomacy, 1973), p. 3.

31. P. C. Hall, *Law and Population Growth in Singapore,* Law and Population Monograph Series no. 9 (Medford, Mass: Fletcher School of Law and Diplomacy, 1973).

32. S. E. Beaver, *Demographic Transition Theory Reinterpreted* (Lexington, Mass: D. C. Heath, 1975).

33. Chen, "Planned Population Growth in China."

34. A. Szymanski, "Economic Growth and Population," *Studies in Comparative International Development* 9(1974): 53; and see R. B. Seidman, *Law, Population and Development: A Review Article* (Medford, Mass: Fletcher School of Law and Diplomacy, 1978).

35. Beaver, *Demographic Transition Theory,* p. 45.

36. Davis, "Population Policy."

37. W. J. Chambliss, *On the Take: From Petty Crooks to Presidents* (Bloomington: Indiana University Press, 1978).

38. Chambliss, "Vice, Corruption, Bureaucracy and Power," p. 1132; A. Block, *East Side, West Side* (Cardiff: University College Press, 1980).

39. *Ibid.*

40. Lincoln Steffens, *The Shame of the Cities* (New York: Harcourt, Brace and World, 1904); also, *The Autobiography of Lincoln Steffens* (New York: Harcourt, Brace and World, 1931), pp. 357-361.

41. Frank Tannenbaum, *Crime and the Community* (New York: Columbia University Press, 1938), p. 128.

42. Report by the Commission to Investigate Allegations of Police Corruption in New York City, Whitman Knapp, Chairman, August 3, 1972, p. 1.

43. Chambliss, *On the Take;* Alan A. Block, *East Side, West Side* (Cardiff: University College Press, 1980).

44. Chambliss, *On the Take.*

45. James P. Brady, "A Season of Startling Alliance: Chinese Law and Justice in the New Order," *International Journal of the Sociology of Law* 9(1981): 41-67.

11

Bureaucracy, its organization, and the legal order

The state and its bureaucracy dominate our world. Though not of our choosing, they structure our arenas of choice. Laws arise frequently because bureaucracies want them enacted; invariably, bureaucratic organizations implement them. (As we pointed out earlier, the bureaucratic structure of modern legal orders requires them to have secondary as well as primary rules.) Courts, police, regulatory agencies, legislatures, prisons, state hospitals, public schools and universities, armies: All of the state's manifestations have a bureaucratic configuration. Bureaucracies constitute the mechanism by which the legal order structures choice and thus seeks to ensure complying behavior with rules of law. They come to be principal agencies as well in the creation of law. An understanding of the relationship between law and society requires that we explore why bureaucracy behaves as it does.

Several threads woven together in the preceding chapters form a pattern that defines the appropriate questions to ask about the role of the state in the legal order. One thread concerns theory: To what extent does a ruling class determine the shape and content of law and the legal order? Another concerns obedience to law: Given a bureaucratic structure, what will increase or decrease the likelihood that those whom a particular law addresses will follow its prescriptions? Yet another thread concerns the organization of law: To what extent does the bureaucratic nature of the legal system affect the legal process?

In one way each of these threads ends at the point where we take up the role of the state. If the legal order responds to contradictions and conflicts in society, how does it resolve them? If the legal order constitutes a normative system for solving problems, how does the state structure affect its outcomes? These issues make the focus of this chapter.

11.1 BUREAUCRACIES AND LAW: THE CONTRADICTION BETWEEN THE LAW-IN-THE-BOOKS AND THE LAW-IN-ACTION

In the legal order, bureaucracies serve a variety of functions. They implement law; they adjudicate claims; they develop ideas for new laws. In the blueprint that prescribes how bureaucracies should work, they must always act *instrumentally*. They serve, they tell us, as a perfectly flexible tool of democratically elected policy makers. The elected legislature creates the laws; bureaucracies implement them according to the law. In the course of implementing the laws, the rules in them come to the attention of bureaucrats. They then formulate suggestions for new laws, and submit them to the policy makers for decision. Always, they do not make policy; they serve the policy makers.

So reads the law-in-the-books. The law-in-action varies from it, sometimes quite sharply. Bureaucrats and bureaucracies systematically violate the law. The police act illegally; housing authorities discriminate against blacks; welfare departments sometimes deny applicants benefits that the law grants to them—anybody can make a list several pages long. Bureaucracies, far from serving as the subservient, obedient instruments of policy, make policy. They apply the law in a particular way, and thus create law; in some cases, they actively agitate for their own ideas and persuade the policy makers to create new laws in the bureaucrats' interests. In this section we present a brief general explanation for the divergence of the law-in-the-books and the law-in-action.

Max Weber first perceived the important role bureaucracies and bureaucratization played in industrial society.[1] More than any other sociologist, he devoted time and attention to the characteristics of bureaucracy and its effects on society. He provided us with a conceptual framework (a language) for thinking about bureaucracies that since has dominated the subject. For Weber, the chief identifying characteristic of bureaucracy consisted of its clearly specified areas of jurisdiction, (usually) ordered by explicit rules—either laws created by the state or regulations stipulated by administrative units. Persons who occupy positions within the bureaucracy enforce the rules, and supposedly adhere to them themselves. These persons gain their authority because of their organizational roles. They do not have authority because they have inherited it (traditional, not rational authority); they do not have authority because people chose them as leaders or because they can sway people to follow them (charismatic authority). According to Weber, their authority rests on the role they occupy with its specified duties and obligations in the bureaucratic structure. Their authority Weber characterized as neither traditional nor charismatic, but legal-rational. Their power

BUREAUCRACY, ITS ORGANIZATION, AND THE LEGAL ORDER

does not rest on coercion, but legitimate authority. Thus legitimate authority becomes a defining characteristic of the positions that constitute the bureaucracy.

R. Nisbet sums up other characteristics of bureaucracy of importance to Weber:

From the basic principle of fixed and official jurisdiction flow such vital practices and criteria as the regularization of channels of communication, authority, and appeal; the functional priority of the office to the person occupying it; the emphasis upon written and recorded orders in place of random, merely personal commands or wishes; the sharp separation of official from personal identity in the management of affairs and the superintending of finances; the identification of, and provision for the training of "expertness" in a given office or function; the rigorous priority of official to merely personal business in the governing of an enterprise; and finally, the conversion of as many activities and functions as possible to clear and specifiable rules; rules that, by their nature, have both perspective and authoritarian significance.[2]

Weber's analysis goes farther than simply this description of bureaucracy. The process of bureaucratization "becomes for Weber a powerful manifestation of the historical principle of rationalization. The growth of bureaucracy in government, business, religion, and education is an aspect of the rationalization of culture that has also transformed . . . the nature of art, drama, music and philosophy."[3] Weber's followers have often translated "rationalization," meaning "good," in contrast to "irrational processes," meaning "bad." Surely no one would want to argue that irrational authority serves society better than rational authority. But Weber in fact did just that: "It is horrible to think that the world could one day be filled with nothing but those little cogs, little men clinging to little jobs and striving towards the bigger ones."[4]

The "little cogs, little men clinging to little jobs and striving towards the bigger ones" become the role occupants in the Occupational Safety and Health Administration, the population councils, the law enforcement agencies and legislative committees who interpret, apply, sometimes circumvent and always influence the "law." They do so within the constraints and resources of their world, including the organizational matrix of the bureaucracy. They influence the entire legal order; but to what extent? Do the state and its bureaucracy act autonomously? Or do they merely do the bidding of those with power and privilege? What mechanisms give those with power and privilege more than a fair share of influence?

Social theory divides on this subject along several critical dimensions. Some theorists adhere to a rather narrow interpretation of the classic statement by Karl Marx that the state and its bureaucracy "is but a committee for managing the common affairs of the bourgeoisie." Others argue that the state acts autonomously in its own interests and representing only itself, its perpetuation and growth.[5] We adopt a third position that we believe supports the data and analysis presented in this book. The state, the bureaucracy, and society have a dialectical relationship. Like the legal order generally, laws that create and circumscribe the boundaries of bureaucracies place limitations on the activities of the role occupants but they do not determine them. Similarly, bureaucracies create their own interests, but they do so within a context of social classes and power differentials.

The problem of bureaucratic behavior constitutes an example of the more general problem of obedience to law. Conformably to the general explanation earlier advanced, a person obeys law if, but only if, a determinable rule exists, he knows about the law, he has opportunity and capacity to obey it, it lies in his interest to do so, and he subjectively believes that he ought to do so or that his interest so demands; it becomes more likely that he will obey if he makes the decision to do so in an open, public, participatory process. To the extent that the rules directed to bureaucracy give bureaucrats discretion, to that extent can they maximize their personal interests and act in accordance with their personal biases rather than in the public interest to advance that which the law endows them with discretion. To the extent that the bureaucratic structure itself constrains their decision-making capacity, they may lack opportunity or capacity to decide conformably with the law. Their own interests and ideologies constitute powerful drives that may push them to violate the law. Finally, bureaucracies mainly operate in secret. They decide whether or not to obey the law not in open, participatory processes but in the very opposite.

We explore these concepts in the case studies that follow. We begin with the case that most clearly capsizes the traditional concept of bureaucracy's instrumental, subservient role in the legal order, that is, the case in which the bureaucracy not merely implements the law, but also creates it.

The Role of Bureaucracies in Law Creation

The dialectic suggests that there should exist a two-way effect between law enforcers and lawmakers. Our model implies that bureaucracies, nominally law implementors, serve as active agents in the creation of law. The data argue that they do. They thus capsize the relationship with the politicians that the law-in-the-books prescribes.

French historian M. Foucault's study of madness illustrates bureaucracy's role in creating law.[6] Foucault shows that prior to the fifteenth and sixteenth centuries, Europe had many leprosariums (mostly in France and England). France alone had about two hundred. In the late fifteenth and early sixteenth centuries these leprosariums emptied. The hospitals and their administrative machinery stood unused or in danger of becoming unused. By various royal decrees, reflecting the economic conditions of the times, the leprosariums of a decade before began to house a whole host of misfits—beggars, criminals, insane and diseased persons—whom the labor force did not require. The bureaucracies that formerly dealt with lepers tended to perpetuate themselves by becoming institutions for housing the criminal, sick, insane, and vagrant.

The Middle Ages endowed madness with a touch of the divinity. People whom today we would call "insane" were viewed merely as existing on another plane. It characterized the madman as fool, jester, perhaps genius. Sometimes people put fools on ships, left to drift from port to port. After a town had looked and had the ship remind it of foolishness, it would shove it again out to sea. Hence the name "Ship of Fools." In the literature one finds madness as a voyage—another country. Madness did not imply depravity. From a voyage of exile one may always return "home."

As Foucault shows, moral degeneracy and depravity did not attach themselves to the concept of madness until *after* asylums for incarcerating the insane became institutionalized. The institution itself shaped the concept of madness. The confinement brutalized its victims. Boredom and abominable conditions led to illness and pain. Even those who did not become physically sick became less coherent after years of chains and damp walls. Society did not perceive the insane as ill. Rather, it viewed them as beasts, forfeiting their humanity. From the Middle Ages, however, the "touch of the divine" hung on, except that now society perceived in the insane not a touch of genius, of eccentric inspiration, but the touch of doom, of "falling from grace," of falling from humanity into bestiality—a God-given, inborn weakness in character.

Economic forces in combination with the pressure to use an established bureaucratic structure created a host of "social problems." The bureaucracy created the laws and the law changed the social definition of the behavior involved.

Almost universally as bureaucratic organizations come into being, expand, and protect their own interests, a similar process occurs. Bureaucracies contain bureaucrats and their interests push them to expand their power and resources. They express their interest by trying to grow larger and to take an ever-increasing range of events under their purview. In criminal justice policy, for the past ten years a trend has arisen to develop alternatives to incarceration for adult and juvenile offenders. This movement has created ways that society could deal with offenders "in the community." The achievement of this goal would necessarily reduce reliance on institutions—i.e., already existing bureaucratic organizations with a staff, space, and an institutionalized role established to house and isolate persons accused of crime. Thus the decarceration movement threatens some established bureaucratic interests while at the same time enhancing the power and scope of control of others.

Initially, the decarceration movement reduced the number of people sentenced to prisons, reformatories, and borstals.[7] Consistent with Foucault's generalization from his study of asylums, however, in the last few years the decarceration movement's major impact has increased the number of people actually handled by the control agencies.[8] Rather than a substitution for imprisonment, courts now sentence to community treatment programs people whom heretofore they would simply have released. In this way the established bureaucracies expanded their arena of control without real loss of clients.[9]

A more recent study by Foucault[10] develops the thesis that bureaucratic organizations in part reflect the continuation of a logic of bureaucratization that operates independently of the interests of the people involved. In an analysis of prisons Foucault proposes that the concept of imprisonment reflected a shift in notions of how to deal with criminals. Earlier forms of punishment dramatized evil through public executions and punishment. By isolating deviants, imprisonment placed them in a category outside the mainstream of normal social intercourse. Historically, Foucault argues, societies considered deviance a normal part of existing social relations. Public punishment resonated with that conception. It served vivid reminder to everyone, especially the lower classes, that no matter how justifiable, partaking in deviance could result in horrible consequences. This policy meets the needs of the ruling classes in an explicitly stratified, unequal society in which the ruling class perceives the underclass as less than human—the British in Ireland, the aristocracy in France, white colonialists in Africa, slave owners in the American south. With the growth of capitalism, its attendant legitimating myths of equality and equal opportunities influenced the new ruling strata to separate deviants from the mainstream and treat them as people who differed significantly from the normal and hence merited significantly different treatment. Thus emerged the bureaucratic organization of prisons and what Goffman calls "total institutions," which for varying lengths of time incarcerate, isolate, and separate from society those whom the system identifies as deviant but human.[11]

Today we can observe the result of these institutional changes. Police and prison bureaucracies transform the law to meet their own organizational goals and to serve the interests of those who occupy positions in the organizations. Not only does this occur in law enforcement (as we saw in Chapter 10), it also occurs in law creation. The interaction between police, prison officials, and judiciary and legislative bodies assures that the same people who must enforce the law participate deeply in its creation.

In Chapter 7 we saw how the drug enforcement agencies intervened in the lawmaking process to "mobilize in" some areas of drug abuse and to "mobilize out" others. We can now expand on that analysis to underline the role of bureaucracies in lawmaking.

Antidrug Laws

Largely due to the efforts of the Federal Narcotics Bureau (later renamed the Bureau of Narcotics and Dangerous Drugs and called today the Drug Enforcement Administration), in 1937 Congress enacted the Marijuana Tax Act:

Prior to 1937 Mr. Anslinger [then the director of the Federal Narcotics Bureau] and the Bureau of Narcotics had spearheaded a propaganda campaign against marihuana on the ground that it produced an immense amount of violent crime such as rape, mayhem, and murder, and that many traffic accidents could be attributed to it.[12]

The state agency that would have the responsibility for the enforcement of the law spearheaded the campaign for it—and paid for the campaign with agency funds. Congress passed the bill with little discussion. Congress apparently assumed that the Bureau of Narcotics knew all about drugs. It did not believe it necessary or wise to call for outside testimony. In a classic case, the organization's position enabled it to expand its domain and to justify its need for greater resources by controlling the information available to the lawmakers.

The Narcotics Bureau created public support for antimarijuana legislation by feeding to magazines and newspapers stories on the dangers of marijuana. Becker's comparison of the number of articles dealing with marijuana for the years preceding and following the 1937 Congress reveals the emergence of media interest in a previously dormant issue.[13] The Narcotics Bureau fanned this media interest. The articles contained cases supplied by the bureau as well as "data" distributed by bureau personnel.

The lawmaking function of the bureaucracy extended to the state level. Through the production and distribution of information and through personal influence the Bureau of Narcotics activated state and municipal law-enforcement agencies. In most of the states it succeeded in obtaining the enactment of antimarijuana laws duplicating the federal laws.

The laws governing the use of opiates in the United States show a similar pattern. In the United States prior to 1914, addicts could and did readily obtain drugs from pharmacies, physicians, and even mail-order houses. In 1914 Congress enacted the Harrison Act as a revenue measure and "to make the entire process of drug distribution within the country a matter of record."[14] The act did not make addiction or using drugs a criminal offense. Administrative orders of the Federal Narcotics Bureau and the bureau's careful selection of court cases in effect translated the Harrison Act into a law that punished drug addicts for their addiction and medical doctors for prescribing opiates. The Federal Narcotics Bureau through administrative practices—even in the face of laws contradicting these practices—pursued a policy of arresting and prosecuting selected medical doctors who provided drugs for addicts. These practices effectively created a law by administrative practice that no legislature or appellate court created. In the end, the policies and propaganda of the Federal Narcotics Bureau also created public support for its policies.[15]

An analysis of juvenile-court legislation in California also shows the power of law-enforcement bureaucracies in creating law. Lemert's analysis of the emergence and functioning of the California Youth Authority makes clear how bureaucratic needs may determine the shape of law:

The pressing need for a budget to support the C.Y.A.'s Division of Institutions has meant that where the choice has had to be made between upgrading juvenile court operation through new legislation and maintaining dominant organizational interests, the latter has prevailed. . . . The need to support and administer existing institutions, as well as construct new ones, soon established budgetary priority for the Division of Institutions, and came to occupy the largest share of time, energies, and attention of administrators and staff. Recruitment practices, in-training programs, and job assignments tended to preserve a custodial pattern of action within the Division of Institutions, despite the California Youth Authority's informal dedication and official allegiance to the purposes of individualized treatment.[16]

These cases expose some of the more visible examples of bureaucratic involvement in the creation of laws. The general hypothesis of law creation that emerges holds that bureaucracies will use their resources, power, and influence to obtain passage and suppression of laws that represent the interests of the bureaucracies themselves.

Bureaucracies perpetuate their own interests by processes often subtle and always obscured behind a smokescreen of ideological justification. The need for secrecy among police, the rule that a police officer never informs on a fellow officer, the strong inclination of police departments to cover up known cases of corruption to protect the public image of "the force"—the police justify all these by lofty principles centering on the protection of the community from lawlessness. The true source of these values in the interests of the bureaucracy and the police thus disappear behind a smokescreen.

In recent years universities have experienced an unprecedented assault in the courts by faculty claiming discrimination; blacks, Chicanos, and women have taken universities to court claiming that universities discriminated against them. For the most part the litigants (the people claiming they suffered discrimination) have fared rather poorly in their efforts to obtain satisfaction in the courts. We examine below why universities have often fought the claims of discrimination and why the courts rarely found in favor of the litigants. By this example we hope to demonstrate simultaneously the importance of bureaucracy in law and the dialectical relationship between consciousness and bureaucratic decisions.

11.2 UNIVERSITIES AND SEX DISCRIMINATION

In 1971, when Congress considered amendments to Title VII of the Equal Employment Opportunities Act that first placed universities under that Title, the House of Representatives committee report on the legislation stated:

Discrimination against minorities and women in the field of education is as pervasive as discrimination in any other area of employment. . . . In the area of sex discrimination, women have long been invited to participate as students in the academic process, but without the prospect of gaining employment as serious scholars.

When they have been hired into educational institutions particularly in institutions of higher learning, women have been relegated to positions of lesser standing than their male counterparts. In a study Kaplow and McGee, the Academic Marketplace, Anchor Edition: Garden City, 1965 . . . it was found that the primary factors determining the hiring of male faculty members were prestige and compatability, but that women were generally considered to be outside the prestige system altogether.[17]

Senator Birch Bayh found the evidence of sex discrimination in colleges and universities "truly appalling."[18] Senator Harrison Williams characterized it as "gross" and "blatant."[19]

Since the 1972 amendment, about forty academic women, to whom their universities denied tenure, brought actions under Title VII for redress, claiming sex discrimination. Until 1979 none of these women succeeded in winning a court order for tenure. Not until 1980 did an appellate court find that a university had unlawfully discriminated by denying a woman tenure.[20]

For purposes of this discussion, we assume that not all of these forty cases involved women who failed to receive tenure because of their own inadequacies as teachers or scholars. It defies the probabilities to suppose that, although Congress found massive gender discrimination, not one of these women plaintiffs suffered sex discrimination.

After 1972 university administrators did begin to hire more women, but the percentage of women achieving tenure did not change appreciably.[21] One would expect that if no discrimination existed, the percentage of tenured women academics in any field would approximate the percentage of women Ph.D.'s of the relevant age group.

They do not. The inference plainly exists that despite Title VII many university decision-makers continued to discriminate. Indeed, many universities fought tooth and nail against claims of discrimination, at enormous cost and in situations where in other litigation one might ordinarily expect a compromise solution. Why did higher-level university authorities so vigorously resist claims by academic women that lower levels in the university had discriminated against them? Why did academic women so singularly fail in their litigation?

The language of Section 703(a) (the 1972 amendment) commands the university administrator only negatively. As we have already seen, the ordinary rules of property and contract law gave university administrations ample power to employ whomever they wished and for whatever reasons they chose. Section 703 carved out of that unlimited discretion only a small exception.

The content of that exception remained thoroughly ambiguous. Did the injunction not to discriminate bar only the conscious use of criteria in the forbidden classes? Or did it bar the use of criteria, however well intended, that nevertheless had the consequence of making women as compared with men swim upstream? Earlier litigation under Title VII established a standard with two prongs, disparate *treatment* and disparate *impact*. Of the former, the Supreme Court said: " 'Disparate treatment' . . . is the most easily understood type of discrimination. The employer simply treats some people less favorably than others because of their race, color, religion, sex or national origin. Proof of discriminatory motive is critical."[22] Of the latter, it wrote that disparate impact discrimination includes those practices which, though "facially neutral in their treatment of different groups, . . . fall more harshly on one group than another and cannot be justified by business necessity."[23]

Title VII therefore commands university administrators not intentionally to discriminate against women academics and not to employ any standard, however apparently neutral, that falls more harshly on one group than another and cannot find a justification in the demands for the job. (For example, discrimination against women exists in many graduate programs. The Ph.D. degree, practically invariably required for an academic post in the United States, falls unevenly upon men and women. Most universities argued, however, that without the Ph.D. or evidence of equivalent study nobody could satisfactorily serve as a professor, and in the United States equivalent courses of study to the Ph.D. usually do not exist.) The discriminatory impact standard, however, rarely applies in academia, where the criteria for promotion and tenure have always received vague articulation since high scholarship, excellent teaching, and well-regarded service to the university and the public are all facially neutral, all so vaguely defined that any university administrator or faculty with a heart so inclined can readily find in them a cloak for discrimination. University faculties traditionally have had wide-ranging discretion in deciding who should receive posts, promotion, and tenure. Title VII's negative command hardly diminished their power.

The complex, many layered decision structure of universities gives them space to discriminate. Universities make decisions about employment and tenure through search committees, departments, deans, divisional committees, presidents, and trustees. Each of them gets a chance to review appointment and tenure decisions. Each of them applies their own subjective criteria. The opportunity for discrimination with impunity multiplies as the number of layers in the bureaucracy multiplies.

Intuitively, it would seem that the multi-layered decisional process minimizes the effect of a discriminatory minority; the committee system and successive levels of review surely would eradicate impermissible bases for decision. In practice, serious disagreement by even a small minority of those involved in the decision-making can de facto blackball a candidate. The multiplex decision process can maximize the power of the discriminatory few, who manage successfully to masquerade their prejudices in adverse subjective judgments about scholarship and teaching.

Universities par excellence, so the myth has it, embody the ideal of meritocracy, where individual academics advance as they produce excellent scholarship and (in some universities at least) demonstrate their excellent teaching and serve well the university or public. Subjective biases aside, it seems difficult to identify a specifically male interest in discriminating against female academics.

University administrators, however, have strong organizational interests that impel them to resist any challenges to university decision-making. For centuries, universities have immunized themselves from accountability for academic decision, usually under the claim of academic freedom. Individuals have challenged university employment decisions on a variety of grounds since the earliest days of the Republic (in 1790, the Virginia Court of Appeals upheld William and Mary College's dismissal of a professor).[24] In Title VII litigation, a well-defined pattern of litigation to the limits has developed. Brown University reportedly spent $800 thousand in lawyers' fees to litigate a Title VII claim in the face of evidence so massive that, after calmer heads in the Board of Trustees intervened, Brown settled the case with a far-ranging consent decree—probably the most favorable decree for women in all U.S. academia. The university surely could have won a much easier consent decree at much less cost had the administration treated the matter less litigiously.

University administrators resist claims of discrimination because accountability impairs power. Practically none of the highly educated, highly articulate men who constitute the administration of most U.S. universities will admit to sex biases. Most know that the law forbids discrimination on grounds of sex. They have, however, become accustomed through long tradition to making their own unassailable judgments about hiring, always masked under claims of excellence. So subjective do academic judgments become that no doubt most university professors and administrators really believe that they make their judgments solely on the basis of "objective" criteria of achievement although the frequent bitter disagreements among academics about the worth of a colleague's scholarship or teaching give that claim the lie. So believing, university senior personnel have no difficulty in believing that distinct differences exist between the scholarship teaching of a woman and of a man candidate. That subconscious biases may distort their judgment they do not admit.

Senior administrators have another reason for defending the university against claims of discrimination. Every Title VII action asserts that somebody discriminated.

That charge constitutes an insult. The senior professors, departmental chairs, deans, or provosts whom a women's suit charges with discrimination have sufficient clout with higher administrative officials to persuade them to defend the suit. The person who discriminated does not have to pay a lawyer; the university administrator who authorizes the continuing litigation has little at stake if the litigation continues, but can lose internal support if the university negotiates a settlement. In the event, universities litigate Title VII cases as though all the world depended on it. In *Sweeney* v. *Keene State College*, the woman plaintiff originally brought an action to protest a failure to promote her to full professor. During the litigation, she received her promotion. After that, only the question of back pay remained. To defeat that claim (and therefore to defeat the claim of discrimination) the university litigated the case to the federal District Court and once again to the Court of Appeals. One would guess that the amount spent in lawyers' fees vastly exceeded the amount of damages at issue.

Much research has demonstrated the sexism that permeates our culture. Academics suffer from the same disease as the rest of us. Given the excessive discretion in employment that property and contract law grant to universities, subjective biases and sex stereotypes easily mask themselves. That when opportunity existed American senior academics tended to discriminate with regard to gender ought to cause no wonder.

Federal Judges and Title VII

The behavior of university administrators seems readily explicable. Why would federal judges so rarely find in favor of women, when by all odds at least some of the cases should have gone the other way?

In the original enactment of Title VII, the great legislative battle raged over the enforcement mechanism. One model existed in the many federal agencies—the National Labor Relations Board and the Federal Trade Commission, for example. In each of these, primary responsibility for enforcement lies with the administrative agency. Complaints of unfair labor practices or unfair trade practices lie with each of them respectively; agency personnel prosecute the cases, the principal factual hearing takes place within the agency, and the agency then issues a decision on the merits of the case, ordering an appropriate remedy—for example, in the case of an unfair labor practice, a cease and desist order, plus an order to rehire an unfairly discharged worker and to give back pay. If the accused party (the employer in an unfair labor practice charge, for example) disputes the agency finding, he declines to obey the agency ruling. The agency then petitions a federal Court of Appeals for an order requiring the accused party to obey the agency's order. A hearing is held before the Court of Appeals that resembles in many ways the ordinary hearing of an appeal from a federal trial court. In that way, the administrative agency serves the function—and more—of the federal trial court, which thus has practically no role to play in the determination of issues within the competence of the administrative agency.

In the maneuvering over Title VII's original enactment, that process was altered.

The legislation did create a new administrative agency, the Equal Employment Opportunities Commission (EEOC). Once it had determined that the employer had discriminated, however, it could not *order* the employer to do anything. It could only "endeavor to eliminate any such alleged unlawful employment practice by informal methods of conference, conciliation, and persuasion."[25]

Any claimant under Title VII must first bring his complaint to the EEOC. Only when it has either decided against the claimant or exhausted possibilities of conciliation may the claimant bring an indepedent action against the employer in federal District Court. In the case of the National Labor Relations Board model the agency bears the burden of litigation; under Title VII, the individual litigant does. The commission or the attorney general *may* initiate the action; in practice, they practically never do so. Instead, within ninety days after receipt of notice from the EEOC of either a rejection of the claim or failure to reach a satisfactory accord, "a civil action may be brought against the respondent named in the charge (A) by the person claiming to be aggrieved."[26] That action lies before the appropriate U.S. District Court. The Supreme Court held that that trial must constitute a brand new *de novo* hearing, whatever the proceedings or recommendation of the EEOC. After that *de novo* trial,

if the court finds that the respondent has intentionally engaged in or is intentionally engaging in an unlawful employment practice charged in the complaint, the court may enjoin the respondent from engaging in such unlawful employment practice, and order such afformative action as may be appropriate, which may include, but is not limited to, reinstatement or hiring of employees, with or without back pay (payable by the employer, employment agency, or labor organization, as the case may be, responsible for the unlawful employment practice), or any other equitable relief as the court deems appropriate.

In any action or proceeding under this subchapter the court, in its discretion, may allow the prevailing party . . . a reasonable attorney's fees as part of the costs.[27]

The rule seemingly requires a straightforward duty from the judges: find whether discrimination existed; if it did, fashion a remedy from the range available. Given the context of judicial decision-making, however, this provision gave the courts great discretion. They tended to exercise that discretion in deference to university power-holders, not women. To understand why the seemingly straightforward rule in practice granted judges great discretion, we must examine the capacity of judges to decide. (We assume that the law gets communicated to the judges—if not to them, then to whom? We also assume that the Title VII cases gave them opportunity to decide either way.)

The judge's discretion in fact-finding comes from the structure of trial courts. In an adversary system, each side proves its case through witnesses. In most cases, witnesses report what they heard or observed: the traffic at the time of the accident, the weather, the speed of the defendant's car, the movements of the plaintiff just before the accident, what part of the defendant's car hit the plaintiff, the tire marks, the position of the defendant's car after it came to rest, the plaintiff's injuries and treatment, his costs and other economic losses. Usually, plaintiff's and defendant's witnesses disagree about many of the matters. A judge must therefore decide whom to believe.

Sometimes that turns upon the credibility of the witness: whether he seems truthful and had opportunity and capacity to observe, remember, and report the incident to the tribunal. (If the witness places himself at a point where he could not see the accident because a large tree stood in the way, his testimony becomes less creditworthy.) Mostly, however, we decide creditworthiness by seeing how the testimony fits into the general fabric of the testimony in the case. (If no doubt exists that a plaintiff saw a doctor immediately after the accident, and that the doctor observed gross contusions consistent with a claim of an automobile accident, a defendant who insists that his car never hit the plaintiff has an uphill battle to persuade a trier of fact that his testimony deserves credit.)

In some circumstances, however, an expert witness may not only report what she observed, but give her expert opinion about some matter in issue. A psychiatrist may report whether in her opinion a criminal defendant suffers from insanity. A doctor may report whether in her opinion a plaintiff has permanently lost the full use of an injured arm, and the percentage of loss. A real estate assessor may give his opinion about the fair market value of real property. They can give these opinions because their expertise tells them, based upon their present knowledge of the facts in the matter, the probable outcomes. (Given symptoms A, B, and C, the probable prognosis for the injury is X.)

In Title VII litigation concerning academic women, the critical testimony generally comes in the form of opinions. In that litigation, the burden of proof lies on the woman—that is, she must persuade the judge by a preponderance of the evidence that the university discriminated against her (disparate treatment) or used an employment practice that hit men and women unequally (disparate impact).

In most academic cases, the disparate impact criterion rarely comes into play; the standards of scholarship, teaching, and university and public service seem neutral enough. Practically all those cases claim disparate treatment, that is, the differential invocation of these vague standards. The Supreme Court described the procedure that a court ought to follow. First, the woman must prove a *prima facie* case of discrimination by proving that she falls within the protected class, that she had the formal qualifications for the position, and that the university hired a male with lower qualifications, or paid a man with similar or lower qualifications more than she received, or promoted a man to tenure less qualified than she. The university then must "articulate" a legitimate, nondiscriminatory reason for its adverse action regarding the plaintiff—usually, that her scholarship or teaching fell below the standards it had otherwise established. The woman then has to go forward with evidence to persuade the court that the claimed legitimate, nondiscriminatory reason in fact only served as a pretext to hide discrimination. Most Title VII litigation centered on that final step: did the claimed reasons for the differential treatment only hide discrimination?

Those reasons usually claimed that the woman's scholarship or teaching did not reach appropriate standards. That, however, depended almost entirely upon opinion evidence. So subjective become the judgments of excellence in scholarship that often scholars with great reputations in a field will disagree vigorously with each other's assessment of a candidate's work. The very structure of a Title VII academic lawsuit, therefore, makes it easy for an academic with a mind consciously set on discrimination to mask his illegal motives. In this day and age, few academics consciously discriminate. Nevertheless, discrimination continues. Sociologists have demonstrated how sex stereotyping seizes men and women in our culture. If a man explodes at a secretary, he runs a tight ship; if a woman does so, she obviously too easily falls prey to emotionalism. In one case, Brown University denied a woman economist a named chair partly on the ground that she had never previously held tenure in a major university. At the time, of the 845 tenured chairs in the 43 major American economics departments (i.e., those that concentrated on research and graduate instruction), women held *fourteen*.

Judicial difficulties with penetrating academic judgments, however, had even another burden to bear. The subject matter of the decision required seemed far beyond the ken of most laymen. A judge who participates in a number of negligence trials in time acquires enough knowledge of medical terms at least to follow a doctor when he gives his opinion about the consequences of an accident. How can he do so when the subject matter of the opinion lies in the most abstruse areas of mathematics, microbiology, nuclear physics, or seventeenth-century Japanese epic poetry?

In the result, the vague standards for employment permitted by Title VII, the mode of proof in academic cases, and the arcane subject matter at issue combined to make the judicial forum a poor one for adjudicating academic Title VII claims. Judges understandably tended to throw up their hands. In *Jepsen* v. *Florida Board of Regents*, the trial court went so far as to say that it would reverse a university only if the woman showed that the university had abused its discretion—a standard probably impossible ever to satisfy.

Toward the end of the 1970s, a number of federal courts of appeal expressed their dismay at that result. The First Circuit stated:

We voice misgivings over one theme recurrent in those opinions: The notion that courts should keep "hands off" the salary, promotion and hiring decisions of colleges and universities. This reluctance no doubt arises from the courts' recognition that hiring, promotion and tenure decisions are most appropriately made by persons thoroughly familiar with the academic setting. Nevertheless, we caution against permitting judicial deference to result in judicial abdication of a responsibility entrusted to the courts by Congress. That responsibility is simply to provide a forum for the litigation of complaints of sex disrimination in institutions of higher learning as readily as for other Title VII suits.[28]

The difficulty, however, lay not in the judges' sense that they ought to defer to academics. Under the circumstances what else could they readily do? (One judge tried. The actual trial of the case, involving a physicist's claim for tenure, took seventy-two trial days. Taxpayers pay about $5000 a day to keep a federal courthouse open, and that does not take into account lawyer's fees at somewhere between $50 and $150 an *hour*.)

No obvious interest spurred judges to favor universities against women claimants. Federal judges have life tenure; most do no more than aspire to higher judicial office; unlike the commissioners of administrative agencies, their future careers do not depend upon the favor of one of the litigants. More subtle interests, however, may operate. University administrators move in the same elevated circles as federal judges. Frequently, they went to the same elite universities and law schools, belong to the same elite clubs, support the same charities, sometimes marry each other's sisters or daughters, and, of course, are almost all men. It cannot come easily for a judge to assert that an administrator in his own circle violated the law, for that may forfeit his friend's approbation.

Federal judges are predominantly white, middle-aged males, who before becoming federal judges practiced in elite law firms or the U.S. attorney's office. In general, they cannot easily avoid having the same domain assumptions as others with that background. If a female semiskilled worker claims that an employer discriminated by refusing to promote her to a higher paying but still only semiskilled job, it violates no domain assumption of upper-class men to assert that she should have been promoted; from an elevated position, the difference between the two jobs hardly seems breathtaking. To maintain that a woman can competently do what a judge perceives as a task on his own level of competence, however, must tend to violate his sex stereotypes, i.e., one of his domain assumptions.

Vague standards, the requirements of opinion evidence, and arcane subject matter combined to give judges great discretion in deciding Title VII cases. Where judges have discretion, plainly subjective factors tend to play a greater role in decision-making than they do when the situation calls for more narrow, fact-based judgments. And so women's Title VII cases floundered, rarely succeeding in producing more than massive lawyers' fees and frustration for women academics.

One may be inclined, in view of these findings, to throw up one's hands in despair. The male chauvinism, the institutionalized biases, the structured disparity between the individual's potential for a fair hearing and the universities' ability to pay gigantic lawyers' fees, combined with the judges' inability to make a decision against the university, bode poorly for satisfaction in the courts on charges of sex discrimination in universities. But note the dialectical relationship in the foregoing analysis. Judges increasingly express concern over their inability to make a judgment on reasonable grounds. Women continue to demand fair treatment in universities and elsewhere. The struggle for equality assaults basic institutions and attitudes and today takes place throughout society. There is no doubt that the present circumstance must change, probably too late for many of the individuals involved in present-day litigation, but ultimately for the improvement of women's position in universities and elsewhere. The universities, given the coincidence of bureaucratic and personal (role incumbent's) interests in continuing discrimination, will doubtless fight hard and long against the changes. The courts, however, given their relative independence from university interests (though judges share many of the same biases as male administrators) will likely change most quickly. For these reasons we take exception to those, like Weber and Foucault, whom we mentioned in the beginning of this chapter, who argue for the inevitable dominance of bureaucracy over everyone's lives. Like the dominance of feudal lords, mercantile capitalists, or corporate managers, the dominance is historically specific and will change when those dominated refuse to live by the rules laid down in the interests of established authority.

11.3 CONCLUSION

In this chapter we have looked at the effect of bureaucratic organizations and the state on the implementation and creation of law. We have argued that the bureaucracy mediates and affects the legal order, but does not control it. The people who occupy roles in the bureaucracy respond to the resources and constraints of their world and in so doing alter and influence the quality and characteristics of the laws that the legal order requires them to implement. In the end the law-in-action systematically differs from the law-in-the-books.

Max Weber perceptively anticipated how agencies speckled with "specialists," organized hierarchically, with one-way communication (from the top down), and circumscribed by rules—i.e., bureaucracies—would come to dominate the social organization of modern industrial societies. Weber also outlined how bureaucracies would develop a life of their own independent from control by the people or by any social class. Like Dr. Frankenstein's monster the "fully grown product" bears only a passing resemblance to the ideas and hopes surrounding its birth.

In this process "the state" and the government constitute the underlying social organizations which circumscribe the particular bureaucracies. We propose here a dialectical model of the state and law. It takes as its starting point the objective relation between the economic and the political in a capitalist society. The capitalist state provides the conditions for capital accumulation, but it must also respond to the conflicts engendered by those very conditions. This response takes the form of administration, bureaucratization, and legislation, that is, the state and its functionary, the legal order. The nature of the response depends in large part on the *source* of the conflict (i.e., whether it originates in protest or as a direct outcome of the system's contradictions) as well as historically specific conditions of the political economy. However the response or "solution" temporarily serves, it can best do only as a stopgap. Ineluctably it will generate further contradictions and conflicts.

NOTES

1. M. Weber, "Bureaucracy," in H. Gerth and C. Wright Mills, eds., *From Max Weber: Essays in Sociological Theory* (New York: Oxford University Press, 1946).

2. R. Nisbet, *The Sociological Tradition* (New York: Basic Books, 1966), p. 46.

3. *Ibid.*, p. 146.

4. *Ibid.*, pp. 292-293.

5. J. T. Winkler, "Law, State and Economy: The Industry Act of 1975 in Context," *British Journal of Law and Society* 2(1975):103-128.

6. M. Foucault, *Madness and Civilization* (London: Tavistock, 1967).

7. Andrew Scull, *Decarceration: Community Treatment and the Deviant–A Radical View* (Englewood Cliffs, N.J.: Prentice-Hall, 1977); see also Andrew Scull, *Museums of Madness: The Social Organization of Insanity in Nineteenth Century England* (London: Allen Lane, 1979).

8. John H. Hylton, "Community Corrections and Social Control: The Case of Saskatchewan, Canada," *Contemporary Crises* 5(1981):forthcoming.

9. *Ibid.*

10. M. Foucault, *Discipline and Punish: The Birth of the Prison* (London: Allen Lane, 1975).

11. Erving Goffman, *Asylums* (Garden City, N.Y.: Doubleday, 1961).

12. Howard Becker, *Outsiders: Studies in the Sociology of Deviance* (New York: Free Press, 1963).

13. *Ibid.*

14. Alfred R. Lindesmith, *The Addict and the Law* (Bloomington: Indiana University Press, 1965).

15. *Ibid.*

16. E. Lemert, "Legislation Change in the Juvenile Court," *Wisconsin Law Review* 1967(1967):421-448; E. Lemert, *Social Action and Legal Change* (Chicago: Aldine, 1970).

17. House of Representatives No. 92-238 (to accompany HR 1746) June 2, 1971, 2 U.S. Congressional and Administrative News, 92d Congress, 2d Session, 1972, 2155.

18. 118 Congressional Record 117 (1972).

19. *Ibid.*

20. *Kunda* v. *Muhlenberg College*, No. 79-1135 (February 18, 1980, 3d Cir.). A few women succeeded in winning more or less favorable negotiated settlements.

21. *American Economics Association Journal* 21(1979):414.

22. *International Brotherhood of Teamsters* v. *U.S.*, 431 U.S. 324 n. 15 (1977).

23. *Ibid.*

24. *Bracken* v. *Visitors of William and Mary College*, 3 Call. [574] 495 (1790), Virginia Court of Appeals.

25. Pub. L. 88-532, Title VII, sec. 706 (b), 42 U.S.C.C. sec. 2000e-5(b).

26. Title VII, sec. 706 (f).(l).

27. Sec. 706 (g) and (k), 42 U.S.C. sec. 2000-e5(g) and (k)o.

28. *Sweeney* v. *Board of Trustees of Keene State College*, 569 F. 2d 169 (C.A. 11, 1978). See also *Davis* v. *Weidner*, 596 F. 2d. 726 (C.A. 7, 1979).

12

The state and the legal order under capitalism

In recent years, the study of law and society has experienced a heady growth. From rather tentative explorations in the mid 1960s it mushroomed, experiencing an outburst of creative scholarship. New vocabularies, methodologies, perspectives, and researches presented a challenge to assumptions previously held sacred.[1] That outburst reflects a fundamental change in the "domain assumptions" of law and social science. In turn, that change reflects fundamental changes in the world view and material reality of our present era.

12.1 AN OVERVIEW OF LAW AND SOCIETY STUDIES SINCE THE 1950s

In some ways, for the social sciences the 1950s seem an enviable period. Almost complete agreement existed on the vocabularies, methodology, and perspective appropriate to the study of human behavior and society. Except for a few who marched to a different drumbeat, most scholars employed concepts like role, status, stratification, social system, social action, actors, progress, and consensus. Positivism spawned the methodology: a belief that we could reduce social reality to individuals' responses to questionnaires and that from attitudes expressed in response to carefully constructed and analyzed questions put to them by trained social scientists we could predict the respondents' behavior. In the 1950s "all health consciences" shared the perspective of functionalism: that we can best understand society as analogous to a living organism with its own needs for survival and an ability to produce social relations in accordance with those needs.

In the late 1950s, the revolt of African, Latin American, and Asian people against their European and American colonial masters shattered the functionalist vision. Demanding independence and an end to European and American imperialism, these people reminded the world that not everyone shared the values and world view of the West and that "social progress" and "the needs of society" did not supply an appropriate perspective for understanding the exploitation and repression of two-thirds of the world's peoples. The functionalist-positivist vision received yet another blow when blacks, Chicanos, Native Americans, and poor whites in America and Europe began demanding the opportunities that supposedly they already enjoyed. Their leaders analyzed American and European societies from a different perspective.

That forced many social scientists to reflect on the accuracy of a perspective that argued that those with the most talent necessarily received more than those with less talent and that this, and this alone, explained "social stratification."[2] In the late 1950s C. Wright Mills suggested that sociologists should investigate the usually ignored subject of power.[3] He even had the perspicacity to argue that a "power elite" with a military-industrial base controlled the United States. To add insult to injury, Mills's methodology challenged positivistic principles, sacrificing as it did statistical sophistication for substantive importance—an act many sociologists then considered heretical.

Ralf Dahrendorf supported Mills's attack on the hegemony of functional-positivistic social science. In a seminal article appropriately titled "Out of Utopia" he argued that we should use a vocabulary that employed concepts like power, conflict, and struggle rather than one that spoke only of consensus, equilibrium, and evolution.[4]

The former colonies in Africa and some neocolonies in Latin America (Cuba in particular) obtained their independence. The civil rights movement grew larger and more violent. Social scientists and lawyers alike could no longer ignore the law's importance or the role of power and conflict in the legal order. People's struggles to survive in and change the real world changed scholarly consciousness.

Conflict sociology and a renaissance of the study of law and society arose almost at the same moment. Two of the first efforts to bring together extant readings in law and society studies had almost identical perspectives and contents. After decades of silence on the subject by both social scientists and lawyers, these two volumes appeared within six months of each other.[5]

Early efforts led to a pluralistic perspective that conceived society as splintered into numerous divisions—social class, power, wealth, prestige, privilege. These divisions generated conflict. That perspective saw control of the legal order and the state as a prize that everyone sought but only a few obtained.[6] It saw the legal order as representing one group or class while repressing others. By contemporary standards that model seems simplistic. It did, however, make a critical break with the functionalism it sought to replace.

The 1960s brought the repressive, violent, and illegal practices of the police into sharp relief. It also underscored the absurdity of some of our laws—those that sentenced people to long prison terms for smoking marijuana, for example. The media showed us mace, tear gas, and nightsticks crashing down on the heads and bodies of students demonstrating against a war that a majority of the people increasingly opposed. The Vietnam war and the repressive actions of the police did not fit nicely into functionalist theory. The behavior of the police in suppressing students and workers, as well as their response to blacks, Chicanos, and Native Americans, exposed more than the seamy side of police work—it exposed characteristics of policing as an enterprise that called for explanation.

The pluralist view gave way to a perspective that postulated the importance of a "ruling class." In the 1960s the United States fought a war opposed by large numbers of people but steadfastly refused to deal effectively with poverty and injustice at home. The first cut at an explanation held that a small elite created the legal order to maintain its own power and privilege. Ralph Miliband exposed the role of the state as a handmaiden of the capitalist class.[7] C. Wright Mills reminded us of the rich tradition of studies of elites, oligarchy, and the state.[8] T. B. Bottomore, Ernest Mandel, Paul Sweezey, Herbert Marcuse, Basil Davidson, E. P. Thompson, Franz Fanon, and Jean Paul Sartre—to mention only a few—resurrected the works of Karl Marx for the Western world. These scholars enriched the study of law and society, becoming ever more complicated as they struggled to describe and explain a world itself grown more complicated.

Current Debates

The 1970s were a time of deep-seated change within the capitalist societies and a time of turmoil in the less-developed countries of Africa, Latin America, and Asia. In the United States the decade opened with Watergate, stumbled and drifted aimlessly (and for the most part secretly) through the presidencies of Ford and Carter, and ended with the election of Ronald Reagan. In the less-developed world revolutions raged as people struggled for their humanity and for a place at the table. Mozambique, Angola, and Guinea gained freedom from the last European colonists as revolutionaries forced Portugal to give up one of the bloodiest and longest wars in colonial history. Revolution tore Zimbabwe and Namibia. South Africa became an armed laager. Zimbabweans succeeded in forcing the minority white government from power; in the rest of southern Africa armed struggle continued.

As the shortcomings of ruling class and pluralist theories became apparent the study of law and society grew increasingly concerned with historical and comparative analyses. Althusser and Foucault resurrected functionalism under the guise of Marxism; others continued to advocate ruling class theory.

The debate increasingly came to focus on the relative utility of theories emphasizing the role of ideology, legitimacy, and the inevitable process of history in contrast to theories that emphasized material structure (the economic and political forms), human volition, and class struggle. All of them increasingly came to perceive the centrality of the role of the state and the legal order.

12.2 THE STATE AND THE LEGAL ORDER

Until recently most analyses of the state focused on its bureaucratic nature. As the preceding chapters indicate, one cannot underestimate bureaucracy's role. Another dimension of the state and government, however, has come to the center in studies of law and society. We begin with a brief caution. We earlier referred to sociology's tendency to reify abstract constructs like society, social order, and law. Discussions of the state and government sometimes suffer the same fallacy. For all of their importance to the modern world, these concepts only abstractly depict social reality. Save for the positions, roles, obligations, and actions of people engaged in day-to-day activities, "state" and "government" have no concrete content. This does not suggest, however, that the analysis must focus solely on the motivations and decisions of individuals. We employ the abstract concepts in order to deal systematically with the social relations and social forces that circumscribe and constrain individual actions. In that process we must not come to see these abstractions as any more nor any less than useful ways of carving up the world so we can more *understandably* deal with it.

The Instrumentalist Perspective

The publication of Miliband's *The State in Capitalist Society* and C. Wright Mills's *The Power Elite* suggested a paradigm that stressed the importance of the ruling elite in determining the resources and constraints of everyone else. Harkening back to the works of Marx, Pareto, Michels, Machiavelli, and Weber, many social scientists conceived society as an arena within which some few people gained economic and political dominance and wielded power. Some denoted this view as the "instrumentalist" theory.[9]

Applied to law and the legal order the instrumentalist theory sees the state and government as the handmaiden of the ruling class. It takes as its starting point the observation by Karl Marx that "the modern state is but a committee for managing the common affairs of the whole bourgeoisie." The "ruling class" consists primarily of those who own and manage the productive forces (financial and industrial sectors) of the economy.

Theory stimulates research. Following instrumentalism's articulation, a vast array of researches conducted in Europe, the United States, Africa, Latin America, and Asia generated findings that seemed to validate it. Throughout the world researchers discovered the existence of cohesive, socially connected elites who communicated with one another and unduly influenced government and state decisions—including the law.[10]

Instrumentalists found a close relationship between capitalists and the state elite. Miliband found that since 1889 the largest single occupational group in the cabinets of the United States consisted of businessmen,[11] and that since 1961 businessmen have composed over 60 percent of each cabinet (whether the Republican or Democratic party was in power).[12] Domhoff demonstrated empirically how those who sit at the top of the financial and manufacturing sector of the economy attend the same schools, marry into one another's families, vacation at the same resorts, and appoint one another to high-level decision-making positions at all sectors of American life: the media, government, state, business, banking, education, and even "commissions" designed to advise government on long-range internal and foreign policy.[13]

Scholars operating within the instrumentalist paradigm found data suggesting the importance of money in perpetuating elite control over state and government. Money determines the outcome of elections at all levels—from city council to the presidency.[14] The immense amount of money required for a successful political campaign—several million dollars to run for Congress or a governorship, over sixty million to run for president—provides a built-in bias in favor of the economic elite for influence and control over elected and appointed government officials and in turn career officials in the state apparatus.

These and other research findings demonstrate the importance of an economic elite controlling the state and government. But not all the facts fit that theory quite so comfortably. Theory stimulates research and research in turn corrects theory. We noted earlier (see Chapter 6) that the instrumentalist theory could not account for significant segments of law creation. Mollenkopf makes the same point: he notes that an entire body of U.S. legislation in the 1930s known as the "New Deal" was strenuously opposed by a large number of powerful capitalists.[15] G. William Domhoff in *The Powers That Be* points to the National Labor Relations Act (1935) as difficult to account for in terms of instrumentalist theory.[16]

If the state and government simply reflect ruling-class interests, then the members of the ruling class must have a significant degree of agreement over what their interests demand. Scholars in what some call the structuralist school, particularly Offe and Poulantzas, offered data demonstrating intra-ruling-class conflict,[17] thus attacking instrumentalist theory. Capitalists' interests do not always mesh. Even Domhoff, who convincingly demonstrates the degree to which the capitalist class shares a common consciousness, recognizes a split between "ultra conservatives" and the "moderates."[18]

Theoretical objections to instrumentalist theory also suggest limits to its utility. Poulantzas's argument is as follows: Instrumentalist theory resembles an empirical generalization rather than an explanation. That a ruling class has influence and control over state and government, even if empirically true, does not give us a very profound explanation of the relationship, why it exists at this historical period in capitalist development, and how it will change. Instrumentalist theory ultimately becomes a static interpretation suggesting a deterministic view of history and society.

Structuralist Theory

The late 1960s and early 1970s saw the development of an alternative paradigm that retained some of the strengths of the instrumentalist view but attempted to overcome some of its shortcomings. This "structuralist" perspective argues that a "structural, 'objective relation' between the state and capitalism . . . guarantees that the state within the limits imposed by inherent contradictions and the class struggle, will operate in the long-term interests of the capitalist class, independent of the direct participation of individual capitalists."[19]

A state that "in the long run" perpetuates the interests of the capitalist class has as a primary function the promotion of "capital accumulation."[20] The state must protect the process of capital accumulation for several reasons: (1) for its survival the state depends, via taxation, on the production of surplus capital, (2) political stability depends on economic stability, and (3) the survival of the state and the interests of the capitalists coincide in that both depend on maintaining the viability of the economy and political stability.

"Capital accumulation" and political stability depend on the promotion of what is variously called "political integration,"[21] "social harmony,"[22] and the "cohesion of the social formation."[23] These different phrasings all argue that the state and government must legitimize the existing political and economic arrangements in order to provide an atmosphere in which capitalist accumulation and production can continue. The system can continue only if it convinces people of its worth—i.e., that it serves their interests. To serve the interests of the ruling class, the state must create that feeling among the people. Thus it follows that the law, as the principal mechanism for legitimizing existing social relations, will respond to the needs of capitalist accumulation and predictability.[24] In this view, capitalists do not directly control the state and the legal order. On the contrary, the state and the legal order best fulfill their function as legitimizers when they appear to function as value neutral organs fairly and impartially representing the interests of everyone.

The structuralist position resonates more closely with the theory we advance in this book than does instrumentalist theory. Structuralist theory suggests a dynamic relationship that gives a central place to the state's relative autonomy and to attempts to resolve the problems of structure inherent in capitalist democracies. Some problems, however, remain. First, most structuralist theory tends to reify the "state," giving it a life of its own, independent of the people who occupy various positions and make decisions.[25] Second, some structuralists overemphasize the stability of the system. Althusser, particularly, seems to suggest that the state inevitably handles conflict so as to ensure the survival of capitalism.[26] Capitalist societies, however, frequently experience rebellions and riots. These evidence an underlying tension which the capitalist state has historically been unable to eliminate. Third, other structuralits err in the other direction: O'Connor, for example, stresses the constancy of crisis in the capitalist state. His notion of capitalism's underlying instability seems belied by capitalism's survival for the past three hundred years. As Alan Wolfe points out: "To accept the cleverness and omnipotence of the rulers as the major explanation of public policy is to ignore the political struggles that went into its creation. Liberal democracy did not, as with some omniscient Zeus, spring full-born out of the forehead of the ruling class."[27] Nor does the "state" omnisciently respond to maintain "the system" by serving the long-range interests of capitalists.

Finally, structuralist theory distinguishes itself from instrumentalist theory by stressing that the state has "relative" autonomy. That central insight lacks content, however, unless one can specify the mechanisms of ruling-class control over the state and how these mechanisms lead not to complete but to "relative" control and hence to "relative" autonomy of the state.

We conclude that neither contemporary instrumentalist nor structuralist theory adequately captures the relationship between the state and the legal order on the one hand and society on the other. We propose instead a dialectical, institutionalist theory that we believe meets the three difficulties in structuralist theory that we have identified.

Dialectical Theory

The observed paradox. Instrumentalist theory predicts that the state will respond to the demands of the capitalist class. Structuralist theory agrees that it will do so "in the long run," but that from time to time it will take steps seemingly against those demands—that is, the capitalist state has "relative autonomy." The structuralist perspective matches reality in a gross way. As soon as one examines the various ways in which the capitalist state acts inconsistently with the interests of the ruling class, however, it appears that the relative autonomy of the state varies radically in different sectors of the polity and with respect to different issues. For example, if a capitalist sues a consumer on a debt arising out of a sales contract, the various minions of the law will act in the capitalist's interests to collect the debt. If, however, the capitalist as employer too blatantly discriminates against a black in industrial employment, the same minions may discipline the employer in the interests of his black workers. The same Congress that enacts a budget that favors the rich and powerful may enact a statute extending the rights of black voters in the South, overriding the claims of entrenched interests to do so. How can this extraordinarily variable "relative autonomy" be explained? Unlike instrumentalist and structuralist theory, we begin not with macro phenomena, but with an analysis of what it means when one says that the state acts with "relative autonomy." First we define what we mean by "state" and "government."

"State" and "government." Structuralist theory frequently reifies the state. Treating the state as a single entity with its own life and consciousness, it does not look very much into the interstices of the state to discover why it acts autonomously in some instances and not in others. We meet this problem by defining the concepts "state" and "government."

"State" has no clear, unambiguous, universally accepted meaning. The concept suggests bureaucratic organization, centralization of power, decision-making by elected and appointed officials, career public servants, war making, international affairs, budgeting, social control and law enforcement, and a host more. We therefore must stipulate what we mean by the word.

A convenient starting point distinguishes between "state" and "government." We use the word "state" to mean the collectivity embodying those roles, positions, and statuses that career employees occupy. We use the word "government" to mean those whose roles, positions, and statuses have been achieved through election or political appointment. Thus, in our vocabulary, the position of Secretary of the Interior forms part of government (the secretary is appointed by the president and Congress), but the bureaucracy the secretary manages forms part of the state apparatus. We make this distinction because conflict often exists between state and government, but simultaneously each always influences the other. Every president from Franklin Roosevelt to Ronald Reagan has complained about the difficulties a president faces in getting action out of "the bureaucracy." Paradoxically, however, every president and every elected and appointed government official has in many important ways influenced that immovable bureaucracy while at the same time being influenced by it.

These definitions emphasize that the state does not constitute an abstract, noncorporeal entity with a life of its own. It consists of living, breathing, and very human people occupying roles. To explain the behavior of the state as a collectivity we must explain how these various role-occupants behave.

These definitions serve another purpose: they explain how government and state can act in contrary ways. Nowhere does this appear more forcefully than in countries in which a revolutionary government takes office either by way of election or after armed struggle. It appears in the sharp contrast between the motivations and ideologies of members of the government and members of the state. In the African country now called Zimbabwe (formerly Rhodesia), after a decade of armed struggle by liberation forces, a negotiated settlement and consequent elections brought the revolutionaries into the seats of power. The civil service bureaucrats, the judges, and the senior police and army officers, however, did not change from the previous regime—all remained whites.

In the role of consultant, one of the authors attended a meeting of Zimbabwe's Minister of Justice and Constitutional Affairs with the chief justice, the attorney general, the solicitor general, the Secretary (i.e., the senior civil servant in the ministry), the chief magistrate, and about a dozen other senior civil servants from the ministry. Except for the minister, every person in the room had a white face; except for the chief justice and the consultant, they had all served the old Rhodesian government that had hung, imprisoned, tortured, shot, and bombed the people who now formed the government.

The contrast between government and state in the circumstances of a country like Zimbabwe appears even more significant if we examine the norms defining the several roles included in the two. Immediately after a revolutionary change in government, the officials of the state continue to follow the norms laid down for their positions. That requires them to enforce the laws as they then exist. Until the government changes the law, the old laws continue. Thus the members of the state find themselves enforcing the old laws.

In Zimbabwe, the new black majority-rule government that replaced the old white minority-rule government espoused a socialist and nonracialist policy to replace the old government's capitalist and racialist policy. The first law of every revolutionary government, however, requires that the old laws continue until changed. Those old laws directed the members of the state—the civil servants, the police, the judges, and so forth—to implement and enforce the property, contract, and even the racialist laws that defined the old capitalist, racialist policy that the government had pledged itself to overthrow. The new revolutionary socialist, nonracialist government found itself presiding over a capitalist, racialist state.

As we have argued earlier, every decision-making structure has institutions and procedures that perform the range of potential decisions. A capitalist state has procedures and institutions that make it difficult or impossible to generate decisions appropriate for a socialist polity (and, of course, vice versa). Thus the new socialist, nonracialist governors of Zimbabwe found themselves in command of a state that not only enforced capitalist, racialist laws, but whose decision-making procedures stubbornly resisted efforts to generate new laws to change the state. Yet until the government radically changes the state's decision-making machinery, and ultimately the legal order itself, the role-occupants in the state structure would *necessarily* continue to act as they had before the revolution—and that would happen whatever the color of the role-occupant's skin.

If by "revolution" one means a change in the state structure, plainly a change in government does not itself amount to a revolution.

"Relative autonomy." When the state or the government as a collectivity makes a decision, it appears that the decision emerges from the actions of a few defined actors. A new law emerges from the decisions of a few hundred bureaucrats, Congressmen, their aides, the president. A court, its clerks, and its sheriffs enforce a contract and collect a debt. A zoning commission gives a steel mill a variance from the zoning laws that will allow the mill to do serious damage to the quality of life of the poor who live in the neighborhood. A lone investigator in the Pure Food and Drug Administration single-handedly fights a giant drug company to prevent the marketing in Africa of Thalidomide, a drug that produced sadly deformed babies in the rest of the world. In each of these cases, in a sense the government or the state made a decision. In fact, specific actors made the decision in the title of government or state.

By state "autonomy" we mean the power of government or state officials in a particular case to make a decision that goes against the interets of a particular fraction of the capitalist class, usually in order to carry out the interests of the state or government officials as a defined interest group, or to carry out the interests of other classes or strata in society. To explain how these role-occupants behave, we refer to our general model of law and behavior (see Chapters 6-10).

Role-occupants act by making choices within an arena of constraints and resources that includes rules and sanctions of the law. To understand the amount of autonomy that a particular member of the state or government has, one must examine his or her particular arena of choice—including, of course, the legal constraints and resources, but also including all of the other factors that we have earlier suggested bear upon the choice. If we examine these constraints, we suggest the following hypothesis: Where the decision of a role-occupant affects *relations of production*, the role-occupant will have relatively little autonomy. Where the decision *affects the amount of profit* (i.e., capital accumulation), the role-occupant will have relatively greater autonomy. We first justify this hypothesis on logical and theoretical grounds, and then we give some examples to show how we believe this hypothesis works.

The dialectic of the state, the government, and the legal order. We have earlier argued that the very process of solving one set of social problems gives rise to new conflicts and creates new forces that will, unless restrained, create new and equally devastating social problems. Some structuralists argue that the capitalist state intervenes in the process of capital accumulation in order to ensure the survival of the capitalist political economy. Even in the short run, that alone does not exhaust the essential function of the capitalist state. Capital accumulation requires maximization of profit. The very conditions that provide for and result from the maximization of profit in many cases threaten the stability upon which the political and economic systems depend. For example, to increase the profits of capital frequently requires a reduction in the labor force's return for its work. Some U.S. industrialists demanded unrestricted immigration in order to create a cheap work force. This policy promoted (1) economic instabilities, such as strikes and high labor force turnover (as was the case in 1921)[28]; (2) social instabilities, in the form of nativist uprisings and protests (as was the case in the 1830s); and (3) political instabilities, by way of the electoral process (by 1900 some feared that the foreign born would soon have enough votes to "rewrite the Constitution") and by way of radical political movements (a fear, much more imagined than real, that among other responses led to the infamous Palmer Raids of 1920).

At any particular time, conflicts arise from the contradiction between some industrialists' need for profit maximization and the general need for system stability. For example, during the 1830s, 1840s, and 1850s, some industries demanded an increasing supply of cheaper labor.[29] These demands led to riots and protests against the influx of cheap labor (which in the 1850s was primarily Irish Catholic labor). This influx of cheap labor led other capitalists to demand the cutting off of easy immigration, for the riots threatened *their* capital accumulation.

We thus state the following general proposition: The state's efforts to protect and enhance capital accumulation must lead to protest by the working class; these protests must threaten system instability; thus, measures to further capital accumulation for the benefit of one fraction of the capitalist class must lead to protest by another fraction of the capitalist class whom the particular measures do not benefit. Organized protest thus sometimes achieves substantial results. To the extent that protesting groups can, until the state satisfies their demands, threaten the normal working of the political economy, they may force significant change.[30]

On the other hand, a great deal of state action concerns not the enhancement of profit for a particular fraction of the ruling class, but the maintenance of relations of production that make capitalism possible. Capitalism depends upon capitalists' making the basic decisions about the use of their property and defining the norms of economic interchange in their own interests. On maintaining the underlying structure or property relationships, all fractions of the capitalist class agree. We would expect that on issues concerning the accumulation of profit for one or another fraction of the capitalist class, the state would have relatively great autonomy; on maintaining the relations of production, the state would have relatively little autonomy.

Contract and property law. Members of the state structure most clearly do the bidding of members of the ruling class in a direct, instrumental sense when (1) the members of the ruling class themselves formulate the norms of behavior they want the members of the underclass to obey, and (2) they can regularly require members of the state structure to employ coercive devices to compel that obedience. That occurs most clearly with respect to contract law. As we have seen, in the case of contract, in practice the economically most powerful class dictates the norms that the contracting parties will follow. Once a breach occurs, the aggrieved party can call upon judges and sheriffs to enforce the contract.

Contract law forms the basic law of a market economy. To the extent that contract law does so, the state's role-occupants necessarily have relatively less freedom to refuse to act in the immediate and direct interests of the ruling class.

A ruling class's capacity to control the economy through contractual relations depends upon its control over the means of production. In a capitalist society, that depends mainly upon property law. Again, we would expect that the norms of property law would admit of relatively little discretion on the part of the state functionaries. Criminal law constitutes the first defense of property—and as we have seen, a victim does not bargain with a thief. She calls the police. In general, the stability and certainty of the law, held by many to constitute one of its most desirable attributes, reveals itself no place more forcefully than with respect to property. Long ago, Sir William Blackstone held that the law's central concern lies with property. Things have not changed so much, after all.

In the United States at least constitutional constraints forbid meddling too far with the basic relationships of production. The Contract Clause of the federal constitution forbids states from impairing the validity of contracts. The Due Process Clause has received an interpretation that forbids too great an inroad into private ownership. A state cannot take private property without just compensation, thus forbidding the nationalization of enterprise without paying for it. At point after point, where the law touches upon basic relationships of production, barriers exist to require the state and its role-occupants to defend the basic relations of production. With respect to those, the state has relatively little autonomy.

In most areas of law, however, discretion remains the rule. Practically any change in the law that relates to the economy will favor one set of capitalists against another. A zoning change, a change in the minimum wage law, a law against discrimination in employment, immigration law, even minor tampering with the law of contracts to protect consumer interests will affect entrepreneurs unequally. A law that raises minimum wages does not affect industries whose employees receive wages well above the minimum. A law protecting consumers against fraud does not affect Big Steel. A law giving the Federal Communications Commission power to award a rich television franchise to one rather than another operator most immediately affects a few broadcasting companies. In all of these cases, the state and the government have relatively great discretion to decide how to behave. Legislators have discretion about what laws to enact, administrators have discretion about how to enforce the laws. In these areas, as our hypothesis suggests, the government and the state have relatively great autonomy.

In the long run, however, discretion must of course favor the rich and powerful. As we have earlier demonstrated, administrators exercise discretion to maximize rewards and minimize strains for themselves and the bureaucracies in which they serve. Legislators exercise their discretion for the same reasons. The rich and the powerful have the greatest capacity for maximizing rewards and minimizing strains for government and state personnel. Thus governmental and state discretion will favor the economic ruling class.

Legitimacy, mystification, and symbolic law. Thus far, we have described the state and the legal order in their relationships with the ruling class and the underclass in instrumental terms—as though changes in the law come about only because the various role-occupants intend their consequences to favor this class or that, this fraction of capitalists as against another. That overstates the case. We must also explain the many cases in which the government enacts a law seemingly in response to a demand by the mass of the population, only to have it prove ineffective. We must explain rituals in the law that seemingly have no instrumental consequences. It is useful to understand these concepts of legitimacy, mystification, and symbolic law.

Legitimacy. Althusser and his followers argue that the state rules in the interests of the ruling class, but that, paradoxically, it can do so only to the extent that it has "relative autonomy."[31] Thus it is argued the state exists to serve the interests of capitalists. In order to retain control, however, it must create a perception of legitimacy in the eyes of "the people." To manage this the state must possess some autonomy from the capitalists. In this way Althusser and others account for the disparity between the idea that the "ruling class" controls the state and the empirical fact that the state sometimes passes and enforces laws contrary to ruling-class interests.

As with any theoretical model, we must guard against rendering our explanations of social phenomenon incapable of being disproven. Althusserian notions of legitimacy come dangerously close to a theory valid not because it fits the facts but because its logic is closed. Althusserian theory argues that even when the state appears to act in ways seemingly incompatible with ruling-class interests, it in fact acts consistently with their interests. By having an appearance of independence of the ruling class, the state expresses its dependence on the ruling class. One cannot disprove so tautological a theory. If the state acts in defense of capitalist interests, it acts because of capitalist control of the state. If it acts against capital interests, despite appearances, the state still acts in capital interests. A theory that data cannot conceivably contradict—that is, a nonfalsifiable theory—tells us very little.

Max Weber introduced the concept of legitmacy into the sociology of law. In his view, a legal order helped a ruling elite to maintain its rule by satisfying the disinherited masses that governance proceeded through general rules, applied equally to everyone without fear or favor. In most capitalist states it seems unlikely that legal-rational legitimacy maintains the rule of the elite against the mass. British Colonial Africa, for example, "received" English law. Some English lawyers gurgled that Africans did not rebel because they loved the rule of law that supposedly governed them. Empirical research demonstrates that Africans, like the poor elsewhere, enjoyed few of the benefits of the rule of law. Instead, the English colonizers used mainly naked force and unlimited discretion.

In general, the sorts of social control that lead to legal-rational legitimacy—the rule of law, due process, the civilized rationality of judicial process as against the irrationality of rule by a police officer's nightstick—govern the lives of the middle class, but not the mass. Governments and states use legal-rational legitimacy as a way of disciplining dissident elements of the ruling class, not the working class. For that, other methods serve better.

Mystification. Everywhere, the legal order shrouds itself in weird rituals, outlandish costumes, incomprehensible language. It clothes itself in mystification. Many of these forms arose in other historical contexts for reasons that then seemed valid. Why do they continue to this day? We suggest that many of the forms of mystification serve to persuade both dissident elements of the ruling class and the mass of the population that the law lies so far beyond their understanding that they can only accept it. E. P. Thompson made the same point in his study of eighteenth-century courts and law.[32]

Symbolic law. A third technique for persuading both dissident fractions of the ruling class and the mass not to threaten stability lies in the use of what some have called symbolic law—that is, the enactment of law that seemingly responds to a particular demand, without it inducing in its addressees the behavior that it prescribes. For example, despite antitrust law, the United States economy remains largely controlled by monopolistic or ologopolistic enterprises. Antitrust law constitutes the symbol, not the actuality, of antitrust. If people protest against flagrant monopolization, the authorities point to the antitrust laws and respond, "We do what we can." Why agitate for a law against monopolies when one already exists?

In general, symbolic law concerns laws that the legislature enacts but that the members of the state do not enforce. These different lawmakers have significantly different areas of choice, as our original model of the legal order suggests. The formal, operative processes of lawmaking take place in full public view—in the chambers of the legislature, in legislative committee rooms, in the public statements of presidents and governors. Enforcement decisions—the sorts of decisions that members of the bureaucracy make—take place mainly in their offices, behind closed doors. What the public learns about can affect the legitimacy of government and the state. What the public does not learn about cannot affect legitimacy. The state nowhere appears so autonomous as in the lawmaking process. It nowhere appears so little autonomous as in the law-implementing process.

12.3 CONCLUSION

We believe that the dialectical, institutionalist model that we have advanced helps solve problems that are inherent in other theories of law. Our model avoids the determinism of other versions, for it admits of struggle and some successes by the mass of the population even within the framework of capitalism. It explains how both relative stability and relative instability become normal for the capitalist state, depending upon the vigor and determination of the state on the one hand and the mass of the population on the other.

A theory of the state and government that tautologically argues that the state in capitalist and present-day socialist societies exists to legitimize existing social relations will not do. Such a theory calls our attention to a great deal that simple instrumental theory ignores. But it obscures the fact that the state consists of a complex set of bureaucracies and political managers with its own interests to which, along with the political interests of the ruling class, it responds. The state has some autonomy which currently manifests itself in a tendency toward increasing control of the economy by state and government (elected) officials. The state, however, is not independent from the capitalist class or from class struggle, even in states such as Sweden or Great Britain where the state has a greater role in the economy than it has in the United States or Canada.

People, we reiterate, make choices, respond to realities, and struggle against oppression. Those at the top act as a class to perpetuate their privilege; those sprinkled below do likewise. The contrary interests generate conflicts, in response to which the government and the state promulgate and enforce laws. The relationship between state, legal order, and government becomes complex, interactive, and ever-changing. In a word, it is dialectical.

NOTES

1. See, for example, W. Aubert, *The Hidden Society* (Totowa, NJ: Bedminster Press, 1965); W. Aubert, "Competition and Dissensus: Two Types of Conflict and Conflict Resolution," *Journal of Conflict Resolution* 7(1963): 7; and William J. Chambliss, "A Sociological Analysis of the Law of Vagrancy," *Social Problems* 12(1964): 46-67.

2. Kingsley Davis and Wilbert Moore, "Some Principles of Stratification," *American Sociological Review* 10(1945): 242-249.

3. C. Wright Mills, *The Power Elite* (New York: Oxford University Press, 1956).

4. Ralf Dahrendorf, "Out of Utopia: Towards a Reorientation of Sociological Theory," *American Journal of Sociology* 64(1958): 115-127.

5. W. J. Chambliss, *Crime and the Legal Process* (New York: McGraw-Hill, 1969); and Richard Quinney, *Crime and Justice in America* (New York: Little, Brown & Co., 1969).

6. W. J. Chambliss and Robert B. Seidman, *Law, Order, and Power* (Reading, Mass: Addison-Wesley, 1971).

7. Ralph Miliband, *The State in Capitalist Society* (New York: Basic Books, 1969).

8. C. Wright Mills, *Images of Man: The Classification in Sociological Thinking* (New York: George Braziller, 1960).

9. D. Gold, C. Low, and E. Wright, "Recent Developments in Marxist Theories of the Capitalist State," *Monthly Review* 27(October and November): 29-43, 36-51.

10. C. Wright Mills, *Power Elite*; G. W. Domhoff, *Who Rules America?* (Englewood Cliffs, NJ: Prentice-Hall, 1967), and *The Powers That Be* (New York: Random House, 1978); Miliband, *The State in Capitalist Society*; G. Kolko, *The Triumph of Conservatism* (New York: Free Press, 1963), and *Railroads and Regulations* (Princeton: Princeton University Press, 1965).

11. Miliband, *The State in Capitalist Society*.

12. *Ibid*.

13. Domhoff, *Who Rules America?* and *The Powers That Be*.

14. W. J. Chambliss, *On the Take* (Bloomington: Indiana University Press, 1978).

15. J. Mollenkopf, "Theories of the State and Power Structure Research," *Insurgent Sociologist* 5(1975): 245-264.

16. Domhoff, *The Powers That Be*, p. 119.

17. C. Offe, "Political Authority and Class Structure: An Analysis of Late Capitalist Societies," *International Journal of Social Sciences* 2(1974): 73-108; N. Poulantzas, "The Problem of the Capitalist State," *New Left Review* 58(1969): 67-78.

18. Domhoff, *The Powers That Be*, pp. 64-87.

19. K. Calavita, "A Sociological Analysis of U.S. Immigration Policy," Ph.D. dissertation, University of Delaware, 1980, p. 37; Alan A. Whitt, "Class-Dialectical Model of Power," *American Sociological Review* 44(1979): 81-99; W. J. Chambliss, "On Lawmaking," *British Journal of Law and Society* 6(1979): 149-171.

20. J. O'Connor, *The Fiscal Crisis of the State* (New York: St. Martin's Press, 1973).

21. R. Friedland, F. Piven, and R. Alford, "Political Conflict, Urban and the Fascist Crisis," in Douglas Ashford, ed., *Public Policy: New Approaches and Methods*, Yearbook in Political and Public Policy (Beverly Hills: Sage, 1978).

22. O'Connor, *Fiscal Crisis*.

23. Poulantzas, *Political Power and Social Classes* (London: New Left Books, 1973).

24. C. Sumner, *Reading Ideologies* (London: Academic Press, 1979).

25. E. Cashmore, "The Social Organization of Canadian Immigration Law," *Canadian Journal of Sociology* 364(1978): 409-429; Chambliss, "On Lawmaking"; Friedland, Piven, and Alford, "Political Conflict"; F. Piven and R. Cloward, *Poor People's Movements: Why They Succeed, How They Fail* (New York: Pantheon Books, 1977); Offe, "Political Authority."

26. L. Althusser, "Ideology and Theological State Apparatus," in *Lenin and Philosophy* (New York: Monthly Review Press, 1971); Poulantzas, "The Problem of the Capitalist State." And see E. P. Thompson's critique of structuralism in *The Poverty of Theory* (London: Merlin, 1978).

27. A. Wolfe, *The Limits of Legitimacy* (New York: Free Press, 1977), p. 6.

28. Calavita, "A Sociological Analysis of U.S. Immigration Policy."

29. *Ibid.*

30. See Chapters 6 and 7.

31. L. Althusser, *For Marx* (London: Allen Lane, 1969); L. Althusser, *Lenin and Philosophy and Other Essays* (New York: New Left Books, 1971); L. Althusser, *Politics and History* (London: New Left Books, 1972); L. Althusser and E. Balibar, *Reading Capital* (London: New Left Books, 1970).

32. E. P. Thompson, *Whigs and Hunters: The Origin of the Black Act* (New York: Pantheon Books, 1976).

Name index

Friedland, R., 317
Friedman, Laurence, 3, 10, 19, 20, 63, 81, 116, 135, 137, 140, 160, 162, 166, 168, 169, 217, 235, 239, 240, 247, 264
Friedman, Wolfgang, 52, 167, 238
Fuller, Lon F., 5, 20, 66, 81, 213, 214, 221, 239, 245, 263

Galbraith, J. K., 112, 116
Galileo, 244
Garfincle, A. M., 146, 167
Garrison, L. K., 81, 239
Genovese, E., 83, 145, 167
Gerth, H. H., 137
Gideon, 147
Girovord, Sir Percy, 168
Gluckman, Max, 24, 31, 47, 48, 52, 53
Gold, D., 317
Goldschmidt, 260
Goffman, E., 290, 301
Goldwater, Barry, 278
Gorz, Andre, 186
Gouldner, Alvin W., 20, 137
Goulds, Jim, 104
Gower, Sir Ernest, 121, 136
Graham, F., 167
Graham, J. M., 153, 166, 205
Gramsci, Antonio, 82, 131, 137
Green, Leon, 231, 240
Griffin, S., 167
Griffith, John D., 194, 195
Grossman, J., 226, 240
Gulliver, P. H., 45, 46, 53
Gunningham, Neil, 152, 153, 154, 167, 168
Gurr, Ted Robert, 172, 173, 203
Gusfield, J., 152, 188, 205

Haeore, Q., 82
Hall, Jerome, 166, 176, 177, 203
Hall, P. C., 283
Hand, Learned, 225
Hanson, Norwood Russel, 20, 163, 169
Hargreaves, 185
Hart, H.L.A., 50, 51, 56, 80, 171, 209, 211, 213, 215, 217, 230, 238
Harvey, William B. Harvey, 4

Hay, Douglas, 136, 179, 204
Hayek, Friedrich von, 209, 238
Heck, Philip, 33, 52
Hegel, G. A., 63, 71
Hobbes, Thomas, 25, 26, 52, 179
Hoebel, E. A., 4, 19, 29-33, 52
Holmes, Justice Oliver Wendell, 19, 68, 81, 177, 216, 218, 239, 259
Horwitz, M. J., 93, 115
Huggins, Martha, 168
Hume, David, 11, 20
Hunt, Alan, 81, 166
Hurst, J. W., 204, 264
Hurst, Willard, 116, 239
Hutchinson, Anne, 198, 199
Hylton, John, 301

Ilbert, C., 136
Ingersoll, John, 193
Inkeles, A., 20

Jefferson, Thomas, 119, 135
Jeffrey, C. Ray, 174, 203
Jex-Blake, Sophia, 146
Jhering, van, 64
Johnston, Sir Harry, 157, 168
Jordan, M., 136

Kamenka, E., 281
Kant, Immanuel, 209
Kaplow, 292
Kelsen, Hans, 56, 73, 76, 83, 209, 238
Keon, A., 136
Kennedy, Mark, 203
Keyfite, N., 283
Kirchheimer, O., 82
Klare, Karl, 142, 166
Knapp, Whitman, 283
Knight, M., 238
Kolko, Gabriel, 141, 166, 187, 204
Krader, L., 81

Ladinsky, J., 81, 160, 162, 168, 169
Langdell, 228
Laski, Harold, 65, 81, 249, 256, 264
Laslett, Peter, 52

Pound, Roscoe, 5, 32, 35, 65, 66, 81, 244, 256, 258, 259, 261, 264

Quinney, Richard, 166, 281

Radin, Max, 239
Radzinowicz, L., 180, 204
Ramazzini, Dr., 196
Ranulf, Svend, 187, 205
Rapson, I. J., 240
Reagan, Ronald, 305, 310
Rechtsstaat, 210
Redfield, Robert, 24, 31, 52
Reinarman, C., 205
Renner, K., 117
Rheinstein, Mas, 80
Robertson, John M., 20
Roby, P., 205
Roosevelt, T., 142
Roosevelt, Franklin, 259, 310
Root, Elihu, 129
Rosen, R. C., 283
Rubenstein, R. E., 83, 168
Rumdm, Max, 52
Runciman, W. G., 52
Rusche, G., 81
Russell, T. G., 7, 11, 264

Sachs, Albie, 82, 167
Sartre, Jean Paul, 16, 305
Savigny, Friedrich Carl von, 29, 30, 31, 81
Sawyer, A., 6, 20
Schmidt, J. A., 167, 226, 227, 240, 244, 245
Schubert, Glendon, 240
Schulder, D. B., 146, 167
Schwartz, Richard D., 43, 52, 53
Scull, Andrew, 301
Seagle, William, 29-31, 37, 52
Seidman, Robert B., 20, 80, 166, 239, 283, 317
Shaftsbury, 179
Shapp, Milton, 278
Sharlet, R., 20, 82, 83
Shumann, Karl F., 178, 203
Sinclair, Upton, 141
Slawson, W. D., 96, 115

Smith, Adam, 18, 20, 59, 82, 86
Smith, G. N., 82
Spencer, Herbert, 6
Spitzer, S., 43, 53
Stalin, Joseph, 24
Stammler, R., 81, 82
Stearns, L. R., 205, 282
Steffens, Lincoln, 277, 283
Stephen, Justice, 128
Stewart, Justice, 254, 262
Stone, Julius, 52
Stone, Chief Justice, 257, 259
Strangeland, P., 282
Sumner, Colin, 82, 166, 168, 317
Sumner, William Graham, 32, 52, 63, 81
Sweezy, Paul, 305
Sykes, Gresham, 81
Szymanski, A., 283

Tannenbaum, Frank, 283
Teitlebaum, P., 20
Thompson, E. P., 116, 136, 178, 204, 305, 315, 318
Thring, Sir Henry, 124, 126, 127, 128, 129, 130, 136
Tocqueville, Alexis de, 2
Trubek, D., 80, 81, 116
Turk, A., 281
Turkel, Gerald, 43, 53, 116, 137
Twining, W., 177, 203

Vinson, Chief Justice, 225

Wade, J., 160, 168
Wadsworth, Senator, 142
Wasserstrom, Richard A., 239
Weber, Max, 24, 56, 60, 61, 62, 80-82, 131, 171, 286, 299, 300, 306
Weinstein, James, 187, 204
Weise, von, 24
White, J. B., 136
White, Justice, 264
Whitt, Alan A., 116, 154, 155, 168, 317
Willard, Samuel, 201
Williams, Harrison, 292

Subject and case index

British
  Board of Trade, 129
  mining industry, 272
  statutes, 126
  system of costs, 233
  welfare system, 82
Brown v. Board of Education, 8, 10, 20, 47,
    235, 239, 246, 250, 251, 252
Bureau of Narcotics and Dangerous Drugs,
    193, 195, 290, 291
Bureaucracy, 153, 272, 285-301
Bureaucratic ethic, 165

California Youth Authority, 291
Capital accumulation, 159
Capitalism, 59, 60, 61, 93, 303-318
  contradictions, 70, 85, 279
Capitalist development, 150
Capitalist economic system, 109, 155, 176
Capitalist production, 160
"Captain Swing," 185
Carrier case (1473), 175, 177
Caveat emptor, 178
Charles II, 200
*Chamberlain v. Milwaukee and Mississippi
    Railroad Co.*, 239
Child labor reform, 187
Child-saving movement, 185, 186
Chin's systems model, 249, 254, 255
Choice model, 33, 132
Civil action, 216
Civil Aeronautics Board, 5, 107
Civil Rights Act of 1964, 246
Civil Rights Act of 1967 (see Title VII)
Civil rights movement, 304
Class conflict, 153, 197-202
Classical model, 109-110, 111
Clean Air Act, 153, 154
"Clear" cases, 216-220
Colonial expansion, 176
Colonization, 57, 58
Command economy, 50
Commerce Clause, 105
Common law, 58, 82, 174, 207
Commonwealth v. Pierce, 218
Communist party, 91, 164
  in America, 255

  in China, 280
Compensation law, 162
Complex technologies, 25, 41
Comprehensive Drug Abuse, Prevention and
    Control Act of 1970, 193, 196
Conflict view of society, 34, 35, 36
Consensus in norms, 37
Consensus myth, 7
Constitution, 101, 183, 211, 250, 253, 261
  of Ghana, 128
Contingency fee, 233
Contract, 47, 59
Contract clause, 259, 313
Contract law, 92-96, 247
  laissez-faire, 94-99
Conversion processes, 220, 238
"Core" cases, 217
"Core" meaning, 213, 214
Corporate
  power, 86-112
  profits, 268
Corporation law, 99-107
Corporations, 1, 86, 89, 95, 141
  health hazards, 87
Cost of litigation, 232, 233
Court of Appeals, 295
Court structure, 207-209
Courts, radical change, 249
  Sudanese, 236
Criminal
  action, 216
  behavior, 172
  law, 172, 181-185, 266
"Crises" cases, 234
Critical criminology, 266
Cui bono, 177-178
Custom and law, 29, 30, 32, 63-64
Custom laws, 108

Dartmouth College v. Woodward, 101, 116
Darwinism, 24, 142
Davis v. Richardson, 93, 115
Davis v. Weidner, 301
Defense of insanity, 218
Delinquency laws, 185
Dennis v. United States, 239
Department of Agriculture, 5, 142, 153

Department of Health, Education, and Welfare, 246
Department of Labor, 234
Desegregation (see *Brown* v. *Board of Education*)
Deviance, 265, 266
Dialectical materialism, 70-73
Dialectical model, 154, 180, 300
Dialectical theory, 309-316
Discrimination, 7, 9, 15, 16, 61, 71, 145, 146, 149, 261, 295, 297, 298 (also see Racism, Title VII, Women's rights)
Disparate impact, 296, 297
Disparate treatment, 296, 297
Dispute-settlement, 39-46, 248
Divorce, 48, 233
Dodge v. *Ford*, 106, 116
Domain assumptions, 299
Drafting bills, 129-130
Driscoll v. *Allis-Chalmers* (1911), 161
Drug Abuse, Prevention and Control Act of 1970, 188
Drug Enforcement Administration, 290
Drug industry, 194, 196
Drug laws, 192, 290
Drugs, 193, 279
Due process clause, 183, 259, 313

Economic elite, 307
Economic stratification, 44
Elitist model, 154, 155
Embezzlement law, 176
English common law, 57-59, 174, 236
and colonies, 37
Enlightenment model, 66
Equal Employment Opportunities Act (see Title VII)
Equal Employment Opportunities Commission, 296
Equal Pay Act of 1970, 12
Equal protection clause, 261

Facilitative law, 86-88
Factory safety and health, 268-274
Federal Bureau of Investigation, 279, 280
Federal Communications Commission, 107
Federal Employer's Liability Act of 1908, 161

Federal Narcotics Bureau, 192, 290, 291
Federal Trade Commission, 107, 295
Fellow-servant rule, 160, 223, 224, 257
Feudalism, 58, 91, 144, 156, 174, 175, 176, 178, 179, 258
in modern law, 256
Fifth Amendment, 252
First Amendment, 104, 259
Ford Motor Company, 106, 110
Form-books, 130
Formal law, 69
Fourteenth Amendment, 104
Free market, 93 (also see Capitalism)
"Friend of the Court." 247
Functionalist theory, 304, 305

Gambling, 276, 279
Gault case, 250, 253, 254, 262
Gebeitsverband, 266
General Motors, 86, 87, 88, 106
General Electric Co., 108
"Grand theory," 18
Great depression in Britain, 149
Grundnorm, 210

Hadley v. *Baxendale*, 97, 115
Harrison Act, 192, 291
Hart model, 215
Haymarket Square Bombing (1866), 161
Heuristic (propositions), 13, 14, 15, 16, 19, 36, 44, 55
Henry II, 174
Heroin, 194
Hoffman-LaRoche Laboratories, 194
Homestead strike at Carnegie Steel, 161
Homosexuality, 5, 6, 189, 212
Hotema v. *United States*, 218
Hoyt v. *Florida*, 167
Human rights, 259
Hutchinsonian movement, 198, 199

I.B.M., 106
I.W.W. strike (1912), 161
Illegal business practices, 193
Immigration laws, 142, 143
Imprisonment, 289
Income tax laws, 259

McBoyle v. *United States*, 219
McCarthyism, 91
McClelland Committee, 278
Machine-smashing, 185
Marijuana, 192, 193, 194
Marijuana Tax Act, 290
Market power, 87, 114
Marxism, 18, 63, 70-73, 144, 305
Marxist, jurisprudence, 80
   theorists, 131
   theory, 140, 141, 142, 144, 147
Matter of Gault (see *Gault* case)
Meat inspection laws, 141, 142, 144, 153
Meat-packing industry, 141
Mechanical solidarity, 41, 43
Mercantile class, 175, 185
Mercantilist theory, 58
Middle-class indignation, 187, 188
Mines and Quarries Act of 1952, 273
Mining industry, 196
Mining Safety and Health, 272
Miranda v. *Arizona*, 148, 214, 250, 252, 253,
   261, 262, 264
M'Naghten case, 218, 244
Monopoly, of barber chairs, 108
Moral entrepreneurs, 188, 252
Mosely v. *Chamberlain*, 239
Mystification, 315

National Association for the Advancement of
   Colored People, 188, 222, 252
National Association of Manufacturers, 162
National Coal Board of Britain, 273
National Commission on Law, 278
National Institute of Mental Health, 194
National Labor Relations Act, 307
National Labor Relations Board, 5, 295
National Livestock Association, 141
National Motor Vehicle Theft Act of October
   1919, 219
Natural law theory, 66, 177
Navigation Acts England, 58
Neo-classical model of capitalist society, 17
Neo-Malthusian theory, 209, 276, 277
Neo-Kantian idealism, 209
Neo-realism, 260
New Deal, 307

New York Civil Liberties Union, 190, 191
Nixon administration, 193
Norm creation, 29
Norm enforcement, 39-45
Normative judgments, 5
Normative myth, 7
Normative systems, 6, 24-38, 38-51, 77
Norms, 30, 74-80, 210, 211
   of conduct, 214
   hierarchy of, 209-211
Nuer, 26-29, 39

Occupational Safety and Health Administra-
   tion, 287
Office of Parliamentary Counsel, 126
Office of Safety and Health, 272
Office of the Legislative Counsel of the Con-
   gress of the U.S., 129
Opium addiction, 159
Organic solidarity, 41
Organizational interests, 231-235
Organized crime, 276

Palmer Raids of 1920, 312
Papachristou v. *City of Jacksonville*, 182, 204
Parker v. *Hannibal*, 161
Parliamentary Counsel, 126-129
Parole evidence rule, 96
Paul v. *Neecham*, 115
Penn Central Railroad, 108
''Penumbra'' of the word, 213, 214, 219
People v. *Roberts*, 218
People v. *Schmidt*, 263
Pharmaceutical industry, 144, 193, 194
Philosophical anarchism, 177
Plague, 159
Platonic Ideas, 4
Pluralist theory, 140-144, 154, 155, 304, 305
Police, 279, 305
   corruption, 278
   malpractice, 222
   and vagrancy laws, 184
Policy, 223-226
Political pluralism, 18
Poll tax, 157
Pollution laws, 152-155
Population control, 274-281

Statute of Labourers (1349), 159
Steel Seizure case, 235
Stevens v. *Fidelity and Casualty Co.,* 115
Stratification, 304
"Strike by rioting," 185
Structural-functionalist model, 35-36, 254
Structural reform, 186
Structuralist theory, 307-309
Subsistence economy, 25, 41, 49
Study of law, 228
Sullivan law, 135
Supreme Court; 8, 9, 223, 234, 235, 246, 250
  comprehensive change, 250-255
  constitutional position, 251
  liberal tendencies, 258
  racial discrimination, 147, 148
  radical trend, 250
  status quo, 259
  women's rights, 145-147
Sweden factory safety, 197, 269, 270, 271
Sweeney v. *Board of Trustees of Keene State College,* 295, 301
Swing riots, 185
Syllogistic reasoning, 260, 261
Symbolic law, 315
Systems engineering, 4

Tax cases, 251
Tax depreciation, 108
Tax of oil industry, 108
Taylor v. *Goodwin,* 219
Thalidomide, 311
Third World, 1, 113
  population growth in, 273, 275
Title VII of the Equal Employment Opportunities Act, 9-11, 13, 17, 18, 61, 62, 64, 66, 72, 75, 78, 80, 292-299
Traditional myth, 220
Theft, 175-178
Theories of the middle range, 14
Thomas v. *Collins,* 264
Three Mile Island, 87
Times Square cleanup campaign, 190
Tort law, 248
Trial by jury, 158
"Trouble" cases, 216, 218, 219, 220, 235, 244

Trusts, 221
Trust law, 221

Uniform Commercial Codes, 123, 136
United Nations, 2
U.S. Steel, 110
U.S. Supreme Court (see Supreme Court)
United States v. *Caroline Products,* 264
United States v. *Philadelphia National Bank Company,* 107, 116
Universal laws, 44
Universal rules, 247
Upper class, 270
Utopia, 56

Vagrancy, 158
  laws, 181, 182
Valium, 194
Value choice, 33
Value-consensus, 187
Value neutrality, 113-114
Volition, 210
Volksgeist, 30, 32, 63-64, 72

Wagner Act, 142, 143, 147
Warranty, 95, 96
Watergate, 305
Water rights, 245
Weberian theory, 62, 71
Welfare state, 49
Whig party, 178
William v. *Ellis,* 239
Wills, 120
Winner-takes-all, 39, 236
Witchcraft hysteria of 1692, 197-201
Wolfe v. *Shelley,* 136
Wolfenden Report (1957), 189
Women's rights, 145, 146, 147
Work conditions, 159-163
Workmen's Compensation Commission, 234, 248
Worker safety, 196, 197, 268
Working class, 153, 160
Writ of certiorari, 223, 234, 235

Youngston Sheet and Tube Co. v. *Sawyer,* 240

Zero population growth, 275
Zimbabwe, 310, 311